G

Marius Kociejowski, poet, essayist and travel writer, lives in London where he works as an antiquarian bookseller. He has published four collections of poetry, *Coast* (Greville Press), *Doctor Honoris Causa* and *Music's Bride* (both Anvil Press), and *So Dance the Lords of Language: Poems 1975–2001* (Porcupine's Quill). Most recently he has published *The Street Philosopher and the Holy Fool: A Syrian Journey* (Sutton Publishing, 2004), *The Pigeon Wars of Damascus* (Biblioasis, 2010), and an anthology, *Syria through Writers' Eyes* (Eland, revised and enlarged edition, 2010). A collection of short prose, essays and feuilletons, *The Pebble Chance*, will be published by Biblioasis in 2014. He is currently working on a book as yet unclassifiable, *The Journals of Arcangelo Riffis*.

MARIUS KOCIEJOWSKI

God's Zoo

Artists, Exiles, Londoners

CARCANET

First published in Great Britain in 2014 by
Carcanet Press Limited
Alliance House
Cross Street
Manchester M2 7AQ

www.carcanet.co.uk

FSC
www.fsc.org
MIX
Paper from responsible sources
FSC® C014540

A CIP catalogue record for this book is available from the British Library

ISBN 978 1 84777 266 4 limp
978 1 84777 448 4 cased

The publisher acknowledges financial assistance from Arts Council England

Supported by ARTS COUNCIL ENGLAND

Typeset by XL Publishing Services, Exmouth
Printed and bound in England by SRP Ltd, Exeter

For Bobbie

Contents

How shall we sing the Lord's song in a strange land?

Psalm 137:4

God's Zoo: An Introduction

This book is the record of a world journey through London's cultures, or, more accurately, through those people whom I take to be *emblematic* of those cultures. What they have in common is that they are poets, novelists, artists and musicians, occasionally some combination of these, and, all in all, well equipped to give voice to their experiences. They are also people who have a healthy mistrust of language. They are all but one of them inhabitants of London and that includes faraway boroughs of which we know little. They have come here from other countries.

London is the main character even though it sits and watches silently for most of the time. London is what the people I've journeyed through appeal to, their frame of reference, and, like God, whether or not it responds to them remains its prerogative. I thought at first I might make London show its legs but it won't even get up on stage. It will not be forced. Sometimes one senses in it, within this living city, ghosts of other cities. The parts of London in which my subjects live are often, to some extent, the suburbs of elsewhere, or else the city for them is not so much a geographical space as it is a mental one. Admirable and lovable though they are, I do not walk with the psychogeographers, picking up spirit traces. When, on the other hand, worlds appear to run in parallel, and, at least for one of the people I have written about here, the Tigris really does seem to flow through London, I have been quite shameless in exploiting those connections.

What follows is not strictly about exiles: it is about émigrés too; it is also about people who are wary of defining themselves either way, who quite simply are no longer in the countries in which they were born and raised. Often they are here merely because they did not return home. It's true of many of the people about whom I write that the words 'exile' or 'émigré' hardly ever come to their lips and when they do it is usually in order to remove any taint of disgrace. The words are used mostly by *other* people. Most problematic is the word 'exile': nowadays it is employed with scant attention to its original meaning, which is *banishment*, from the Latin *exilium* or *exsilium*. An *exsul* was a banished man, one commanded to quit his native soil. Ovid was such a figure, Dante another. True exiles are now rare. Solzhenitsyn was bamboozled out of Russia. Pasternak almost certainly would not have been able to return had he gone to collect his Nobel Prize. The most debased use of the word is when one hears of tax exiles, when exile is synonymous with a Bacardi nightmare. A favourite buzzword of journalists, pollsters, demographers and sociologists, the term 'exile' has been stripped by them of any metaphysical dimension and is therefore the most unsatisfactory of handles. Whenever I use it, I do so reluctantly.

The modern exile is someone who has been forced to leave his country because of war or economics or is unable to return for fear of punishment or starvation. And even if we accept this limited, limiting definition, we are looking at something that is substantially different from what it was even half a century ago, when the decision to leave, or not to return, was considerably more drastic, almost certainly irreversible. The sense of isolation is no longer felt to quite the same degree. The letter that once upon a time took several weeks to arrive, which, after being tampered with by the authorities at the other end, might have brought news of birth or death, has been largely rendered obsolete. Communication is now immediate, and as such it has altered the very condition of exile. Space and time are no longer the obstacles they once were. What does remain the same, however, although in ways more difficult to measure, simply because things are not as clear as they once were, is the internal shifting of one's tectonic plates. I want to know what happens *inside*.

Artists are already exiles of a kind, which is to say the position they occupy in society is not what it used to be, when, say, a poet was his country's conscience. This is not strictly true, of course, because in some parts of the world, where there are no government subsidies other than those provided for the forging of prison bars, a man of words can still deliver strong punches. What a meltdown there's been, though, in the affairs of men. We are truly bound 'in shallows and in miseries'. Artists have become, at the very least, internal émigrés, retreating further and further into themselves. And being fiercely individualistic, most of them, they are wary of sharing too much with their compatriots and indeed there are often tussles over cultural space. Only rarely are they willing members of ethnic communities except, of course, when there's money to be made. Our cultural institutions go to great lengths to ensure there's always some kind of jamboree. The danger for any artist in such a position is the slippery slope of compromise, and nowhere is this more in evidence than within closed circles. There one may offend one's peers a little, but only if one does not push at mutually agreed upon boundaries. All, ultimately, must eat from the same plate. Generally speaking, then, creative people are not easy to drop into tidy ethnic scenarios. The Turk is not to be seen anywhere in that part of London where daily staples are advertised in words with undotted *i*'s. The Iraqi seems perfectly happy to live among Poles with their truncheons of smoked pork sausage. The Iranian lives in a predominately West Indian neighbourhood. The Zimbabwean lives in Harare North.

§

Such rules as I made, I soon broke, such that maybe the breaking of them was my only rule. There were a number of things I swore I wouldn't allow myself to do, which I went ahead and did anyway. It was almost as if by first wrapping myself in chains I'd earned myself the right to wriggle free of them. At first I had decided that on this zigzag journey through London's cultures I would address only those people working within their own languages. And problematic though this was, I would extend this to include both visual and musical language. This 'purist' approach fell apart almost immediately. My Turk, upon arriving here, began to write in English. What he had committed was, in E.M. Cioran's phrase, 'heroic treason'. This does not seem, however, to have invalidated the 'Turkishness' of his prose. Moreover, the subject is not only a Turk but a Jewish Turk, or a Turkish Jew, which puts him in the position of being a *double*-exile, but then this, too, is probably untrue because what writer is not at very least a *triple*-exile? Another was a Hungarian who, on occasion, lapsed into something approaching the incomprehensible in any language although, all in all, he was pretty sharp. (It is with sadness I speak of him in the past tense.) The Iranian remembers nothing of her Iranian childhood and is firmly rooted in the English language. She is, however, so *very* Persian.

A too rigorous system of enquiry, when applied to people, will not allow for the accidental seepage, the trickle of a phrase, that shows up in it more microcosms than the ocean it feeds into. 'You would play upon me; you would seem to know my stops; you would pluck out the heart of my mystery,' says Hamlet, and he exclaims, ''Sblood, do you think I am easier to be played on than a pipe?' Whether he whispers or bellows this is something for a good director to determine, but there can be few lines that argue more effectively against the academic marshalling of human nature. It was this very line, incidentally, which in Pasternak's translation won the applause of Soviet audiences. They waited breathlessly for it, seeing in this a coded reference to their own plight. That plight is, really, everyone's.

So fine, then: I betook myself, small blue MZ-N707 Type-R Walkman recorder in hand, through a city which, in cultural and ethnographical terms, is the world's most diverse. Whenever possible I allowed myself to be guided by circumstance. Sometimes this amounted to no more than a gut feeling that here was somebody with whom I could converse. The choices I made were not always the most logical ones. If I did not write about the most obvious figures maybe it was because enough has been said about them already, so often I approached people who have not had the attention they deserve, but in the main I went for those whose stories intrigued me. Absolutely imperative was that I felt sympathy for their work, because without it I'd rapidly decelerate and finally splutter to a stop. If they happened to be people with whom I'd already crossed paths once or twice, then so much the better. What it meant was that something about them had stuck in the brain and, such is one rule of thumb, what sticks there is probably worth sticking onto the page.

Absolutely paramount to any understanding of my intentions is that this is *not* a book of interviews. It is, rather, a series of 'constructions' based on many hours of recorded conversations. I made it a point of principle never to go to any of my subjects with prepared questions. This is because I believe that the words of greatest value arise from *good talk* rather than interrogation. Such questions as I did ask belonged wholly to the moment as they would in the natural flow of any conversation. There are stretches of direct speech that I have allowed to stand without significant change, otherwise, and quite without shame, I pulled together fragments of conversation from here and there, splicing them together, and I shifted materials to where I felt they would make the greatest impact. There are several instances, I will not say which ones, where I sought to reconstruct, to the best of my abilities, what people would have said had they been saying it in their own language, which is a roundabout way of saying I tweaked their English. Also I think it is impolite to duplicate other people's mistakes. Sometimes editing of this kind has the curious effect of at first striking a false tone, and then, with further polishing, suddenly returning the subjects to themselves. As with an invisible mender, the surest guide to success was whether or not my subjects themselves would notice. I wished, above all, for the *character* of a conversation to be preserved. This was the ideal towards which I strove.

§

Of the various writings I have had recourse to perhaps none is so profound, so poetically charged, as the Polish writer Józef Wittlin's 'Sorrow and Grandeur of Exile'. Actually it is the text of a talk delivered at a meeting of the American Branch of the International PEN Club on 27 February 1957. It haunts the writing of this book although not to such a degree that I have had to crib from it. The sense, rather, was of finding myself sitting with him at the same table. Wittlin, born 1896, was a novelist, poet, essayist and translator not just of Joseph Roth and Rainer Maria Rilke, both of whom he knew, but also of Homer's *Odyssey* which, in his earliest versions – there were many – he sought to reproduce in hexameters. After his experiences during World War I, as an infantryman in the Austrian army, he became a pacifist, and so it is unsurprising that the Homer he first began to translate, in 1914 of all years, was not the Homer of the *Iliad* but the Homer of vagrant heroes. 'The fatherland of Homer,' Wittlin wrote, 'is the pain which is everywhere.' Józef Wittlin died in New York City in 1976. All the tragic currents that run through the twentieth century ran through him, but exile for him was not a wholly lamentable state of affairs. There is even, he suggests, unlimited freedom for the émigré writer. 'Solitude,' he writes, 'is a miraculous soil on which the ability of an objective view of human affairs is born.'

One passage from his piece is of particular relevance:

> In Spanish, there exists for describing an exile, the word *destierro*, a man deprived of his land. I take the liberty to forge one more definition, *destiempo*, a man who has been deprived of his time. That means, deprived of the time which now passes in his country. The time of his exile is different. Or rather, the exile lives in two different times simultaneously, in the present and in the past. This life in the past is sometimes more intense than his life in the present and tyrannizes his entire psychology. This has its good and bad aspects. An exile living in the past is threatened by many dangers. For instance, by the danger of pining for trifling things whose real or alleged charm has gone for ever. He is threatened by the danger of pining even for the stage properties employed by older, today no longer living, worlds … The life of the exile, like the life of any other person, speeds onward to its end, but an exile, as it were professionally, moves backwards. Hence, often serious and even tragic, conflicts arise. It happens that the émigré lives in a complete vacuum which his imagination fills exclusively with phantoms of a dead world.

Time, or the loss of it, is one of my themes. What happens, say, when people move from Arabic to World Time? What happens when even the countries they've left behind enter World Time? What does one have to do in order to preserve one's creative voice inside Greenwich Mean Time? What happens to those whispered promises of love at closing time? Time plays havoc with most people, especially as they get older, but I think it does so all the more with people who are exiles or émigrés. There would appear to be a tendency in them to recreate time not according to what it actually was, or is, but to what it *might* be. (My Hungarian provided a masterclass in imaginative historical reconstruction.) Wittlin remarks on the dangers of being too passionately rooted in one's time because to be so is to be its slave. 'Only a *destiempo*,' he concludes, 'can be really free.' This journey, then, is not always an unhappy one. Quite a few of the people I spoke to are pleased to be here. Some found their artistic voices only after they came to London. Sorrow may be in attendance, but rare is the artist in whom it is not.

What strikes me about the stories I've gathered here is how often, and with hardly any prompting, the shades of grandparents tiptoe onto the scene. This, I believe, is inextricably connected with the matter of time. It's something addressed in these pages by the Uzbek writer. Almost always, in his poetry and prose, there is a scene with an elderly man or elderly woman and a young boy. What's missing is the generation in the middle. Spiritually, the elderly preserve in themselves something that was all but destroyed during Stalin's time, whereas their children, born in the 1930s, were the shiny new products of a Soviet atheistic culture. Authenticity is the preserve, therefore, of those who had at least a glimpse of traditional life. It is to them that younger Central Asians, and for that matter Russians as well, go looking for examples of wholeness, or, as my informant puts it, *unbrokenness*. The foregoing describes an extreme, of course, but it is a situation repeated in varying degrees throughout many of these stories. There is the natural reticence that comes, or ought to come, when speaking of one's own parents, and with the absence of various kinds of psychological barriers the channels between grandchild and grandparent are usually more open in any case, but there is another reason why those elders loom so large in the memories of exiles and émigrés and that's because at a double remove they are what their children, so rooted in time, could never be: the custodians of lost worlds, emperors and empresses of the invisible.

§

So why do I call this book, this place, these people, *God's Zoo*? The phrase appears as a quotation, unacknowledged alas, in Paul Tabori's *The Anatomy of Exile: A Semantic and Historical Study* (Harrap, 1972). I wish I could run it down to its source. The words leapt from the page, hovered for a bit, tickled my senses. Then a couple of people – not anyone in this book, though – said it could be read as offensive. Who, among my subjects, foreigners all of them, and therefore deeply sensitive to such issues, would wish themselves inside a zoo?

I'd been, they said, wildly inappropriate in my choice of title. So I went back to being without one, desperate for a single hook from which to hang a multiplicity of stories. I came up with all kinds of verbal infelicities. Still, that old phrase kept humming in the ear. (It fed the eye too. I liked the *zed*. Polish is rich with them; English, by comparison, is impoverished.) Months later, I mentioned it to one of the subjects in the book and, while admitting it might draw fire, she loved it as a title. Others liked it too, and then I realised just how lazy my earlier acceptance of other people's interpretation of it had been. Surely what it meant was that as creatures are to men, so are we to God, and that in this respect it defines the human condition: we are all in God's Zoo.

Semantically the phrase doubles up to mean where we all live. Although the gates to the city may be open (even if a couple of people here would dispute this) we are confined to it through circumstances, whether they be family or social ties, profession or even the absence of one. Most of us are in there for the duration. We'd sooner choke on its fumes than sniff the roses elsewhere. We are even lured into the illusion that civilisation is here, barbarism outside. Our behaviour, in this packed environment, is not quite as it is in Nature. It is, arguably, both better and worse. Where, in Nature, will you find long-stemmed glasses? Where, in this city, can one, with impunity, skin a rabbit? This may be the Devil justifying his position, but the phrase, when originally coined, did refer to this London of ours.

As Tabori notes, and he is speaking of the different forms of exile, the phrase also serves to describe our 'infinite variety'. What struck me when gathering these stories was how different they all are. I had initially feared they would be straitjacketed by a common theme. The results demonstrated quite the opposite: containment, it seems, set those voices free. Already, though, I have begun to drift a little. There's somebody I've got to see, and, as luck would have it, he's cooking for me. The dish he promises is one from his childhood in a faraway place. Will he be able to find the spices by which means he'll recreate all things gone? *God's Zoo.* I, for one, will be there at swilling time.

The Poet, the Anarchist, the Master of Ceremonies

Whose Tale Contains a Desk Inlaid with Midnight Blue

John Rety's eyes twinkle like cut diamonds tossed onto a haystack darkened by several weeks of rain. They make him look younger than his 77 years. I should think that, like me, he does not own a comb. The accent could be from anywhere east of a certain longitude. It's not easy to say from where exactly because the years of speaking English have made of it a kind of mélange. The madness, which he has in abundance, is of a species that could not be from anywhere other than what used to be called Eastern Europe. *Mitteleuropa* really, but because of the Iron Curtain it was twice removed and sealed into a ghetto for our Western fantasies. We wanted those countries free, but only in captivity did they ever really shine. When he's not scowling, which these days seems to be most of the time, Rety scintillates. Short and stout he may be, but, as my wife can testify, because she danced with him once, he is fleet of foot, and although on that occasion the music was an Irish pub band whose cheeriness is of a species that never fails to depress me, he seemed to

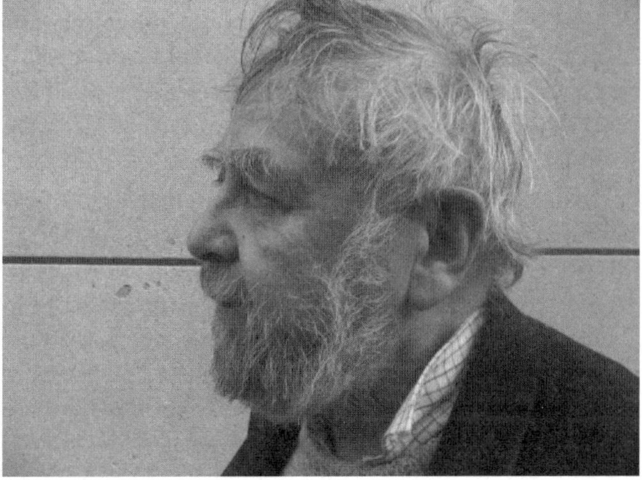

move to another music altogether and indeed may have been a Habsburg waltzer in a past life. When I told him on the phone that my world journey through London had brought me to Hungary, or at least that part of it which is to be found in Kentish Town, there was a terse silence.

'What about it?'

As is so often the case with people who adore the limelight, Rety packs a great deal into the shadows of a previous existence.

'Will you be my Magyar?'

§

The autobiographical note John Rety produced for his most recent pamphlet of verse *In the Museum* (Hearing Eye, 2007) reads:

> John Rety was born when he arrived in England in 1947, two years after World War II and at the age of seventeen. He came by the Alberg [sic] Express from Budapest where he was born on 8.12.1930. After a period of 4 years of various employment he began to have work published and became the editor of various literary publications, having had a book of his short stories published in 1951 [sic] (slated by the *Catholic Herald* and praised by the *Morning Advertiser*). He turned to poetry around 1980 having finally decided to give up painting when in 1977 his studio was broken into and all his paintings were stolen. In the poems printed here a judicious reader will be able to adduce underlying incidents and other significant details of the writer's life.

Will trains ever again sound our inner disturbances? What better illustrates our rootlessness, an unresolved love affair, or the swoop of time than a train's whistle? There was an Austrian movie *Arlberg-Express*, directed by Eduard von Borsody and produced the same year John Rety made his departure. The single mention of it in the British Film Institute archives describes 'a criminal adventure about a stolen jewel and a young musician who returns home from being a prisoner of war'. The film itself is not available. What one hears of it is enough, though, to evoke a Europe in post-war turmoil, an endless stream of people on the move.

What gives Rety his public face, and which has made him something of a legend in literary circles, although not always a lovable one, are the Sunday evening poetry readings he organises at the Torriano Meeting Hall in Kentish Town. The late Julia Casterton, poet, describes the atmosphere thus:

> The Torriano Meeting House is a mixture of a Quaker quiet room, but not quiet, and a Spiritualist Church, but with the spirits alive rather than dead. There are readers from the floor in the first half, lots of them, and the place gets very hot, with a little air blowing through the Virginia Creeper that festoons the one window; and in the second half, two 'known' poets, though as everyone in the audience is a poet too, it can be more of drama than two solo performances, and there can, on occasion, be some very intelligent heckling. John Rety, as master of ceremonies, is very strict. If the poems from the floor are no good, he shouts at everybody and tells them they should read more good poetry if they're to avoid writing rubbish. The atmosphere is something between the beginning of an Aldermaston March and Brendan Behan's aunt's tea party, because everyone's actually very nice, in a pugilistic, revolutionary sort of way.

Rety takes issue with that Virginia creeper, saying it creeps *on the outside.*

On the publicity brochure for the readings are written eight of the most dangerous words ever to have been committed to the English language: 'All poets present are welcome to express themselves.' And express themselves they do, sometimes at considerable length, or so it feels, and it brings to mind Leopardi's anecdote about Diogenes the Cynic who, upon seeing a poet endlessly reciting his verses come to a blank page, cries out, 'Take heart, friends. I see land ahead.' It has to be said, though, Miss Casterton's quite right: as master of ceremonies Rety usually puts a stop to any poets outstaying their welcome. Sometimes they give rise to his virulence: 'We had Sir Stephen Spender here once and he had to wait three quarters of an hour while poets spoke from the floor. If William Shakespeare himself walked in, I'm sure he'd have to wait a couple of hours.' Often, just before the invited reader takes the stage, the would-be poets, their weekly vowel movement done, take to the street, which brings to mind yet another story Leopardi relates: when the poet Martial was asked by someone why he wouldn't read his verses to him, he replied, 'So as not to hear yours.' I would say there is nowhere in London where bad poetry comes closer to touching the sublime, and this, I believe, is because of the way the words move through that rather special atmosphere. This said, it is also a place where very good poems get an airing. The hot furnace of the Torriano has been the tempering of many a fine poet over the years. Also it has acted as a platform for poets as diverse as John Heath-Stubbs, Dannie Abse, Ken Smith, John Arden, David Halliwell, Lotte Kramer, Mimi Khalvati, and James Berry.

John Rety is other things too – poetry editor for *The Morning Star*, honorary member of some new manifestation of the Theatre of the Absurd, 'Toyota Corolla' in the Icelandic Car Choir, a professional chess player (a Hastings Master in 1956), and he has even written a play, *To Hell with Heaven*, which, so legend goes, he offers people £5 to read. Actually when speaking to him one does enter a kind of theatre, the absurdities flying back and forth, but recording him is another matter: he is faltering, shy even, seemingly unable to distinguish between what has value and what doesn't, but then he claims he is much quieter than he used to be. This he puts down to old age, but, really, I don't believe him. All one requires is a match, and, once struck, a small flame travels in silence to where memory explodes, and suddenly, by the flash it makes, if one is quick-eyed, one gets a picture of things as they once were. In the theatre of operations that has been his lifeline for over a quarter of a century now, we turned the clock back to when John Rety was Réti János and then pushed it forward again to when he was born, aged seventeen.

§

War disrupted a life that hitherto gave no cause for complaint. For reasons that still elude him, Rety was sent to an English nursery school in Budapest. 'Wee Willie Winkie' he remembers, but no equivalent Hungarian rhymes. One of his early memories is of being allowed to take over the steering wheel of the school bus, which really was more like a lorry, he says, and such recklessness of spirit brings to mind the saying that God made Hungarians in order to sit on horseback. All vehicles are extensions of horses or at least that's the case the further east one goes.

Rety's grandfather, Réthi Lipót Pál, was an impresario, head of the First Hungarian Theatrical Agency, and among the people he brought to Budapest in 1907 was Enrico Caruso. Aged 80, Réthi was deprived of the aristocratic 'h' after a court hearing designed, it seems, to bring him one step closer to the proletariat. It seems no Réti or Rety, even an aitchless one, ever strays too far from the stage. Rety's father, István, took over from his father as director but only for the 'metal albatrosses' to intervene.

My mother wore a paper shirt
My father wore a hat –
The metal albatrosses
Soon put a stop to that.

I see them faintly smiling still
And a bit surprised at that

For mother sweet was fond of her shirt
While father was at one with his hat.

But fate and destiny jointly declared
An unequal war on my mother's shirt
And their metal albatrosses
Destroyed my father's fine hat.

('World War Two')

The 'metal albatrosses' require no explanation, but that paper shirt may strike some readers as a bit obscure.

'My mother, Ilus, was full of ideas. There was no soap available, so she decided to make some. It looked like soap, it smelled like soap, it had the hardness of soap, but when you added water it didn't lather. Still it was a great achievement. Then she decided there was lots of paper about, and so why should anybody wear cloth shirts when in summer it was warm enough to wear paper ones. She made these beautiful shirts, always out of the best paper, which you wore for a while and then threw away. She made them for anyone who wanted them. Sometimes she decorated them in different colours with geometric woodcut decorations. Those shirts made their own music, which is to say that when you walked you could hear them crinkle. She was that kind of woman, inventive – a brave woman too, braver than most people in that she took no notice of the bombings, and would never go to the shelter. One day the bombs were falling and she was polishing her nails, and she said to my father, "I have run out of acetone. Go and get me some." My father said, "But, my dear, the bombs are falling." "What are you worried about bombs for? I need some acetone to remove my nail varnish." Another time, we were making tea. She said, "There is no lemon." My father said, "But darling, all the shops are closed, the greengrocers are all gone, and anyway there's not a single lemon to be had in the whole of Budapest." "János, prove your father wrong and get me a lemon." So I went. There was an air raid, people running about, and I knocked this person up, saying to him, "Lemon? Have you got a lemon?" "Yes," he said. So I bought it and ran all the way back through the falling bombs. She said, "How much did it cost you?" I told her. "What, you paid *that much* for a lemon!" That was her all over. She should have written poetry, not me.'

The war, as Rety describes it (and this is so often the case with childhood accounts of battle), is curiously remote. This was in fact largely true of the first years when the country was under the often controversial leadership of Admiral Miklós Horthy, who tried to keep Hungary out of the war, although that sometimes meant striking deals with Hitler, even to the extent of passing a series of anti-Jewish measures. Admiral Horthy also, whenever possible, rescued Jews. Given the fact that Rety's family were nominally, though not religiously, Jewish, their position was precarious to say the least. Things changed when the Americans began their carpet bombing of Budapest, which, though the Americans did not know it, put a temporary stop to the deportation of Jews to Auschwitz. The actual physical fighting started later. It was not until March 1944, when Hungary tried to make a separate peace, that the Germans invaded, kidnapped Horthy's second son, which, after the horror of losing a first son on the Eastern Front, forced the father to abdicate, and the fascist Arrow Cross Party took over. The true horrors began.

'There were some people, very few, who stood up against the tyranny. My father was in hiding somewhere, my mother elsewhere. I took no notice of the restrictions. I went wherever I wanted to. I carried messages for what I now realise must have been the Resistance. I did that while the bombs were falling. The shrapnel whizzed past me, and sometimes I'd pick up a piece that was still hot. I suppose young people living in war zones grow up thinking it is a natural thing to go and see a friend and find only a demolished building. The Russians encircled the town and you could hear gunfire coming closer and closer and all of a sudden they entered, first Pest and then Buda. There was no food. If a horse collapsed on the street people would rush to cut up the carcass. Soon you began to see human bodies all over the place. The bridges were bombed and there was utter chaos. A young person doesn't really care about those things, and I began to believe that was part of my life. I was valet to Captain Gyuri Pukás, a quite well-known actor, son of my family's barber. As it happens my father was his agent. After the war, he was tried by a Hungarian court for being of some rightwing persuasion. I was the only person to go and testify for him. They laughed their heads off because I was only sixteen and they took no notice of what I was saying to them. Pukás was a marvellous person, very handsome, and he got me to stay in some deserted barracks where there lived only a cook and one other person, *me*. Barcza cooked a huge meal each day for all the would-be assembled but it was just us two. The rest of the town was starving and we had all this meat which he cooked in a huge cauldron. Then Barcza would ring a bell at which sound nobody came, we'd eat, and then we'd throw the rest of the food in the gutter. I asked him why he did this and he said, "Orders are orders. I have been told to cook 200 dinners. I'd be shot if I didn't." I suppose these experiences formed my ideas. I became a lifelong anarchist. I don't believe in nationalities, I certainly do not believe in religion, nor do I believe in rulers and I regard the people who rule over populations as either mentally ill or criminal or both. I am prepared to speak English at the moment, but if there was another language I'd be quite happy to speak it because I do not believe in any superiority of any one language over another.'

'Were you ever in danger?'

'I was in another building just a few months before the war finished and this man from the 7th District – his name was Hartyáni, a tailor by profession, a lifelong communist, and, as far as I understood it, district commander for the Resistance – said to me, "Go downstairs to the gate." He opened the gate and gave me a big kick on my backside and said, "Go on, run!" "Where to?" I cried. "Anybody you know because it's not safe here any more." Later, I learned there was a huge police raid on the building and I would have been arrested and put in a camp. Hartyáni survived, or so I believe. I should be grateful to him because he saved me, but I don't know why he had to give me a kick on the backside. After the closure of the barracks, where the cook and I lived, Captain Pukás gave me the address of a devoted friend of his, a bedridden woman called Julia. She was the last person to shelter me. I had to bring her provisions and after a while she began to believe I was her son. When the war finished she was very upset I had to go.'

'Did all your family survive the war?'

'My father survived, my mother too, but unfortunately my beautiful grandmother Sári was shot dead on 11th January 1945, only days before the Russians came. There was some young thug in Nazi uniform, a Hungarian fascist, and she said to him, "Look, boy, you had better remove your Nazi armband and disappear because the Russians will be here soon. Save yourself." There were witnesses to this. He took her into a corridor, and all they heard was a pistol shot. That's one reason why I never went back to Hungary because I couldn't face those people again after what they did to my grandmother. A civil servant, a friend of my grandmother, told me what happened to her. "By the way," he said, "she left a bag of beans. If you come along each day, I will make us lunch." Food was scarce. We ate in silence for about a month. One day he announced, "I'm afraid the beans are finished, so there is no reason for you to call tomorrow." So that was that. When I heard what happened to my grandmother I ran and ran, kicking all the stones, swearing and cursing humanity and everything else. That woman was very precious to me. The reason I'm here at all is because just before the First World War, during one of the pogroms, she swam across the River Drava from what would later be Yugoslavia, with the two small children strapped to her back, my mother aged one and her brother aged two. Meanwhile, my grandfather Schaffer jumped up and down naked on the bank of the river so as to draw the attention of the soldiers who were firing at her. They shot him dead and she made it across to Hungary.'

Years later, Rety's daughter, Emily Johns, produced a linocut of that scene.

'She was a lovely woman. She used to take me to the park and on the way she would stop at a pub where she'd blow the head off a glass of beer and, drinking it in one swig, say, "Don't tell your mother."

She had a machine with which she produced these cloth buttons. She was the poorest of the poor, but she made some money out of these buttons which she sold to the department stores. I would go with her. It was good fun going to those stores because they had some kind of doorless lift that went up and down, which, if you were lucky, you would jump into, otherwise you ended up nowhere. She was the one who did everything. She cooked for all the family but never ate with us. I used to sit with her while the others were guzzling. She would stay in the corner by the window with a Bible in her hands and, being an educated little boy, I said to her, "But granny, you've got the Bible upside down." She said to me, "Don't tell your mother otherwise I won't have five minutes' peace and quiet." She realised that as long as she had a Bible in her hands and gave the impression of being a pious woman they wouldn't disturb her, this despite my family coming from a very atheistic crowd. In some ways I resemble her. I've never been able to keep my mouth shut.'

The Russian army entered Budapest on 17 January 1945, although it would be another month before the city, under the control of the Arrow Cross, capitulated. The Battle of Budapest would be one of the bloodiest sieges of the war. Some 40,000 civilians perished. Rety and some other people were taking shelter in the basement of a tenement building at 40/42 Rákóczy út. The future Hastings Master was sitting on his own, setting out chess pieces on a board, when a group of German soldiers burst in, looking for civilian clothes in order that they might disguise themselves. One of them saw Rety alone at his chessboard, sat down with him and began to play. Rety recalls that he employed the King's Gambit. The German was close to winning when his companions shouted at him to leave with them as quickly as possible. Rety was left staring at his unfinished game. A few minutes later, there was a sound of boots on the stairs and a Soviet soldier burst in, extremely tense, and covered the civilians before him with his machine gun. A woman screamed. The soldier swung round, saw the chessboard and sat down to complete the game.

'And being the man in the middle, I was soundly beaten,' Rety muttered, fully aware of history's ironies.

Rety returned to the other shelter where he had been with Hartyáni. On the floor above, some women and children were having a celebration when a drunken Russian soldier entered, waving wildly his Shpagin PPSh sub-machine gun, which the Magyars nicknamed the 'balalaika' on account of its shape. When Rety went up to see what the commotion was one of the women whispered to him to run upstairs to the seventh floor and ask the woman called Ada to come down, saying she was the only person who could ease the situation.

'Ada practised whoredom on the seventh floor.'

'Practised what?'

'*Whoredom.* She was our local prostitute, a very beautiful, very fussy woman who spent hours making herself up for her next customer. I went to fetch her. I can still remember the room, which was to the left of the door, and there she sat, staring out the window, a little dressing-table in front of her. She was surrounded by gentle lilac colours, soft furnishings. She wouldn't make a decision until she'd heard the full story, which I had to do quickly, and even then she thought about it for a while. She allowed me to watch her put on her makeup. Then she got up, threw a dressing gown over her negligee, put on her slippers, and said, "Let's go." There was now quite a crowd of people standing around the Russian. She sidled up to him and the situation changed immediately. She didn't speak Russian. It was her hands that talked. Theoretical, isn't it? She understood the man was drunk and because she understood that just then he was no better than a dog she acted as a woman who understood men. There are very few women capable of understanding a man in all his moods, their sudden changes, and she dealt with the situation beautifully. The Russian fell asleep in her lap. We have been prudishly made to believe that certain women are saintly and certain women are prostitutes. My advice to a woman who doesn't understand a man is not to live with him because he will not be able to explain to her who he is. These prostitutes, however, they *know*! If Ada's case had been better advertised, she would have been made a saint in the Roman Catholic church.'

'So did it become sexual?'

'It is *always* sexual when a woman calms a man down.'

'Yes, but did he go upstairs with her?'

The queen is a most versatile figure, against which the pawn only rarely has a chance. Fornication, Rety assures me, did not take place.

§

After the liberation, Rety's mother had another brainstorm and devised a poster.

> COME FOR A COMMUNAL BATH, ALL OF YOU. I WANT TO SEE YOU ALL, NAKED AND UNASHAMED. I SHALL WASH YOUR BODIES CLEAN AND TEND TO YOUR SORES. ALL THAT DIRT OF HATRED AND OF CRUELTY WE MUST NOW WASH FROM OUR BODIES AND FORGET FOREVER.

'I don't know if this was ever enacted, but philosophically she was right and certainly it was the right place to do it because Budapest was full of thermal baths. Also we were surrounded by all these bloody priests and their novices. The war was such a long time ago. If you hadn't reminded me, I wouldn't have known it happened.'

'And what of the peace?'

'I must say there is a lot of anti-Soviet propaganda, but I still hold with affection those Russian women soldiers who ran Budapest after the liberation. You never saw women like that, in the middle of the road, with outstretched hands, stopping all the traffic, telling people which way to go. There was no nay-saying to them. Those Russian women *were* the Russian Revolution as far as I was concerned.'

'How did you feel about Soviet forces coming into Hungary?'

'They were a breath of fresh air. I was in the Resistance, hoping for someone to liberate the place. The last three or four months, when all the scum came to the surface, was when the real atrocities took place. In only four months they managed to deport hundreds of thousands of people – Jews, gypsies, political opponents, anyone they disliked.'

> Why did he leave her behind, they were made for each other, they were in love. He could not remember the moment of their parting. 'Shall I see you tomorrow as usual?' 'Not unless you come and see me in London.' She laughed and thought it was one of his jokes.
>
> ('Banal Incidents from My First Period')

'The woman in my "Banal Incidents" is really an amalgam of all my past friends and loves, but she could also be this woman I met just three days before I left Hungary. Viera was married to some distant relation of mine, a man who wrote penny dreadfuls, sometimes two a day. She was a mathematician. She attached herself to me and spent her whole time feverishly writing out long equations. She wanted to make sure I understood all there was to know about mathematics. She gave me, for example, a very simple formula, which I still remember, on how to solve quadratic equations:

$$x = \frac{-b \pm \sqrt{b^2 - 4ac}}{2a}$$

You see, the more unknowns there are, the more difficult it is to find the solution. If there is only one unknown, then it's very simple. The point is everybody wants some kind of ally, somebody with whom he can discuss his ideas. I don't know what happened to that woman but clearly she should have said to me, "Don't go to that foreign country. Stay here. I want to make you into a mathematical genius. I will leave my husband and I'll pump you up with mathematics for the rest of your life."'

§

> There were people who were alive and those were the ones he left. He left them where they were. He didn't take them with him. How could he have put all his acquaintances into one suitcase and carried them across Europe on the Arlberg Express? How could any brain put up with such cargo? One ticket transports one person only, but the suitcase is packed full of ancestors, kin, friends and ex-countrymen. 'Carry your

bag, sir?' 'By all means, as long as you can lift it.' 'But it is as light as a feather.' 'For you it may be, for you don't know, can't feel what's inside.'

('Banal Incidents from My First Period')

'I have no idea why, but I was the first person to be granted an English visa that year. It was guaranteed by a man called György Tarján who was an actor with the National Theatre in Hungary and later became head of the Hungarian Service of the BBC. I met him just the once after my arrival but I was never offered a job or anything. I have no idea whatsoever as to why it was I came to this country. My parents thought it would be a good idea for me to come to England and to continue studying English, but I didn't realise I'd be stuck here.

'It was really going from one war-torn country to another. My aunt who'd lived here most of her life was waiting for me at Dover. There was silver service on the train going from there to London. The city was very poor. The snow was very high that year and there was hardly any heating. There was still rationing, and the whole place was a bombsite, even more so than anything I saw in Budapest, with whole areas levelled. But people were very cheerful. You could still hear Cockney voices, which you don't any more. The point is this:

the first nine years of my life were halcyon days, but once the war started it was not so much the bomb damage which affected me as the fact that everybody around me had gone completely mad. Their behaviour became strange to me. I tried to keep to my own interests and walked the streets of Budapest as if nothing was happening but most people were terribly afraid. I tried not to give in to that but when I arrived in England it was as if all of a sudden I had left a mental hospital and was now living in a free-speaking country. I have never regretted the move. I have become very fond of this place and am probably more anxious about it than most people who were born here. There are signs now of complete dereliction. Almost immediately after I arrived, my aunt burnt my Hungarian passport so I couldn't go back. The British authorities gave me permission to stay for as long as I wished. My first job was in publishing with an old man called Eugene Prager who was also a refugee – from Prague, as it happens; a very lovely man who published some nice books but because he couldn't speak a word of English he didn't know *what* he was printing. I thought I was set up but suddenly he decided to stop and I found myself without a job in 1951, the year of the Festival of Britain, so I hung around the coffee houses until I was asked by some people to edit a new magazine called *Intimate Review*, which published people like Colin Wilson for the first time.'

Elsewhere Rety describes the *Intimate Review* as 'a bohemian newspaper without offices or staff. Its headquarters was a table in the newly opened coffee house in Northumberland Avenue.' Then came his first literary break.

In 1953, Rubicon Press published Rety's first book, *Supersozzled Nights, or, Htuoy's Backward Youth*, an epistolary novel, which in the second half appears to forget it is one. The book doesn't end: it stops. The illustrations by John Addyman are in a satirical vein, and the one on the dustwrapper depicts a young, rather fey, figure at its centre, whom I go excavating for in an older man's features. Ah yes, the uncombed thatch, it's got to be him. It is too early in the history of the human race to be able to say what *Supersozzled*'s literary value is, but maybe it would suffice to say it resists the temptation to become great literature. It is, rather, a relic from bohemian Soho at a time when even its whores were the creatures of a monochrome world. Almost every time I open the book there is a fresh tear at the edges of the pages. Could it really be destined for extinction? Certainly the Soho it depicts is gone, or, rather, it has been displaced by the unaffordable. *Supersozzled* has its moments, but these are like separate cars of a train that comes without a set of tracks, and, at times, is rendered in the slightly laboured English of the foreigner whose disadvantage is to speak it too well for common usage. There are impressive passages, though, such as those contained in a chapter about going to an exhibition of a sculptor whose identity is not important, although it would be nice to know, and which begins, 'There are sculptors, and eminent ones, with their crowing of cocks understandable only to hens.'

> My friends were impressed with his work and I did not tell them my thoughts, they would have called me a purist, with the best not good enough for me. It is true I am apt to speculate now and then, but I try to be fair. I always try to be kind to mediocre people. I praise them and usually make them feel good and on top of the world. I despise the bad and expect miracles from the best, though. I expect the best to surpass themselves, in humility to their fellow beings and because they are the hope of the human race and it is only by their standards that it is worth while to live. Thinking that, I followed them to the bus-stop and decided to go back on my own to continue my meditations. However, as I looked at the back page of my newspaper I saw that the horse which I picked with such optimism was placed third in a field of similar number. Suddenly I forgot all about art and correct and incorrect living and the image of the horse came into my mind and I began to laugh and my friends began to laugh, the way they thought my system of picking winning horses is not good enough.

> Now, I thought to myself, life is complex. There is art, there is fate and there are your cows. Your cows are very important because they complete the picture. They are slow and quick at the same time. They seem to do nothing yet all the time they are producing milk and getting ready for their last day. Their presence is obvious, though seldom noticed. They are the essence of life, all around us and nowhere at the same time. One makes profound statements and the horse he tips to win finishes last and leaves his profundity behind like another umbrella or glove.

'I can still read it, but I wish I wasn't imbued by fiction. That is to say it was all about real people I met in the coffeehouse era of the 1950s, although some of it was made up. I had the idea a story had to be something with a middle, a beginning and an end and which pleased everyone. I wish I'd been less inventive, but I feel it is as good a bit of writing as that from any of my contemporaries although none of them could really write. My situation was that I became more an editor than a writer. If there was a blank page, I quickly filled it with fiction, usually under a different name, but more and more I began to regard myself as a handmaiden to the arts. I then co-edited with the late Peter Everett a magazine called *The Fortnightly* that ran for four issues. It printed people like Elizabeth Smart, Burns Singer, Doris Lessing, Philip O'Connor who wrote as "Caliban", Tom Blackburn and John Heath-Stubbs. I met Louis MacNeice and Francis Bacon and others. There was Peter Brooke who wrote under the name of Anthony Carson, an excellent writer but now completely forgotten. He was a very big chap suffering from some kind of cold and we put him up on our floor where he stayed for three days and suddenly he woke up, dragged me to his bank where he walked up and down with the manager until he got a hundred pounds out of him. Then we had something to eat. I remember him sitting in the French in Soho and scribbling while the printer's devil waited for his weekly article for the *New Statesman*. Francis Bacon, you'd never see him completely sober. Everybody said "Francis is here" or "Francis is gone", but he was always there somewhere. John Deakin the photographer used to be there.'

Meanwhile, in Hungary, there was revolution. One of the victims of 1956 was Rety's father who was walking down a road when the sound of gunfire from a tank startled him and gave him a fatal heart attack. When I asked Rety his feelings about the Hungarian Revolution, I was treated to a dose of his famously contrarian nature.

'I was very happy in England. I really distrusted the so-called Revolution altogether. My impression of the political elite of Hungary was that they were very rightwing, supremacist, and they hated everyone who was not what they called "a Hungarian". They hate the Romanians, they hate the Yugoslavs, they hate the Turks, they hate the Jews, and they hate the gypsies. If all those people did not exist they would invent someone to hate. They didn't like the idea of living in some kind of state, however bad it was, where there was a common education, a common currency, and where people had as much chance to live as the next person, and were adequately housed. They love the colour of their flag, but I wasn't convinced by the Revolution and I am *still* not convinced, especially when I hear about what is going on at the moment. They haven't changed at all. They are just as rightwing and vindictive as they have ever been. I don't like the idea of any kind of state and certainly I don't like police states, but at least under the Soviets they didn't have racial disharmony at the top of their agenda. If I didn't come out of Hungary I'm sure I would be dead now because those disgusting people with their lies would either have killed me or bored me to death. I don't know why I ever had the misfortune of living in their midst.'

Soon after the death of his father, Rety's mother came to London where they lived together for a while.

'One day she said to me, "I would like to get married, so could you disappear from my life. Nobody will marry me if he sees I've got a bearded son." I did see her once more. I was in the Inverness Street Market, in Camden Town, queuing for vegetables, and there was a woman in front of me who I thought looked very much like somebody I knew. I kept jumping the queue, sidling up, and the closer I got to her the more she wanted to disappear and then I followed her and she turned and was about to slap me in the face for molesting her. She stopped, and said "Oh, Jancsi, it's you." She gave me her card, saying she was married, and told me to be careful what I say when I phone her. I never saw her again. My aunt found out from some friends in Budapest that she'd dropped dead two years earlier on Pond Street, in Hampstead. I made enquiries, but I don't even know where she is buried.'

§

After Rety's Soho existence, he and his wife, Susan, opened a furniture shop in Camden High Street. Many of the people who lived in the area were stalwarts of the Soho scene – Jonathan Miller, George Melly, John Roberts and Alan Bennett – and were surprised to find him there. 'What are you doing *here*?' they'd ask, but Rety had now forsaken literature for furniture.

'We used to lend our furniture out to little groups like the Unity Theatre. They were putting on *Hedda Gabler* by Ibsen and decided on this beautiful writing desk, which they put on reserve, but before it went to them this American woman came into the shop and said she wanted to buy it. She was very beautiful and looked to me like she was quite well to do. I can still smell the perfume she carried with her into the shop, which had a very springy scent. I said that for the time being we couldn't sell it because we had promised to lend it to the Unity Theatre. After a while, the desk came back and she still wanted to buy it. It was a little Edwardian writing desk, very suitable, I suppose, for a woman. It had a red leather inlay that was slightly frayed at the edges and she told me she wanted it replaced with one of Midnight Blue. So I sent it to the leatherers, J. Crisp & Company, in Hawley Road. She kept coming in, asking whether it was ready because she was writing on her knees. I was rather surprised by that expression. I didn't know what she meant by it. After a while, the desk came back from the leatherers. All cleaned up and polished, it looked very nice. I telephoned her but there was no reply, so I went along to 23 Fitzroy Road, just on the way to Primrose Hill. There is a plaque on the wall for W.B. Yeats who lived there.

'A man in shirt sleeves opened the door. "Could I speak to Mrs Hughes?" He said, "What do you want?" I said we had the desk ready for her and this man looked at me, and said, "The woman is dead and you fuck off." Which I did. What else could I do? I went back to the shop a bit disturbed about the whole thing. I told Susan what happened. "Who *was* this chap?" I asked her. I should have known but I took very little interest in poetry at that period. I could tell you whether something was made in 1830 or 1910 or whether it was Jacobean or Edwardian, but because I do one thing only at any one time I devoted myself to that side of things and forgot all about literature. She never actually introduced herself as Sylvia Plath. She just gave the name "Mrs Hughes". When the story broke in the local newspaper, Susan realised that it was her. She was not all that famous yet. She was *Ted Hughes's wife*. It was very curious because two other people from the same household used to come in, the Wevills. They bought furniture from me and later I helped them move to Highbury Fields. Assia Wevill was very beautiful and, come to think of it, it must have been her who introduced Plath to our shop. I was never a confidant to their relationships, of course.'

'Presumably when Hughes said this to you he was in a state of some anguish.'

'I think he looked upon me as some tradesman, bothering him. Years later, I met him at the Festival Hall, in the company of Danny Weissbort, and I thought of reminding him, but he had become quite a different person, relaxed and charming, so maybe I had caught him at the wrong moment. After a while, I began to blame myself because instead of going along with this woman and doing all these things to this wretched table – sorry, this *very beautiful* table! – I should have asked her a simple question, "But, Madame, why are you writing on your knees?" And then maybe she would have answered and I could have forwarded myself twenty or thirty years into the kind of thinking that would have allowed me to understand what she was talking about and she would still be alive. She would not have committed suicide, and I would have realised that she was not just talking in parables, but thinking to herself, "Look here, poor man, but I just don't know what I'm doing." What kind of phrase was that, *writing on my knees*? She must have been in a terrible condition, but she didn't look it. She was very beautiful, collected, well-dressed, and, as I said, her perfume still remains in my nostrils after all these years. What else could I have done?'

I wonder, though, if there is not another explanation for Ted

Hughes's outburst, which may be found in his posthumously published *Birthday Letters* (Faber and Faber, 1998), in a poem titled simply 'The Table':

> I wanted to make you a solid writing-table
> That would last a lifetime.
> I bought a broad elm plank two inches thick,
> The wild bark surfing along one edge of it,
> Rough-cut for coffin timber. Coffin elm
> Finds a new life, with its corpse,
> Drowned in the waters of earth. It gives the dead
> Protection for a slightly longer voyage
> Than beech or ash or pine might. With a plane
> I revealed a perfect landing pad
> For your inspiration. I did not
> Know I had made and fitted a door
> Opening downwards into your Daddy's grave.

There really was such a table. At the end of the poem, there is a bitter reference to those 'peanut-crunchers' who'll now be free to examine Plath's writing desk as well as her life, which, as well as being doubtful poetry, is both odd and justifiable. Who does he accuse, then, here, on *this* page? I relate only what was told me, although this may not be, is hardly ever, excuse enough. I plead John Rety's case. As a warning against intruding into matters unknowable Hughes is, of course, absolutely right and there can be few writers in recent times who suffered more the finger-wagging of others, most of them absurdly remote from the scene, but nevertheless his admonishment does sound a bit strange coming in poems which themselves are so intimate. The private, here, intrudes upon the public. Whether well versified or not, it hardly matters – those poems simply had to be.

So what really did happen on that winter's day in February 1963, when, maybe for the first time ever, a Hungarian acted in complete innocence? (I am sorry for the jibe. After all, it has been said of Hungarians that only another Hungarian can love a Hungarian. Also, given that I'm partly of that vicinity, and may even have some Magyar blood in me, I'll say what I like.) To summarise: the table Ted Hughes made for Sylvia Plath a couple of years earlier, in

September 1961, would have been left behind at Court Green in Devon, a sad token of a broken marriage. She had needed another table upon which she'd write the poems that would knock those still floundering in the typescript of *Ariel* into the shade. After all, she was only 31 and new to her mature voice, on the brink, as it were, and she'd already found the table that was completely *hers* or would be once it got back from Crisp & Co., newly inlaid with Midnight Blue. As 'peanut-crunchers', we may allow ourselves to believe it was her favourite colour. She had already painted her floors in it.

After her suicide on 10 February 1963, Ted Hughes moved from Soho into 23 Fitzroy Road in order to take care of their children. At night, lying awake in his dead wife's bed, he could hear the howling of the wolves in their cages at Regent's Park Zoo. Their terrible voices seemed to carry messages, and so they would to someone as morbidly sensitive as he was. 'What are they dragging up and out on their long leashes of sound,' he wrote, 'That dissolve in the mid-air silence?' Small wonder, then, that the daylight intrusions of a furniture man might have sent him over the edge, and it must have been so terribly galling, as well as painful, for him to discover that a writing-desk was Sylvia Plath's final purchase.

'I don't know why these things happen to me,' Rety continued. 'There was a play by J.B. Priestley, *Dangerous Corner*, which my father brought to Budapest in 1946. Something fatal happens in it and the playwright goes back to that moment and tries to change events, the idea being that if somebody had said something other than what was said then the whole sequence of events might have been different. It must have made an impression on me because later it made me think, "Ah, if only I had known who Mrs Hughes was."

'Another strange thing happened to me after I published Colin Wilson in *Intimate Review.* He had become famous because of his *The Outsider* and in November 1956 he invited me to go to the Royal Court Theatre where he, Wolf Mankowitz and Arthur Miller were to have a public discussion on drama. Kenneth Tynan was in the chair. I arrived late, so I was taken upstairs where there was a bar with the grille pulled down, and by the grille there was a blonde woman in black, sitting with her back to me. The man asked me to wait until there was a moment when he could slip us inside and then he said to this woman we would have to wait until the lights were down because the management didn't want the audience to notice she was there. I took no notice. We were taken in and she sat in front of me. There was a huge row on stage about the meaning of *macrocosm* or *microcosm*. Colin Wilson was white with fury, Arthur Miller was sucking his pipe, and Wolf Mankowitz was trying to be funny. I noticed the woman in front of me left before the end. And then I was told it was Marilyn Monroe. The point is this: Marilyn Monroe committed suicide. Now, if I had chatted with her in that bar I could have asked her, "Why is it that you don't go in as the star you are? Why do you have to take second fiddle to this man talking about microcosm or macrocosm?" Maybe one should just say that at every moment in one's life one has to be as collected as possible, so that one does the right thing, and alter events there and then, say "yes" or "no" at the right moment, and behave accordingly. These two stories stay together in my head. It was such a long time ago nobody will be hurt by this any more. Miller is dead, isn't he, and so is Monroe, and so are Plath and Hughes. I read somewhere that Kafka was frightened of coincidence.'

'But you are looking upon these events as opportunities.'

'Opportunities lost! It is too late. There is somebody else who has caused me sleepless nights. Who was that shabby little man I met in Brighton in some old Lyon's Corner House? He came up to me, and, putting something in front of me, said, "What do you think of this?" And he kept doing these quick sketches, one after the other, drawings of the earth, showing the roundness of the horizon, and things coming from elsewhere. Later, I was told there was this man living in Brighton who'd set up Britain's radar defences. I should have had the courage to say to him, "Who are you? Why are you talking to me? What's all this about a four-minute warning?" And here he was, working out whether it was possible to have defences against a nuclear attack. Such a shabby little man, who was he? You walk about and then somebody comes along and says, "Help me across the road. You can make three wishes." It happens. Everyone must have memories about meeting somebody who was trying to tell him something.'

§

'I like what you said about being born when you arrived here.'

'Well, *John Rety* was born – there's no doubt about it. I had problems with this. The people who printed the pamphlet contacted me, saying I should change the blurb because it was a complete nonsense. "How can anyone be born *aged seventeen*?" they said. They have no sense of humour, but "John Rety", both as a name and as an entity, did not exist until I came to this country. I am very conscious of that.'

'Do you still think in Hungarian sometimes?'

'As much as I *think*. I don't think a lot any more, but it used to be that I'd ask myself a question in Hungarian and then ask myself the same question in English, and I'd find the answers weren't always the same. Each language *thinks* differently. I've tried it. I had to make some important decisions in my life, and so I asked myself the same question in both languages and I got contradictory answers.'

'Such as?'

'Well, one said "Do it" and the other said "Don't".'

Coda (2011)

It was an uncombed atmosphere. Can there ever have been an occasion that so captured a man whole? The anarchists were there; the Stonehenge hippies; poets and actors; chess players; musicians, among them Hylda Sims who sang a rollicking ballad of her own composition, 'Mooching in Soho', Soho from the days of skiffle. It was, in short, a fabulous rabble. The commemoration for John Rety took place at the Art Workers Guild in Queen Square on 19 March 2010. It may be the very last event of its kind, not so much because of the man whose life we had come to celebrate, although it is hard to imagine its equal, but because it captured a London that is all but gone. One could be forgiven for thinking bohemia was alive and well and not smothered beneath chummy surrogates. Also it demonstrated that John Rety was bigger than the Poetry Society, bigger than the Arts Council, bigger than all those sleek organisations whose sole purpose it is, often under the guise of 'the shock of the new', to house-train the arts. The space from whence he came, and which, together with his partner, Susan Johns, he had helped to create, was a zone where poetry *happens*, not because it is fuelled by subsidies but because of the generosity of spirit that underlies such things *when true*.

A couple of days after he died of heart failure, on 3 February 2010, I happened to be on Kentish Town Road. I saw and felt him everywhere. I passed the eccentric sandwich bar, Tolli, which was a favourite spot of his. This sparked a memory of sitting with him there, cocooned on the upper level, going over his corrections to the piece I wrote on him. Quite suddenly, he looked directly at me, and said, 'Will I live long enough to see this published?' It was not always easy to disentangle the serious from the theatrical in him and I have to confess I opted for the happier option. A world without him seemed, just then, inconceivable. There was, though, something awfully tired in his face. The piece appeared before he died, in *PN Review*, and so he had the satisfaction of being able to say to people I had created 'a marvellous fiction'. If it was a fiction, it was one that he perused and corrected at every stage. I never thought that he, avowed anarchist, would be such a stickler for detail. We came to a complete halt over whether Admiral Miklós Horthy was a goodie or a baddie.

There was struck a most lovely note, one among many, that night in the Grand Hall of the Art Workers Guild. It was one that touched on yet another of his concerns. Had I known about it before, it would most certainly have entered my piece. In a way I'm glad it didn't because its absence demonstrates the fact there is always another facet in the man's character waiting to be revealed. (And still I'm finding them: among the various comments posted by people on the internet was this one: 'I remember John blowing up and popping brown paper bags on Whitehall, to protest the sonic booms of the Concorde airliner!' I wish, too, he had told me about the anti-war play he wrote and performed on the steps of the Hungarian Parliament just after the war, when it was decided that Budapest was not perhaps the safest environment for a young man of ballooning anarchic sensibilities.) Ah yes, that note: John Rety's daughter, the artist Emily Johns, read out a letter which he had published in the September 2009 issue of *Peace News* (London), written in response to the recent and disgraceful treatment of Roma people in Belfast. It was, for me, the high point of an evening packed with surprises. I reproduce it in full, as a testament to its author's humanity:

> Although I am not a habitual letter writer, I am so dismayed and emotionally moved by the news of the savage maltreatment of the Roma people in Ulster that I feel I must try to add my feeble voice to what I hope might become a thunder against ethnic violence in our midst. The government is first and foremost to blame for not having carefully explained to the local population that these poor people were trying to find a sanctuary in this country. The shameful killings and political attacks on gipsies in Romania and Hungary are shameful, horrible and despicable. But I also grieve for the Roma for a very special reason. I was a 14-year-old boy in Budapest in September 1944 running errands for, what I now realise to have been, the resistance. A message that I had to carry took me into a hideout for persecuted people full of misery and despair. I happened to look out of the window; opposite there was a building site and I saw there a beautifully dressed Roma woman carrying bricks. As the sun came out of the clouds she put down her bricks and started to sing and dance. I was certain that she was intending for us to see her. For me in all this gloom and wretchedness of the shelter there came a shaft of light, a sudden presence of Hope. This I shall never forget, and in my gloomiest moods her image of humanity comes into my mind. I hope people of peace in Northern Ireland will rise up and defend this poor persecuted people.

The anarchists, the poets, the actors, the musicians, the chess players, the body-bejewelled Stonehenge people all applauded. The evening was completely his, and, even in absentia, maybe his best of many good performances.

John Rety is dead. John Rety lives.

Swimming in the Tigris, Greenford

The Poetical Journey of Fawzi Karim

Greenford is not where one might expect to find one of Iraq's most esteemed poets, and, in truth, I'd never quite registered the place. The likelihood of my going to Baghdad was just a bit less remote than that of my ever finding reason to go to Greenford, although I *have* been to Perivale. Young Poles have largely taken it over, such that 'Green*fort*' is spoken of in Katowice, and even Gliwice, as a borough of promise. Although it sounds, and looks, like a modern suburb, it is first mentioned in a Saxon charter of AD 845 as 'Grenan Forda' and almost 200 years later it appears, verbally congealed, in the Domesday Book with a named population of twenty-seven people *and one Frenchman*. There were no Poles. An Iraqi was unthinkable. Another interesting thing about Greenford is that its tube station is the only one in London to have an escalator going from street level to platform level and it is also the last escalator to be made of wood. The others were replaced with steel in the wake of the King's Cross fire. True to its name, Greenford boasts expanses of green across which I saw not a soul move.

Greenford, Middlesex. It slipped into one of John Betjeman's verses.

I first met Fawzi Karim at a party in Kensington for a New York writer who is legendary for emptying the contents of other people's refrigerators, as he did mine once. Also, when bored, which is often, he flings his hearing aid on the dinner table. The party, all in all, was not such a bad one. I was enthusiastically introduced to Fawzi by the poet Anthony Howell, co-translator of his long poem *Plague Lands*, which shall here serve as a template for his life. We spoke for ten minutes, maybe more, and although this was over a year ago, when it came time for me to seek out an Iraqi for my world journey through London it was Fawzi who first came to mind. Something about him had greatly struck me, which may have been the quietude of one in whom exquisite manners blots out the boorishness of barbaric times.

(I might have said 'civilised values' but as of late the term has been hijacked by besuited savages.) And there was something, too, about Fawzi's quiet, slightly gravelly, voice, which could be heard above the world's noise. It was quite without pressure. Also, although this did not unduly influence me, he made kind remarks about a series of articles I'd written on Damascus, a city he knows well and which, on occasion, stands in for the city he is not able to return to.

I arrived at his home in Greenford just as a Bach toccata was coming to a close. One wall of his living room is shelved with CDs of classical music, including almost every opera in existence. Fawzi, as I would soon discover, is one of the very few Arab authorities on Western classical music. Also, there is an ancient wind-up HMV gramophone with a golden horn, similar to the one that was in his family home in Baghdad. Fawzi told me how, as a child, he listened endlessly to an old 78 of the Egyptian singer, Mohamed Abdel Wahab, and memorised the lyrics, repeating one line over and over, little realising he was duplicating a skip on the record's surface. There are a good many books, many of them biographies of composers, and poetry, of course, in English and Arabic. And then there are the oil paintings that serve to demonstrate that Fawzi might equally be considered an artist. But then, why not *both*? Why not get over this Anglo-Saxon prejudice of allowing people only a single vocation in life? The paintings are, in spirit and theme, perfectly aligned with his poems, and indeed Fawzi speaks of the paintings collectively as 'a poet's mirror'.

One canvas in particular haunts me.

The poet swims naked in the Tigris, the same age he was when he did the painting, in his late fifties. Fawzi, though, has not, at least in the physical universe, swum in those waters since his early teens. The image, even before one learns this, is dreamlike.

'The sense I get is that the Tigris, even more so than the city it divides, is the great force behind your poetry. Correct me if I'm wrong, but it would appear it also flows through London.'

A serious man, Fawzi laughs only when he means to.

'It may run even stronger here than at its source in Turkey because it belongs to memory rather than to reality which belongs to time that is completely gone. An important thing to remember about Iraq is that when dealing with memory and experience most

people there belong to small, enclosed areas and not to the country as a whole. I grew up in the Karkh area of Baghdad which is on the west side of the Tigris. My actual district was al-Abbasiyya, which is now completely gone. It was destroyed in order to make way for Saddam's palace gardens. It was a beautiful area, natural and simple, full of palm trees. Many of its inhabitants were poor, their livelihood dependent on fishing, farming and dates. We would climb those palm trees, and the smell of the dates when they were not yet ripe, a stage that in Arabic is called *tal'a*, was like human semen, a smell that still reminds me of growing into adulthood. The ancient Egyptians regarded the palm tree as a fertility symbol and from ancient times Iraqis have believed that palm trees contain souls. There is a famous book in our literature, an epistolary work by a group of tenth-century scholars and philosophers who called themselves *Ikhwan al-Safa* ("The Brethren of Purity"). To this day we do not know who they were, or who the compiler of their book was. Their encyclopaedia dealt with all aspects of existence, from the inanimate to plant life, to human, and the various stages in between. They spoke of the palm tree as being the last stage of plant life and first stage of human existence, which is why nobody would ever dream of cutting down one of those trees. There is even a legend of someone cutting into the crown of a palm and hearing a high-pitched voice coming from inside. Those trees are thought to have souls. During the war with Iran many hundreds of thousands of them were lost and then, in our area, Saddam cut them all down. There was an island in the middle of the Tigris, which we'd cross over to in our boats. We would plant things there. We built temporary houses with *hasir*, which is made from reeds. The young people spent their nights there. I spent much of my childhood fishing and swimming in the river. Later, because it was too close to the palace, Saddam banned all boats and even swimming was forbidden. I had no experience of the river as a whole, only of the half kilometre or so which belonged to our area. At the same time, this water was a mythical thing that belonged to Sumerian civilisation. Myth cancels or diminishes the idea of time, so that you find yourself living in the same dimension as the Sumerians. That's why in *Plague Lands* Gilgamesh and Enkidu are actually *there*.'

'The Tigris will nudge us with its epics,' writes Fawzi. Several pages into the poem, Gilgamesh appears beside the river in disguise. 'What happened before will happen again,' he says, to which the authorial voice in the poem replies, 'Yes, but why the modern dress, Gilgamesh?' Gilgamesh, looking over the embankment, sees corpses floating down the river, his own among them. Another image that appears early on in the poem relates to the ancient Iraqi custom of placing lit candles on plates made from rushes and floating them down the river in celebration of that most mysterious figure of religion and folklore, al-Khidr, a Muslim saint whose Christian and Jewish counterparts are St George and Elijah, and whose mythic origins may pre-date all three religions. It had been my intention once to pursue the subject of al-Khidr through the minds of the people who most revere him. It was a pleasant surprise to meet him again in Fawzi's poem. As a figure who might serve to make all three religions tolerable to each other, there is none more appropriate.

'I put a certain light on it now, of course, but I recognised that mythical dimension even at a very early age. Sometimes you understand things without language, as a kind of music inside you, which only much later becomes words. All that I have, even my relationship with the Book, has its origins in al-Abbasiyya. We had a Shi'a mosque there called Hussainiyya, which I belonged to because of its library. As a young boy I became manager of that library. So I began there, with the Word and the Book, although not really with the information contained in those books, and even now I feel some separation between words and their meaning. I loved and collected books, often reading from them in my high voice. The Arabic books, especially the old ones, came mostly from Beirut and Cairo, and had uncut pages that one had to open with a knife. You could smell things rising from those pages. I could smell the shapes of words as they rose, and even their meanings had their own shapes. There was no separation, no paradox, between things. When later, insensitive to the religious atmosphere, I introduced volumes of modern poetry and prose, some of it quite irreligious, I was asked to leave.'

There is a paradox which remains at the very root of Fawzi's thinking. One needs first to understand the layout of a typical Arabic home, the greater part of which is hidden from public view. Its rooms surround an open space, a small garden paradise suggestive of the greater Paradise that awaits those of high moral virtue.

'When I was a child we had two trees in the courtyard of our house. There was the mulberry which was full of light, beneath whose spreading branches my aunt who was blind took shelter from the sun. I used to climb up between the leaves, and there the light flooded in from all directions. The other was the oleander which was the mulberry's extreme opposite, a dim and closed tree, which never accepted our human presence. Its sap was bitter to the taste, sticky, and attracted flies. I like both these trees, but to which do I belong, the mulberry or the oleander? One is bright and open and extroverted, while the other absorbs the light and keeps it there. Although the worlds they represent are for me totally separate, I feel I belong to both of them. I think I prefer the first one, but it's the second which pulls me more. When I speak about music and literature, the difference, say, between Tolstoy and Dostoevsky, or Hemingway and Kafka, often I think of those two trees. Dostoevsky is the oleander because his dark journey is contained *there*. Among painters, the Expressionists belong to the oleander, unlike the Impressionists who belong to the mulberry, who go outside to play amid colour and light. When I listen to Brahms and Wagner, I am again reminded of my relationship with those trees. They are ideal models in a sense. They inhabit the same time period but are of wholly contradictory natures. Brahms is the autumn between two seasons, his love for Clara, though hidden, flashing like the light of the sun between the branches of the mulberry tree. Wagner, on the other hand, prefers the dark places of the soul. He is able to see there as do certain animals at night. His is a special light generated by darkness itself – no need, for him, of sunlight. The love of Tristan and Isolde is a love of death too. Wagner is the perfect oleander. This is my struggle. I do not *like* the oleander – nobody can like it – so why am I obsessed by this dark, secretive tree, even though as a boy I belonged, body and soul, to the mulberry? Always there are these two directions between which I can't choose. That's why from the very beginning I felt it was impossible to believe, either religiously or ideologically, in any one thing. I am divided on the inside. While I may have been a Marxist once, in my early adulthood, as an ideology I knew Marxism was impossible. Marxism is a dream of thought and, like all dreams, is impossible to apply to real life. If you try to force theory onto real life what you get is a swamp of blood such as we had for much of the twentieth century. I can appreciate Plato's *Republic* as a great work of imagination but to make this republic real would be to create a hell for people. I think my poems reflect this inner struggle or what the painter Kandinsky calls "the inner necessity".'

We would salute that oleander, hot with our uniqueness.

That oleander of Fawzi's childhood, whose shoots so often take root in his verse, was chopped down for firewood. This was when Saddam's henchmen took over and destroyed people's houses in order to make room for his palace. When Fawzi said the oleander's sap was bitter to the taste, I wondered *whose* taste. The oleander contains toxic compounds, including cardiac glycosides, only a small dose of which can cause the heart to race and then dramatically slow down, often with fatal consequences. There is no part of the plant that does not contain a deadly poison, and its poisons are various. A single leaf can kill a child, and the bark contains rosagenin which produces effects not dissimilar to those caused by strychnine. The seeds may be ground up and, as has been the case in southern India, used for purposes of suicide. A small amount of sticky white sap causes the central nervous system to collapse, with resultant seizures and coma. What is especially poignant here is that its burning wood produces highly toxic fumes, which, as a symbol for a country in flames, could hardly be more apposite.

'When I think back on my childhood on the Tigris, I realise there were all these great benefits. All the symbols became real, full of life and mythology. It is a river that continues to run through my poetry and which makes me realise that poetry does not deal directly with history but with myth. It is why I criticise most Arabic poets. A poet does not bow to the winds of history. The myth is generated from personal experience, from his struggle with history. The greater percentage of Arabic poetry pays lip service to this history, is like a mirror reflecting it, and too little comes from inner experience. These poets are believers, coming with their dogma, knowing well in advance what they want to say. Poetry, however, deals with something else. A poet has to neglect historical time and go beyond it – he has to make his legend compared to which history is a mere shadow.'

Maybe what makes this image so arresting is its perspective. Fawzi, seven years old, stares not into our but into his own distance. It's as if everything in the photograph is set to his gaze. It is 1952, presumably winter – well, cool enough for him to be wearing a coat – and he is returning home from the school which, so I am told, is hidden somewhere in the shadows behind him. A smudge behind the vehicle, as if the ghost of some greyer architecture, is the old parliament building, which later was replaced by the National Assembly, and it will be on the road from there, six years hence, that Fawzi will see something terrible, which will direct the course of his life. The ditch filled with water – there is another hidden from view on the opposite side of the road – belongs to the ancient irrigation system that channels water directly from the Tigris to the gardens of the houses. Water is, for obvious reasons, a dominant theme in Arabic literature. (Worth noting is a famous hadith in which the Prophet Muhammad says one should never waste water even when sitting beside a river.) One of the buildings to our left of Fawzi is the local café. A bit deeper into the future, when Fawzi is seventeen and already plagued with verses, its owner will doubly, triply wipe the tea glasses clean, and, soon after, he would even break them because the lips that touched them were those of an Unbeliever, that is, if we are to equate a poet asking questions about existence with atheism.

What is even more interesting, and I mean no disrespect to our subject, is the ewe a few yards behind him. It belongs to a woman who lived in one of the houses nearby. The ewe is called *Sakhlat al-Alawīyah* which translates, somewhat clumsily, as 'the sheep of the woman of the family of the Imam Ali', and because it is so illustriously connected it is considered a sacred creature, which may go wherever it likes, whether it be into shops or houses, and almost always with a treat in store. Ill fortune comes to anyone careless enough to shoo it away. Fifty years later, a childhood friend of Fawzi's, looking at this photograph, will remark, 'Why, this is the ewe of the holy woman!' There is nobody of that time and place who doesn't know that creature. What the photo represents for Fawzi is not just a lost world but also, in the relationship between the ewe and the people among whom it so freely moves, forever safe from the butcher's knife, a metaphysical one. It is a world in which a nearby tree, a Christ's thorn, is believed to harbour a djinn that at night throws stones at people who come too close. It is a world of mystery and between it and its inhabitants there is an easy correspondence. Such questions as will be asked are the poet's prerogative. The boy would already appear to know this. The ewe certainly does.

§

There are some people whose lives may be read as narratives, and others, Fawzi's among them, whose lives can be seen as clusters of images. A Caesar demands a narrative; a Virgil is all images. We began with Fawzi swimming in the ancient waters of the Tigris. What is a river, though, without its bridge? A bridge is one of the most potent of images. It can symbolise a link between the perceptible and the imperceptible, a connection between direct opposites, or it can represent a transition from one world to another, or, with its destruction, a sundering between them. In 1952, when Fawzi was seven, his father worked on the construction of the nearby Queen Aliyah Bridge, which, after the Revolution of 1958, was renamed the Jumhuriyya Bridge or 'The Bridge of the Republic'. There Fawzi would take his father picnics in the three-tiered container that has a Turkish rather than Arabic name: *safartas*. Fond though those memories are, they also contain an incident responsible for one of several violent passages in Fawzi's poem, all the more terrifying for being presented in a flat conversational tone.

> My father has been working on the bridge.
> 'Today a man fell,' he tells us.
> 'Landed in the pillar's rod-mesh guts.
> Didn't have time to draw breath.
> The mixer tipped and covered him quick
> With the next load of cement.
> A bridge has to have its sacrifice, I suppose.'

Those lines seem to connect to the construction, between 1931 and 1932, of the White Sea–Baltic Sea Canal, when approximately 100,000 gulag prisoners perished, their bodies used as fill by their Soviet masters who, much to Comrade Stalin's pleasure, completed the work four months ahead of schedule.

'This bridge became an important symbol in my writing. I was from a small, unknown area, and when, aged sixteen, I started publishing my first poems in magazines, nobody knew where I was from. There were no intellectuals in my area who could put me in the direction of poetry. I was the only person in my family who was a keen reader and painted and made sculptures. I grew up relatively isolated and my contact with books was with only the most traditional ones. I didn't realise then how good this was for me. It was only later, aged nineteen or twenty, I went "across the river" to the Rusafa side and mixed with the Sixties generation. Crossing that bridge became symbolic for so much in my life. There, on the other side, each group had its own café. There was one café for Communists, another for Trotskyites, and yet another for Maoists and then there were still others for Ba'athists, Pan-Arabists and so forth. One café was named after the singer, Om Khalsoum, and yet another was for blind people, many of whom played their instruments there. Those cafés were a very important part of our culture, but in some ways it was a dark scene. All the time I kept asking, "Where is *my* café? Where's the café that represents my sense of perplexity and wonderment and separateness?" Everyone belonged to a political party or artistic direction. The writers who enthused about modernity behaved very much like ideologues, even to the extent of creating their own enemies. I could find no space between them. Those people of the 1960s with their readymade ideas remind me of the Russians of the 1860s. Dostoevsky wrote about them in *The Devils* and so did Turgenev in his *Fathers and Sons*. Of course we didn't have a Dostoevsky or Turgenev in our culture who could give voice to these matters. Our situation was similar to theirs in that we too had our devils, real ones, who with their crazy ideas sought to recreate the world on their level, who forced the people to think along similar lines, making them believe their problems could be resolved quickly through revolution. This is why Iraq was completely destroyed, and in precisely the same way the Russian radicals of the 1860s were to blame so too were the Iraqi intellectuals of the 1960s.'

There comes in the poem a strange passage in which Fawzi and a friend are in a boat near the bridge when they witness some turbulence: 'Yards away, some buckled chunk of shrapnel / smashes into the water's face.' It took me a couple of readings to determine where, chronologically, the reader is supposed to be. The temporal haze is deliberate. Although the scene is set in the early 1960s, the object the boys see arrives from thirty years or so in the future.

On 17 January 1991, at the beginning of the operation known as Desert Storm, Major Joe Salata flew his sleek, bat-like F-117A Nighthawk, which the Saudis nickname *Shabah* or 'Ghost', through Baghdad's night skies. At the dropping of those first bombs Salata made the utterance that was heard on news broadcasts all over the world and which reappears, slightly recast, in Fawzi's poem: 'The city lit up like a Christmas tree.' Grossly inappropriate though the image may be, it was not the first time people have located beauty in destruction. Salata, speaking further of this event, says, 'I can remember one target in Baghdad – it was a bridge. My objective was to drop the bridge into the water. It wasn't to kill everybody on the bridge, but I saw a car starting to drive across the bridge, and I actually aimed behind him, so he could pass over the bridge. If I had hit the left side of the bridge, he would've driven right into the explosion. Instead I hit the right side. You can pick and choose a little bit in the F-117 … I think the guy made it safely across the bridge, but you can't really think about that when you're at war. You could drive yourself crazy, thinking of those kinds of things. If you have a target to hit, you hit it.' Joe Salata, only two years Fawzi's senior, made a perfect strike, what in military jargon is called 'placing steel on target'. The column of the bridge, around which Fawzi used to swim, becomes, in the poem, the image of an uprooted tree.

> It's time to deepen
> the gulf left by the roots.
> A tree uprooted grows tall.
> Vacating its place of planting,
> it grows, and then it vanishes
> Like smoke:
> On the water's face
> nothing but the shiver of a breeze.
> My friend and I are in a boat.
> We lean over and lift the shiver
> Off the face of the water,
> making a net of our hands.
> The fish quiver, leap and vanish.

The bombing of that bridge was something Fawzi watched on television, in Greenford, and now, at a curious point in our history, where communication is both remote and intimate, a quick search on the internet reveals the name of he who fired the missile.

§

On 14 July 1958, when Fawzi was thirteen, General 'Abd al-Karim Qasim marched into Baghdad and within hours effectively put an end to Iraq's Hashemite Dynasty. The coup, which was welcomed by the majority of people, was one of the most savage in recent Arab history. The young King Faisal and twenty members of his family, including women and children, were butchered. The evening before, when the world seemed at peace, a Pakistani magician had put on a show for the children, among the entertainments a couple of trained turtle doves, one of which pulled the other in a small cart. They flapped their wings and picked up small objects when told to. Where did those doves go? There is an Arabic term *sahel*, which means to humiliate a person by dragging his corpse through the street. *Sahel* was the Iraqi Revolution's guillotine. It became symbolic of what happens when a people temporarily, and collectively, goes insane. The corpse of the Crown Prince, 'Abd al-Ilah – 'hound of the imperialists', according to slogans of the time – after being cleaved of its hands and feet, was then further mutilated and dragged over the Aliyah Bridge to the gate of the Ministry of Defence where it was hanged. After the souvenir hunters had their way with it, there remained only a piece of backbone. Prime Minister Nuri al-Said ('lackey of the West'), who once rode with T.E. Lawrence, attempted to make his escape dressed as a woman but was spotted when the bottoms of his pyjamas showed beneath the *aba* or black gown. There is still debate as to whether he was shot or committed suicide.

'It is very hard to speak of this because I did not fully understand what was going on. I was very young. They took Nuri's corpse, burnt it, dismembered it, dragged the pieces all over the streets of Baghdad for three days, and after that they hung them from the bridge. The burning thigh I saw with my own eyes, close to my house. All of us ran after it and started shouting revolutionary slogans but I returned home quickly because of the smell of the burning flesh. You can't imagine from where such hatred comes.'

> We saw the world with its trousers down and laughed.
> We opened vents for the smell in our shackled bodies
> And the smell disappeared within us.
> That revolutionary summer had just such a smell.
> And my father said, 'Whoever goes sniffing out corpses
>   would want to be rid of their stench.'

'And because I actually saw this, it came naturally into my poem although there, of course, it takes on a different hue, one that suits the imagination of someone like me. Most of what we have seen since in Iraq is a variation of what happened in the course of that single day. This event produced a great crisis in my unconscious.'

'You spoke earlier of having crossed the bridge to the Sixties, yet you remain critical of them.'

'What happened with my generation happened everywhere. This

is why I criticise the Sixties altogether, whether they were in America or Paris or Iraq. That generation didn't look to the earth but rather to their own thoughts which seemed so bright at the time.'

'Surely, though, the Sixties in Iraq must have been very different.'

'Completely, but it *tried* to copy the Sixties in the West. I am speaking of the intellectuals, of course. They were dreamers full of hate, whose great ideas went ultimately against humanity.'

'You speak of modern Arabic poetry as not being able to embrace the truth and as having become a vehicle for hate.'

'The ideological mind has a clear way. It knows where it ends. The dogmatic person sees clearly the future, which is why he urges people to look there and to neglect the past and present altogether. That's why our countries prefer anthems that sing of the future. This mind in order to give meaning to the struggle must create an enemy especially if there isn't one already there. It got so every idea in our society was a political one. You *had* to be Communist or Ba'athist or, in later years, Islamicist. If poetry does not have the capacity to build a party with guns and knives, then at least it can manipulate the emotions to inspire hatred. One of our best poets, 'Abd al-Wahhab al-Bayyati, wrote a line, "We will make ashtrays out of their skulls." Another poet wrote, "I made from the skin of my enemies a tent to shield myself from the sun" and yet another warns that when he gets hungry he will eat the flesh of his enemy. These may be strong images, but really they are the opposite of strength. They have nothing to do with *real* poetry.'

'Clearly you are outside the mainstream of modern Arabic poetry. When did that separation begin?'

'I think it was there from the start. My first collection of poems, *Where Things Begin*, published in 1968, when I was twenty-four, did not speak of anything ordinarily dealt with at the time. Those poems as a whole were a kind of song without words and as such constitute a brief romantic period in my creative life. The separation was already there, not because of the intellectual atmosphere or the life I was leading but because of something in my own nature. Even the book's title points to a profound difference between me and my generation. When I think back on the titles of other collections published at that time – *Ashes of Bereavement*, for example, or *Dead on the Waiting List* or *Silence Does Not Bother the Dead* – they may sound nice in Arabic but they are empty of meaning. What is reflected in them is the disappointment that hit at their authors' dreams of changing the world through "great ideas". The revolutionary parties to which they belonged failed them although even then they didn't learn. I preferred to start with the things in life and nature that surrounded me, which were close to the earth.'

'You had a great mentor at that time.'

'Yes, the Iraqi poet, Badr Shakir al-Sayyab. I had been looking for new things, especially those coming from Europe via Beirut. Adonis was an important poet for me, but his brightness and greatness belonged not to my own experience but to Modernism. There is nothing from his *inner* experience, nothing unique. That is what I want from a poem. What I realise now is that the "newness" I was after had another name: *timelessness*. I get the "new" only when I start digging into the past. When one is young it is a beautiful thing to think about the world and to interpret it in a different way, but with experience the poet looks behind the surface, conversing with what is hidden there. Likewise, he writes his poem for the hidden reader. I am not *modern*. When finally I realised this, I went back to al-Sayyab. When I was young I would sit with my friends, most of whom were not writers, by the Tigris singing his poems, and even now I sing them. A great poet is one who can make dialogue with me. A poet with whom I am unable to do this is not *my* poet. Al-Sayyab became a Communist but later the Communists hurt him deeply and so he became a Pan-Arabist but, really, he didn't believe in either. He believed, rather, in his own weakness, his isolation among poets who thought of themselves as prophets. He died in 1964, aged thirty-eight, destroyed by everything – the politics, the intellectuals, the women, none of whom loved him although now some of them write memoirs about their warm relationship with him. He was someone who could elevate history with mythology such that even his village, Jaykour, has become a mythical place. If you mention Jaykour in Syria, they will say "The village of al-Sayyab." But it is not the Jaykour of real life. If you mention the Buwayb River everyone will tell you this is the river that runs through al-Sayyab's poetry, but if you go to Basra you'll find it is only a tiny stream. This river became for him a mythical thing, a part of his underground world which he could belong to rather than to this world.'

'You say the intellectuals were largely responsible for the country's demise.'

'We did not have journalists as such at that time. They were mostly intellectuals – poets, writers, or critics. They were the only ones who stood between culture and the people, between ideas and the people. Such ideas as ordinary people had were all taken from the media – TV, radio and newspapers – or else from the political parties, all of which were run by intellectuals. When I describe the café scene as terrible, it is because there were no people there, only ideas. There were answers but never any questions in those places and yet each coterie had its own answer as to what the truth is. I will give you an illustration. I had a good friend, a typical Communist writer, a very nice man whose ideas were so clearly put they didn't allow for questions. This friend was born in the al-Shawaka area of Baghdad. Baghdad has many districts which are either Sunni or Shi'a. So here we have al-Shawaka which is Shi'a and al-Joiafir which is Sunni and separating them is a narrow street, al-Shuhada, which has a lot of doctors and pharmacies. When life was relaxed there was no difficulty between those two sides. When the ideological crisis came, al-Shawaka became Communist and al-Joiafir became Pan-Arabist. The first preferred tomatoes because they are red, Communism's colour, and the second preferred cucumbers because they are green, the colour of the Pan-Arabist movement. I said to my friend, "Try to use your imagination. Suppose you were born fifteen metres away from here, just across the road, what do you think you would have become? You would have been a Pan-Arabist, not a Communist! You are seventy now and you have clung to this illusion simply because, satisfied with readymade answers, you want to be free of having to ask questions. Yet so many people were killed for this illusion."'

'This brings us to the subject of your first escape from Iraq.'

'When the Ba'athists came to power in 1968, I went to Beirut. At that time I left my job as a teacher of Arabic, which I had greatly enjoyed. A lot of boys became good readers simply because I was with them for those nine months. The secret police came to my school, asking questions about me. At that time the Ba'athists began to focus on teachers, and because I was neither Communist nor Ba'athist I was more suspect. If I were taken into custody, there would have been no party behind me. I was accused of stepping outside my lessons and of talking to my students about literature. This was my style of teaching. I talked about Arabic writers and because my students lived far from the centre of Baghdad, I brought them books. A number of students whose families were Ba'athist informed on me. They said I spoke about the devil or the angel and that I had caused them to stray from their studies or that I had advised them to read certain writers. They accused me of being a liberal – *librale* – which was very dangerous accusation because to be liberal meant that one belonged not to any single ideology, Ba'athism or Communism, but to the West. Luckily for me, a relative of mine was then head of the Department of Education and had all the records on me. He warned me to take care, saying information was being gathered on me. So I went to Beirut. My family knew nothing about it. I was twenty-four at the time. I had already published my first book in Baghdad and so I was known in Beirut. Also I was published there in *Sh'ir* and *al-Adab* magazines. At first Beirut was a paradise. It was like Paris. There I read Sartre, Camus and Eliot although I didn't really know how to be modern. I went deeply into things that were never really part of my inner life. It was like watching a lovely American film in darkness and then stepping out into the light and seeing life as it really was. I stayed in Beirut for two and a half years. The poet Yusuf al-Khal was there. Adonis helped me. But a lot of things in Beirut began to destroy me. I started to drink. Alcohol was cheap. Then, in 1971–72, in Iraq, there was a coalition between the Ba'athists and Communists. There was a sense of relief and that maybe now things would get better. So I returned there.'

The story of that return provides what in the poem feels like a sweet hell of dissolution – of endless booze, of evenings spent in debate at the Gardenia Tavern, now long gone, which in Fawzi's writings has become a kind of spiritual home, and of sleeping rough on park benches.

> The waiter sees the mud on my galoshes
> And sweat, from a wank, on my brow.
> A reek, as from the underwings of bats,
>   wafts out, freed from my armpits.
> The waiter tries to head me off.
> Ah, but the summer urges me

> To trample fields not trampled on before
> Or take the shape of a beast from another time.

The irony is that for Fawzi and others of his generation it was a kind of blighted paradise, a hallucinogenic lull before all hell broke loose.

'Yes, but it wasn't such a hell really. Compared to what would follow, it was rather beautiful at that time. We had a safe, if brief, existence. After we left the taverns the best thing was to sleep outside beside the river. This was normal. That was a good period in our history. After the British companies left, the money from the oil was all ours. The Ba'athists showed another face, although at that time I knew Saddam, this man who when he was sixteen killed his own cousin, to be a filthy man. The Communists had to defend him, saying this was *our* man. Only a couple of years later, Saddam's black cars, eight of them, without licence plates, with black curtains in the windows, became a symbol of terror. They drove everywhere at high speed, and from any one of those cars men would leap out and grab somebody, taking him God knows where. If anyone went near one of those cars, he would be arrested. People had no idea if Saddam was in any of them or not. Saddam's name became more important and terrifying than the President's. I knew this man would be the realisation of all my darkest fears.'

'You must have witnessed many tragedies, writers who thought they could embrace one ideology or another and were subsequently destroyed by those choices.'

'They paid no attention to the idea of truth, even if there wasn't any truth to be found, or to the idea of asking questions even if there were no answers. I broke with a couple of friends when they joined the Ba'athists. On the other hand I had many Ba'athist friends, a couple of whom protected me several times, but they were mostly people who were in it from the beginning and not like those who later became Ba'athist just so they could have money and power. These people I avoided. The Revolution destroyed people. People were murdered or else killed themselves.'

> My generation's had to put up
> With its fair share of knocks.
> One hid his head inside a shell

And lived below the surface for a while;
Another died within his coat as he tore at his insides
In a country where brigades of fans
Just blow away the dunes.

'There is nothing I can say about the people I knew that wouldn't apply to the many thousands of others who died. Actually, most of my friends died of other causes, drink, for example. I dedicated my *Collected Poems* to twelve people, some of whom were killed, others who simply died young, but I say all of them were *killed*. They were victims.'

One poet Fawzi remembers in particular is 'Abdul-Amir al-Husairi whom he describes as 'the hero of his own dream'. This *poète maudit* has come to represent for Fawzi and for others of his generation the dying gasp of a romanticism that may owe more to the bottle than to verse. Al-Husairi came from Najaf which is one of the centres of religious learning, home to the Imam 'Ali Mosque, whose resplendent dome is made of 7,777 golden tiles, and which for Shi'a is the third holiest shrine in existence. For a young poet deeply rooted in classical Arabic literature, the move, in 1959, from such a pious atmosphere to Baghdad, now capital of revolution, was a traumatic one. In a new world that demanded of every intellectual that he be aglow with ideological passion, al-Husairi, oblivious to the political circus, saw only that life was increasingly getting worse for most people.

'A very talented poet, he was surrounded by some of the best writers of the time. A romantic, which is how I see myself, that is, belonging to a struggle that involves the duality between freedom and necessity, individuality and responsibility, al-Husairi was, symbolically speaking, the last of his kind. We all drank, of course. Alcohol was an important dimension of any poet at that time. If al-Husairi drank more heavily than us, it was probably because he didn't belong to anything and so, in his alienation, drank all the more. A man of dreams, he was in despair, and finally the drink swallowed him. He lived in a cheap hotel in al-Maidan and every morning he would begin his journey from there, across Baghdad, to Abu Nuwas Street where our Gardenia Tavern was. You need at least an hour and a half, walking in a straight line, to get from where he was to where we were. It took much longer, of course, because he stopped at every bar on the way. Everybody in those bars knew and accepted him. "Here comes al-Husairi!" they'd say and so he would sit with them, drinking one or two glasses of *arak* before moving on, and so, stopping at each place, he would finally come to us at the Gardenia. He would settle there for a while, very proud inside his dream, and spoke like a god, and this we accepted although we wouldn't have done so from anyone else. Then he would continue the rest of his journey by the end of which he would have consumed roughly two litres of *arak*. We all knew that one day soon we would hear of his death. When it came, in 1973, he was still a young man. The great thing about this character was that everybody, even the ordinary people on the street, knew him. This popularity was of a kind that has completely vanished from Baghdadi existence. Al-Husairi was the last glimpse of a great period now gone forever. He was the scion of a great village called Iraq. I did a drawing of him naked.

'With regard to this recurring image of nakedness in my work, I did a large painting once, of an imaginary festival in Baghdad, which depicts a brass band playing, people dancing, people preparing food as if for a special occasion, and in it everybody is naked. Why naked? The naked ones are the dead coming back to life and what you have in the painting is a whole city putting on this great festival in order to receive them. When I drew al-Husairi naked, I believe I did so unconsciously. This is how the image came to me: *he was naked because he was dead*. When I make drawings of al-Sayyab, I also do him naked. So nakedness for me is an image of something coming from another world, from death itself. I even did a painting of myself naked in a room, with a bottle of wine.'

'And then, of course, there were those who went the other way.'

'You need to be very sensitive and talented in order to feel deeply about this tragedy. Most people weren't. Others simply became bad people. I do not wish to mention them by name. Still others tried to get on as best as possible. I will give you another example. One of my friends is a good short story writer who writes about the inner struggles of people, or about the struggles between them and their fate, or about their condition, which is that of always looking for the light. One of his stories is about a man seeking death because for him the height of desire is to vanish. We had all these voices, saying life's problems could be resolved through ideas and ideologies, and then along comes this writer who speaks about things which are so deep. This is what writing should do, teach us how to live. Anyway, it was impossible for such a man to involve himself with politics. At that time Saddam started to support writers, often giving them expensive gifts or money. Saddam sent my friend a Mercedes-Benz. A car in Baghdad is very expensive to run and the Mercedes-Benz was worth more than his house. This was a gift from Saddam, so what could he do? He couldn't refuse this gift coming from someone so terrible. Also he couldn't drive. He couldn't give the car to anyone else to drive nor could he sell it because if the secret police found out he'd be in trouble. So he moved the car inside his house and from then on he spent much of his time on it, cleaning it every two or three days because it was not good to leave the engine. He did this for a couple of years and, after a while, when the tyres started to sag from disuse, he propped the car up on stones. All this was just so he could avoid problems. Chekhov could have written a story about this nightmare. It is such a dark and beautiful theme, what the Russians call "a smile between tears", and all this poor man could do was grimace.'

§

Fawzi, it has to be said, is a good cook. It must have taken him ages to stuff the tomatoes, peppers and courgettes with herb-infused meat and rice, a Baghdadi speciality. Our move to the dinner table, in a room flooded with light, where a wasp flew in circles, also provided a natural turning point in our conversation, which now focused on his decision to leave Baghdad forever.

'I did so because I wanted to survive. I desired another language, true, but this was not the main thing that drove me out. It was in order to survive. When I returned from Beirut I wrote for a weekly magazine. I received a fixed wage, although I was not formally employed, either as a worker or a journalist. I preferred this. If I wanted to leave the country, however, I had to get written permission from my head of department, which I couldn't do because I wasn't working officially. So I persuaded a Ba'athist friend to ask the director who, by the way, was a well-known poet, to give me this paper granting me leave to travel for two weeks. My friend tried several times and each time was refused, the director's excuse being that once I was on the outside I'd write a poem against the regime. He said this even though he knew I wasn't a political writer! One day, without realising it, he signed the paper. It was the end of the day, and he wanted to go home, and so, without looking at them, he hurriedly signed all the papers in front of him. The following morning a nice old man who brought us tea said, "Fawzi, this is for you." I told my friend, and he said, "Don't tell anyone!" I got my passport in a couple of days.'

> My friend, take off your shoes.
> Take off your shoes and go barefoot,
> For this is the last time we tread
> The ground of our country.
> Tomorrow the footwear of exile will fit us both.

'First I went to Paris which is "the city of light", where everything's on the outside. Paris, the Latin Quarter in particular, is traditionally the first choice of Arab intellectuals. I stayed there for a month. I can't criticise Paris which, after all, is the heart of Europe, I had come from Baghdad, which was very poor and simple, to the great city of Sartre, Camus, Rimbaud and Mallarmé. But I didn't really like it there. The French are so very fashionable, changing all the time, and with the Arabs it's the same. Every couple of years or so, we have a new school of thinking. I hate all that. My time does not move. In Arabic we call it *dhar* or, in English, "eternal time". When I came to Dover the policeman asked me, "Why are you visiting Britain?" I didn't have the English words with which to answer him. "Holiday?" he asked. Still I couldn't understand, so I started looking for a small dictionary I'd brought with me. I couldn't find it. "Okay, okay," he said, "You're on holiday," and let me pass. It was like a dream. When I arrived at Victoria Station, I knew immediately this was my city. I felt something here embrace me. I had left a country where I spent five years in darkness, which was not safe, where anything could happen to you. I was frightened, of course.

'Again I go back to those two trees. Paris is the mulberry tree, full of light, all my friends sitting and chatting in the cafés, while London is the oleander where everything is wet and dark or else hidden behind walls. When I begin to compare them, I can see why I love London more. It's because it brings me to myself, to what is deep inside me, and to what I need. Here was a country which had Romanticism for two hundred years and also there were the same red double-decker buses that we had in Baghdad. I worked as a proof-reader for an Arabic newspaper. I didn't work as a journalist, which was a good thing because I didn't have to mix my poetic language with journalistic language. I started writing articles on music. I got a bicycle. I had one in Baghdad. It was not often you saw a poet on a bicycle there. They called me "Abu Bicycle". With time, I came to love London in a real way and also, of course, the English language. London is a very generous city. If I belong to any city, it is this one. I appreciate its humanistic side even though, in 1981, I was attacked and badly beaten by skinheads in Earls Court. I was on the way home from seeing *Rigoletto*, carrying my bright red programme. There are bad people everywhere. This city gave me, for the first time in my life, a place to live. In Baghdad I lived in cheap hotels, seedy rooms in poor areas. And then, in the first year I was here, I had a serious heart attack. My friends said, "You fled Iraq only for this to happen?" I lost all hope. I felt this was the end of life. Strangely, though, this awful experience greatly benefited me. Maybe it gave me more than life itself gave me. Death had come so simply. The word became real, maybe deeper than reality itself. All of us speak about death, but really it's only words. What is the difference between words and experience? You may have a lot of things but not the fruit that comes from them. A great man may know death without experiencing it – he does not need to be on a deathbed to understand that without death life is nothing and that it can push the poet or thinker onto a road of knowledge and wisdom that previously had seemed inaccessible.'

'You say you have not been able to swim in English time.'

'Sometimes I feel I am not really living here and that for these past thirty years I have been inside a great library. I go to the shelves, remove a book, and then replace it. I may enjoy this, but it is not really life. I think that in order to feel he is alive a writer needs to know that somebody somewhere is talking to him. A reader who likes what I write *speaks* with me. Maybe this is what I have lost or what I miss most living here. I am not English. I do not *live* among English people. I do not have English friends. I met some English poets, but with them it was mainly sitting and talking arbitrarily about things on the outside, nothing ever really in depth, and then nobody contacts you afterwards. Still I don't feel I'm so terribly isolated because my close friends are books and music. I need at least double this life to obtain half of what I want. This isolation is not life, however, and maybe to say I am living in a great library sounds a shade dramatic. Sometimes, though, I feel I am waiting, like Godot, at a train stop. A train comes every minute, full of people, and there is no space for me. So it is very hard to speak about this and to which time I belong when I don't belong to any. Maybe this is the tragic side of my life or, because I feel it so deeply, it might even be the most enjoyable side. The richest part of my intellectual life has been spent here. Modern English poetry is still hard for me, and much of what I see is, I think, very provincial. You need to be a Londoner to understand a London poet. I am involved with a metaphysical dimension, which is why I prefer poets like Czesław Miłosz who are similarly engaged. Only there, in that dimension, do I find someone to speak to.'

'When you first came here, did it take a while to find your poetic voice again?'

'I think I stayed silent for just one or two years, but then I busied myself with a lot of other things. I studied language, and I tried to read English books. When you first came here from Canada it was, in a sense, like going from one village to another, both of which had similar cultures, the same poets and the same philosophers, but coming from a place like Baghdad meant I had to cross a much deeper divide. And now my friends are dead or else they have become old and the places I knew are gone, the Gardenia Tavern, for example.'

The Gardenia belongs to Fawzi's massive store of images. When he returned to Baghdad for the first time, in 2004, he found it closed and it has become yet another place which he can revisit only in painting and verse. It is the subject of one of his most powerful canvases. The empty space at the lower right-hand corner is where the poet al-Husairi should be.

'When I say my time is gone, I speak as a poet. It is not difficult for me to go to Damascus and to re-enter Arabic time, which means just happily sitting there and watching, and thinking about nothing at all, and going towards nowhere in particular. I need this sometimes, but I couldn't live there. Anyway, as you said to me earlier, Arabic Time is disappearing – it is being replaced by World Time.'

'Away from your audience, what enables you, or pushes you, to write? Who are you writing for?'

'Sometimes I feel I write for nobody at all but at least in some corner of this world, and I have experienced this several times, there are people who read my poems and like them and feel they have a dialogue with them.'

'So maybe being here has helped you.'

'It has helped me a lot! If we both understand what we mean by the word "exile", I am not an exile in the way many people like to think. I'd sooner say I was already an exile in Iraq when I began to write. I felt language to be an obstacle, and not a thing I needed, and that it was impossible to push language all the way to its roots. Often I tell people if I could be anything else it would be a composer and this is because music is abstract and as such it is where my passion and my struggles lie. Words alone just won't do it for me. When dealing with language, a poet has certain problems because the words he uses are the words everybody else uses. We know language is the only tool of communication between people. So I come to words, wishing to use them in a completely different way, but will the language go easily with me? Will she accept me as a visitor and allow me to use her differently from, say, how a scientist does? The important point here is that rather than settle for the language we all use, I dream of going back to its very roots, to the very origins of language. When a human begins to give expression to something he starts with movement – words come later. At the beginning there was no gap between the word and the thing it describes. With time, that gap became bigger and bigger and the words became symbols for many other things as well. So when a poet deals with language, he dreams about returning to its source, when the word *was the thing*, but already he is an exile because there is a gap between the thing said and what he desires. He struggles to close this gap, but it is impossible. This is the first dimension of exile. If we go to another dimension, another level of exile, here you are, someone who thinks and feels and sees differently from the people around you. This is the problem between the individual as poet and his society. It's not easy really.

'When I was quite young I dropped everything and went to Beirut. Most of my dreams at that time contained my mother and father because I hadn't yet finished with them, I still needed them, but I needed to leave too. So this, in addition to the other two I have just described, was another form of exile. When I returned to Baghdad, I knew something was forcing me. It wasn't really a matter of choice. It was partly the illusion that everything there was about to improve, the political coalition being a new step towards paradise, but I knew this to be foolish. Also, I needed to return because I was tired of Beirut and of being without work or money. All the while I knew it would be going back to hell and so, for another six or seven years, I struggled inside this hell. The other day I wrote a poem in which time becomes a boat on the Tigris and it goes with the current to the sea and there vanishes completely. So I came to London. I watch the Thames here, full of boats and with no space for any smaller ones between them. It is not my time at all. That's why I say it is not so bad to live without time. And this is what I mean about exile inside language, that there is some great source which is forever lost. We are exiled from the origins of language. So it's not really true when I say I have written a new poem. There is no *new* poem. One just repeats things, adding a little bit here and there to the great store of poetry that has been available since *Gilgamesh*. If the "new" happens, it does so only on the surface or with technical matters. For thirty years now, I have had this familiarity with English or Western poetry – I do not differentiate between England and the rest of Europe because for me the West is one huge country.

'If I have familiarised myself with Western art and poetry and philosophy and music, and I'm still pursuing things as yet unknown to me, I have failed to do the same with people themselves. I think this is not only a very deep exile but also a tragedy. And – this is the terrible thing – I enjoy it! If I could choose, if I could be familiar with the people who love their culture, it would be a great thing, but it seems impossible now, especially at my age. This is hard for me and yet this gives me depth and courage. I do not feel I am dealing with ordinary things but with the exceptional. So it is not necessarily a negative exile. When I think about exile, it is not in the ordinary sense of the word. It is one of many dimensions. I remember once looking at a map of the universe, with its millions of galaxies, surrounded by this great darkness from which it is impossible to derive any answers, and I felt there was no space for our galaxy with its sun and earth and of course there was no space for me. This gave me a deep sense of universal exile. Suddenly I felt this great loneliness and a sense of no longer being safe. It was as if I were a child seeing his house for the first time without his father and mother. This sense of not belonging anywhere is what provided me with the first glimpse of a metaphysical dimension.'

'And being surrounded by the English language, has that in some way helped purify your Arabic?'

'Yes, the English language has greatly benefited me, not just with the logical structure of its sentences but also, most importantly, with its sense of justice. In Arabic, there are many words which I'd call "unjust". For example, often when we speak about something or someone we'll automatically add *'alā al-itlāq*, which means "absolutely". We use this word all the time and yet it doesn't allow space for either the speaker or the listener to understand his limitations. Arabic puts great value on the sound of the voice, the tone of the rhetoric. What is said in Arabic is so abstract, so boundless, whereas in English you don't employ more words than you require. This has affected my poetry, which is why when I return to my old poems I see in them a lot of meaningless space. The great classical eighth-century writer, Al-Jāhiz, said that one shouldn't care too much about the meaning, that meaning can be got anywhere on the streets, whereas what is more important are the shapes and sounds of words. Our critics repeat this still.

'I will give you another, perhaps more direct, example. We have Arabic states led by dictators everywhere, from Morocco to Iraq. I am talking about the last hundred years. We have no democratic states. These dictators stand and speak to the people and even if what they say sounds nice you feel some sort of command in their talk. This has been reflected in our literature. When we write, we do not think about the listener or reader as being another part of the conversation. This takes from the very soul of writing itself. It is undemocratic. We are excluding our audience from the dialogue. When I write a poem I want to feel somebody somewhere listens to me and converses with me, thereby giving life to the poem. This is almost a dead issue in our modern literature. I already gave you a couple of examples of strong images, which to my mind merely denote hate. This is something terrible we have in our language. The poet says what he does not really mean, which has nothing to do with his experience, and which he himself does not believe. It is not necessary for him to believe in what he says but rather to present a strong image. That is why even our great classical poet al-Mutanabbi is full of these lies. They may be powerful images, but I read them as expressions of strong hate. This is what I mean by justice. As a consequence of being here, I have become very close to the idea of the simple sentence, one in which there is no exaggerated feeling or idea or belief. It is better to leave things just as they are. Once you add these other things you misjudge, you become *unjust*.

'The Arabic poetry of the last forty years has become so empty, such that with many books you can't even get past their titles. You then go inside them and there is no solid basis of knowledge, no dialogue with surrounding experience, nothing there is *settled*, and yet the language stays afloat like a balloon, growing inside itself. There is no weight of human experience. This covers almost seventy per cent of Arabic writing in that it is artificial and empty. You have these post-modernists imitating New York, and even now, in these terrible times, they are speaking in the same tone. This is the height of carelessness. It is not necessary for Baghdad to become Paris in order that good poetry be written there. This is the story of my struggle with Arab intellectuals, which is why most of my books do not go down well with them.'

We barely quarried the mountain of food Fawzi made. There was enough to see him through for a week or so. We moved back into the relative darkness of his living room where I suggested we end where we began, with the painting of him swimming in the Tigris, which depicts him as an older man rather than the child he was when he last swam there.

'Painting for me is a relaxation from writing poems. Writing makes me tense, whereas painting is like going for a walk in wide open spaces. It is a working of the soul and body together. Some friends of mine who are painters say this is not painting in the way they understand it because usually one starts from colours, shapes and lines. They say I know how it will end in advance. This is not strictly true, but always the *image* is the first thing to come to me. I remember that the sense I had while painting this was of a man dreaming he is still swimming in the Tigris. As I said before, I do not live as others do, inside a current of ordinary time. You can see in the upper corner of the painting a wooden boat, called *belem* in the local dialect, which at that time was a principal means of river transport. Those boats are no longer in existence. Saddam forbade their use. The secret police destroyed my brother's boat and then beat him. The water in this painting has a double nature. It reflects a richness of life which at the same time is horrible. It is like the Will of Schopenhauer, a blind force that gives life and death at the same time. When you read Sumerian literature, the water there has another life. In the marshes in the south of Iraq, where the Tigris and the Euphrates meet, you get this still water, the stillness making it seem all that much darker. The ancient Sumerians believed it was at that place one crossed over to another world. It was where, each year, the god Thammuz began his great voyage to the underworld. Al-Sayyab felt instinctively that this water was a current of hidden time. It is pretty much the same with the water in my poetry. I call these paintings "the poet's mirror". Sometimes what he sees is devilish in nature, a madman with a dark figure behind him or a naked man sitting in a strange, empty room with his bottle of wine. I think you can deal with these paintings in the same way you deal with my poems.'

'Would you ever go back to Iraq to live?'

'I don't think so. Even if everything settles down in Iraq, and I go back there to live, I'd swim in a time that has nothing to do with me any more. Simultaneously this encourages me. It gives my poetry a new dimension. The idea that my time is dead is not really such a bad one. I have not swum in English time either. A friend of mine, a good writer, tells me this is wrong, that I must belong to what I have now. "You should write in English," he tells me. Maybe he is right, but even if that were possible I don't think I could give in English what I can still give in Arabic. The fact that I can give at all is because I am in a void. This is no bad thing. Most people need time. A poet doesn't need time.'

Always the gentleman, and also because a dicky heart requires he take exercise, Fawzi put on his cream summer blazer which, maybe because of his dark complexion, makes him look so handsome, and accompanied me to Greenford Station where, uniquely for London, although commonplace for those who live there, one goes up to the train platform on a wooden escalator which has been granted, to the joy of rail enthusiasts everywhere, a stay of execution. This, too, was a journey outside time.

Old Turk, Young Turk

Moris Farhi and his Journey to the Fountain of Youth

I hope he will not be offended by the title. It is not to suggest that Moris Farhi is old, which he is not, or that he is particularly young, on which matter I'll hold my tongue, but that in him, as in most writers, the imagination, a promiscuous creature, is no polite observer of age. There, in the country which it explores, young and old entwine. Moris, or 'Musa' as his friends call him, after four decades of projecting himself onto the geographies of elsewhere, has at last revisited, with startling effect, the land of his youth or, more specifically, Ankara when it was still a fledgling capital – 'a small town of no importance' according to the *Columbia Lippincott Gazetteer* of the time. *Young Turk* (Saqi, 2004), which here serves as a template for my enquiries, is 'a novel in thirteen positions', a description that not only reflects the different perspectives from which it is told – some of whose narrators are the author, or, rather, bits of him in various guises – but also the fact that for Musa the road to Paradise runs through women's bodies. (He is also the author of some erotic verses.) When asked about the images dearest to him the one he returns to is Gustave Courbet's *L'Origine du Monde*, a painting whose overt eroticism even today rarely fails to shock.

Curiously, for all his sexual gung-ho, he was a bit thrown by my first question.

'Musa, how is it the women in your stories are always so willing?'

'Are they?!'

There is something of the pasha about him, a corona of whitish beard and swept hair, a boyish twinkle in the eyes, a mellifluousness in his voice that allows one to feel the red carpet to the deepest chamber of the heart has been unrolled especially for this and for no other occasion. Are those ladies willing? *Indeed, indeed.* The thing about fiction, of course, is that in it one can get one's women to do as one likes.

'I think, when speaking of Turkey's eroticism, one finds a great awareness of sexuality despite the pressures from Islam. The atmosphere there is so imbued with masculine sexual thoughts that the contagion spreads to women as well. They do not, of course, have the freedom we have. Women are sacred whereas it is expected for husbands to go to bars and be unfaithful. The great tragedy of fundamentalism is that it insists on suppressing women's sexuality. It can be only detrimental and, I think, unnatural. The boldness with which a man and a woman will look at each other in Turkey is registered in some bubble, its import being that in other circumstances, in a different world perhaps, he and she would be lovers. There is always that initial assessment as to whether the two *could* conjoin. Certainly no one expects an easy victory but sex, or, rather, the hope of it, is in the air one breathes. Whenever I am in Turkey and looking back on my youth there, the idea of a sexual paradise strikes me as being of Sufi heritage, the becoming as one with somebody or with the godhead. Certainly the Turkish *hamam* about which I wrote was a paradise, the women there totally unselfconscious about their bodies. They walked about as if in a dream, so comfortable in themselves.'

> But, of course, above all, you note the bathing women, the cornucopia of breasts of every shape and size. Those for whom modesty is a virtue at all times wear *peştamals*, transparent aprons which, rather than veil the glories of their flesh, emphasize them saliently. The rest are completely naked, except for bracelets and earrings, and look as if they have been sprinkled with gold. Tall or short, young or old, they are invariably Rubenesque.

So maybe those Orientalist artists were right, after all, only how did they ever gain admittance to the *hamam*? The answer, quite simply, is that they didn't. They relied on reportage, or, better still, imagination. Musa was able to get inside only because, as a young boy, his precociousness was not yet visible, or, to put it more bluntly, his testicles had not yet dropped.

§

At the beginning of *Young Turk* is the ghostly figure of Gül, a Jewish girl described as a *pîr*, a designation normally applicable to a Sufi elder or shaykh. She initiates Rıfat, the figure who may be the closest Musa comes to the directly autobiographical, to the mysteries of sex: she shows him *hers* and he shows her *his*. The world of carnality, though, is one through which she merely glides. She is made for something else, something terrible. Somewhere between child and woman, holy fool and clairvoyant, Gül is empowered to see when and where death strikes, and the terror of her situation, from which only her own death will release her ('God be praised! I know how to stop seeing'), is that what she sees ahead of her is human carnage on a hitherto unimaginable scale. Was Gül based on an actual figure? And if so, what did she look like? Was her death as Musa describes it?

'You are asking me about matters from sixty-five years ago! *Gül* means "rose" as in *Gulistan*. I can't say I knew her well. There is a kernel of truth in just about every story in *Young Turk*, based either on things I saw or was told. Otherwise I had to invent much of her story. All girls of one's early youth are attractive to start with but she had something others did not have. This may be hindsight, of course, but she had a quality, which I can only call an aura, that appealed to, and engaged, people. This was also true of the adults amongst us in that they, too, found her special in one way or another. I wouldn't know if she was pretty – I can't now bring up her features – she was certainly taller than me, slimmer, very athletic, and I think she had beautiful hair of a sort certain young people have, which undulates as they walk. Maybe that was part of her appeal. From what little I can remember of our conversations one minute we'd be talking about mundane things, maybe about the soup her mother made, and the next she'd be very quiet and pensive although without in any way excluding you. Still you felt she was thinking about something that did not concern you. I probably did ask her "What is the matter?" or made some remark like "Look at that bird flying!" and although I don't remember what her verbal responses were, she would then snap out of wherever she was and come back to quotidian things.

'We are talking about memory here. What one preserves is perhaps only partly true or else embellished. There is, for example, one strange childhood memory I have of something I did not actually experience but which has never stopped haunting me. One day my father – I must have been about three or four at the time – came home with a huge bloody bandage across his head. I remember freaking out. He had a jalopy which he loved to drive and earlier that day a plane flew very low over his car, making him lose control of it. Strangely I have always imagined I was in the car with him. I can see this plane coming straight at us and yet I wasn't there.

'And so it is with Gül in that I can't be absolutely sure about my memories of her. She might have been a tomboy, which she was to some extent, but it is her remarkableness, the fact that she could see into the future and into pain, that stays with me. I remember her being instrumental in somebody's recovery from illness, although it was not, as I have it in the book, my brother's. She may have been instrumental in bringing the gypsy who healed my brother of severe jaundice, who did so by making a cut in the shape of a plus sign on his forehead. My mother was horrified but he was withering away and all other treatment had failed. She insisted that the blade be sterilised. A couple of days later he was completely cured. Although Gül was very different she was never excluded as a stranger or an alien *other*. We lived in a society where any supernatural gift – the gift of prophecy, for example, or the reading of coffee dregs or broad beans thrown onto a zodiac – was much admired. The mad were considered wise. She may have had problems I was not aware of. She might have been excluded from certain communities, perhaps the bourgeois ones, but in the early forties, apart from a nucleus of government people, some intellectuals and commercial people, and the young who had to go to primary school, much of the population was still illiterate, particularly in the newly introduced Latin alphabet, and so, in this atmosphere, these superstitions prevailed. I always liked that, not that I was superstitious myself, but I was fond of people who did not conduct witch hunts. Gül was a person who made an impact. Ah yes, and she had beautiful legs.'

'Did she really undress for you?'

'No, she didn't.'

I detected a tremor of disappointment in Musa's voice.

'That was a boyhood wish. I telescope many things in order to make a story but what I can say is that I remember to this day how when I went to bed it would usually take me quite a while to get to sleep, and it was then I would fantasise about saving Gül from something or somebody. I was the great hero of all those fantasies.'

'You speak of her as having predicted the Holocaust.'

'I think it may have been a memory of people telling me she foresaw it. I don't know if she herself ever told me. I may even have heard different things, which I have now conflated into one.'

'Do you have any recollection of how you heard about her death?'

'No, but I remember going to her house after she died, which is described in the book. Ankara was a small place back then and word got around so quickly, so the news could have come from anywhere. She really did freeze to death. This was not uncommon. I had to walk about two or three kilometres to school and the shortest path was through a park. In those days the winters were severe, minus 30 degrees sometimes, and you would occasionally find homeless people sleeping on benches, who'd salute you or ask you to bring cigarettes, which we would then pinch from our parents and take to them the next day. Occasionally one or two of them disappeared and you learned later they had frozen to death. Certainly I did not find her body in the park nor did I see it at any other time. The fact that she froze to death really shook me, though, and probably the awfulness of her fate still gnaws at some part of my unconscious. That she should have died like that I find quite unbearable.'

'It sounds as if she didn't know enough to come out of the cold. After all, she did have a home to go to.'

'Again people say she knew of the Holocaust about to take place, which is the story I use, but nobody knows for sure what happened. There may have been some looming tragedy in her family. It's all so very dark now. I think the family moved away. Maybe it was some domestic strife she could not endure.'

The reasoning world, which has little time for the fool who is wise, will consider Gül insane. The philosopher Jacques Maritain speaks of 'the finality of the useful', a deliberately chilling phrase, and the painter Cecil Collins, in his great essay *The Vision of the Fool*, writes: 'Our society has rejected the Fool. Not only because he cannot be exploited, not only because they judge everything by its usefulness; but they are frightened and disturbed by the Fool, because he is the child of life, and not of abstract virtue.' Gül is most certainly a child of life, the pity of it being she is born into the wrong time. She who sees so deeply into the future must also bear the immediate suffering of her age. The date of her death in the book is given as February 3rd 1940, and, although the author alone knows why he chose this date, on that day in Gostynin, Poland, the Nazis murdered the inmates of a mental home, who, according to them, were worth only as much as the food they ate.

§

'What sort of family background did you have?'

'In many ways it is a sad story of two wonderful people who just couldn't get on. My grandfather was a customs officer in Ruschuk on the Danube, in Bulgaria, which was then part of the Ottoman Empire. After he got ill, he came back to Turkey and settled in Izmir where my father was born. When my grandfather died my father left school, aged twelve, and with a mother, a younger brother and sister to look after he was forced to work. He was a remarkable man who, with no formal education, spoke eleven languages and wrote in seven alphabets. English he picked up when he came to visit me in England. Greek he knew because my mother was from Salonica. Their marriage was arranged by their respective uncles. My mother, who was also Jewish, came from a wealthy family. Her father was a solicitor, a violent man who used to beat my grandmother. Once he threw her from a balcony as a result of which she had a broken hip and was lame for the rest of her life. Another time my mother pulled out her father's hunting rifle and said, "If you touch her again, I'll kill you." My mother went to the conservatoire and could play the piano and sing as well. I think she felt she had married beneath herself and often she would reprimand my father for lacking in culture, my father who could speak several languages, but really it was because he was working class and my mother was bourgeois. Actually my brother and I think she became, after the Holocaust, somewhat unstable of mind. She had lost nearly all her family in Salonica, nineteen members, including her father and her sister and children, all of whom were sent to Auschwitz. She was always waiting for letters from them, her sister in particular, and eventually they came to an end. The chapters in my book, "The Sky-Blue Monkey" and part of "A Tale of Two Cities", are very much based on what my mother went through at that time. The final letter she wrote describes how the house had been taken over by the Germans. They had to go up to the castle and live in tiny shelters.'

> Fortuna's letter was like that of a dying person, without a trace of the billowing fury with which she normally faced adversity. Her husband, Zaharya, one of those impressed for road construction, had suffered a heart attack and died. Viktorya and Süzan, her daughters, aged eight and ten, had become the family's breadwinners. Every morning before dawn, they would leave home – which, these days, was a corner in a disused warehouse – and climb to the lower slopes of Mount Hortiatis where they would collect wild flowers. They would then run back, at breakneck speed, to reach the city by noon and sell the flowers, often in competition with equally destitute Gypsy children, to German officers relaxing at the waterfront tavernas.

'They didn't dare send the boy out because he was circumcised. That was the last letter my mother received. In 1946, we moved from Ankara to Istanbul. My childhood friend, Asher, had moved there the year before. His father who worked for the Ottoman Bank was a member of the Jewish Agency, and was always in danger to some extent, transporting Jewish refugees from Europe, through Turkey to the Syrian border where from there somebody else took them to Palestine. The Turks shut their eyes to this for a while. Asher's family had a small flat in the Taksim area. The day after we moved to Istanbul, we went out for a walk, and, passing their house, we decided to pop in and say hello as one does in Turkey. Because they weren't expecting us Asher's father had all these photographs of

Auschwitz on his desk. Asher and I were playing ball outside when we heard an awful scream, such I had never heard before, and we rushed inside. There was my mother holding a picture of corpses piled high, only their skulls visible. She was screaming and pointing at a head in the middle of this pile, saying it was her sister. This became one of the peripheral wounds in my parents' relationship. They both died sad people.'

Perhaps it is a little too tempting to see the Erzincan earthquake of 27 December 1939, one of the worst in the country's history, as a portent, especially when the Nazis themselves, or at least some of them, saw it as divine retribution for Turkey not joining the Axis forces. Portents are what we choose to make of them. One survivor, whom Musa cites in his book, described the earthquake as 'the Devil shaking the earth as if it were a die in a heated game of backgammon'. The initial shock claimed 8000 lives, but with successive earthquakes and floods the death toll reached well over 30,000. Although its epicentre was in the east of the country, the tremors could be felt hundreds of kilometres miles away, in Ankara, where a father stood in the doorway of his four-year-old son's bedroom, telling him not to move, which was all very well given the cot was rolling from wall to wall, its laughing occupant thinking this was all a game. Musa, most oddly, turns that boy into a distant relative and, odder still, he buries his mother in that earthquake.

§

Admittedly I have had a prejudice against Turks for their treatment of minorities, the Armenians in particular, and yet a reading of Stanford J. Shaw's *Turkey and the Holocaust* (Macmillan, 1979) forces me to concede that Turkey's behaviour with regard to the Jews was one of the most heroic of any country in existence. From their side, Jewish Turks responded positively to Atatürk's insistence that Turks be proud of their Turkishness and even went so far as to avoid (willingly) speaking Judeo-Spanish in order not to offend native Turks.

When Atatürk gave refuge to Jews from Nazi Germany, who had been thrown out of their jobs in 1935, among them was a doctor who would play a heroic role in the country's future and, more specifically, in Musa's life. Albert Eckstein was a communist and

World War I hero. Between the years 1935 and 1950, while working at the Numune State Hospital in Ankara, he revolutionised paediatrics in Turkey. All hospitals in Turkey are based on his. During the summers of 1937 and 1938, at a time when the infant mortality rate was about 50 per cent, he and his wife travelled throughout Anatolia in order to report on health and the living conditions of Turkish children. Also he was a gifted photographer. One of his images, a group of women in the village of Bürnük in the northwest of Anatolia, was reproduced in 1942 on the ten-lira banknote. This was the first time women appeared on a Turkish banknote.

'My mother spoke of him as if he were a god. I had had diphtheria. After recovering from it I went back to school, was inoculated there and then got it again. The second time, in 1941, was apparently touch and go. My mother went to Dr Eckstein. I remember lying in bed and there being this oxygen cylinder which stood from floor to ceiling – it must have weighed a ton – which Eckstein brought in somehow, and also I recall my mother and father saying that if I survived the night I'd be okay. Eckstein saved my life.'

The tolerance which was the hallmark of Atatürk's rule suffered a tragic setback after his death. In 1942, the new Turkish president, İsmet İnönü, who ought perhaps to be remembered not so much for this as for his part in saving European Jews, introduced the *Varlık Vegisi*, a 'wealth tax' designed to raise funds for the country's defence in the event of its being drawn into the war. Although aimed at the wealthy in general, it had the effect of targeting non-Muslims in particular, in short the Jews, Greeks and Armenians who controlled much of the economy. Unable to pay the exorbitant tax, about 2000 men were sent to forced labour camps such as Aşkale in eastern Turkey. One person who could not pay the tax was Musa's father, who was sent to Sinop on the Black Sea, but not before the bailiffs removed everything or *just about everything* – the law stipulated that families so punished be allowed to keep a single mattress. The bailiffs, perhaps a shade kinder than others, allowed them to keep the stove as well.

'I remember my father just before he was taken away coming in with a single apple, saying "This is all we have" and then giving it to me. When the men were taken away we were in great fear because for six months we didn't know what had happened to them. We didn't even know where they were. There were rumours that with the men gone the women and children would be unsafe, but I never really felt in danger. This was true of my non-Muslim friends as well. All we were told was that my father was going into the army and in a way that actually was the case. As labouring soldiers they were given uniforms. My father was all right because he could read and write in several languages. While the others were taken for labour, the camp commandant made him a secretary. Meanwhile, we stayed in the flat where we were, which was a rented place. And yet, despite it being a difficult time for everyone, it being the middle of a war, I never went hungry. I still went to school although one had to pay to go and my little canteen was full every day. We were helped by freemasons on the one hand and by our Turkish Muslim neighbours on the other. They agreed they would now have to feed these Jewish families. It was not so much a question of honour as of doing the right thing according to Islamic tenets, that is, you did not abandon people who sought help or refuge. We had a staple diet of bread, cheese, onions and olives. That was lunch, dinner *and* breakfast. And it's still my favourite meal. We survived.

'One day my father came home on leave, quite emaciated. The way my mother describes it is that she had to wash his uniform ten times because it stank so badly. The great thing about my father is that I got my love of books from him. When he returned from the labour camp and got back his job in a textile shop, one day he came home, saying, "Go downstairs, there is a parcel for you." It was a ten-volume encyclopaedia for children, which he bought with his very first wages. That was my dad all over. I kept it until 1986 by which time, of course, it was quite out of date. That year my mother broke her pubic bone in Istanbul so my brother who lived in Paris and I took turns to be with her and in the meantime a neighbour found her a wonderful woman to look after her, who did the cooking and the cleaning, and she had a young son, so I gave it to him. There were always some books in the house, the early works of Nâzim Hikmet for example.'

'Would I be right in thinking that being a Jew in Turkey in a way made you a double exile?'

'This was a dark period in Turkish history. On the other hand only twenty-eight Jews died, mostly old men breaking stones in Aşkale, who were exposed to the cold or else had heart attacks. This, when compared to what was going on in Europe, was a tiny number of casualties. After the *Varlık* caused a great scandal in America, with articles appearing in the *Herald Tribune*, they rescinded it and pardoned everyone. Most of the people were able to go back to their old jobs because the Turks who had taken them over kept them for their friends' return. My father was a great lover of Atatürk and of the poet Hikmet too, both of whom were from Salonica, and he would not say a word against Turkey. At the primary school, which I went to from 1941 to 1946, we were called "Atatürk's children". We were committed to turning the country around, beating poverty and disease, and making it a model for all countries. We were very idealistic. When I went to college in Istanbul the college dormitories were full of Greeks, Armenians and Kurds. Nobody ever said "Dirty Jew" to me or whatever. After the state of Israel was created, one or two people would ask questions like, "If Israel and Turkey went to war, whose side would you be on?" But it was a question that came out of ignorance. They didn't know which was more important, religion or the place where you were born. Apart from that I never actually experienced any anti-Semitism. I have a huge number of Turkish Muslim friends who, fifty-three years on, are still bosom friends, so I can't say I ever suffered as a Jew in Turkey. With the *Varlık* one felt there was discrimination against minorities, but in a way it was like the tortured who comes to blame himself rather than the torturer. We thought we were culpable and weren't doing enough to be true Turks and that we had *other* traditions. We knew Ladino, the Spanish-Judeo language, but didn't speak it because it would mean not being sufficiently proud of being a Turk. Still the *Varlık* did leave one with a scar because at some level one was discriminated against, but then you can say anti-Semitism was everywhere.

'There's something in the Turkish psychology that is used to having minorities and in a way there is great respect for their cultures. Muslim friends of mine would go to an Orthodox mass or to an Armenian wedding, so they were accustomed to a life where minorities lived among them rather than in ghettos. In the neighbourhood you might have the fishmonger who was Greek and the baker who was Armenian. I remember the sugar festival at the end of Ramadan when we'd go around to Muslim friends, taking sweets, and it was the same at Jewish New Year when they came to wish us well. Maybe it is a romantic thought but I have a belief that somewhere within the Turkish nature there lies a greater tolerance of other cultures than in many other countries, perhaps something even more than tolerance, a respect and appreciation of other people's art and culture.'

§

Do people, especially those in exile, seek to rewrite not just their own, but also their countries' histories? It's not a question that can ever be fully answered, and to even attempt to do so would be to wield a yardstick where nothing is measurable, and yet it seems to me that the exile or émigré, more so than the people among whom he lives, is prone to this desire, and quite often he enters a realm where things of the past are set right. A novelist has carte blanche to do as he likes, of course, but I wonder if in *Young Turk*, when Musa projects himself into an old scene, he does so as some kind of corrective. There are two linked stories in *Young Turk*, which would seem to do just that, which involves some boys and their bid to rescue members of their Jewish family in Salonica, which, as we already know, ends in failure.

Salonica, 'the Pearl of the Mediterranean' (actually the Aegean), was one of the great Jewish cities and for centuries was part of the Ottoman Empire. Although there had been a Jewish population there since the third century BC, it was not until the fifteenth century that it became predominantly Jewish. When the Jews were expelled from Spain in 1492, Sultan Bayezid II remarked: 'They tell me that Ferdinand of Spain is a wise man but he is a fool, for he takes his treasure and sends it all to me.' Of the 56,000 Jews living there in 1941, 45,000 died at Auschwitz.

'I had a cousin a few years older than me, Mordecai, who was a dwarf. He was just like a djinn, an absolutely wonderful figure, and he used to work part-time, running errands between shops. One day

Mordecai came to me, saying he'd found a man, a Levantine owner of a fish restaurant and a small fishing fleet, who could smuggle my relatives out of Salonica. We went to see him. It was morning, the restaurant was not yet open, and we asked the waiters whether we could see him. This man saw us and said, "Come, boys". There he was, this powerful figure seated between three chairs. He said, "What do you want?" We told him. "How many are there?" "Nineteen." "Come next week, they will all be here." Mordi and I were just stunned. We couldn't speak and then I said we didn't have much money. "Don't worry about that. Give me a bottle of raki, that'll be enough." We found ourselves dancing in the street, saying, "Could it be so easy?" We believed him hook, line and sinker. The following week we found him sitting in the same position. "Sorry, boys, I have been very busy and just haven't had time. Come next week." This went on for five or six weeks and at the end we realised he was just humouring us. One of our national traits is that we can never say no. We realised this, so we stopped. My story evolves from the premise: *what if he were serious*. As I said, there is always a kernel of truth somewhere in my stories. The business about the boys going to Salonica is imaginary, but the boy who dies has elements of me in him because after the war I would put myself in his situation, this cousin my own age who died in Auschwitz. What separated us was only the comparatively short distance between Salonica and Istanbul.'

§

Another figure in *Young Turk* who fascinates me is Saadet, the mysterious woman whom the boy Yusuf, yet another of Musa's fictional disguises, meets on a ship going to France. She is on a journey to discover whether someone whose identity I will not reveal here had survived the war. On the way, the ship stops in Naples where Saadet takes Yusuf to see Pompeii. There she screams at the sight of a figure preserved in ash in the museum. This may be a fiction, but it is one powerful enough to be, where such matters circulate in the soul, true.

'*Saadet* means "happiness", ironically enough. Here again, hers is a mixture of several stories. My father's brother and sister went to France in the late 1920s because there was no work in Turkey. They made a good living there and then the war came and there was no further news of them. After the war, in 1946, my parents received word they had both survived along with their families. My aunt and her children had gone into a nunnery as Catholics; my uncle had been hidden by a farmer. When my father learned this he said we would have to save up money to go to see them. By 1947 they had saved enough but because I was at school I was not allowed to leave with them. My father arranged that I would join them as soon as school finished. In 1947, he booked me a berth in the dormitory of the hold of a Turkish ship, a huge space one side of which was for women and the other for men. I set out from Istanbul, aged thirteen, to Marseilles where my uncle would meet me. On the journey we stopped in Piraeus and Naples. At both harbours there were sunken ships all over the place. I was the only child on my own. The others were all families, mostly Armenians and Jews, going to see whether their relatives had survived. Because I was on my own I became a sort of mascot, both for the sailors, who would take me to the first-class section and give me food there, and for the people who were in the dormitories. There was one matronly lady – actually she was only thirty-five or so, which at the time seemed old – and she became motherly towards me. She would ask the sailors to give me more food and then she took me on an excursion to the Acropolis. When we arrived in Naples she told me to buy as many packs of cigarettes as possible from the ship's store. I think I bought four, which was all I could afford. We went to Pompeii and on our return from there, at the harbour, were all these poor people selling bags made of straw. I was able to buy some as presents for my aunt and cousins, all on four packets of cigarettes. This woman whose name I can't remember was going to look for a relative. I suspect she may have been Armenian.

'That was the first story. The second story, which in my book I linked with this one, relates to when my parents returned to France about three years later. A distant cousin of my father's called Ner came to my father, saying, "I have a son in France, named Salvator, who I'm told has survived. He is in an asylum near Lyon. Could you please visit him." On that trip we drove. As I said my father was a great driving enthusiast and so we drove right through Greece and Yugoslavia. When we arrived in Yugoslavia it was the day before the Turkish Prime Minister was due and the whole place was full of Turkish flags. Thinking we were an early arrival from the Turkish government they immediately received us as royalty and gave us an amazing suite. The roads were ghastly and on the way there we had two punctures. That evening we went walking. I remember it was some kind of ritual, all these people walking and not saying anything, and then we sat down at a café where this man appeared at our table. He lifted his arm and there were numbers tattooed on it from Auschwitz. He said to my father in Ladino, "I need to live so if there is anything I can do for you I'm ready to help in any way." In those days a Yugoslav transit visa meant you could only stay in one place for a single night. You had to move on. So my father replied, "Well, it's a good thing I bumped into you because I've got two punctures that need repair." The man asked if my father had anything other than money with which to pay him. Fortunately my father had a spare can of engine oil. With that can of oil we bought a new tyre to replace the one that had been torn to shreds and we fixed the other one.

'We got to France and my father said, "I have to see someone." So I went with him. We came to this asylum place where we did manage to see Salvator, a very handsome man but totally out of his mind. He had been in some camp – I can't remember which one – and he was just blathering away. The whole ward was full of disturbed people. Very few times have I ever seen my father cry. He was in many ways an intrepid man and a great optimist, but when we came out of the hospital and got into the car I saw tears running down his face. The other times I saw him cry were when he and my mother quarrelled and things got a bit too much and when Atatürk died. There is yet another element in this story in that there was this Turkish woman who had gone to Paris with a Jew who became successful as a trader. If I am not mistaken they were taken to Drancy and all I heard was that she managed to come back from there because she was Turkish. Whether or not the Nazis actually got her husband I don't know. The Turks rescued quite a number of Turkish Jews from France, eighteen transports which went through war-torn Europe from Paris to Istanbul.'

§

Another chapter in *Young Turk*, 'When a Writer is Killed', is about the planned rescue of the great Turkish poet, Nâzım Hikmet, another literary fantasy in which the author projects himself onto the rescue bid and, once there, somehow misses the opportunity. When the Democratic Party came to power in 1950, writers and intellectuals petitioned the government to include Hikmet in the political amnesty list. After his release from prison in 1950, alarmed by threats against his life he fled on a freighter bound for Romania and from there he went to Russia where he remained for the rest of his life. There is still considerable contention with respect to his politics and to this day, even though he is widely revered, the government will not allow his remains to be brought back to Turkey and buried.

'I did see Hikmet once. It was in 1951, in that very brief period of about a year, between when he came out of prison and just before he escaped to Russia. One of our teachers said Hikmet was going to read his poetry at a wealthy friend's house. We got very excited but of course we couldn't get inside. We did go to the house, which I remember as having a large garden and orchard, and from behind iron bars I saw him at a distance, a tall man with reddish hair. He looked like a god! We couldn't even hear him. I have listened to recordings of him. He was not such a great reader of his own poetry and he didn't have what I would call a strong voice, such as Atatürk had, but he was such a beautiful poet. I left Turkey at a troubled time. I had become involved with the distribution of Hikmet's poetry. We printed them out on a Gestetner machine and took them to nearby schools. Often we went to this *meyhane* or wine tavern where poets would congregate and swear at each other in verses. Those poems which were composed impromptu were invariably crude, sometimes brutal, and, as the Turks would have it, served to insult their antagonists' sexuality. Anyway, thinking we were safe there, the police found us and took us to the police station. They asked us what we were doing and we said we were distributing poems. "Are they legal?" they asked. We said we didn't know, so they gave us a couple of smacks, told us not to do it again, and sent us on our way. My father got very frightened about this. When I left I think it was already in my mind not to return because in terms of freedom of expression the situation in Turkey was getting worse and worse.'

§

'When I first came to England, in 1954, aged nineteen, I might have landed on Mars. At 6.30 the streets were deserted, most men went to the pub, and nobody would invite you to his home. I was in a different universe. There were good sides as well – the tolerance, for example. You could say whatever you liked, which was what made me fall in love with this country in the first place. I had really wanted to do drama at Yale. There was a scholarship floating about, but somehow I missed the deadline. Also, my father didn't want me to go to America and it was then that he decided I should stay in England and study his business, which was textiles. So he took me to the technical college in Bradford and there put me on a wool scouring course. You took a fleece and fed it into a machine almost a hundred yards long and it came out at the other end, absolutely clean. It was so boring sitting there, watching this fleece. Bradford had these funny orangey lights, and also, with all the cotton mills there, it was terribly polluted. I had gone from sunny Turkey straight into this pea soup. Within six weeks I ran away from there. My friend Asher who, alas, is dead now, was studying medicine in London and it was he who arranged for me to get an audition at the Royal Academy of Dramatic Art.'

Asher, Musa's boyhood friend from Istanbul, was one vital element in keeping alive for him, in foggy climes, the Turkish flame.

'Asher was a deeply sensitive boy. His mother had a heart condition dating from when she was first married. The doctors advised her never to have children but after thirteen years she couldn't bear it any more and said that even if it killed her she would have one. As I mentioned earlier, Asher's father worked with the Jewish agency but later, towards the end of the war, when Turkey joined the Allies and the British began to exert pressure on the matter of Jewish refugees going to Palestine, he was arrested and put in prison. Some of the men who had come back from their imprisonment or forced labour somehow managed to collect enough money to get him released. He returned to his job at the Ottoman Bank. Meanwhile, doubtless brought on by her husband's imprisonment, Asher's mother's health had deteriorated to the degree that by 1946 she was too ill to leave the house. By the late 1940s Asher and I met every day after school and our first task was to make his mother a meal which usually was just boiled fish, unsalted rice and potatoes. We would settle her down on the sofa, cover her with blankets and give her a book. I loved her. Sometimes I think I loved her more than my mother. One Saturday morning the telephone rang and my mother answered it. It was exam time and the arrangement was that during the exam period Asher would stay at our house. We were in my room. Asher announced, "I have to go home now." I said I'd go with him. When we got there we discovered his mother had died. He had known when he heard the telephone. It could have been anyone because the telephone rang all the time. Soon after, Asher developed a spot on his lung and was sent to Switzerland for nine months. We wrote each other letters every day and he told me how much he enjoyed the sanatorium because he made friends there with the doctors who told him all about tuberculosis and heart disease. The treatment worked and he decided he would be a heart specialist.

'Asher came to England a year before me. The reason I went to London was because of him. We led something of a dissolute life. Asher because he was studying medicine had access to countless nurses. He would say to me, "I'll bring you five." We had a flat, with only two rooms, which had a special lighting system, a red and a green light. When it was green you could go in and when it was red you couldn't. There was this one funny episode. Asher said, "Look, we'll have an orgy. I'll bring nurses from all parts of the world, Africa, Asia, the Middle East, South America. Choose your colour and enjoy yourself but on one condition: you have to cook." The party started and there were maybe twenty girls. I looked at them and said I didn't mind which one I slept with. So I went into the kitchen to cook spaghetti. The problem was we had just one pot and I could make enough for only two people at a time. I began at eight o'clock and by eleven I was still serving spaghetti. When finally I served the last person, Asher's girlfriend, everyone else had gone. No orgy!

'Asher completed his studies, got good marks, and then had to find a place in a hospital as a medical student. In 1954, priority was given to Commonwealth students. Once they were placed, for those who remained it went alphabetically by country and of course Asher was way down the list. When his father retired at the end of 1956 he said he couldn't support him any more. I think that broke Asher inside. The whole idea of being a heart specialist was something he felt he owed his mother. Later he became the director of a successful travel business but there was always this immense sadness in him that somewhere along the line he had missed what he had come to earth for. He would have been a wonderful doctor. I have always seen Asher as a beautiful soul. It may be the romantic streak in me but I am a sucker for unsung heroes, those people who do good things and never boast about them.'

Asher, who died on 8 May 2004, the day before his 70th birthday, still haunts Musa's dreams. It remains to be seen whether he ghosts the pages of some future work.

§

Musa's great passion was for the stage, and the idea was that he would go back to Turkey and be involved in the theatre there, but when he graduated in 1956 it was a time of cultural suppression at home. A theatre director had been arrested and tortured and playwrights and actors who had always been in the avant-garde were now denied free expression. Musa's father wrote him a letter advising him to stay in England a bit longer.

'So this, then, is what kept you here?'

'No, it is what prevented me from going back. It was, to a major extent, cowardice on my part because of what was happening over there. I was scared. The choice was either to stay here or to join my father's textile business in Istanbul and give up theatre altogether. It would have been an easy life. Although to begin with my father was against my studying drama, in the end he respected my wishes and said, "It is good you are learning English and maybe you will start writing." So he was very liberal although he was always concerned for my welfare because of the erratic earnings of a writer. He helped me. Cheques would arrive. He was a wonderful person. He would say to me, "What happens when I go?" "Don't worry," I'd tell him, "I will survive somehow." So I stayed and got married to my first wife who didn't want to go to Turkey, which meant I had to make my place here. I tried to work as an actor and wasn't very successful at it and of course I had this atrocious accent. You had to be able to speak the Queen's English. The worst thing was when you were made to recite Shakespeare's iambic pentameter because – it's the most uncanny thing – your accent comes right back. Even I could hear it. They offered to let me carry a spear for a season.'

I reminded Musa that Victor Mature's definition of acting was to be able to hold a spear and look devout. I could see, though, that we had come to a critical point in our talk, a crossing over which for nearly everybody I'd meet on my world journey through London would bring a catch in the throat or a glistening to the eyes.

'My not going back was, in a sense, a quadruple betrayal – a betrayal of my father because he wanted me there, a betrayal of my mother because I might have been of some positive influence in a bad marriage, a betrayal of my brother who was only eight years old at the time and so had to take the brunt of the conflict at home, and, of course, a betrayal of Turkey because as a child of Atatürk I should have gone back and battled things out. After all, *we* were the ones who were going to make it a light unto nations. We had been taught that we were the inheritors of so many cultures, so many beautiful things, ideas and poetry, and so my not going back was a betrayal of that vision. Also there's the guilt of having lost a culture that I greatly admire. I don't think that sense of guilt will ever leave me although in some ways it fuels my writing. Somehow it always gets in there, so that my themes are very much involved with betrayal and abandonment. Like any writer I'm trying to work this out for myself and although I will never succeed I do think it brings something to my work, which is a consolation. Sometimes, though, the guilt is terrible, particularly when I go to Turkey, especially these days when the country is so precariously balanced between the two evils of nationalism and Islamic fundamentalism.'

After Musa decided he wasn't cut out to be an actor, or at least not in England, not with its iambic pentameter tripping up an oriental tongue, he wrote screenplays, including a series for *Doctor Who*, that were never produced, and several novels, the fourth of which, *Children of the Rainbow* (Saqi, 1999), touched on a theme dear to him, the plight of the gypsies.

'I have a great love for gypsies and spent my childhood with them. We lived on the outskirts of Ankara, and beyond us was a brewery and behind that were fields with trenches where the gypsies lived. We used to play in these shelters, which were almost like World War I trenches. The great thing about these children – again we are talking about poor times – they would say, "Come to our place", which would turn out to be a shack with an aluminium roof or sometimes just a tent. There would always be a piece of cheese or something given to us by their mothers. When I first suggested to my mother that I should invite some of those boys she was horrified. "Gypsies in *my* house!" she cried. That was another source of guilt for me, that I could never bring them home. Then, of course, when details about the Holocaust came out we learned how the gypsies had suffered equally. They called the Holocaust *Porajmos*, which means "the devouring". Some years before her death, my mother asked me what I was going to write next and I told her I was working on *Children of the Rainbow* which was about gypsies. She replied, "I am very glad." She told me that she had been in a hospital in Paris and was sitting next to a gypsy woman who had been an inmate in Auschwitz. She had been experimented on. She told my mother about these twins she had looked after. By then my mother had completely turned around so the gypsies were our brothers and sisters.'

Most gratifyingly for him, Musa was awarded the *Amico Rom* ('Gypsy Friend') and the 'Special' prize from the Roma Academy of Culture and Sciences. That he should have fixed upon outsiders is hardly surprising. A good part of his life has been devoted to people in distress. He has campaigned for many writers who have been imprisoned for their writings, and in November 2001 he was elected Vice President of International PEN, a year that would also see him appointed a Member of the Order of the British Empire for services to literature. Among the shorter works he has produced is an essay that provides a key to his thought, 'All History is the History of Migration', which was first published in *Index on Censorship*.

> Many years ago, whilst collecting material in Ethiopia for a novel, I met an Italian septuagenarian in the Eritrean port of Assab. *Tio*, 'Uncle', as everybody lovingly called him, declared himself an *insabbiati*. The term refers to people 'caught in the

> sand', like fish, and was coined for those Italians who, having participated in Mussolini's invasion of Ethiopia in 1936, chose to stay on after Italy's defeat at the end of the Second World War … *Tio* kept offering the image of the *insabbiati*, those 'caught in the sand', as the perfect representation of this caste. He said we were creatures facing death with a much greater awareness of the frailty of life and thus with an enhanced compulsion to survive; creatures that could not – or did not get the chance to – live in their native matrix and, consequently, desperately sought to make a new life in unknown lands and under harsh conditions; creatures that often became fodder for the people in power in their new environments, thus providing the hosts with good nourishment. Since then, the image of the *insabbiati* has served me both as a guide and as a metaphor. As a guide, it has helped me to struggle against the depression of the exilic condition, the harsh realities of exclusion, the longings for my native land, and the free-floating angst of feeling worthless because of the difficulties of integration and acceptance. As a metaphor, it has given me a perspective on history by recognising that displacement – or, to use the gentler word, migration – is not only a condition that rules much of the animal kingdom but also much of humanity, that, as the title of this paper brashly declares, all history is the history of migration.

This seminal work explores the predicament of the *other* – the exiles, refugees, immigrants, displaced people, outsiders, outcasts, strangers, untouchables – and, of course, artists and writers, who, according to Musa, chronicle true history.

'What I am leading to is this question of *otherness*,' I ventured. 'I am not sure I can fully subscribe to the psychoanalytic interpretation you give it later on in the essay. I would always opt for Rimbaud's "*Je est un autre*." Would you care to expand on this? Your experiences with gypsies must have given you at an early age a sense of otherness. It is what makes us artists in that we identify with these people.'

'There are good sides to otherness, but strangely enough I have become more aware of the *other* in Europe than in Turkey. Let me put it this way: being the *other* in Turkey was quite an open matter.

You were a Jew. Your name was different. As soon as you said your name it meant you were a Jew or Armenian or Greek. Your otherness was almost like a Star of David on your chest, whereas here it was so much more underground, so much more hypocritical. In Turkey you could be the *other*, and somehow you integrated, but here, in certain parts of Europe, France especially, although nobody says it outright they would stop you from joining them. The *other* can be used as a scapegoat. There are good sides to being an individual – we are all *others* because we are all individuals – but to actually categorise people, whether by race or religion, it is *that* idea of otherness I'm so very much against. If you push it far enough then even the Holocaust becomes justifiable. And it is happening again with all this Islamophobia. All Muslims are being labelled as "terrorists". There is an element of good in otherness, but then something about this really scares me. You might go to a poetry reading that fills a stadium and you will see all these big men, real macho types, crying their eyes out because the poetry is so beautiful and then a minute later somebody comes along and says all the problems that you have heard about today are caused by Jews, gypsies, Armenians, Greeks, whatever, and suddenly you see that same delicate, deeply sensitive, mob suddenly turn to brutality. My fear is that the *other* or otherness is used in a demonic way by politicians. And coming back to Turkishness and Atatürk's notion of what it should be, it was arrived at with the very best of intentions. Here was this newly truncated Turkey, and when Atatürk said, "We don't want any other territory, we just want this area", what he needed to do in order to unite the various peoples living there was to invent this idea of Turkishness. This is what all nationalists do. You may start with good intentions but when put in the wrong hands they become lethal. We can learn a great deal if we can accept otherness and if others accepted *our* otherness. There would be an enormous exchange of cultures and ideas but it is hardly ever applied in that way, certainly not in my experience.'

'Not even in the literary forum? Wouldn't there be an automatic understanding of otherness?'

'I would like to think they'd understand but remember, England is to some extent a more sophisticated country than Turkey in that it distinguishes between different forms of otherness, but this is not the case in a Muslim country where any non-Muslim is considered the *other*. Islam was at its most clement during the Ottoman Empire but this evolved from political necessity because they had to keep all these different peoples in some sort of harmony within the empire. They became autonomies of various sorts, but the way a mob can turn at the least provocation, especially in the Middle East – and I would include Israel in this – really frightens me. Yet in the main these are decent people. They don't mean to harm anyone, but if a faith or a people are to survive then the *other* becomes something that needs to be exterminated. According to their thinking, they are right. That begs the question: does religion really help the people? I am inclined to say "God save us from religion", because there are too many ills, not just in Islam but also in Judaism and Christianity. Too many injustices have come through religion. On a simple level, the subjugation of women, the inequality that women have suffered in the western world and continue to suffer in the eastern, all have come through religious dictums, the tenets of a patriarchal society. I am sympathetic because there are some wonderful as well as awful aspects in any religion, but parts of the Old Testament I find almost obscene. Apart from certain sections, like *Isaiah*, it is all about war and conquest and extermination. And then they exhort you to continue with this sort of destruction.'

§

In the penultimate chapter of *Young Turk*, 'He Who Returns Never Left', which takes its title from a line of Pablo Neruda, a woman who might or might not have become the speaker's lover says to him:

> One other thing. Even crueller because it concerns your soul. Wherever you go, whatever you do, you'll find you've stayed here. You'll realize you've never left our soil – neither our country's nor mine. Or if by chance you manage to transplant a limb here and there, your mind will always return. Your conscience will be more unforgiving than my body.

'Was that based on a real conversation?'

'No, that's my judgement of myself, that's the guilt showing. I suppose it also reflects my guilt about the girl I promised to marry and didn't, partly because in London I got a taste of the dissolute life and also because I wasn't ready to get married. My first marriage, when I was twenty-three, was a disaster for that very reason. Something else, though: Turkey, the country itself, has always been feminine in my mind. *Anavatan* means "motherland" in Turkey as opposed to "fatherland". *Ana* is the Turkish word for "mother" and *vatan* the Arabic for "country". This notion of Turkey is in some respects oedipal. Then there is Hikmet's wonderful poem *Kuvai Milliye* (*The Epic of the War of Independence*) in which he describes how the women carried cannon shells and were just as heroic as the men, fighting side by side with them. They had posters similar to those of the Communist regime of big-bosomed women representing the heroism of the people. What I realise more and more is that the resources women have, their determination and their diligence in whatever they do, whether at home or at the office, makes them, if not physically so, stronger than men. I am always amazed at the resilience of women and even more so at the fragility of men. The latter is like mica: you press it and it cracks. All these factors have perhaps unconsciously depicted Turkey for me as a woman. I can't say that about England. There is something about the Turkish psyche and it may well be that the stoicism I have seen in Turkish peasant women, such as one sees on that banknote, their hard labour and how they uncomplainingly maintain family, farm or husband, are the very epitome of human endeavour and survival. I imagine, too, one has a very early, even pre-natal, erotic impression of the soil where one was born, as it being a place of fertility where everything grows. I think it may be part of the collective unconscious about the earth. My idea of God, if I were a believer, would be God as a female. The woman I left behind or, rather, could *never* leave behind, is the country in a metaphorical sense. My vision of Turkey has always been this boyish dream of saving your loved one, of being a man and strong and saving the weaker sex. As the days go by, I think I become more Turkish.'

Musa's story ends as it begins and as it will continue, with a woman or, rather, with an idea of womanhood that for him finds its most succinct expression in Courbet's painting.

'I really do think God is inside the vagina,' he concludes. 'Certainly woman's soul is. When it is freed, it's Paradise.'

Once Upon a Time in County Cork

One Woman's Journey from There to an Area of Manifest Greyness

The Irish poet and novelist Martina Evans (née Cotter), when it came time for her to paint her living room, sought to replicate the blue of the covers of the Shakespeare & Company first edition of *Ulysses* (1922). James Joyce permeates, no, *soaks*, her talk. 'Chrysostom is mentioned on the very first page,' she told me with all the zeal of one who has just opened up a pharaoh's tomb. 'What Joyce is actually referring to are the gold fillings and the well-fed mouth of Malachi Mulligan. A bit later, in the Proteus episode, he compares his own teeth to empty shells and calls himself "toothless Kinch, the superman". Joyce had terrible problems with his teeth. When he went to Paris he screamed with every mouthful of French onion soup.' She paused. 'What do you call it? *Onion* soup? You don't call it *French* onion soup when you are in France, do you?'

When she speaks – softly, quickly, cramming more words into a minute than many people do in five – even the asides have asides. And there's the lovely turn of phrase too. She mentioned some woman having eloped with a sewing machine. What can it mean, I ask myself. What does it matter though? There is a zone where all such verbal felicities are poetically rather than literally comprehensible. It set me to wondering whether in this world journey through London the most unfathomable of all countries is not the one from whence my subject comes.

'Anyway,' she continued, 'when he was drinking *that well-known Paris delight* he would scream in agony because his teeth were in such a bad state. Dental envy lies behind the whole first chapter of *Ulysses* and people don't see that! They make all these references to "Golden Mouth" but – '

'Surely,' I interjected, 'the epithet relates to Chrysostom's gift for oratory.'

'It is about that too, but what Joyce is *really* saying is that

Mulligan is well fed, properly looked after. There are so many references to poverty in *Ulysses* and in particular that of the Dedalus family. Bloom is conscious of that too, when he looks at the ragged children in the street. Buck Mulligan talks about it in the very first episode when the old woman comes in with the milk, saying that if everyone could have good milk like that the country wouldn't be full of rotten teeth. Money and teeth – they're very connected.'

Odontology may form the greater part of Martina's psychological profile. She thinks teeth, she talks teeth. She writes about teeth. *Can Dentists Be Trusted?* is the title of one of her poetry collections and staring from its cover is a terrifying-looking nurse with Richard E. Grant eyes. The poem 'Gas' speaks of how 'cold thin air / breathed through a mask / changed the din of the drill / into the pure art / of Jimi Hendrix's guitar.' Another poem about dentists describes 'the ones you only visit once'. She even dreams about them. She relates a dream in which there is an IRA-like funeral for one of her extracted teeth, a tricolour over its minuscule coffin, balaclava'd men firing a salute over it. The subconscious, she tells me, is a funny place.

She loves westerns. Cowboys adorn her bathroom, a whole posse of them above the sink – the images or, rather, the *idea* of them, always preferable, she admits, to the grizzled reality from whence they come. She not so long ago watched *Rio Grande* because she had heard that at some point in the film a UFO appears in the sky behind the actors' heads. ('I was looking out for it but was so blown away by the chemistry between Maureen O'Hara and John Wayne I missed the UFO episode.') She kept rewinding the video but each time, swept up by the romance, she missed it. The Old West took her back to James Joyce. She had been watching the commentary on the filming of *The Wild Bunch* when one of its makers said that all the while he was reading the *Iliad*. Thus spurred, Martina read it and, after that, the *Odyssey* which in turn, after a hiatus of twenty years, led her back to *Ulysses*.

The cats rule, though. Donny, Dora and Alice are bigger than James Joyce, bigger than John Wayne. A conversation with her is, by extension, a conversation with them. The garden behind is, or will later be, their cemetery. Martina gave me pinkish brandy made from the elderberries that grow above one of their graves. We drank the blood of Eileen Murphy who one day confabulated with her, or at least did so in one of Martina's most celebrated poems, 'The Day My Cat Spoke to Me'.

> I was surprised not so much by the fact
> that she spoke
> but by the high opinion she had of me.
> 'I think you're great,' she said
> and it was at this point
> I looked at her in surprise.
> 'I mean,' she continued, 'the way
> you've managed to write anything at all!'

Eileen Murphy, 'her yellow eyes opening wide / before narrowing into benevolent slits', addressed Martina at a major juncture in her life, her divorce.

'It's a dark place to go,' she said, 'I appeared in court sixteen times.'

She pointed to the crucifix she was wearing, its purpose, I suspect, more apotrophaic than religious. It was a posthumous Christmas present from Eileen Murphy, the purchase of which was aided and abetted by Martina's daughter, Liadáin. Christmas saw Eileen Murphy in the grave. Martina took up wearing crosses because, she says, she has always had a problem with boundaries.

'This is my church, the Church of Eileen Murphy. It would be a kind of *Boy's Own* way of learning to live your life. If you are in a situation you would ask, "What would Eileen Murphy do?" She might hit you with a belt or a stony silence, one or the other, or maybe just a miaow. Those are probably the only responses you need in life. She is an alter ego for me. I really would like to have her kind of character, one that doesn't stand for any nonsense. I am always getting involved in nonsense.'

The walls are not quite the right shade of blue, at least not to my eye, but maybe the more she penetrates the heart and soul of her Book of Books the closer she'll come, with the next coat, or maybe the one after that, to achieving that special Greek flag blue. She was quietly amazed when I told her that in 1984 I handled the diagonally striped blue-and-white tie that Joyce wore, which he presented to the printers of *Ulysses* as the blue of his choice. The tie he later gave to his close associate, the Jewish-Russian émigré, Paul Léon, and decades later, after its stopover at the London antiquarian booksellers for whom I used to work, it is in Tulsa, Oklahoma, along with such treasures as the corrected proofs of *Finnegans Wake* and a white porcelain lion, a punning gift which Joyce gave Léon, who only a few years later perished in one of the Nazi death camps.

A chunk of Irish landscape crackled in the fireplace, one of the *Bord na Móna* (Board of Turf) peat briquettes that Martina buys here in London. When I looked out of the window onto Balls Pond Road, what Peter Ackroyd in his *London, A Biography* describes as 'an area of manifest greyness and misery', a phrase which Martina adopted for the title of one of her poems, I wondered at how in a very few lines she manages to set the tranquillity of inside against the noise of what goes on outside.

> I sleep high on the bird's nest.
> Trucks and lorries shake the house
> and make the bricks tremble,
> roaring tidal waves rock the bed
> and put me to sleep.
> There are odd wrecked Georgian houses
> beached between tyre shops and takeaways.
> Sometimes people are murdered.
> Police sirens shriek up and down all day
> like seagulls chasing sandwiches.

Disquietude is never far away, just an ably thrown pebble's click against the boarded-up front of what used to be the Turkish community library directly opposite, TOPLUM KÜTÜPHANESI, where not so long ago a young man working there hanged himself. Martina spoke of the ambulances, the police, the young Turkish men in black walking up and down the street, sorrowing for one of their tribe. Meanwhile, in her poem, 'the uniformed Catholic children / slip along the wet pavement / like blue fish / swimming down the Balls Pond Road.'

§

She comes from a village not far from Mallow in County Cork. One might be forgiven for thinking Burnfort is a mythical place. So small it has escaped the cartographer's eye, it takes its name from an ancient ringfort known as *Ráth an Tóiteáin* ('Fort of the Burnings') of which all that remains is a souterrain; unless, of course, one wishes to include the shield on the BP sign that swung throughout the whole of her youth beside the Cotter residence, which was home, shop, bar and petrol pump all rolled into one. The family lived upstairs, a child's fantasy of a place, which in the 1940s had been owned by a scrap merchant who added all sorts of curious features – a fireplace edged with black-and-white tiles of Grecian figures, wooden panelling from a luxury liner that had been wrecked off the coast of Cork, with the cabin numbers **118**, **117**, **116** still visible, in black against ivory plates, a section of railway track holding up the kitchen ceiling and other oddities. And with it being Burnfort's social and mercantile centre it is also the setting, although nowhere does it say so, of Martina's as yet unpublished book, *Petrol, a Poem in Three Acts*.

A couple of things make this image special: the extensive creases and the long shadows of those who are no longer about to throw them. One of the major strands in Martina's work is that by making them talk, talk and talk she brings those shadows back to life.

'There is a lot of sound in it,' she said of her new work. 'The BP sign, the big one in the picture, swings all the time. What made me think of it is the opening scene of the movie *Once Upon a Time in the West* where all the different noises make their own music. The cowboy setting, the Deep South, the music and everything, can be related in so many ways to Ireland, to Burnfort in particular. It's about voice too. Voice is everything for me. It was Joyce's favourite instrument. I'm nothing like him, of course

– I'm so simple and he's so complicated – but my first novel *Midnight Feast* is very much about voice. There are true incidents in *Petrol.* A magician came to the school once. I was grown up to the size I am now, maybe thinner … I grew to my full height when I was thirteen and went around for years thinking I was a giant. The magician had a big fluffy white rope and said he would hang me upside down from the ceiling where everyone could see my figure. These images come back to me, especially that awful feeling when you are young and vulnerable and everyone is about to look at you and how terrible it is going to be. The book is about how adults can confuse and terrify children. I was terrified for months after this experience. I wasn't sure if this man wouldn't come after me with his rope and force me to hang upside down. After all, he was supposed to be a magician.'

'What about your parents?'

'They went to Australia with five children, came back with seven and left two behind. They paid full price to go there, while everyone else went there for a tenner. They didn't know about the Australians offering Irish immigrants almost free passage. It was an expensive cruise. My mother told me that all the while they were on the ship they entertained people. All the children would get up and sing for them. They were in Australia for ten years. My father got sick there. They never talked much about what they did there but it was difficult for my mother, possibly difficult for my father too although he made it sound romantic when he came back. There were all these lovely aboriginal names and of course he spoke about the birds and the wildlife. He was always imitating the laugh of the kookaburra.

> My father's lips pursed with pleasure
> when he uttered the name of a place called Geelong,
> as if he was getting ready to blow
> into an invisible didgeridoo.
>
> (from 'The Australian Rug')

'They lost money hand over fist and barely got back to Ireland with enough to make a fresh start. They went to County Cork. They were originally from County Limerick where they had a big farm. The farmhouse was supposed to be haunted. My poem "Stones" is about how the stories about it haunted me:

the horse that went mad from a brain haemorrhage
circling and circling around the hawthorn-ringed field,
the riding accidents, bodies on the railway tracks,
Johnny the dead dog the children buried up to its neck.

'They sold it to a man and six months later he was thrown from a horse and killed. My brother spoke of footsteps on the stairs. Maybe it was difficult for them on that lonely farm but they had it hard in Australia too. My father was struck down by rheumatic fever for most of a year and then he was knocked over by a drunken driver. He was fifty-eight and my mother about forty when they returned to Cork, which was when I came along, the *mistake*. They didn't know anything about running a business but they opened up the bar, shop and petrol pump. It was the focus of everything. People would come down from church, funerals, weddings, the hunt, the creamery, and it was run very haphazardly. Can you imagine, starting all over again at that age? And then a tenth child arriving just when they must have thought they had enough?'

'What about your childhood?'

'Dreamy. I had a world of my own but then I'd talk my head off if I got a chance. I had a lot of friendships with older men, which I suppose is bound to happen when you grow up in a pub – lovely old men like Tom Twomey who would play cards with me, and there was Gerald Regan, a solicitor who would bring me beautiful children's books. Rilke says the source of all poetry is childhood and dreams. We drink from the well until we drink it dry. I think that is really true. There's an interesting Graham Greene essay about how the books we read in childhood are books of divination. I believe some of the things that make us sad when we are young do so precisely because we know they are going to happen to us. And then Declan Kiberd has written about how Joyce fell in love with the story of Ulysses when he was twelve – it was the children's version by Charles Lamb that originally captured his imagination.'

In her poem 'Facing the Public' the daughter captures the mother whole; or could it be, rather, that with so much of the poem hijacked by her voice, the mother captures the daughter whole?

My mother never asked like a normal person, it was

I'm asking you for the last time, I'm imploring you
not to go up that road again late for Mass.

She never had slight trouble sleeping, it was
Never, never, never for one moment did I get a wink,
as long as my head lay upon that pillow.

She never grumbled, because *No one likes a grumbler,*
I never grumble but the pain I have in my two knees this night
there isn't a person alive who would stand for it.

...

She didn't do the Stations of the Cross
she sorrowed the length and breadth of the church.
And yet, she could chalk up a picture in a handful of words

conjure a person in a mouthful of speech ...

There is very little in Martina's poetry that does not come from either her own or her mother's memories. The poem becomes a study in embarrassment. It is about the mother acting out scenarios in private and then being embarrassed when she is overheard. Anyone who comes from a small place will know how there the echoes go on forever.

Never, never, never would she be able, as long as she lived,
even if she got Ireland free in the morning, no, no, no
she would never be able to face the public again.

'That poem came when one day my daughter Liadáin was going on about something or other and I said to her, "Don't be so dramatic". She said, "Oh, *I'm* dramatic, am I!" She made me laugh and then I thought of my mother. And the poem just came out. The strong ones tend to, but really I'd been writing it for years. She was a larger-than-life character, a woman who ran everything. When I told her my first book was accepted she said, "Oh, a book!" When I added that it was poetry, she replied, "Oh, poems ... I thought it was a *book*." And then she'd say things like, "As Peggy Looney said to me, 'What a book you'd write, Mrs Cotter, the interesting life you've led, if you only had the time.'" Now I feel she is writing mine. Her voice is present in so many of the poems, especially the recent ones. She will always be renewing herself through them, I suppose. A strong light casts a strong shadow. She was fantastic in a way but terrible as well. You could ring her up and put the phone down, go off, water the garden, go to Sainsbury's, come back, sweep the house, and she would *still* be talking. She wouldn't have drawn breath and if you did try to interrupt her, you'd get from her, "Will you let me *speak*!" My mother always felt she had to jump into a conversation with *something*. She had to fill in the spaces, juggle with words, and entertain people. Eileen Murphy doesn't feel that pressure, does she? She doesn't need to say the "right" thing. She just stares at you.'

§

The burnings of historical memory, 'the fort of the burnings', might be said to have been later ghosted in the domestic activities of Martina's father, who loved to set fires.

> He was a quiet man,
> a secret man, who liked to be alone,
> and he had ten children.
>
> He couldn't bear to cut down his trees
>
> Every Christmas he defiantly brought in
> the worst pine, with the scantiest branches,
> and his family spent the whole Christmas
> trying to cover it up.
>
> Passionate about fires, inside or out,
> he spent summer evenings tending crowds
> of them in a field full of sunset.
>
> (from 'A Quiet Man')

'There's something very pagan in those lines,' I said.

'He was a *real* pagan! He loved fires. There is another short poem, "Burning Rubbish", in which I describe him as standing still among the blazes like a Roman general. Before he died it seemed some mad dream to be a writer but his death was the catalyst. Daddy died when I was twenty-seven and I was devastated. I didn't expect it … he was an old man with cancer … his time had come. I dreamt that I was stitching his dead body up, trying to make it come back to life like with Pangloss in *Candide*, which I was studying at the time, but he just smiled and shook his head as if he was very tired. I was so upset and in all my madness and ranting, the self-consciousness melted away. Life was too short for that and so I started writing poems. The original impulse was to write a poem about him. I couldn't do it. I had made many attempts but they all fell flat. It wasn't until I was close to completing my fourth book that I was in Waitrose one day and wrote "A Quiet Man" in two minutes on the back of my shopping list. It came out just like that. It must have been growing inside me. You could say that poem took two minutes to write or it took nine years. He was quite a bit older than my mother, a background man, not a big talker, although until he was seventy he worked really hard at some job or other as well as tearing round, looking after the garden and all the animals. A really lovely, cherubic-looking man with beautiful skin, all smiles, he'd walk our dog Fifi to the church. People would say of him, "Mr Cotter is always the gentleman, no airs or graces about him, every day going with his little dog to the church." Fifi loved the church, especially at Christmas time with the crib and the straw. The Three Wise Men arriving on January 6th always made him bark. He seemed to think they were a sinister addition. Most of all he loved to roll on the strip of orange carpet before the altar. I went up with them once. Fifi lifted his leg and Daddy just stood there, beaming with pride as Fifi pissed on the carpet. He told me it was "only a small bit", shook his head as if to say, why would anyone mind. Anything Fifi enjoyed was fantastic and sacred and probably a tribute to the orange carpet. The way my father was, well, he was a bit tangential or whatever, not exactly your normal or conventional character. All this stuff with the cats and the dogs, they were more real to him than people. My mother used to say, "There's more thought of cats and dogs than Christians in this house." Probably the same could be said for *this* house. In some ways my father never grew up. He did not want to go to school, resisted it violently. I heard the story that he rolled in the mud of the schoolyard in his new suit and eventually his mother just kept him at home. He lived in a world of his own, which made it difficult for my mother who was always branded as the bad one, but although she was tough and hard at times *somebody* had to rule, I suppose. She was super-sensitive as well … we all were. It made for lots of dramatics and my father would have his hand on the handle of the back door, always looking to escape our racket.

'The three-card trick men used to come to the horse fairs. My father must have remembered them from when he was little. There

was a famous horse fair in Cahirmee and the three-card trick men would go there, rangy-looking fellows in flat caps who'd go to all the fairs and carnivals. You would have to *find the lady*, guess which card was where. They would first come to the pub in Burnfort and ask my father for a cardboard box, which they'd set up for their cards, and my father would go weak with excitement. A man in his seventies, he'd cry, "They're here, the three-card men! They're here!"'

'Were they tinkers?'

'They were what my mother would describe as "next door to tinkers". I don't know if they were tinkers. She told me a story once about a real tinker and Tom Twomey and Lord Harrington and how they all sat by the fire, discussing horses. And because it was about horses the class differences completely melted away. That story always struck me. That's what's so important about being a poet, the *passion*. You see the most awful people, once they begin to speak of such things they are completely transformed.'

It seems as good a way as any to describe Martina's poetry, as a process of transformation which comes through allowing people their say, where even the Paddy Caseys of this world are given a shot at redemption, their awfulness made sublime. It is also a poetic world in which people tug hard at their leashes.

'My mother was much more in thrall to those particularly Irish Catholic inhibitions than my father was. I used to think it was just his personality and also the fact that women tended to be the more religious ones when I was growing up, but somebody told me that the Catholic church had been more relaxed, more Italian, before De Valera came to power and, with the help of his henchman, Archbishop McQuaid, ruled Ireland in that particularly moralistic way. My father grew up before that time, whereas my mother would have had the full weight of their influence. It was so repressed. Also De Valera was born out of wedlock, sent home from America by his mother to be brought up by his grandmother in Limerick. My poem "Reprisal" begins, "Never trust a Palatine or a Bastard." They used to say that in County Limerick "the Bastard" referred to De Valera. His mother went on to have a legitimate family in America but she never sent for him. That could be the root of his conservatism and control freakery – a personal interest in keeping women at home by the fire. You could say the political came from the personal.'

Martina pulled a 1950s Australian bible from the shelf and thumped it down in front of me. The dust rose from it and landed mote by mote in my glass of wine. I opened it onto a garish colour plate captioned 'Queen Assumed into Heaven', the Virgin Mary as I had never seen her before, a Tallulah Bankhead figure, the synthetic blue of her robe clashing with the synthetic pink of her dress, not colours such as one might find in nature – although maybe that was the point, that those chemically induced hues only served to emphasise the supernatural. Maybe, though, they were merely the colours of a tacky decade.

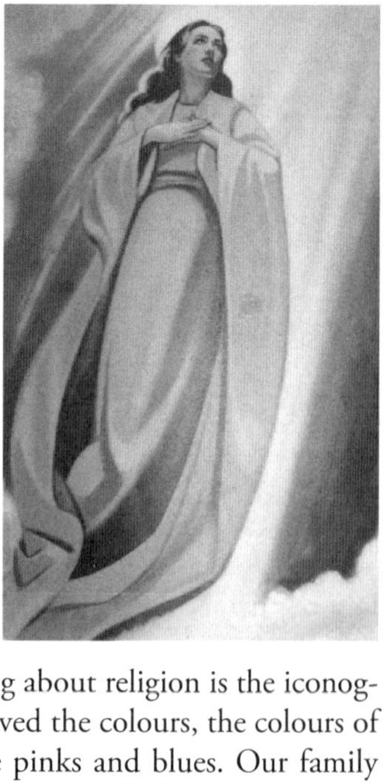

'Oh yes, I think that is so very Disney. It reminds me of *Sleeping Beauty* when at the end of the film she twirls round and round, her dress going pink and blue, pink and blue. You will notice a lot of pink and blue in the house. The thing about religion is the iconography. Ever since I was a child I've loved the colours, the colours of suffering, the Virgin Mary blue, the pinks and blues. Our family bible has exactly the colours I like. There is a whole generation very nostalgic about the iconography, especially those of us who have left the Church. We spent ages looking at this stuff. We had no choice. We should have come to hate it but because we got away, looking back on it now we can love it. Everything seems to come full circle.'

'So God's still kicking about your psyche?'

'I would never be so foolish as to think I could ever escape Him,' she whispered. 'There is a poem of mine "One Morning in July" which laughs at my younger self thinking I could strike out as an atheist. But I think I've left the Church. Ireland is in a very bad state with it, it's reeling at the moment. I heard the bishop isn't coming to the latest confirmation in a particular parish. Somebody said he'd be afraid to come because he'd be lynched. This is because of all the recent scandals, the bishops covering up for paedophiles. The feeling is *that* bad. Originally Ireland was a matriarchy with very strong female figures. Brigid was a goddess before she became a saint and it can't have been good when these powerful, pagan, rounded, female figures had to be squeezed into a virgin mould. All the stories about St Patrick and St Brigid are very interesting, with his being all about sexual repression and suffering and hers about abundance. When the goddess Brigid passed cows they would give three times the milk. She was like a corn goddess. She could hang her coat on a sunbeam. She was very much associated with the sun, with fertility, with abundance, with snakes, with giving milk … and then St Patrick arrived. One of the stories that really sums him up relates how one of the chieftains decided to convert to Christianity and St Patrick had this crosier which he went to stick into the earth but it went through the chieftain's foot by mistake and the chieftain, thinking this was part of the Christian initiation rites, did not utter a word throughout the whole thing. *That* set the tone for the way we were going to be from then on. I have no time for St Patrick.'

So, then, it was a tussle of war between Christian male and pagan female. The latter never really goes away, though. It might even be argued that the goddesses are back in force. There was one spotted not so long ago on Wandsworth Common. What Martina could have added is that Brigid was also considered the goddess of poetry or what the ancient Irish deemed 'the flame of knowledge'. According to the Middle Irish collection, *Lebor Gabála Érenn* (*The Book of the Taking of Ireland*), Brigid was herself a poet. Lady

Gregory in *Gods and Fighting Men* (1904) describes her as 'a woman of poetry, and poets worshipped her, for her sway was very great and very noble. And she was a woman of healing along with that, and a woman of smith's work, and it was she first made the whistle for calling one to another through the night. And the one side of her face was ugly, but the other side was very comely. And the meaning of her name was *Breo-saighit*, a fiery arrow.' The Christian Brigid seems to have imported a good many pagan elements. According to the chronicler, Giraldus Cambrensis, she was associated with the eternal sacred flame at Kildare, which was surrounded by a hedge. Any man attempting to cross the hedge would go insane and die, either that or his *dingle-twang* would wither. The fact too that the goddess Brigid was associated with hill-forts and fire would suggest that Martina's mind was unwittingly seared at an early age.

'The story about St Patrick driving the snakes from Ireland … when I was a child I was terrified of snakes. My first ever poem "There is a Snake in My Bed" was published in a swanky magazine called *Celtic Dawn*, edited by a man operating out of the Bee Gees' castle, in Thame, in Oxfordshire. Terence DuQuesne was some kind of Egyptologist and magic man who was friendly with Robin Gibb's Irish wife, Dwina, with whom he co-edited the magazine. My first experience of being published was being invited to the Bee Gees' castle. If I thought poetry was going to be sex, drugs and rock and roll, it was all downhill after that. Admittedly I got a funny feeling when the man at the drawbridge got on the telephone to Terence, "Put down that donkey, will you. Your visitor is here."'

And not only does that snake not go away, it grows in size too. A recent poem 'Boa Constrictor' would suggest difficulties of an ophiological kind in County Cork. The 'big fat body of him', which Martina observes behind thick glass in the Dublin zoo, escapes. It is heading, as do so many of Martina's poems, towards a particular place.

I saw the road from Dublin disappearing
under his muscular body as he went past
signposts, no need for such a diabolical fellow
to check where he was going –
cleverly travelling at night, arranging himself

carefully in ditches for sleep by day.
Every so often, he might stop to open his mouth for a sheep like
the picture I'd seen in World Book Encyclopaedia.
He knew where he was coming all right –
the village of Burnfort.

All roads would seem to lead to Burnfort, which on the map remains invisible.

§

'What about life in the pub, shop and petrol pump?'

'My mother could never refuse anyone anything. People were always coming, begging for the last bit of whatever we had or else looking for drink.'

Christmas Day and Good Friday
were the only days that the pub closed.
And yet they came –
trembling strangers, under hats and caps,
lapels turned up against the slanting wind
or hiding a dog collar.
(from 'Desperate Men')

'She would be easily persuaded to give away her last bit of whatever it might be, often taking things out of the kitchen for people who knew they could work on her or even stuff that was not hers to give. Some people used to book their papers in advance, pay on yearly account. There was a local bachelor who took himself very seriously and would order the local papers, the *Cork Examiner* and the *Evening Echo*, and when he came he expected them to be there waiting for him. Invariably my mother would have given away one of the papers to someone else. "Oh, my God," she'd cry, "Christy Callaghan is coming!" We'd be sent flying out the back door to a neighbour with a two-shilling piece to buy back the newspaper and then somebody else would be out in the back kitchen, ironing it, straightening out the pages, and putting it together, and Christy, who'd experienced this one too many times before, would get all edgy. "Where's my newspaper?" he'd cry. "All I want is a drop of whiskey and my newspaper. Is it too much to ask for?" Sometimes it *was* too much to ask for. There were seventeen cats out back of the house … that's an approximate number because they came and went … and there was Fifi. My father wasn't allowed to feed them the best meat in the fridge. So I would aid and abet him. We had an electric meat slicer and I would watch out for him when he snuck in with a non-electric knife so as not to make any noise and he would be sawing away all these big chunks of meat which he would then run out to give to the cats. And because he'd be in such a rush the meat was left in a terrible condition and we couldn't sell it to anyone. Now I think of my poor mother but at the time I thought she was the arch-enemy of the cats. I don't think we had much business sense. Every now and then my mother would talk about the bailiffs coming. Somehow, though, they did manage. We were sent to boarding school, for instance.'

'And the publican side of things, what was that like?'

'Singing was a big thing when I was growing up but with the coming of TV and bands all that has died out. One person might have had a musical instrument but generally speaking people would just get up to do their party pieces and of course you knew what everyone's piece was going to be. I learned all the words to "Harper Valley PTA" and performed it. Do you know the lyrics? "Mrs Johnson, you're wearing your dresses way too high. / It's reported you've been drinking and a-runnin' round with men and going wild." The customers would be thinking *what the hell*. I didn't know what it was about, but for sure it wasn't some lovely song about the IRA. Years later, someone in the bar said, "Ah, for the days when people sang!" and my older sister got really mad. "Oh, I remember them all right," she said. "*Bloody hell!* So-and-so would come down from the mountain and would have to sing his bit and we'd be all bored out of our heads and then Mr So-and-so would glare at us while Mrs So-and-so sang, she who didn't have a note in her head, and, God, I'd be afraid to even touch a pint glass because Mr So-and-so would, like, give you such a vicious look." So you always had this other side to the lovely singsongs.

'We were definitely considered oddballs. I think we had it in spades. My brother Tom was on his way to boarding school

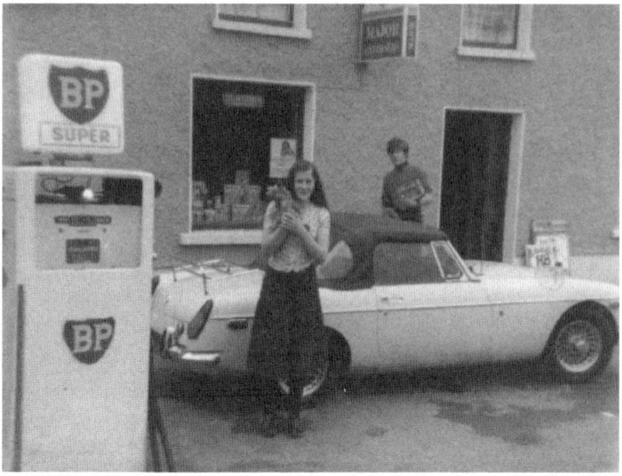

when he met a man on a train and the man said "Where are you from?" and Tom said "I'm from Burnfort" and the man said "Oh God, I *know* Burnfort. There is a pub there." And Tom opened his mouth to say he lived in the pub when the man continued, "Jesus, there is a funny family living in that pub. Do you know them?" And Tom said yes, and let the man talk away, entertain him all the way from Mallow Station to Limerick Junction on the foibles and eccentricities of the Cotter family. And then when Tom got up to change trains at Limerick Junction he said, "Before I go, I had better tell you I'm one of the funny ones." And he left the man with his jaw dropped down to his ankles.'

'It would seem literature came late to you.'

'It was *always* with me. I learned to read very young and that became my refuge. I was able to remove myself at the age of three. That's the irony of the whole thing: the end product of the reading is becoming a writer and *what* do I write about? All the things that I obviously *didn't* shut out despite having my head stuck in a book all the time. That's what it is, the fairy tale, the return in the myth. I got into a lot of trouble because we were always supposed to be minding the shop and the bar and the fact that I was always reading was a bone of contention. There was one big row with some woman. I was rolling half a dozen oranges over the counter with my left hand while holding a book with my right hand, reading it. As a teenager I used to keep diaries which were just dire. I wish I'd kept them because they would be hilarious to read but they were really emotional and melodramatic. I tore them up because they disgusted me. I used to write out Maupassant stories in French, pretending they were mine. I can see now that this was a good way to learn to write and to this day if I really like a poem I'll write it out in longhand. It is like inhabiting it. You get a sense of its structure. But I wasn't thinking that at the time. I was just pretending to be Maupassant and very sophisticated because I was writing in French. So it was always there. Also my family were absolutely brilliant storytellers. My mother was always telling stories in public and in private. She'd drive us mad sometimes going off on tangents – free association, out of control – but sometimes the words and the way she said them was like a glove on the hand fitting just right. My sister Bernadette was very funny, with a great memory, and we would tell each other stories and like my mother she would be hungry for detail, asking exactly how people looked and asking me to repeat what they said and *how* they said it.'

'All this would appear to be connected to the very idea of Irishness, the gift of the gab.'

'And the feeling you *have* to entertain. I grew up with that. It was very much in the family. My mother would say, "Go down and talk to the customers", but with my head always stuck in a book I think I was hit and miss.'

'There is the boredom too, which in your writing acquires an almost mythic quality.'

'Yes, when boredom is heightened to a state of fascination, this is what art does. There is madness in it too. It is almost hysterical boredom.'

§

A growing strain in Martina's poetry, particularly in her most recent collection, *Facing the Public*, is Irish history, often the interstices where it and family history become one. The poems, many of them imbued with what she calls the 'black note', are often told aslant, their revelations unintentional although that is precisely what they are meant to be. A boy suspected of informing for the Black and Tans is dragged by a horse and cart for forty miles, Ernie O'Malley of the IRA is given his say, and in prison her Uncle Tommy writes a letter about a grey mare, yearning for 'the day she'd come again / drumming her hooves'. Very rarely is anything spelled out in black and white. Martina shuns the propagandistic line. She brought out her family album of photographs, pausing at one, saying, 'We were doing a nativity play. I *think* I was the Virgin Mary.' As the photos moved from colour to monochrome, a history in reverse, the figures who flit in and out of her poems stared at me from their fixed places.

'These are my maternal grandparents. Her family refused to hang the picture because they didn't like *him*. Richard Cotter was very well educated. Sometimes, when I hear stories about him with his moustache, I think of James Joyce's father, John. They were from roughly the same era and of the new rising Catholic middle class. Catholic Emancipation came in 1829. They'd both been to early Catholic boarding schools, John Joyce at St Colman's in Fermoy and Richard Cotter at St Michael's in Listowel. What I heard was that Richard Cotter was a silver-tongued devil and she, Elizabeth Cowhey, was a long-suffering woman with a lot of money. Look at that waist … it must have been uncomfortable … I wonder where her teeth are … she is keeping her mouth clammed shut … I have been to the dental museum in Wimpole Street and seen Victorian false teeth, wooden. Anyway I'm not going to go *there* … She and her sister, Mary, were followers of Parnell who haunts the pages of Joyce. They were big tenant farmers who got involved in Parnell's Land War campaign. This is going back to the late Victorian period and the beginning of the rise of the Catholic middle class. The plan of campaign was that the tenants would refuse to pay the landlords. You had to be brave. You would be evicted and then you would fight the eviction. It was decided that *she* would do it because she wouldn't get a long sentence like a man would. It would have been your typical eviction scene. All the

windows on the first floor of the house were bricked up. She and her sister, Mary, went upstairs and they poured kettles of boiling water mixed with Indian meal down on the soldiers, the landlord, the bailiff, the battering ram, fixed bayonets. Eventually she was carried off to prison.

'When I visited Kilmainham Prison and inspected the various cells I discovered women weren't treated as political prisoners and that she would have been thrown in with the prostitutes. No one ever mentioned that! My mother, who really admired her, said she was a lady and that when she was in prison she refused to drink out of a tin mug and so they had to bring her a China cup and saucer. My mother also spoke of how she would darn socks for the workmen on the farm. Servants weren't often treated that well. As a child I was told she met Grandfather Cotter in prison. He had been imprisoned for cutting a rope bridge from under an RIC [Royal Irish Constabulary] man. One Sunday afternoon the RIC man was reclining on a rope bridge, watching the river and the minnows dancing in the sunlight off the water, and Richard Cotter snuck up on him, cut the ropes, and down went the RIC man among the minnows. That was his great blow for Irish freedom. Anyway there he was with his silver tongue and when they met apparently he didn't think all that much of her but after his release, when he found out she had three brothers all of whom died young and that she had ended up inheriting the farm, he hurried to Ballybunion where she was convalescing at her aunt's hotel, courted her, and married her. Who knows for sure what happened? Economics are always a consideration and maybe people were more honest about mercenary motives back then. He was called "Ould Cotter" by some people and I remember being thrilled when I came across a character called Ould Cotter in *Dubliners*. My mother was the one who told me everything. Her voice goes right through those stories of the War of Independence. When she was growing up in the late 1920s she listened to those stories and soaked them up like a big piece of blotting paper. You would think she'd been there and actually witnessed the events. My poem "Two Hostages" is about my mother and my father being taken hostage, on separate occasions, by the Black and Tans, "one of them claiming that he couldn't *get over the brown eyes of the Irish*." My father never told me that story, my mother did.'

Martina turned another page in the album.

'Here's a lovely picture of Daddy and my Uncle Tommy in 1910, with their Eton collars. Daddy's on the right.'

'Why did your father go silent on all this history?'

'He was a quiet man. They were all traumatised. When he was dying of brain secondary all through the end he spoke about the Civil War – he was reliving it. That was even *less* spoken about. The Irish War of Independence *was* spoken about. It was a one-sided view of heroes, the David and Goliath thing, the IRA being David and the British Empire Goliath, and in a way it was, but it wasn't the *full* story. The Civil War, on the other hand, couldn't be discussed at all because it was too horrendous. My father was on Michael Collins's side. Somebody from the Republican side, a man called Cronin, shot the eye out of my father's uncle's head while he was shaving. Cronin's son became a politician and every time my father saw the election posters for him he'd start rumbling. We used to think it was hilarious when he and his friend Tom Twomey got all obsessed about the Civil War. We also teased them because we knew Michael Collins's followers became Blueshirts, quasi-fascists, with a uniform and – let me put it *this* way – a very distinctive salute. We poked fun at the Blueshirts, which wasn't very nice, but we didn't have much sympathy for their side of the Civil War. Some of them later went and fought with Franco.'

'Was your father involved in actual fighting?'

'Yes. He would have been very young though. That is all I know, he never spoke of it. I remember in the 1970s my brother came home drunk and said to him and his friend Tom Twomey, "You never said what the *other* side did. You never told us about Dirty

Dick and 77 Republicans." Now, any mention of *that* was enough to start everyone off. General Richard Mulcahy, "Dirty Dick", would have been a hero of my father's. An ex-medical student when he joined the IRA, he was on Collins's side and then, during the Civil War, when he supported the Anglo-Irish Treaty, he executed 77 Republican prisoners. Tom Twomey used to smoke a pipe and drink by the fire. My father would be down there too, both of them quite old at this stage. They loved Fifi. When Tom Twomey came in he'd heat his flat cap in front of the fire to warm it up for Fifi who would jump into it and they would sit there admiring him, discussing the weather and talking about old times. So when my brother came in that night, shouting at them about Dirty Dick and the "77", they went berserk. These old men who would never say boo to a goose held him up against the wall. My sister Bernadette who was there told me Tom Twomey's false teeth were clacking with temper.'

'Those are the details I love!'

§

It had come time to shift houses.

'Listen,' she said, 'do you see the chandelier?'

I stared up at the ceiling of the not quite *Ulysses*-blue room in the house opposite the boarded-up front of the Turkish library on Balls Pond Road.

'I got it for fifteen quid from a street trader in Camden Passage – he got it in a house clearance in the East End. It's art deco. I grew up in a scrap merchant's house that was full of salvage, the ship's panelling, for example, and poetry for me is another form of salvage, salvage from the wreckage. And this house too, in more ways than one, is a bit of salvage. It was a complete wreck when I bought it with my husband and I could see after a while I was going to end up doing all the work and with a young child to take care of I needed any spare time to do my writing. I'd worked so hard to get out of radiography. I didn't feel I was up to much more burning of the candle at both ends. Little did I know. Anyway, the roof was leaking, the walls were full of holes – it needed a lot of spare money, something we never had. So when we separated I called the estate agent to put it on the market straight away. I desperately wanted us to be able to get on with our separate lives. The estate agent refused. He was a man called Malcolm Levy, a Jewish Eastender – very witty and entertaining – but he was serious on this occasion. He said he had a buyer on the phone but he wasn't putting it on the market. "It is the ground under your feet and things are going to get very nasty." He was right. The house was such hard work, though, and I had to do it all on the shortest shoestring with a lot of hard work and disasters. Liadáin's ceiling collapsed twice, the Thames Water man got stuck like Winnie the Pooh in the aperture leading to the attic and told me I would have to get a very small, very brave plumber prepared to crawl over the electrics if I was to get the ballcock sorted out. The attic of course was built for smaller Georgian working-class men. Handymen came and went, many of them dubious or plain mad, like the fellow who made me dance the military two-step with him at ten o'clock one night. That's an example of a bit of nonsense there for you. There was a fantastic roofer called John from Cork who was a terrible time-keeper but very kind and he squeezed myself and Liadáin into the cab of his truck (there were always a few of his extended family with him, as well as a severely autistic man he'd met on a building site years ago who'd become completely attached to him) and he drove us all around North London to builders' suppliers getting anything we needed and introducing us to all the London Irishmen who worked in these places. But then Dalston began to change. When we moved in it had been a dangerous run-down area. Now property was rising fast. I could never hope to pay my ex-husband his share and we would have to leave this place when Liadáin's education was finished and we'd grown so mad about it. I decided to change my mortgage to an interest-only one so I could pay my ex-husband. At least it would delay the inevitable sale. I told a very good friend of mine my plan. He told me that I could get an interest-free loan which I could pay off at a very comfortable rate and I thought he was mad. Then he explained. He was also Jewish and I knew his four grandparents died in concentration camps but I didn't know that he had inherited a large amount of reparation money from the German government. It had been paid to the previous generation in his family but they could never bring themselves to spend it. So my friend secretly spends the money doing good deeds for so many people and helping Liadáin and me to stay in this house was one of them. Overnight, I had the strength to clear the garden full of rubble and weeds and in the space of a year turned from Mrs Brownfingers to Mrs Greenfingers. And sometimes when I'm in the garden and I think of how this came about, it does really feel like a miracle. There are iron bars from Clerkenwell Prison upstairs. I dream of houses all the time. They are wonderful dreams because I keep finding more rooms that I never knew I had. Freud said the psyche is like a house. One of the first things young children draw is a house.'

> These houses grow inside us.
>
> I dreamt of a house in Holloway
> in a circle of mountains,
> a green ocean washing the front door.
>
> My daughter talks
> of a house with a stream
> running right through the middle,
> the Salmon of Knowledge
> lepping for joy inside.
>
> (from 'Dream Houses')

'I think *this* is my dream house. Lately I'm dreaming more of gardens. I dream of there being more to my garden, sunny spots I never knew I had, and in them I'm planting roses and fuchsias. If there is any religion that comes to me I think it is through gardening, the magic of things growing, dying and coming back. I don't think it matters *how* we come back. I've been dreaming too about the garden in Burnfort and that makes me so happy because I feel close to my mother like I was when I was a child. I was mad about her then, and with everyone else away at school we'd be close. One dream sounds gruesome. I am kneeling, planting roses, but instead of a box of bone meal beside me there is a corpse and I am breaking bits off it to put in with the roses as fertiliser. In the dream I'm happy, though, and maybe it's a metaphor for writing because I believe we write for the dead.'

Martina is, arguably, the noisiest woman ever to have laid siege to a kitchen. She sliced red peppers for her famous red pepper soup, the clanging of pots and pans and the higher notes of spoons and knives together creating a din through which, on the recording I made, I struggle hard to follow her words. She then put on the rice.

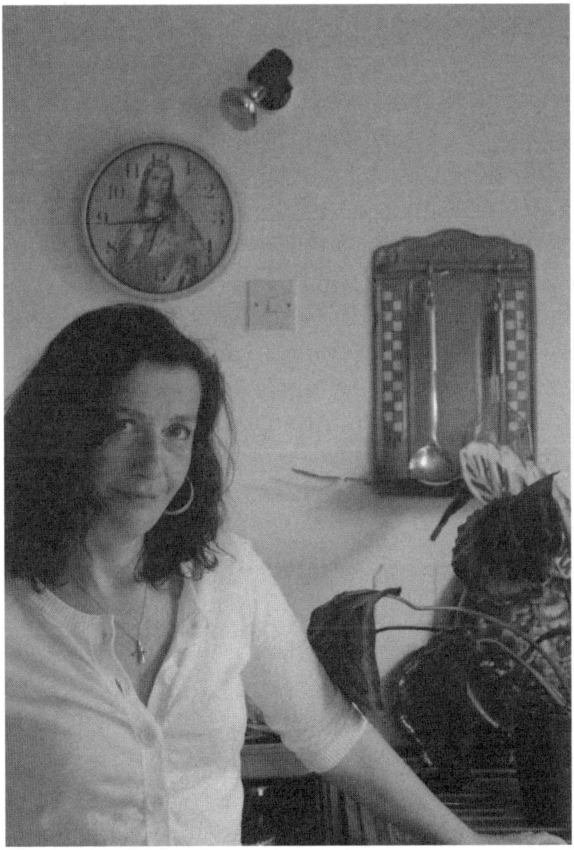

What's missing from the image is the knife she was holding when I suggested she might not be quite the feminist she believes she is. I only narrowly missed being added to the peppers. What I think I really meant to say is that she is uncontainable. There's no ideology that'll keep her in one place.

Martina came to London in 1988 and worked for some years as a radiographer. When I remarked on how masculine nurses' uniforms had become we embarked on a strange disquisition that might have had something to do with the connectivity of form and appearance.

'I can't ever bear to talk about the deterioration of the nurses' uniforms these days! Those awful trouser suits, and there's no sign any more of those lovely big headdresses for the Sisters in Charge. I weep when I think of what is gone. I think the uniforms were very beautiful. A part of me hates all that hierarchy but for me it had glamour, an element of safety. I suppose I'm not being practical as trousers are more comfortable. I'd love it if they brought back the Latin Mass too, but as I wouldn't go to church anyway I'm not entitled to complain. I had an experience once which makes me think of the Circe episode in Joyce, where all these masochistic events happen to Leopold Bloom. That was the thing about James Joyce – he wasn't ashamed to show those aspects of himself – the humiliation, the masochistic bits, all the hallucinatory stuff that goes on in the brothel – he showed every side of the human being. And that's what's so hard about being a writer, what one has to reveal about oneself. Anyway I was with a friend in the King's Head in Islington. We were deep in conversation and alcohol. I have a bad sense of direction and instead of going downstairs to the toilet I went upstairs and entered a dressing room which I didn't know was there. A World War I British soldier – they obviously had some play on – appeared in the room, absolutely incensed, and he obviously wasn't going to get out of character for me. I can't remember what he said but I remember backing out of the room. Perhaps he was enjoying himself, I don't know.'

'Could it be you interrupted a performance?'

'I hope to God not, but I remember getting great pleasure out of the whole thing, after the initial fright, *definitely* in recounting it. Whatever he looked like, now, in my imagination, he is six foot six, blond, wearing a pale khaki uniform. Also he had on these puttees, or if he didn't he has them on now. He's in one of my novels in progress. You remember the girl in my novel *No Drinking, No Dancing, No Doctors* steals a nurse's uniform. When I was a child I wanted one and I liked being in hospitals the few times I was in them – the clean sheets, the nurses with their upside-down watches, those lovely pillbox hats and the strange curvy veils. The thing about wearing a uniform was that I felt I was playing a role. A hospital is, after all, a dramatic place. I don't mean melodramatic but what Robert Frost meant when he said everything is as good as it is dramatic.'

It was here, in London, soon after her father died, that she began to write. It was here that she gave birth to her daughter and it was here that her marriage fell to pieces. And it was here, at the time when the courts were determining whether to overturn the judgements on certain people accused of bombings in the 1970s, that she felt the need to acquaint herself more with Irish history.

'Those were still highly political times because of the reopening of the Birmingham Six and Guildford Four cases. I'd walk into the staffroom at the hospital and people would be saying terrible things about them, what I call "tabloid comments". I didn't really know that much about Irish history and I hadn't been very political, or, if so, only through what my mother told me. Still I couldn't believe people were so ill-informed and could make such ignorant statements about what was happening. I began to try to explain to them about Ireland but they didn't understand. They called me "the IRA". It was hard being called that. One man I worked with, whenever a bomb went off, would ring me up wherever I was and say, as a joke, "Where were you last night?" I was in my twenties then, in my nurse's uniform. I think I've been trying to explain Ireland ever since. What I'm really interested in, though, are people who don't have a voice. This is especially true of the Irish who came here before me, as labourers, who John McGahern called "the silent generation". I became fascinated with all those builders and labourers because I used to X-ray them at the Whittington. These were men who came over in the 1950s whereas my generation came over with more education and confidence. They were incredibly sad and touched something inside me. I was looking back through them to my parents who were very unhappy as immigrants, who had been well-off farmers, middle class with servants, and suddenly ended up in Australia where they were like the rest of the paddies.'

The stories of those Irish who came to England in the 1950s have been captured most poignantly in Catherine Dunne's *An Unconsidered People – The Irish in London* (2003). She describes them as having become 'doubly invisible' in both their own and their adopted countries. The more Martina delves into her country's past, the more she becomes a conduit for what she calls the 'black note'.

'There is this fantastic book, *The Burning of Bridget Cleary*, which is so compassionate, so empathic and so informative. She was an

Irish woman burnt to death by her husband in a fireplace in 1895. They thought she was a fairy. It was a bad time for this to happen. The Unionists had a field day of it, saying, "We can't allow these savages Home Rule." One of the things that really interested me as a writer was the court evidence. There had been a local fairy doctor, somebody else giving advice, various relations standing around and doing nothing to stop this man who'd obviously gone out of his head. The strangest story! They were all in court now and the people there, depending on whether they were pre-famine or post-famine, gave very different evidence. Those who had been born before the Great Famine were generally illiterate while those born after it were literate. The people who'd been to school gave expositions in which they simply related what happened, but when the illiterate people got up in the witness box they went into complete dramatic mode. They recreated and visualised the whole thing for themselves. The best writers are people who can do *that*. A lot of people can't visualise and what they relate just won't come alive.

'The reason why I'm interested in *voice* is because it often chooses the black note. Neruda has it in his "Ode to Death". I can't *explain* the black note. You know it when you hear it and the Irish have a lot of it, with their love of funerals. They relish it. It's what Joyce has in *Ulysses*. The most powerful voice there is Stephen Dedalus who is based on Joyce's father, John, who is from Cork, who is malicious, witty, funny, dark, coarse … an incredible voice that jumps off the page. So much writing comes from the dead. I started writing after my father died. As I said before, I think we write for the dead, we inhabit their voices. Yeats talks about how the dead have wisdom but no power … we have the power and the dead try to make us do their bidding. I don't want to merely repeat what Lorca says about *duende*, but this is why I like the dramatic monologue, when people are unconscious of what they reveal about themselves, hang themselves in speech or whatever. Voices are at their most powerful when admitting the dark in themselves to someone else. A really bland example of this would be somebody launching into conversation with "I am not a racist" and then going on to demonstrate otherwise. I tried to do this particularly in the monologues "Reprisal" and "The Boy from Durras" where the people speaking give an account of what has happened – a terrible dark thing, revenge. You know how in tragedy there is a cathartic sense, a sense of completeness, that this is what life is about, and the voice has a satisfaction, almost enjoyment, about it even as it is telling you something terrible. It is like someone grabbing you by the collar and saying, "Yes, this is what it's like. Have a look." I think most of the time poetry can deal with dark subjects much better than fiction. It can deal with torture, the Holocaust, and compared to it fiction doesn't even come near. It is closer to prayer, on a higher register soundwise. That's why I never like fiction as much because there is an element of judging that goes on, which does not go into poetry. I always felt very exposed when writing fiction because it is about arranging people. You give your view on people, on how they act, on how they talk to each other, on how they react, and that shows how you see people. That makes me feel far more naked than if I revealed a secret about myself, such as I'd killed or robbed someone. I do not judge people when I'm writing poetry. If writing is to do with the relationship between the writer and the reader, the reader finishing what the writer starts, then I think in most fiction it's the writer who finishes it. It's for that reason poetry is more healing to write. It allows us to release some of the darkness in ourselves. I think that's how *duende* comes into people's speech, which is why the story of Bridget Cleary really fascinated me because here were people who sat about, churning milk or whatever, while a woman was burnt to death and they were all thinking to themselves, "Oh, no" or "Go easy on her there." You can see how jealousy, resentment, fear and cowardice allowed this thing to happen. This can happen in any situation no matter what it is – it could be the Rosenbergs in the United States getting executed. There is a play called *The Little Foxes* by Lillian Hellman, where the servant says something about there being people who eat the world and those who stand around and watch them eating the world.'

'You say it took your leaving Ireland to enable you to write …'

'You can't go back!'

'But you do so all the time in your work.'

'Yes, but still you can't go back physically and even if I did there'd be nothing to return to. The pub is rented out, there's no post office in the village. There isn't even a shop any more. It really is a vanished world. I do think you lose something else. You become more of a foreigner there and you are one here as well. Although I'm in a very different situation, I am an exile.'

'You consider yourself so, an exile as opposed to an émigré?'

'The word seems to me the right one.'

'As someone *forced* out of Ireland?'

'On a realistic level that sounds totally self-indulgent but I think I'm telling the truth. The word *sounds* right to me, as if the sound *is* the sense. I suppose it's self-imposed exile … I felt I needed to get away to write.'

'So the years of being here haven't lessened your sense of being an exile?'

'I never entered the Irish *thing* because I don't go to church. I have always felt like an outsider. You know something – the first place where I felt I belonged … I was twenty-eight at the time … was the Torriano Meeting House. There I met the wonderful John Rety and a lot of eccentric people. I recited a poem from the floor. There was a man with a can of beer, holding a dog by a string, sitting on the edge of the stage, very unnerving, and there I was shaking, reading out my first poem. And then he asked me to read it again! But, to go back to your question, I think one responds to the deepest tribal parts of oneself. Edna O'Brien says the exiled writer is joined by a cable to his native country. But then I love being here because I'm free. It is a great escape from who you are. Coming here started me writing as much as my father's death did. My sister Mary brought me here for a week's holiday when I was eleven and I completely fell in love with the place. I have always been in love with London. I think for me it is having this safe little place within the city, my own little microcosm, and then I make little forays out into the jungle. The garden feels like a secret too. *The Secret Garden* was another favourite childhood book, another book of divination. I lie in the hammock under the honeysuckle at the bottom of the garden … and it's a secret … the blackbirds are singing … the cats are around me … and at the same time I hear the roar of the traffic and the police sirens … peace and noise all at the same time. Also for me the world of books was London. I felt I had come to the right place.'

There was a slightly acrid, black, smell in the air. Suddenly there was a panicked look in Martina's eyes.

'I think I've burned the rice,' she cried. 'Isn't that terrible?'

'Yes,' I said, 'and at this stage in life too.'

My Problem with Brahms

And How Nelly Akopian-Tamarina Came to the Rescue

My 'problem' is, or rather *was*, feline in nature. Years ago, I'd heard Brahms got his musical inspiration from torturing cats and that he sought to reproduce in music their dying cries. What emerges of late is that this was a slander made against him by Wagner who sought any means possible of discrediting his fellow composer. Wagner junked Brahms. Brahms junked Wagner. Their adherents behaved likewise. The musical century was ablaze. Still, the charge is a troubling one because it is hard to believe that Wagner, who was so horrified by vivisection that the mere thought of it kept him awake at night, could have played fast and loose with an issue that touched on his own most deeply held convictions. Also, one's inner realm of justice is badly disturbed because it is one of the flaws of human nature that when such a charge is made, somewhere, in the deepest recesses of the mind, it continues to stick even when the evidence demonstrates otherwise.

Sadly my opinion of Brahms was besmirched from day one. I had listened to Emil Gilels play the *Four Ballades*, Op. 10. I'd heard Solomon too, but not even they, great musicians that they are, could dispel my problem with Brahms. And yet, I reasoned, if the *Ballades* owe their conception to such a hideous origin then surely all art is suspect. My doubts were finally put to rest on the evening of 30th January 2008 when I heard the émigré Russian pianist Nelly Akopian-Tamarina play not just the *Ballades* at Wigmore Hall but also the *Three Intermezzi*, Op. 117 and *Eight Piano Pieces*, Op. 76.

Brahms is innocent. The cats may breathe easy for a while. If I give a precise date for my mollification it is because musically the evening was a momentous one. Akopian-Tamarina rarely performs and it had been twenty years since she last performed in London. That something 'special' occurred is beyond doubt but to ascribe any technical analysis to what I *think* I felt is quite beyond my musical capabilities. Some chemistry worked on me at just the right moment in my life. Say, simply, I was moved. Say Brahms might have been Chopin in bearded disguise. Say Nelly Akopian-Tamarina came to the rescue.

A unique performer, she is the most balletic of pianists. She could easily pass for a ballerina, and indeed she might have become one were it not that her teachers advised a pianistic future. Sometimes, while playing, she turns sideways, as if about to float away into the distance on a gradient of approximately 32 degrees. Another thing she does, which I hesitate to call a mannerism for fear it will be thought deliberate, is that she falls away from the keyboard, her spine absolutely straight like a yachtsman seeking to control his craft in a strong breeze. She demonstrates her love for the music physically, or rather she uses her body physically and in the process demonstrates her love for the music. In this respect she is Richter's opposite, the great Richter who sat hunched inside every note. She has been described as the survivor of a 'golden age' when musicians were in absolute obeisance to the music rather than to the careers which their playing it helped create. This is not to cast aspersion on the many fine musicians on the concert circuit today, but they tend to breathe a different oxygen. Akopian-Tamarina is hooked up to a supply from elsewhere. Antál Dorati described her as 'simply a phenomenon' and critic Ateş Orga writes, 'she is a strong believer in allegory as a passport to other worlds and states of mind'. When I heard her speak on a BBC programme for no more than ten minutes what I heard was enough to feed the Slavic side of me, and like red wine spilled over a white tablecloth a shape resembling Russia spread through my thoughts. She would be the emblem of all that her country has had to endure. She plays with what it is made. What I had not bargained for is that she is also the embodiment of her country's many complexities.

She simply *has* to play. The idea of any length of time spent away from the piano is more than she can bear to contemplate – it is even, if one may go to such verbal extremes, horrifying, and, in this respect, it would seem that considerably more than pianism is at stake. It would seem, rather, a matter of survival, both physical and spiritual. 'Slavic madness?' I ask. 'Yes, maybe,' she replies, 'but *don't* overdo it.' There is subtle humour in her voice. She is a woman of rituals, many of them. She keeps upon the piano a slip of paper bearing, in her slanted hand, a quotation from Charles Lamb's *Dream Children: A Reverie*. Curiously enough, she has excised from it words maybe too painful to include:

> We are nothing; less than nothing, and dreams. We are only what might have been, and must wait [upon the tedious shores of Lethe millions of ages] before we have existence, and a name.

Where, exactly, are the tedious shores of Lethe? And for how long must they be endured? Only piano, it seems, dissolves space and time. Only piano brings release. And to try to extricate Akopian-Tamarina from that sonic world is not easily done. She enters it gladly – she leaves it unhappily. It is a process she compares to being inside a bathysphere, which is lowered to the ocean's bottom, slowly, slowly, whoever captains it very gradually adjusting the pressure as to do so too quickly would be dangerous, and then, after finding that place which she thinks of as her true domicile, a true romantic, she will practise there for hours on end, and then, the idea hateful to her, she returns to the material world, the coming back up so very much more painful than the going down. She told me this, or at least some variation of it, which maybe I have simplified or maybe I have complicated, over the telephone, whispering, pleading for more time to readjust to things as they are, or are about to be, which is why she had to cancel yet again a meeting with me. And when I telephoned her a week later, once more I churned her oceanic peace. She said it was not the right time. All told, it would be over a year before I could get her at our table.

'I am difficult,' she jokes, 'even when I'm easy.'

We would later have a discussion on the semantics of the word *difficult*, a dramatic sketch for which goes something like this:

A dinner table lit from above. Night. There are no curtains at the windows.

(*Silence.*)
NA-T: You say I am difficult.
MK: I'm only repeating what you told me.
NA-T: Yes, but only *I* am allowed to say so. What is the opposite of difficult?
BK: (*Aside.*) *Very* difficult.
MK: Easy, accommodating…
NA-T: (*sarcastically*) This is what you like? You prefer easy, accommodating people?
MK: You put me on the spot!
NA-T: So don't call me difficult again.
MK: You will be described so in the piece, whether you like it or not.
NA-T: I *like* difficulties. Sometimes Brahms and other composers provide easier alternatives for extremely difficult passages. I feel reluctant to use them and prefer the original. I like *difficult*. Life is difficult. Getting up in the morning is difficult. So how dare you call me difficult? *Of course* I'm difficult. I would hate to be otherwise.
(*Pause.*)
NA-T: (*brightly*) What about *challenging*? I crave challenge. The challenges in my life have made me into what I am today. Or maybe *complex*? Complex I *like*.
The room darkens. The windows brighten.

Akopian-Tamarina dislikes being interviewed, reasonably enough, and so I put it to her this would be not so much an interview as the record of a conversation, which is why I never go to anyone armed with questions. She told me she went to a clairvoyant once, who within minutes said to her, 'I think the stage is your forte.' She laughs at the memory of this, while admitting that playing piano is an act so transparent it reflects everything inside one.

'It is who you are and it's where you can't lie.'

She can barely operate in the world as it is, but she is not so much the ascetic she will forgo its pleasures. She loves clothes. She loves shoes. She loves them to the degree that they are an expression of her personality, which, in any case, is what style ought to be. She loves 1940s movies, anything with Bette Davis in it, and although classical ballet is her first love she adores Ginger Rogers and Fred Astaire. She also loves the Beatles.

§

'Ecstasy,' Pushkin writes, 'is a glass full of tea and a piece of sugar in the mouth.' The brilliant Russophile, Leslie Chamberlain, writes: 'Of all beverages, tea alone has the proverbial power to relieve *toska*, the sadness and melancholy which traditionally burden the Russian spirit.' Many cultures have a special word to describe their collective spiritual woe – the Turks call it *hüzün*, the Germans *Weltschmerz*, the Poles *żal*, the Portuguese *saudade*, the Finnish *kaiho*, the Chinese *bei qiu* – and it's a curious fact that in each instance it is held to be untranslatable. Is melancholy, then, a local preserve? Or could it be that the English language is deficient in sorrowful modalities? According to Nabokov, 'No single word in English renders all the shades of *toska*. At its deepest and most painful, it is a sensation of great spiritual anguish, often without any specific cause. At less morbid levels it is a dull ache of the soul, a longing with nothing to long for, a sick pining, a vague restlessness, mental throes, yearning. In particular cases it may be the desire for somebody or something specific, nostalgia, lovesickness.' These words come from the notes he made to his translation of *Eugene Onegin*.

Akopian-Tamarina has *toska* in abundance. She also has a wry sense of humour and whimsicality of an order that truly surprises. I poured her some tea. We discussed the business of why it is the English, or at least those of a certain vintage, pour the milk first and whether this is not indicative of a social divide. She pours the milk *after*, she says, because it was important for her to observe, as in music, the tonal shifts in coloration. Amusingly she brought with her a small bag of brown sugar just in case there was none at our place, an act that struck me as quintessentially Slavic in its disquietude.

I had been seeking a symbolic object whereupon one might divine the existence of another culture's transcendent values and so, with tea the subject of the moment, I asked whether her family owned a samovar. The samovar is emblematic of so much – a Russia of godly times, old hospitality, Chekhov, aristocrats in peasant smocks, peasants in obeisance to what Fate has slopped onto their plates, unruly passions, exomologesis on a Dostoevskian scale, a leisurely unfolding of good talk, a rapid escalation of terrible talk, in short, a world *before* Lipton's teabags took over – and when, as I suspected would be the case, she said that yes, as a child she and her sister collected coals for it at her family's dacha I knew then we had entered one of the paradoxes of her Soviet existence.

'Actually, yes, we *did* lead the life of… shall we say… privilege. I spent my early childhood in the USA, in Washington, where my sister and I went to kindergarten. My father was posted there as a government representative for his side of the industry. At home, in Russia, he was director of an institute said to be testing new engines for tractors. After he died, it was rumoured that actually it was for tanks and he worked for the defence industry. A bright young scientist, after he graduated, Stalin noticed him. My father worked under direct orders from him.'

Stalin's written order is still in her possession.

'On the journey home, the ship's captain advised my parents to throw away any evidence of bank accounts in America. I suppose it was naïve of them to return to Stalin's Russia, thinking they could bring such papers with them, and so they dropped them overboard. Years later, my mother would say with regret, "Just imagine the interest we might have accumulated from those days." Our American past was only to be whispered, and English was to be forgotten. We were supposed to be like everyone else, not draw attention to ourselves. And yet, as I said before, we lived in a world of privilege. The elite in the Russia of those days did not mean people with money but those with outstanding achievements, gifted and dedicated to their work. We lived in a style not affordable to most people. My father had a personal chauffeur. We had a flat of our own which, in those days, very few people had. My mother did not have to shop because of all the American trunks full of things. We came back with an unimaginable amount of luggage. If I wanted a new pair of shoes a trunk would be opened. This continued right through to the 1960s. I remember the children in Moscow asking to touch my toys. They hardly had any and my sister and I had amazing things like dolls' furniture. My mother was extremely beautiful and glamorous and when she stepped out looking like Joan Crawford with a feather in her hat, lovely gloves and shoes, she stopped the traffic. Imagine the hungry and devastated Russia of the time. Even some years after the war there were wrecked military cars lying about, which served as our playground, and German prisoners of war *still* being moved from place to place. In the middle of all this, people would sometimes stare at my mother. My father pleaded with her to be less showy but this is all she had, those fabulous clothes.'

Akopian-Tamarina dresses in a fashion that reflects the style of her late mother, her *bijouterie* too, both on stage and at table. When we first met she wore a brooch of three jewelled ballerinas and later, when we met again, the earrings she wore were from her mother. And most elegant they are, too, those clothes – black, always black, but of a black that radiates light. I asked whether her mother lived in another world to go out in Moscow dressed like that, like shiny obsidian amid so much dull slate.

'To be honest, yes, she probably did live in a world of fantasy, which is what I inherited from her. I am still in that world, never knew the way out of it, but the point is that it was natural for my mother because those were the only clothes she had. She was extremely kind, a wonderful heart, generous to a fault. I think her ups and downs in life – in the early days the Revolution and then the war – helped her to be kind and sensitive to others, forced her to be more aware, to look at life in perspective, and to know that the unexpected could come from around any corner. She went through life as a traveller, observing rather than merely looking at things.'

'I have this image of you, a child in this grim world…'

'But it wasn't so for me! I was so protected. I mean you did *know* what was happening. When we came back from America people would whisper to each other "*zabrali*" – "taken". One morning I heard my mother whisper to my father that two of our neighbours had been taken away during the night. *Zabrali*. My mother was puzzled by how it was possible that my father was not taken, how he managed to avoid the dangers. As history now knows, masses of people were taken. My distant relatives were. One night, without being told where they were going, they were put onto cattle wagons. Years later, I met the family in Siberia after giving a concert there. I was told that their mother who, like mine, was gracious and beautiful, aristocratic in her whole demeanour, when they arrived there, simply lay down and never got up again. She lay there for years. It was beyond her psyche to be able to contemplate or take in what had happened. She was brought to things she never knew existed. They had had a beautiful life, in upper-class surroundings, and then to have suffered that journey, to have their lives completely destroyed in a moment. She died in her bed, grief-stricken. They have been rehabilitated since, but you can't rehabilitate a life, can you? And yet when Stalin died, in 1953, we cried. We were in school and all the children were lined up. We cried… everybody cried… the whole country cried. What a paradox. Maybe the secret of his power was that he did not allow the brain to travel. It was to be confined to that box that was called Soviet Russia, and the less you knew the better it was. That is why art was so wonderful because it was the only way one had the freedom to wander into fantasy. Nobody could touch us there.'

'Except,' I interjected, 'if you were using words…'

'True, and even music suffered but being the most abstract of all arts it was comparatively free. People were starving for culture. This explains the tremendous queues for the theatre, the full houses, packed concert halls. When you think of the wonderful performers you could see! In a way one was… I always hesitate to use the word "happiness"… there isn't any such thing as happiness – it's rather the *anticipation* of happiness, a kind of borderline between desire and fulfilment, and it's only there I feel happiness lies. So although I use the word advisedly – and also I take into account youth and innocence – in a way one could be *happy* in that situation. I was happy in mine.'

Arguably the most problematic of all human emotions, happiness (*schast'e*) is especially vexing for any Russian who grew up with it meaning the emotional state that socialism would bring to each Soviet citizen. Andrey Platonov writes in his *Happy Moscow* (in Robert Chandler's translation): 'People had not yet attained the courage of continual happiness – they were only learning.' When Stalin announced, in the face of all evidence, that 'life has become merrier' he was not so much the supreme ironist as the doctor whose medicine was to be taken in massive doses. There is a famous propaganda poster of him addressing a crowd of adoring faces, captioned: **ЛЮБИМЫЙ СТАЛИН – СУАСТЬЕ НАРОДНОЕ** (BELOVED STALIN – THE PEOPLE'S HAPPINESS.) This is not to suggest that matters of the spirit should always refer back to politics, which borders on cliché when one speaks of people who grew up in such regimes, and yet the fact of one's childhood environment, even when the bigger realities did not intrude too closely, is inescapable. I am enough of a Slav, on the other hand, to appreciate that when entering such emotional terrain any talk of happiness causes one to falter, and sometimes even to stumble. There is something in the mind that would rather not admit to it. Misery, by comparison, is pleasure. Over dinner, which was salted with good talk, peppered with laughter, I did suggest to Akopian-Tamarina we were in peril of enjoying ourselves.

'Even our family was a mini picture of the Soviet regime,' she continued. 'My sister and I were brought up in a strict way. Among other rules we never spoke until spoken to, and it stuck with me for life. I find it difficult to initiate a social acquaintance. I hesitate to start a conversation. We were free only to do what required discipline. I often say to my students that liberty is a luxury of discipline.'

When Akopian-Tamarina speaks of what it is to be within such limitations, she traces in the space in front of her a square, which seems to hang there for a while. This was the second of several such squares. The first was a couple of minutes ago.

'It is only through discipline we have, and can understand, freedom. My father placed great importance on this, saying modesty makes a person beautiful and work adds dignity to one's existence. He was black-and-white in his views but then I had this glamorous, exuberant mother who would fill in the spaces with a kaleidoscope of colours. She was amazing with her hands. What she could make with knitting needles is beyond belief and in a rare moment, when she had nothing else to do, she would sit and work with her fingers up to ten threads at a time. Perhaps I have inherited her finger technique! This is not to write my father out of the picture. Over the years, I have come to understand just how right he was when he put discipline above other human qualities, something that he would promote by his own example. He was a workaholic and we would hardly ever see him. He would leave the house before seven in the morning and arrive home very late. I took from him his methodical, scientific and logical approach to things, balanced by my mother's gift for colouring and fantasy. Sometimes, although he supported my mother's pianistic dream for me, I would hear him tell my mother to leave the poor girl alone. Although he was musical himself and could play by ear the most complicated pieces by Bach and Schumann, he took the view that music was more of a hobby than a proper profession. Still he was proud when I became a concert pianist. He was a very quiet man, a man of few words, and maybe because they were so few in number they stuck with me. I was in awe of him, this figure of authority, and when he would come home in the evening, my sister and I had to pretend to be busy because sitting and doing nothing was not something he approved of. Although my mother was equally demanding it was in a different, more feminine way. She was very gracious and had a profound faith in God, but in her own gentle unspoken way. She used to keep a photograph of Tsar Nicolas II by her bed and continued her quiet prayers for the souls of the Tsar and his family. It was her idea for me to become a concert pianist and she dedicated herself to it. This remarkable lady executed her dream single-handedly. She did so against so many no's, so many doors being shut in her face. She had a vision and she followed it.'

§

The Russian piano school may be said to have begun with an Irishman, John Field (1782–1837), first exponent of the piano nocturne. Moscow not only provided him with a concert platform, with the added frills of a wife, a mistress and flowing booze, but also a substantial income from teaching whereby he might support that lifestyle. The Irishman, it seems, had discovered his inner Russian. As a teacher *par excellence* it was he who begat Alexander Dubuc who begat Alexander Villoing who begat Nikolai Rubinstein who begat Alexander Siloti who begat Alexander Goldenweiser whose students included, among others, Samuil Feinberg, Grigory Ginzburg, Dmitri Kabalevsky, Leonid Roisman, Tatiana Nikolayeva, Dmitry Paperno, Lazar Berman, Dmitri Bashkirov, Nikolai Kapustin and… Nelly Akopian-Tamarina. The genealogy is necessarily incomplete because there were other teachers, including, of course, the *other* Rubinstein, Anton, and, springing from them, other tributaries, but taken as a whole one finds there, writ large, the musical history of Russia. Also, among the students, there were composers as diverse as Glinka, Scriabin, Rachmaninoff and Shostakovich. That it should be called a school at all is a bit of a misnomer in that its prime aim, although it was never set in stone, was to encourage individuality, making it more, in the Oriental fashion, a pedagogical chain.

Akopian-Tamarina looks back in awe.

'What is unique about the teaching of music in Russia is that every great artist feels a passion and a duty to pass it on. It is not seen as a lesser or isolated profession. We had these music schools, lots of them scattered throughout the Soviet Union, which, in addition to the regular schools, were for the children who lived in the area. I started at one such school later named after the great Konstantin Igumnov. My first lessons were with a lady who at the time seemed to me very severe, who would slap me on the fingers if I made a mistake. However, I remember her with warmth and gratitude for giving me that all-important start. My sister started at the same school on violin, but later changed to piano. Then we moved to another area and therefore also moved school. There, with my new teacher, I was selected to play a Haydn concerto with the orchestra, which was seen as quite an achievement. However, I must admit it was the time when I did not find music very inspiring and all I wanted was to put a stop to the whole thing but I didn't dare tell my mother. One grew up in a very strict atmosphere and did what one was told.'

There is a memento of her from that time. She appears to be, despite her reluctance, very much inside the music. As was always the case at schools, on the back wall of the stage, although it is not clearly visible in the photograph, there is a Soviet flag bearing the images of

Lenin and Stalin. There is, if one looks carefully, a face in the folds of the cloth, which, like some visual experiment out of a Holbein painting, is distorted to such a degree that it is not clear whose it is, Stalin's or Lenin's, but, the longer one looks at it, it seems, rather, the ghostly image of another face altogether: Franz Liszt's.

'One day, first thing in the morning, my mother heard the sound of piano scales coming from the direction of a neighbouring house. "Nelly, get up!" she said. "Somebody is already playing scales." And it was the same thing every morning, somebody out there, up early, playing scales. Slowly my mother realised that whoever was playing them did so better than her Nelly. She wouldn't have that so she went over to investigate and spoke to the grandmother of the girl who was called Natasha. I started to resent this Natasha. My mother asked the grandmother, "How is it that your Natasha is so good?" She replied, with arrogance, "Well, *of course* she's good because she is at the Central School of Music."'

The Central School of Music for Exceptionally Gifted Children, as it was first called, was established in 1932 by Alexander Goldenweiser and took only the *crème de la crème*. Representatives would go around the Soviet Union seeking out the most gifted students and bring them there. The musical gap between it and the ordinary schools was huge. Anyone who is anyone in music came from that school.

'So having got this information my mother went straight there, saying she had a very gifted child. It was gently explained to her there was no way the Central School of Music could take pupils who came from such a musically humble background and even if this were possible they would have to repeat a year. Now for my mother, with her notions of success, repeating a year equalled failure. She said, "Look, just write down the programme." Then my mother had the nerve to take me out of both schools, the regular and the music one, and found a wonderful musician, Mira Yakovlevna Siver, a student of Igumnov. "This is my girl. I want her in the Central School of Music in three months." My father's chauffeur would drive me there for lessons. Three months later, I played the entrance exam. I was accepted without needing to repeat a year. Not only did my mother push me into that school, she demanded I have the best teacher, Anaida Sumbatyan, whose teenage pupil, Vladimir Ashkenazy, had come back from the Chopin competition in Warsaw with second prize. Anaida Stepanovna Sumbatyan graduated from St Petersburg Conservatoire where she studied with Maria Kalantarova, herself a disciple of Anna Esipova, wife and student of the legendary Leschetizky. At the time she was the most sought-after teacher in the Soviet Union. When I came to her for the first time, I wanted the earth to swallow me. I had hardly played any studies. At the beginning she didn't know what to do with me but kept saying I had a fantastic ear. She preferred to work with more advanced students but slowly grew to love me. She was hugely intuitive, and had the ability to isolate one's particular gift and knew what to do with mine. Although she was very critical of the gap in my preparation, she loved my sound, saying "It is God-given". She used to emphasise the voice of the melody, joining me with her flat hand on a higher register. "Sing, Nelly, sing", she would say. That was my first encounter with the Art of Cantabile. She changed my life and opened for me the magical world of music. I fell in love with it once and for ever. So instead of putting me through the torture of musical studies, she gave me Bach, Chopin and Liszt. When I began with her I was at the back of the queue and by the time I graduated I was number two. We were all numbered. The atmosphere there was extremely competitive but also warm and motivated and it became a way of life. Rather than play with toys children at the school would discuss Chopin studies. My extraordinary mother did the impossible. She pushed me into zones which at the time seemed totally beyond my reach and each time I reached one she would push me into another. And now, thinking back on Natasha, I really owe her a lot. She became a friend for life.'

When Akopian-Tamarina left the Central School to go to the Moscow Conservatory, she became one of Alexander Borisovich Goldenweiser's very last students. Goldenweiser was one of a number of musical legends of whom we hear little here. There survives a short film of him playing a couple of Chopin preludes, looking very much as she would have known him – wiry, white-haired, wrapped in ancient light. As a young man, with a tousle of wavy black hair, a riverboat gambler's moustache, he was close to Tolstoy, often visiting him, and playing for him, at Yasnaya Polyana, and the informal record he kept of his conversations with the writer, *Vblizi Tolstogo* ('Close to Tolstoy'), remains invaluable. Another side of Goldenweiser is presented in an interview with his student Grigory Ginzburg, which illustrates in some detail not only his teacher's methodology but also another of his great passions, which had he moved to England would have helped him to feel very much at home.

> His apartment on Prechistenka at the time was almost a city block long … With rails and switches put throughout all the rooms, Alexander Borisovich would crawl excitedly on the floor with me. Most of all we liked to arrange crashes. Steam engines with passenger cars would be set on a collision course from the opposite ends of the apartment. The switches moved, the engines crashed, fell and a fire would start. A marvellous sight: everything broken, fuel spilled from the burners, the whole floor a mess … Then Alexander Borisovich's wife (Anna Alexandrovna Goldenweiser) would come, a terrible row would start, the fire would be put out, we would be sent out to the back rooms, the oil would be cleared, the floors polished … I could see that Alexander Borisovich was leaving with a heavy heart.

Akopian-Tamarina reveres him still.

'Goldenweiser taught at the Moscow Conservatory for almost half a century, which is a lifetime, and his name was synonymous with an era, a monumental history. I would stare at him in a kind of silent disbelief.'

'Did he speak of Tolstoy?'

'All the time, all the time… tea with Tolstoy… but for us of the Soviet generation it seemed rather funny at the time. We thought of Tolstoy as representative of Czarist times, which were so far away from us. Goldenweiser would still use the old names of the streets, as they were known in those times. He was like a bridge between the old and the new and he succeeded in both. He was nicknamed "Starik" or "Old Man". He was a very small man, almost bent in half, thin shoulders. Our lessons were in Class 42, with that famous black sofa behind two pianos, one of which was only for his use which he kept locked. Each lesson was like a master class with a seated audience. Not only students but also professors would come from faraway cities just to hear what he'd have to say. It was frightening enough playing for him let alone such an audience. You didn't come to it as if to a normal lesson. You always had to be ready and on form. I remember soon after I entered the Conservatory there was a jubilee celebration for him. The delegation headed by the Director came to congratulate him. The room was full of people, among them his famous ex-students Lazar Berman, Tatiana Nikolayeva, Dmitry Paperno and Dmitri Bashkirov who later became my teacher. Dmitri Alexandrovich Bashkirov was one of my very special musical inspirations. I admired his playing and could not wait for his illuminating lessons, which fired my imagination. So Goldenweiser asked a couple of students to play, first Berman, and then he said, "And where is this new little girl who plays Bach?" I played *Chromatic Fantasy and Fugue* in front of all those people.'

'Were you able to talk to him on a personal level?'

'Yes, although maybe that's a slight exaggeration. You had to talk during lessons, of course. Once he invited me to his place. I took cream roses, and we had a conversation which will haunt me for ever. Afterwards he said, "You know, Nelly, that really was a most poignant conversation. When I die, you'll remember it." And so I do.'

'*And so I do*,' she said again as spectres began to gather at our table. At times I begin to wonder if she plays not so much for the living as for all the ghosts in her life. Ancestral spirits need constantly to be fed and they have an otherworldly appetite.

'I remember one lesson in particular,' Akopian-Tamarina continued. 'It was evening and unusually there was nobody else in the room. I played for him Chopin's *Sonata in B minor*. I finished the first movement and because I wouldn't dare look behind me and because he didn't say anything I thought that meant I should carry on. I was too shy to ask him, "Would you like me to continue?" That would have been much too forward! So I played the second movement, again *silence*, and then, after the third movement, I had this horrible thought. One of his students in the same year as me had this stupid joke: "*Starik umer*" – "The old man has died", repeating it every week. Being young, one didn't realise how cruel that was. After the third movement I wondered if he had actually… there was this silence… he didn't say a word. Imagine. What if he had died and I was still playing? … I finished the finale and then he spoke. When he really did die, it was so sad. I remember going up the stairs of the Conservatory. A mirror was covered with black cloth, in accordance with the Russian tradition, and there was an announcement that Alexander Borisovich Goldenweiser had died.'

Akopian-Tamarina, falling back into the present tense, whispered, 'And here we are.'

§

She might have been, were it not that Fate carries a balalaika, born into a flawless scenario. She went to the best schools, the sounds that arose from them some of the greatest interpretative music of the century. She entered the student competitions, a rigorous selection process that only the finest musicians could survive, and which culminated in her winning first prize and the Gold Medal at the Robert Schumann International Competition for Pianists and Singers in 1963. Soon after, she was taken on as one of five new soloists for the Moscow Philharmonie. She recorded for the prestigious Melodiya label works by Chopin and Schumann. She was, in short, a rising star on the Moscow scene.

If she moved among great figures, it was not because she sought them out but because they were unavoidable. Among many, she met Shostakovich.

'I think that for Shostakovich confrontation with authority was not in his nature. Therefore he had to suffer a lot of affronts, but given his legendary name I sometimes wonder whether he might have stood up to them. Maria Yudina, a fabulous pianist and a deeply religious woman, did so. But then I think Dmitri Dmitrievich Shostakovich was a very shy, modest and peaceful man. I met him a few times and that's how he came across. But how forcefully he raised his voice through the power and message of his music!'

The incredible thing about Soviet cultural history is that for all the ghastly products of Socialist Realism – the kitsch, the slogans, the square-jawed workers on postage stamps – there were numerous interstices where absolute power was on nodding terms with truly great art. The aforementioned Maria Yudina was, despite her open criticism of him, Stalin's favourite pianist and when she was awarded the prize which bore his name she gave the money that came with it to the Russian Orthodox Church so that it might go for 'perpetual prayers for Stalin's sins'. Stalin, when he first heard Yudina's recording of Mozart's *Piano Concerto no. 23 in A major*, wept. In 1964, by which point party leaders of not quite so firm a hand had an even less firm grasp of aesthetics, Akopian-Tamarina played at the Kremlin, at a concert to mark Leonid Brezhnev's ascendancy to power.

'I didn't play alone. Five new young soloists were selected to perform and there were five pianos positioned at different levels on the stage. We were supposed to play some piece especially written for the occasion – I remember it was in C major – for five pianos and orchestra. It had little artistic value. I could hear only the instrument next to me and as it was the same for the others we didn't play together.'

It must serve in memory only as a bloated fanfare to a vain man who would oversee a period of economic and political stagnation. Stalin gets all the biographies, Brezhnev the one-liners. And yet, as Akopian-Tamarina points out, it was a system in which things serious, comical and sublime were possible. After all, the concert at the Kremlin signalled an acceptance of her.

'I had it all. I was now a soloist with the Moscow Philharmonie, independent, and yet there was this huge dissatisfaction within me. Sometimes I would play a concert which I didn't think was all that wonderful and because I could not make a connection between what I felt and what the audience heard and applauded I was left confused. Had I arrived at a *cul de sac*?

Such a point, when reached, invites all manner of dark forces, most of them subliminal in nature. A chasm is created. Anything might happen there but nothing could have prepared Akopian-Tamarina for what actually occurred in 1973, when professionally all seemed to be on the rise.

'It was then that my sister Tatiana decided to emigrate with her Jewish husband and their two small adorable children. They were a couple of wonderfully gifted young musicians pursuing their dreams.

Although they went to live in the USA, officially they had applied to emigrate to Israel. That meant that they were immediately stripped of their Soviet citizenship. The shock and tragedy of it was that back then we knew we would never see them again. It had a devastating effect on my parents and myself. It broke our hearts and our lives were shattered. That was Russia at the time. I remember the confusion, everybody offering advice. At the last minute somebody said, "Take a bottle of olive oil." I thought, "My God, they are going for life. How long will a bottle of olive oil last?" Everything just collapsed. I had been playing in Moscow, Leningrad, Kiev and abroad, in most of the important venues, and then, after my sister emigrated, although I was still with the Moscow Philharmonie they began to show their displeasure by not allowing me to play in those main cultural centres. Together with a violinist in the orchestra, I was summoned to a party political meeting at the Moscow Philharmonie. All such bodies had a political committee attached to them. The violinist's brother had also emigrated. We went into the meeting, one after another, and then we compared notes. Obviously from our answers our political views would be assessed. Their question to me was, "Do you denounce your sister?" If I had done so, supposedly I'd have been in their good books. At least that's what one assumed. But there was no way I was going to do so. It had nothing to do with politics but with my sister whom I love dearly. The violinist denounced his brother. I would not denounce my sister. I knew the implications, of course, but what was so ironic in the end is that it made no difference, the results were the same: we *both* were not allowed to go abroad to perform. You could *say* it made no difference, but it made a great difference to me. I think there is something immoral in abandoning one's own judgement and belief. The violinist and I then discussed the question of what manifests strength and weakness, whether it is strong to leave your country or an act of weakness.'

'And your conclusion was?'

'It takes an enormous amount of strength to leave your homeland, but from the other point of view it might be seen as a sign of weakness not to stand by your country.'

'And then what happened?'

'So as to be seen that I was still allowed to perform they would send me to obscure places. There was that famous Soviet slogan *Iskusstvo v massi*: "Art to the masses". Sometimes it would take twenty-four hours to get to some little town in Siberia, and then you'd have to wait for ages for a connection to the next place. But there would always be someone to meet you. I arrived at one place, so small it may not even be on the map. It might have been where Stalin sent prisoners. The woman there looked at me, "Tell me, girl, are you a dancer?" "No, I play piano." "*Piano!* Where do you think I'll find you one?"'

'Gogol lives!'

'Absolutely! Another place, when I finally arrived there, had about a dozen people in the concert hall. It was so cold that I had to play with my fur coat on. You have not experienced cold like that. The food would freeze inside the room. People would warn each other, saying "Your nose! Your ear! It is going white!" Somebody told me in that climate at times the snow storms were so terrible people couldn't see anything and because they couldn't find their way home they would freeze to death only a few metres away from their front doors. At the next town of my tour it was minus 46 centigrade, which is where I turned back home. In retrospect, there was an aura of lightness and humour but those were difficult times.'

One image from those days she sees as symbolic of her whole life.

'I was collected from the train by this bulky Siberian wrapped in sheepskin. I got into his military car, with green canvas sides, open spaces in between, and he was going in that Siberian wind in the middle of winter. We drove for over an hour through an absolute desert, God knows where. I remember a light and then nothing maybe for two or three minutes, then another light, again darkness, and the image of those lights came back later in my life, after emigration, and I thought that's it, that is actual life, a lamppost here, some sparkle, and then nothing, another sparkle, again nothing. One's life is an accumulation of these highlights, the small things which altogether make a picture. Sometimes there is complete darkness where there are things memory does not wish to preserve. Wonderful moments stand out like small pieces of a jigsaw puzzle.'

'Would that image have taken shape had you stayed in Russia?'

'I often wonder.'

When it came to the details of her leaving Russia, Akopian-Tamarina spoke at great speed as if to get through this painful period of her life as quickly as possible.

'After a year spent like that, in 1974, I was told that I was awarded the Schumann Prize of the City of Zwickau. This was a great thing for me, but even though the award ceremony was in the German Democratic Republic at first I was not allowed to go. At the very last minute I was given a passport and was allowed to receive the prize but *not* to perform there. My father knew what this meant. "You are not going to be awarded prizes every year," he said. "We have no choice but to leave."'

A photograph shows her seated at the piano in the Schumann House in Zwickau. She is dressed in black but I shall resist the temptation to quote the opening lines of Chekhov's *The Seagull.*

The official view was that Soviet artists, through their performances, carried moral standards to the audience and that if they wanted to live in the West they had none. The moment Akopian-Tamarina applied to emigrate was the moment she was thrown out of her position as soloist with the Moscow Philarmonie. She was now 'immoral' and immorality could not be allowed to contaminate a Soviet audience. Her world crashed. The family applied as a whole to emigrate only to be repeatedly refused. The second plan, one that was to have tragic consequences, was that if one member of the family went abroad, and then another, the last would surely be allowed to go.

It was a long and dark period in her life during which time she lost not only her job but also most of her personal and professional contacts. The people whom she knew in that empyrean realm pretended they didn't know her. Official references to her name were removed and her recordings were no longer available. Solace, when it finally came, wore a peasant's flowered headscarf. The most important figure at that time was Maria or, in the diminutive, 'Marusia', who had been attached to the family as a helper although, in truth, she was so much more. A stock figure of Russian literature, only now does she enter, as she might a field of snow, the blank page – silently, uncomplainingly, indestructible.

'A peasant from a small village, deeply religious, she became my greatest support, my best friend. She understood the simple things in life while her ignorance was a form of bliss. She was not aware of the world outside, most of which was beyond her comprehension anyway, her idea of happiness being a piece of chicken. With my own existence so suddenly reduced, against that complicated background Marusia demonstrated a pure and simple love. I would secretly go to church with her, Sundays being when she put on her best clothes. A knitted piece her mother made for her is now one of my treasures. She had a wonderful soul. She told me that when she died I would inherit her blanket and pillow. She was so poor and yet she symbolised the true Russian spirit and as such filled a particular space in a bleak time.'

The meek shall inherit if not the earth then at least a drumstick paprika'd.

Another person who became important was a neighbouring woman, an artist who encouraged her to paint. She took her to a studio where every thirty seconds a nude struck a fresh pose. This encouraged a speedy line, as opposed to the hours it would take to realise a pianistic one, and yet for Akopian-Tamarina the division between painting and music is not necessarily a sharp one.

'I have always loved visual art and for me it is closely connected with piano, with sound. As if I can *see* sound and *hear* colour. It was never my intention to become an artist. As I was not allowed to play I painted in order to fill in an emotional void. I had arrived at a point where there was no way out. I was expressing my creativity and was excited when some of my watercolours were selected for an exhibition in Moscow.'

She drew another square.

'The tragedy of it all is that I never wanted to leave Russia. One might have talked about it, about how wonderful it would be to go to the West, but I wonder if I would ever have made that move myself. I was really put in a corner and it was only because I could not contemplate a life without piano that I made an application to leave. The fact is I love Russia deeply. With all its good and bad it is my motherland, my joy, my pain and… I miss it so badly. The scar of leaving it stays with me and will do so forever. I have been back a couple of times since. It was so special to be invited back to play at home after all these years. On stage it felt as if I had never left and yet it felt somehow strange. I am not the same – *they* are not the same. Going back is very emotional, as if in pursuit of an elusive dream. "… À la recherche du temps perdu…" It drains your heart and soul and I come back in a devastated state. Sometimes I am asked, "How could you forgive Russia?" But I still love Russia as dearly as ever.'

'Does Russia love you back?'

'In all these years and with all the changes, there has been no offer of an official memorial for my father or reinstatement of my position with the Moscow Philharmonie or the return of our flat which I simply left behind.'

§

Akopian-Tamarina came to England in 1978. We shall glide over the many intricacies that finally enabled her to do so. There are enough such stories, each with their share of weights and measures, levers big and small, the endless waiting in corridors, petitions and refusals. Officialdom is nowhere better realised than when designed to ensure the happiness of the human race. It was years before she could leave. She left Russia not so much from choice as from absence of choice. Most tragically, although her mother was able to follow her to England, her father was prevented from doing so. The belief that his wife and daughter going first would ease his passage cruelly misfired. He was refused the simple certificate of residence which was needed in order to apply to emigrate. Her father with his knowledge and reputation was too important a figure to be allowed to leave. He even went to the extent of retiring from his job, thinking that maybe then the focus would be removed from him. It was not to be so, and after a life of activity, with a mind always alert, his contacts now gone, he died a slow death alone in Moscow, and, even more tragically, Marusia, who lovingly cared for him in his final days, died before he did. Stalin's 'bright young scientist' was not even accorded a burial appropriate to one of his great achievements.

Akopian-Tamarina continued: 'I would pick up the pieces for years to come. I personally do not know any Russian emigrating to the West who did not have to pay a price.'

'What about the years of silence? Were you able to draw from them?'

'After accepting for all those years the futility of my situation in Russia, psychologically I was quite unprepared to find myself in this country. Certainly playing piano was the last thing on my mind. I had already accepted I'd no longer play. When I tried to, I just couldn't any more. So I had to begin afresh, but one consequence of coming back to it, after so many years, was that I found my inner voice. From very early on, as a pianist I had always been encouraged to express my individuality. In retrospect I think that period of enforced silence provided a background against which I had to find a new way of playing. Silences are not nothingness. They are necessary, like the pauses in music. You have to *live* them. Each concert should be an occasion and the whole beauty of live performance is that as the music unfolds the listeners become participants and that in itself is a miracle. The audience does not need to be musically educated. We all have imprinted in our soul, in our psyche, the ability to see and understand what is true and beautiful. One instinctively *knows* it is not a fake.'

'And in terms of having adopted another language, another approach to life…'

'Music is my first language, the verbal second. Very often the first makes much more sense to me. For words to be able to match the music one needs to be a poet. In music everything falls into place and I could stay there for ever. Whereas when it comes to mundane matters, these seem complicated to me. The more I see and the wider I open my eyes the more I bury myself in piano and live in the world of music. I find solace… I find *everything* there. I am my own teacher. I am the best student I've ever had. It is *my* world and I am unhappy when it is disturbed. During the years when a musician finds his mature voice all I had was silence. And when I returned to music, I fell in love with it all over again.'

'What about the country where you now live?'

'It was by a smile of fortune that I came here. I feel this is my adopted family or rather it is the British who have adopted me. My perception of Britain was obtained in my schooldays, through my parents and through Soviet education which placed particular emphasis on the importance of British art and culture. When I came to this country I was happy to discover things for myself and among many things that attracted me, apart from the traditional cup of afternoon tea, was the reserve in the British character, the famous sense of fair play, and a quiet, undemonstrative patriotism and respect for tradition. After thirty-four years of living in this country I understand why everyone talks about the weather. Just look out of the window. My mother and I were so grateful this country embraced us. My mother used to dream of reaching the age of a hundred so that she would receive the telegram from Her Majesty the Queen and to speed the process started, naively, adding to her age… It is quite right to say this immigration cost me, all in all, a break of over ten years but then I look at my life as being full of breaks – *this* break, *that* break – and maybe it is not necessarily what happened to me but rather how I reacted to things. It hasn't been easy. That I must say. It hasn't been easy at all.'

§

Russian poetry is held to be untranslatable and among the most difficult poets to render into English is Marina Tsvetaeva but nowhere is she *better* untranslatable than in the versions made over the years by the poet Elaine Feinstein. One poet grasps the inner world of another poet and from that beginning is at least able to allow the reader to register something of what is being missed in the original. In Feinstein's version of 'Verses about Moscow' Tsvetaeva writes:

> I lift you up like a
> sapling, my best burden: for
> to me you are weightless.
>
> In this city of wonder
> this peaceful city
> I shall be joyful, even
> when I am dead. You
> shall reign, or grieve
> or perhaps receive my crown:
> for you are my first born!

Akopian-Tamarina takes everywhere with her a volume of poetry, Pushkin being 'god', but also she loves Tsvetaeva.

'Recently, on a bus, I cried unashamedly when I read her. I wonder if it is easier to remain Russian if you are at a distance. There is such a thing as *Russianness*. There is no understanding it – you simply have to feel it. You have to be Russian to know it. Nobody expresses it better than Tyutchev. Sometimes I close my eyes and imagine my youth, see my family, friends, my teachers… and then I open them, retaining for just a few seconds longer those aromatic memories… With friends from my past I don't have to prove anything, whereas in this country I had to start all over again. When I first came here, British audiences were not familiar with my name and my playing. In Russia, I had established my character morally and professionally. That is who I was and then suddenly everything was disrupted. I wonder why people say, "Let's be positive – look to the future. Forget the past!" The past supplies me with everything I need. It is a well of richness. I can draw any emotion from there, my imagination… *everything*. Often I do a mental exercise. If I could play back the film of my life and think, there it is, that is where I made the wrong turning, and stop there, maybe if I had gone not left but slightly to the right, through that forest, then I might have come to a beautiful field of daffodils. When I think in terms of my life being a forest what comes to mind are the opening lines of Pushkin's *Ruslan and Ludmila*:

> On seashore far a green oak towers,
> And to it with a gold chain bound,

A learned cat whiles away the hours
By walking slowly round and round.
To right he walks, and sings a ditty;
To left he walks, and tells a tale…

What marvels there! A mermaid sitting
High in a tree, a sprite, a trail
Where unknown beasts move never seen by
Man's eyes, a hut on chicken feet,
Without a door, without a window,
An evil witch's lone retreat…

'This to me is life. It is full of magic – the mermaid sitting in a tree, signs of animals that never were, a house on the legs of a chicken. I knew this poem by heart when I was four or five. And yet there are also bad things there. A wrong turning will take you to where this awful creature is going to eat you alive. I often think of my life in connection with those verses. I am proud of my origins, my culture, my family, my teachers… I wouldn't trade them for anything else. This poem has been my emotional companion and I never stopped believing in fairy tales. And of course we are also so fatalistic.'

Akopian-Tamarina speaks of the Fates as if they were hatched in Russia. Superstition is there in equal measure. She describes how her teacher, although extremely religious, kept saying to her that if you accidentally drop your music sheets, in order to avoid bad luck you must sit on them while they are still on the floor.

Akopian-Tamarina reached into her handbag for her icon.

'At Wigmore Hall, on either side of the stage, you will see flowers. I hid this icon in the flowers on the left hand side, overlooking the piano. Before the concert the Russian Archbishop Elisey of Sourozh blessed me on the stage and he also blessed the piano. Then I showed him the icon and he blessed it too. I love the magic of Wigmore Hall and nostalgic beauty of its older Steinway.'

Akopian-Tamarina concluded: 'I sometimes wonder if I am in the wrong place, if I have been dropped here by mistake.'

'You mean here in England?'

'No, no, on earth! I'd rather be *over there,* somewhere... or perhaps somewhere on the borders of three countries, where they meet, maybe in the Alps... so one doesn't belong to anything or anywhere... so that one is free. Yes, I would like that.'

I pointed out a line from Rimbaud's *Illuminations*: '*Madame *** établit un piano dans les Alpes.*' The line has been interpreted, wrongly I believe, as illustrative of the author's contempt for bourgeois culture, and, then again, it has been seen as a precursor to surrealism with its playful though mostly futile derangement of the senses. Any interpretation is inadequate. The religious is only one more pitfall: Rimbaud was too much the genius and too much the hooligan to allow phrases such as 'spiritual quest' into his lexicon but if alchemy – and the whole passage from which this quotation comes is alchemical in nature – may be said to represent the transformative or interpretative powers of the artist's imagination then I think Nelly Akopian-Tamarina should be allowed the chalet of her choice. An alphorn will serenade her arrival with a *ranz des vaches*. Maybe our *poète maudit* placed those asterisks, where a name should be, towards some such purpose.

Ana Maria Pacheco's Journey to the Underworld

Or, Misfortunes of a Sardine

Old Kent Road formed part of Watling Street, the Roman Road which ran from Dover to Holyhead. Chaucer's pilgrims made their way to Canterbury along it, and a few centuries later, in 1660, Charles II, coming from the opposite direction, bedazzled his way to power with, according to John Evelyn, 'a triumph of about 20,000 horse and foote, brandishing their swords and shouting with inexpressible joy; the wayes strew'd with flowers, the bells ringing, the streets hung with tapestrie, fountaines running with wine'. The only time I'd ever been on the Old Kent Road is in a game of Monopoly. I am, at heart, a monarch of crumbling edifices. The area, a mishmash of the shabby and the starkly modern, is not without its antiquarian surprises. The converted Victorian school building where the Brazilian sculptor and painter Ana Maria Pacheco lives is wedged between the unhappily-logoed Toys Я Us, its pale brick some kind of Lego surrogate, and the sedate grounds, covering six acres, of what was once the Licensed Victuallers' Asylum founded in 1827 for retired publicans and their wives. Here, the London of brutal architecture rubs up against the London of a more lyrical age. One may read into this, although to say so is almost to spoil the game, a perfect analogy for Pacheco's artistic vision, a steady tug of war between harsh and gentle.

A few days earlier, I went to an exhibition of hers at the small church of All Hallows on the Wall, which is adjacent to the London Wall, and part of which stands on the foundations of the ancient Roman wall. Appropriately its architecture draws on elements of the Emperor Hadrian's *Templum Veneris et Romae* in Rome, a nod in a direction every bit as incongruous and fitting, say, as Dante's sudden invocation to Jove in the middle of *Purgatorio*. There is a layered history here of the kind Pacheco relishes. The exhibition, which she considers one of her most important to date, comprised a sculpted head, which is to say *the head removed*, of John the Baptist placed wittily (if one may use such a word in this context) in the baptismal font, and, in the nave, facing each other, two sets of sculpture, respectively titled *Memória Roubada* ('Stolen Memories') *I* and *II.* They are, and this is to simplify matters a great deal, two wooden cupboards shelved with rows of sculpted heads. When read on one level only, which is not where art likes to be, they are a statement on Brazil's brutal colonialist past.

The heads are, to state the obvious, detached from their bodies. The faces of those in *Memória Roubada I* are more anguished than those of *Memória Roubada II.* They are flushed with colour and movement whereas the latter are more static – a colder, deathlier pale. It is for the observer to decide which disturbs him more.

What is perhaps so haunting about these faces is that they have been caught not at the moment of death but in the fulness of life. What one sees in them, some with furrowed brows, others with pursed lips and sad eyes, is a collective expression of worry. The worry is for what informs most worry: the future. I was reminded of a phrase I picked up elsewhere: *the unstoppability of the gentle.* If there is a message of hope, and this, ultimately, is what shines through the darkness of Pacheco's art, it is that before such humanity all empires must ultimately crumble. On stone floor tiles in front of *Memória Roubada II*, lettered in red, in the original Spanish, are some of the most ironic words ever to have been written with regard to the fate of the indigenous people of the Americas, which are taken verbatim from a directive issued by the great Isabella de Castile:

> And do not consent or allow the Indians who live on the said islands and mainland, whether already in our possession or to be won in the future, to suffer any offence to their person or their goods, but see to it that they are well and justly treated.

The scallop shell is suggestive of several things – the birth of Venus (Rome, again), womanhood, fertility, water, and, according to the ethnomusicologist and symbologist Marius Schneider, it is also 'a mystic symbol of the prosperity of one generation rising out of the death of a preceding generation'. (What is to be said, though, for the prosperity of vanished tribes?) One might wish to add to the list of symbols, a little prosaically perhaps, that of a certain oil company. The gold with which the shell is painted serves to remind the viewer of dark forces, the insatiable greed that drove the early Europeans coming to 'the New World' to hideous extremes.

What is doubly ironic is that the church of All Hallows on the Wall is almost entirely lost in the steely, corporate heart of the City of London, whose street names at almost every turn bespeak empire. There, amid steel, darkened glass and stone, only the fleetest of foot survive. Although Pacheco quite properly dismisses the notion of art as a form of pamphleteering there can be little denying the historical import of these two works, and indeed any serious study of her art must take into account her country's troubled, often bloodstained, past.

Heads, decapitated or otherwise, enter much of Pacheco's work. There is a famous photographic image which, although it was taken some years before she was born, was much reproduced and sent shivers through her childhood. It depicts the decapitated heads of the famous bandit Lampião, his lover Maria Bonita, and nine of his gang of *cangaceiros*, so-named after the Cangaço, the badlands from whence they came. Lampião, which in Portuguese means 'oil lamp', was the *nom de guerre* of Virgulino Ferreira da Silva, who terrorised much of north-eastern Brazil in the 1920s and 30s. The emergence of such figures owed much to the brutality of the large landowners who, with the collusion of church and state, exploited the cowboys or *vaqueiros*, driving many of them to banditry. A folk hero to many, a psychopath to others, Lampião encapsulates Brazil's many dichotomies, the most troubling of which being that he should be considered any kind of hero at all. (The popular *cordel* literature of the country, which at its most colourful has woodcuts of him posthumously fighting the devil, does not extend to descriptions of castration, gang-rape, and the cutting out of a woman's tongue.) Lampião was known to have prayed several times a day, which would seem to suggest that God and brigandage rode the same horse. The story is not without an element of black comedy: after the slaughter of the gang in 1938 their severed heads, crudely pickled in kerosene, after being displayed here and there, were moved to the Nina Rodrigues Museum in Salvador. The families of the deceased appealed to have the heads returned to them in order that they might be buried. The director, Estácio de Lima, after whom the museum was later renamed, responded, saying he couldn't do so because their removal would constitute a threat to the state's 'cultural patrimony'. The dispute was settled only in 1969 and the heads were buried on a hilltop overlooking Salvador. While this grisly image, which I will not reproduce here, informs Pacheco's work, she makes one important distinction: her heads are not severed but *separated* from their bodies. The substance of what she told me is that in the absence of religion and myth, and with a growing dependency on reason, we have been cut off from the depth in our own souls, the prehistoric connection whereupon hangs our history as human beings. The disconnection of head and body, for which one may read mind and heart, is why we are left with this fragmented culture or what she calls 'a façade of empty images'.

The anthropologist Darcy Ribeiro's *O povo brasileiro* (*The Brazilian People*, 1995) provides an excellent, if controversial and at times highly idiosyncratic, thesis on the development of the Brazilian people. The book can be read, a little uncomfortably for some, as a record of who slept with whom. Were it not for the social institution of *cunhadismo*, the giving of Indian girls as wives, there would be no Brazilian people. The tragedy, or what with each succeeding generation would amount to multiple tragedies, is that their offspring, the *mamelucos*, were even more brutal towards their maternal race than were the Portuguese. And then came the black slaves, bringing with them a legacy of yet more misery and violence. The Brazilians are, therefore, a syncretism, a confluence of three streams – the Indian, the European and the African – and, if one wishes to examine each of those streams closely, their many tributaries. Ribeiro writes:

> All of us Brazilians are the flesh of this flesh of those tortured blacks and Indians. All of us Brazilians are, likewise, the mad hand that tortured them. The tenderest softness and the most atrocious cruelty come together here to make us the sensitive and long-suffering people that we are and the insensitive and brutal people that we also are. Descendants of slaves and slave owners, we will always be slaves to the distilled malignancy installed in us, both because of the feeling of the pain intentionally produced in order to give more pain and because of the exercise of brutality over men, women, and children that has been the nourishment of our fury.

A romantic and a leftist, Ribeiro salutes the Indians, saying in an interview, 'I think so much beauty would be unbearable for our culture', and of the blacks he writes that they redeem the blood of the Brazilian people. Most strikingly, and this goes to the very heart of Pacheco's artistic credo, he says, in a documentary series of the same name, that in their art the Africans sought to make visible the invisible.

Ana Maria Pacheco was born in Goiânia, the regional capital of the state of Goiás which geographically is the most central of the Brazilian states. It is no exaggeration to say she is truly one of that city's children. When her parents first moved there it was a fledgling town designed to replace the previous capital, Goiás Velho. Claude Lévi-Strauss, in *Tristes Tropiques*, describes a visit there in 1937 when it was still in its earliest phase.

> On an endless plain, half vacant lot and half battlefield, bristling with electric cable poles and survey posts, were a hundred or so new buildings, scattered in all directions. The largest was the hotel, a cube of cement which, in the surrounding flatness, looked like an air-terminal or a small fort; one felt tempted to describe it as a 'bastion of civilization', not in a metaphorical but in a literal sense, which in the circumstances took on strongly ironical overtones. Nothing could be more barbaric or inhuman than this appropriation of the desert … Only the fear of some disaster could justify the existence of this blockhouse. A disaster had, in fact, occurred, and the silence and

> immobility all around was its ominous aftermath. Cadmus, the civilizer, had sown the dragon's teeth. Out of this land scorched and burnt by the monster's breath, one expected to see men sprouting.

What he seems to imply is that nothing of human value would come of it, and yet for Pacheco's parents, who as children had witnessed their own parents' losses in the Great Crash of the 1930s, it was an extraordinary place, a fresh horizon of opportunity. When they moved there it was still pretty much as Lévi-Strauss described it, but by the time they died it had become a city of two million inhabitants. It is not just trees that grow quickly in the tropics.

§

This brings me, *enfin*, to the smaller geography that is Pacheco's London home. Within, Brazil is everywhere. I could swear I arrived in rainfall but, once inside, an Amazonian sun tumbled down from high windows onto a beauteous array of ethnic art, textiles, books and music. Among the artefacts is an eighteenth-century Brazilian wooden sculpture of Saint Anna, mother of the Holy Virgin, teaching her child how to read. This transmission of knowledge from mother to child, in the light of what Pacheco would have to say about her own mother, is particularly poignant. Also, music is immensely important to her. The viol of Saint-Colombe was playing when I arrived, its chiaroscuro a perfect commentary on her art, almost better than anything words could produce. We spoke across a round wooden table, and, in contrast to the architectural jumble outside, all there, at least for the duration of our talk, seemed unified, a bulwark against unfriendly forces.

An intensely private woman, Pacheco is troubled by what she describes as a tabloid desire to go into people's private lives. What is still worse, she says, is how many subjects are willing to expose themselves. 'Who are we to invent ourselves?' she asks. 'We are nothing in comparison to the bigger picture.' She is equally reluctant to elucidate her works, in particular her sculptural ensembles which stand as her greatest achievement to date. 'If I make a work, it is already there,' she laughs, and she laughs a lot, 'so why should I talk about it twice?' Were she to do so, to explain the meaning of any single work, it would be with the consequence, she argues, that not only another person's but also her own reading of it would be closed. Another reason for her reticence is that she is aware of women artists having to carry some kind of banner, which ultimately has nothing to do with the art. 'I do not want to be seen as a rare bird from Latin America.' This said, she spoke of her life in a manner that elucidates her art more than it exposes her life. We began, reasonably enough, with her childhood or, more accurately, with what filled it up with images.

'We were not as socially engaged as most Brazilians, who on the whole are a gregarious people. This is something I have been able to observe while living here and which probably I would never have understood were I still there. It was slightly as if we were foreigners and I think, too, it had to do with our mother's influence. She came from a different world – she had her own code, which was a Protestant one. What this code means in a general sense is that one has to take responsibility as an individual. There is no bigger thing such as Catholics have, which my father had, of the Church as a feminine entity with a Holy Mother who forgives. This accounts for a lot in a culture. You feel more relaxed about life, more able to enjoy the pleasures of the physical world. People say Catholics alone have all this guilt but this is not quite true. Protestants are much more rigid. There is no way they are going to go along with any of that! According to them, you have to be responsible for your own actions. I think having had a mother who had that masculine approach to life, as opposed to my father's more feminine one, was quite unsettling for me. She was deeply aware of certain matters with respect to social behaviour, a sense of propriety, for example. She was the *other* although it was more subtle than that. A Brazilian, she didn't speak the same "language". She was different even from her own sisters. My father's side of the family never accepted her, their cruelty in that context being gossip. She was full of contradictions like all of us. She was authoritarian but there was this other side, enormous warmth of a kind that was not overly demonstrative but which was more like a glowing ember. It was hard to be herself in a society that was so gregarious. My maternal grandmother was a beautiful woman but with whom I never had any emotional connection. Although both grandmothers died in our house there was always this distance between us. We were severed of any kind of physical contact with them and because of this family divide it was the same with our aunts and godmothers as well. Maybe because of this, with there being nobody else, our connection with our parents was all the more intense.'

There is a striking photograph of Pacheco's father together with his daughter, which depicts him as somewhere between slightly dishevelled and suave, a cock of the walk whose feathers old age had begun to remove. Pacheco provides an earlier, rather more robust, picture.

'The image that stays with me is of him as a much younger man, when he was a *bela figura*, wearing, in the hot weather, his white suit and beautiful brown shoes. He was a visionary, a man of action, unafraid of taking risks. He was more subjective than my mother and when I think about my parents in relation to my work there is probably more of him in it – his passionate drive, for example – whereas my mother was the one who with her mental discipline provided the right conditions for my being able to do it. Actually my parents could not have been more opposite in character. She loved chamber and instrumental music while he preferred opera. She preferred solitude while he loved to dance, not that he was very good it at! He took lessons once and there is a funny story about him and his teacher, a German woman. She kept saying to him he was *duro*, which means "stiff" but because of her accent it came out sounding like *burro* which is the word for both "donkey" and "stupid". He thought she was so rude! Also he liked to play tricks on people. One day he brought a little pig and set it loose in the kitchen. This is the kind of thing he would do. My parents may have been opposites, but they laughed a lot and it was just lovely for me, as a child, to watch them get all dressed up to go to the movies or to a ball.'

One thing I knew about in advance, although only sketchily, was of the disappearance of Pacheco's maternal grandfather, a Baptist minister. Ribeiro suggests that the people of the *sertão* or hinterland – of which the state of Goiás is the geographical centre – are characterised by a religiosity that borders on the messianic and also by a predisposition to violence. It is a heady brew that brings to mind the image of Lampião on his knees. Although Pacheco never knew her grandfather, and in fact this happened when her mother was only five, the impact of such an event could not but have sent ripples down through the generations.

'I can tell you this had profound repercussions on my mother's and, of course, *her* mother's behaviour. The important point is that my grandfather was a Protestant going, in the 1930s, to a small village that had a strong Catholic, almost mediaeval, mentality. You can imagine this would make a good movie, the drama of an erudite man, trained as a lawyer in America, with his beautiful library in the middle of nowhere. There is much about which I'm still unsure. In Brazil, largely because of colonisation, people do not want to know too much about the past for fear of what they might come across there. "Oh my God," they'd cry, "my grandfather was a black slave or an Indian!" My mother befriended an elderly couple, the husband governor of the state at one time and his wife a retired university lecturer. When they discovered who my grandfather was, this man said, "I can't believe this! I was young at the time, but I remember him clearly. He was the most extraordinary orator. People would come from miles around just to hear him speak." How could someone so well-known in the area simply disappear? I'm sure he was murdered. After all, this was *bandido* land. That's where I come from, this interior which was very violent. Goiânia was then a town of foresters, people who did not belong there, and even in my childhood there were the most terrible murders. It was different from urban violence in that it came from a rural life that had lost its groove. So there was always that internal clash in our culture. As children we were not allowed to go out on our own, which, to this day, is one of the reasons I like being indoors. It's the way I've been most of my life. After my grandfather's disappearance the family collapsed, my grandmother was helpless, and there was nobody to pursue the matter, to find out what happened to him. My grandmother was left with all these children, without means, and had to find a job as a nurse. She was so angry with my grandfather for disappearing she got together all his precious books, put them in the garden, and made a bonfire. It is like something out of Gabriel García Márquez. What is a mystery to me is that my brothers and sisters, let alone my cousins, were never curious about this. I wanted to know the full story and so I quizzed all my relatives. My grandmother died when

I was twelve, but she was a difficult woman and I could not have asked her, but I questioned my aunts who each had her own view of the matter. Why was I so curious? I think it's because I have this fascination with beginnings and origins.'

Just when I began to think Pacheco had had a rather painful childhood, she demonstrated the opposite.

'Actually I had the most idyllic childhood. We would have family outings to the most wonderful places. At carnival time, which lasted for three days, we would dress up in fancy clothes and go out for night drives and join the festivities in the street. It was lovely. It may sound at times as if I dislike Brazil but actually it is the other way round: I love it. There is another side to people there, in that despite their suffering, and maybe even because of it, they are full of *joie de vivre*. You would not get that impression from the films they have exported over the last thirty years, which are sensational and crude, either that or the superficial images of naked women on Copacabana Beach. But when speaking of this *joie de vivre*, there is also, in the depth of the Brazilian soul, an element of enormous sadness that we call *saudade*, which is untranslatable, which is a mix of melancholy and missing something you never had. With the three major cultural groups – the Indian, the black and the Portuguese – what they have in common is this thing which comes of having been uprooted. The other thing to note is just how magnificent the nature there is. You cannot but be in awe of the immense skies, and you cannot be completely sad when you wake up in the morning to all the beautiful colours, the birds singing. I think the sheer magnitude of everything must have a positive influence on people. It is becoming less so but when we were young the popular thing was to go picnicking beside the river, not like you do here but for a much longer time. We got this from the natives who were nomadic and would spend six months of the year on the riverbanks. And so in Brazil where rivers were the bridges between places, where even one of the tributaries of the Amazon is so wide you can't see the other side, we have this river culture.

'One time, we decided to join the two families. My mother and my aunts spent weeks making costumes and we would have barbecues, all these people having great fun. It's changed now in that people take fridges and sophisticated camping things with them or else stay in big hotels, but it used to be that they would camp out for maybe three months at a time. This is just one example of our *joie de vivre* and also it points to our ability to enjoy life without having to carry within ourselves, all the time, the notion of work. It is not like it is here. When I came to England, I just couldn't understand this idea of a work ethic. The reason I work is because I have something I have to achieve, but is not with any abstract notion that I *have* to work. Hence the hammock! The greatest joy for me as a child was to be in a garden in a hammock, eating chocolate and reading books. I never had my mother coming and saying I had to do something. When I first came here people would say to me, "Oh, that is *so* self-indulgent!" I wondered what they meant. So there is, despite all the horror in our history and the sadness, another side. When people say "Oh God, you do all this horribly sombre work!" I don't think so. If I didn't have faith and were not an optimist I would never be able to do anything because any work I make is an act of faith.'

'Was your mother an artist?'

'She was not an artist in any practical sense but my love of poetry and music comes from her. She loved music, Chopin being her favourite. She insisted on our being taught music. With most Brazilians it was like the Victorian era in that a child was expected to learn an instrument. At home, however, it took on a rather different dimension. She read poetry all the time, especially the Brazilian Romantics, and her favourite novel was *Don Quixote*. The older I grew the more I began to realise how extraordinary this was, that the intellectual curiosity she induced in me was in a place that was rather crude and barbaric. And because of all we had been given at home I felt very different from my peers at school. I couldn't relate to them. So I withdrew, which is one symptom of the outsider. When I look back, though, what is marvellous is that I was allowed to study whatever I wanted to, so at least on that level I had immense freedom. Although my mother did not intend this – she, too, was very upset when I decided to become an artist – she unwittingly gave me the coordinates by which I was made aware of the possibility of another life.

'One thing about our mother I will never forget is that she would sit us down at the end of the day to watch for the coming of the evening star – I mean what poetry was *that*! I come from a place which is very flat so the sky is huge and because it is near the equator the sun goes down quickly. According to our folklore, the evening star is called *papa-ceia. Ceia* is "supper" and *papa* means "to eat" and so *papa-ceia* is this star that comes to join you at your supper. It is such a poetical idea. We sat there, waiting for that little star to come, at which point my mother would begin to tell us tales. She would also explain that because of our position on the planet the most beautiful mornings are the April ones, the most beautiful evenings the May, which have this rather special, reddish light, and the most beautiful nights the June when the winter sky is full of stars. All this was in order to bring us in touch, in a most profound and poetic way, with the physical world. It was something which she did to perfection. I remember it as being always very dark, probably because of the many power cuts. We would burn candles. Maybe this explains why there is so much actual darkness in my work. Today we don't *see* darkness. We would gather around the table to tell tales, ghost stories, and, scared though we were, there was this feeling of warmth and security, of knowing the grown-ups were there. We would stay at the table long after the dishes were cleared, talking.

'This, for a child, was a most nourishing time. I already carried within myself the tales of three different cultures – the European, of course, those of the black slaves, which were usually moral in nature, and the Indian. There is one fairy tale in particular, an Indian one, which I'll relate it to you just so you may see how different it is from European tales. A grandmother is painting the body of her granddaughter, decorating it as Indians do, and along comes this spotted puma or *onça.* A huge, very dangerous, creature, it appears a great deal in Indian mythology. It says, "I, too, want to be painted", and the grandmother, being a cunning woman, replies, "Well, you'll have to be cooked first." She kills the creature and then tells the child, "Look, you must not eat this meat." Soon after, they are walking in the forest and the grandmother looks and sees the child is transformed into a puma. Obviously she has eaten the meat. When I was growing up, the interior of Brazil was still stuck at the end of the eighteenth century and because it was cut off from the rest of the country the mentality of the people was rich in its connection with the mythical world, with an amazing oral tradition that still prevails there.'

'A lot of that must have fed your imagination.'

'Absolutely! Also we never had that preoccupation, which people from the coast have, of always trying to emulate, or look to, Europe. We took on something else that is neither European nor native but that evolved as a mixture of both. The festivities, the traditional feasts, for example, were a combination of pagan and Christian. When I was about ten a neighbour of ours who worked for an Indian reserve had a visitor, the son of an Indian chief. This man was so tall and beautiful, a real aristocrat, and although he did not speak Portuguese he sang for us in his native tongue. I will never forget that. It was such a beautiful thing and of course it connected us to another world. I have seen the prejudice against Indians. Psychologically they are the *other*, and so, in terms of the practical and political, they are the ones who have to be erased. Another side to all this is that there is a lot of prejudice within people of mixed blood. You have to imagine a power that comes, erases memory, erases language, and then brings the new religion. What you think will happen *does* happen. The people born within that scheme won't like the Indians because they are the lowest on the social scale, the pariahs of society, and so you get even a well-known Latin American writer calling for the assimilation of the Indian population. That is the white man's mentality, which is lethal. The great Spanish composer Victoria wrote sublime music but the culture which produced him also produced Cortés and Pizarro.

'There is a magnificent figure in our Brazilian history and literature, António Vieira, a seventeenth-century Jesuit from Portugal who came during the great period of colonisation. He wrote the most fantastic sermons in which he defended the Indians. He was so against their abuse the Inquisition brought him back to Portugal where he was grilled, although later he did manage to return to Brazil. However, even he could justify slavery! Slavery is the dark stain in our history. Brazil is the country that had the greatest number of slaves and it was the last to abolish slavery. I often think you can never really go beyond your own time. People will speak of such and such a great artist, describing him as being beyond his time, but no, the greatness of a Mozart is that he was a man *of his time*. One of the hardest things is to be aware of the times in which you live. Although Vieira was one of the luminaries of Brazilian literature, not even he could see beyond his time. So how do you square this? It is pretty difficult. I imagine in the future people will look with the same kind of disbelief on people today who believe in market forces. We can't see anything else. It was the same with slavery. They could not imagine an economy without it.

'When I went to Dakar, I visited an island called Gorée, which was where the main slave station was. The slave route started there and ended on the coast of Brazil. There is a museum, La Maison des Esclaves, which is actually quite kitsch but there was one image that haunted me for weeks afterwards. The building is placed on the very edge of the sea and it has all these rooms where they would put men here, women there, children in another place, and there was one room in particular where they put the sick people who were going to die. This room had a door which opened straight onto the sea and these stones. A boat couldn't get anywhere near. It was through this door they would throw out the dead bodies. It was such a Dantesque image, the dark of this room and, coming to this door, the bright light from the Atlantic Ocean. The brutality we see today, the unthinkable, the murder of street children, stems from this and yet nobody cares.'

'You speak of a mythic world whose strands come from the Indians, the blacks and the Portuguese. Were you aware of it at the time?'

'You were not aware of it – you were *part of it.* Only when consciousness sets in do you become *aware*. Obviously this happened as I became older but any *real* understanding came after I left Brazil, when I could articulate it more.'

'Did you feel you were surrounded by something *other*?'

'Obviously I can say so now, but I wasn't aware of it at the time. There is another story I'll relate, which will illustrate the reality there. In many of the Catholic churches there is an area called a "miracle room" or *sala dos milagres.* The ancient Romans had this too, a place where, if you had some problem, you could make a votive offering to the spirits. That's how it got into Christianity. Where I grew up it took quite a different turn. Not far from Goiânia there is a village called Trindade ("Trinity") that is dedicated to the Holy Spirit and which, every July, is the site of a major pilgrimage. The small church in this village, Santuário Basílica do Divino Pai Eterno, has one of these miracle rooms, which is full of all sorts of things – effigies of limbs and hands, discarded crutches, and naïve paintings. There is one painting in particular, which depicts a scene with two hunters, above them a leaping jaguar, and, written in small letters at the top, are the words "Help me, Holy Spirit!" At the bottom of it is a written explanation. The man who gave this painting to the church did so in recognition of the fact that the Holy Spirit saved him. The jaguar ate his friend instead of him.'

Pacheco burst into wild laughter.

'Can you imagine! *I'm saved and that's what counts!* And then, of course, there was Holy Week, *Semana Santa*, which was quite something. I wasn't brought up as a Catholic but this being a Catholic country I'd go to all the big events. There were festivities throughout the year but to me the most poignant, if only because of its emotional charge, was Holy Week. I remember people telling me this was already largely a thing of the past, and they would describe how during that week they would fast and not even brush their hair or clean the house. You have to imagine the grammar of it, when on Good Friday, for example, all the images of the saints were covered in black cloth. This, for a child, was incredible. And then there were the street processions, which I am certain were just like they were in mediaeval times. The most crucial one was on Good Friday, the *Procissão do Encontro*, the "Encounter Procession", when women from one church would go through the streets, carrying an image of the Holy Mother, *Nossa Senhora das Dores* (Our Lady of Sorrows), and from the other church the men would come, carrying an image of Christ carrying the Cross, *Nosso Senhor dos Passos*, and they would meet in the middle. There was no music, just silence, and then there would be the sound of two pieces of wood in a holder, the *cataracta*, a slashing noise meant to reproduce the sound of Christ being beaten. Suddenly a girl with a beautiful voice, standing on a stool above the crowds, would sing, *a cappella*, a Gregorian chant, the *Canto da Verônica*, which symbolises that moment when on the Via Dolorosa Veronica wipes Christ's face. You have to admit that is theatre! Imagine what it was like for a child. I remember to this day all these people walking in silence. It was so dark and everybody there was so sad, and, what's more, they meant it. On Holy Saturday, after sunset, there would be the Paschal Vigil for the body of Christ, with an effigy of him in a coffin. They would spend the whole night in the church, in silence. I think in cultural terms this was a moment of total connection because they were mourning something they could all relate to in their own experience. When people wept over the body of Christ it was a catharsis because they would connect this to memories of losing someone close to them. When my grandmother died there was a vigil for her body in our living room. This carries the most dreadful memories for me – for years afterwards, I couldn't bear the smell of candles. Anyway, at five in the morning, Easter Sunday, you would hear a trumpet. Wherever you were you'd hear this, the *hallelujah* marking the Resurrection, and then there'd be a big carnival, with the burning of Judas. It is like what they have here for Guy Fawkes. I think both come from a pagan world. I remember my cousin would make a figure of Judas, hang him from a tree, light a fire under him and children would be so happy! The brutality of it! When you think in cultural terms how quickly a pattern of behaviour erodes. What I describe is mostly gone. I feel privileged because I come from an era that still had a connection with an ancient past. I think the potency of those rituals comes from something older than Christianity. Somehow we are poorer because we lost it. The most difficult thing for contemporary artists is subject matter because in the old days you had antiquity, myth and Christianity and with them a wealth of images one could explore. After Modernism, we are kind of dry, aren't we?'

'Your father, visionary though he was, was rather against you becoming an artist, wasn't he?'

'Oh, *yes*!'

(Pacheco stretches her *yes*'s and her *no*'s to approximately three and a quarter times their natural length.)

'The idea of a woman artist was absolutely unthinkable. What I said about being able to study what I liked does not equate with any idea of liberality here. This was not Europe – it was South America. A woman still had to have a husband and carry on with the family tradition. My father came from a family of thirteen brothers and sisters and for a daughter of his to be not so keen on pursuing this was pretty terrible for him. At nineteen, I was the oldest child. When I left art school the idea was that I would get married. Art school was taken only as a kind of finishing school. I said no, I wanted to be a sculptor. "What, are you mad!" my father said. "A woman needs to have a man to look after her." He tried to persuade me by all sorts of means. I don't know how I managed to fight him. Cultural forces can be so much stronger than individual vision but probably he was not conscious of this. The norms of society, which he adhered to, this idea of patriarchal society, for example, which he defended so strongly, were such that the idea of a daughter going into the world alone was anathema to him. Not long before he died, however, he capitulated and told me I was right. That was a marvellous thing for him to have done. It removed such a big weight from my shoulders otherwise I might be carrying all this horrible guilt.'

'I had been wondering about you following these two paths in your education, art and music. Was there a point when you were going to fall either one way or the other?'

'Yes, very clearly this was the case. Music is still very much a part of me. It was my mother's greatest dream that I become a musician. So I went along with her and studied music. We could all read music, but my sister and I were the only ones to do a degree in it. At art school it already began to dawn on me that sculpture might be the more fulfilling path for me. But then I decided I wanted to leave Goiânia and, thinking maybe I could extend my musical training, I went to Rio and enrolled myself in a theory course at the National University. I found this wonderful piano tutor who'd studied for many years in Europe, who had been a student of technique in the Russian tradition. I spent a year and a half restructuring my whole piano technique and, difficult though it was, it was a valuable thing to do. It forced me to break old habits. My tutor was well connected and was just about to get me a scholarship to go to Paris to continue my musical studies when I got this invitation to go back to Goiânia to teach at the art school there. So there I was, in Rio, with this marvellous opportunity to go to Europe and faced with the choice of going back to this provincial school in inner Brazil. Fate is strange. I chose the less glamorous option. The other thing about music is that when I had to do exams and musical performances I was a bundle of nerves. I thought, "Hang on a minute! This is not the life I want." As much as I loved music, I didn't like the performing aspect. I suppose it's because I like to be private. *That* was the moment I understood I was not cut out to be a musician. Actually I had no second thoughts about going back to Goiânia but doing so was hard work. There was enormous animosity towards me, especially with all these powerful men there. Aged twenty-three, I was considered too young to be a lecturer.'

'Why I asked you about music is because it strikes me that in your sculptural ensembles there is a kind of musical notation, something like a string quartet.'

'You are absolutely right. There is this element of counterpoint and the string quartet, with its close interaction of musical elements, is very much based on the idea of working together. After all, I spent eighteen years of my life involved in music. There is so much one has to learn that inevitably it becomes a part of one's thinking.'

§

Pacheco's youth was blighted by a series of military dictatorships, often dubbed *Anos de Chumbo* ('Years of Lead'), which lasted from 1964 until 1985. When she left Brazil in 1973 it was under the presidency of Emílio Garrastazu Médici, a period during which many thousands of Brazilians were imprisoned, tortured or murdered.

'I was not directly involved but at university I witnessed horrible acts of brutality to young people. Students of mine were tortured and murdered. One thing we all knew was that there were moles everywhere, so we had to be careful of anything we said. One day we gave a lift to a boy whose back was covered with cigarette burns, and then there was a student of mine whose sister was my contemporary at university and later involved with the guerrillas in the Amazon. My student was murdered, shot in the street. They claimed this was a *crime passionnel* but no, it really had to do with taking revenge on her sister. Another time, the police investigated a lecturer at our university and then went to his home and demolished his library. Once, we were all summoned to police headquarters, which was where they tortured people. We were interviewed one by one and this man showed me a photo of a street protest, saying, "Do you know anybody here?" Of course I didn't say anything. I could hear screams coming from elsewhere. They did this in order to scare you. I had my sympathies, of course – such things make you take sides – but probably I was more concerned about my work. I was in my early twenties. It wasn't until much later that I realised how scared I was. This was nothing compared to what a lot of people had to go through.'

'The reason for your leaving Brazil was still an artistic and not a political one.'

'The irony was that I wouldn't have left had it been solely a matter of politics. It had everything to do with where I was born. When I applied for a scholarship, which is how I came here, I wasn't necessarily thinking about London. The main thing is that I wanted to leave Brazil. *Why did I want to leave?* There is a thing about colonies, which is not necessarily specific to Brazil, and it is that when you live in one there is always the feeling that things are happening elsewhere. As a colony we always looked to the centre that is Europe. You begin to feel you are not in the right place. That is a syndrome of colonisation but that was not quite the reason I wanted to leave. Actually I was quite content to be there but as my work developed I began to feel there was a gap between life in inner Brazil and the things I was learning at art school. After some years, I began to be conscious there was something missing in my work. What we were fed on was a staple diet of Modernism. So what was my situation as an art student in a school in the middle of nowhere, reading essays on Picasso, Impressionism, Kandinsky et cetera? It was madness! I was being taught by people with a European connection, German or Italian, at a school that had the French Academy as its model and which was totally out of sync with the locality. It is important to add that coming from the middle of Brazil my sense of awareness of culture, and what comprises its core, was very different from someone who comes from the coast. Our history is so completely different. There was not only this big gap – there was a further kind of ambivalence, which is historical in nature. When the country became independent from Portugal and things got economically stable there was quite a lot of wealth. The children of rich parents would be sent to Europe. What happened is they became acquainted with the latest in terms of political and social, and consequently artistic, movements, and so this small elite came back to Brazil, bringing with it the latest in terms of the new language, whatever it was. Meanwhile the rest of the country had no idea about any of this and the popular art was unaffected. So these two parallel forces, working at the same time, became ever stronger. The more erudite were always informed of what was happening elsewhere, which in the nineteenth century was Paris, in the twentieth, New York, and now, in the twenty-first, London.

'I am very conscious of Brazilian history and I don't want to make works that are just a mere repetition of what is happening here. Also I am not making nationalistic work – this is nonsense and, besides, it's dangerous. I want my work to reflect what I am. If you go the way of following what's happening in the major centres, then what you have is colonisation revisited. The point I am trying to make is this: in Europe, whenever there was a change in terms of language or visual arts, whether it be Romanticism, Impressionism or whatever, they were reflections of social change. In Brazil, things didn't happen like that. Social change there was not like it is here. Brazilians may like to think this is not so but the people who'd be saying this are from the coast. Say these things to someone from the middle of Brazil and he'll have no idea what you are talking about. It is a big country. There is this assumption that because we speak the same language there is homogeneity but in fact there are great cultural differences. There is not, as has been often suggested, this unity in terms of culture.'

'So what you are against is the mere adoption of European or North American forms.'

'Yes. It has nothing to do with prejudice. It's simply because it has nothing to do with the reality there. You can say, well, I am not living there. But I *am* Brazilian. I came here as an adult. My formative years were spent there so my work cannot but reflect that experience. Another factor is the landscape. My mother was frightened of it. She was worried about being bitten by snakes. She got this from her mother who was not from the area. The landscape is not as friendly as it is here. So there I was, the recipient of two things – one, this terrible fear of the landscape, and, two, being taught things that have nothing to do with it. When I was already in my third year, I decided I would investigate this place which is part of me. I started to draw from the landscape, which was not exactly in the wilds, the *sertão*, but on the outskirts of the city. Today you would not recognise the area because it is now completely urbanised but when I was a student it was still pretty rough. The interesting thing was that here you had people living in the slums who had come from deep in the interior of the country, many of them migrants from farms that had become derelict. I spent ten years drawing these people. They are the roots of my iconography, the visual language of my work. Would I have had a chance to succeed in Rio or São Paulo with this language? I don't think so. I tried to make sense of a world in fragments, but what I didn't expect was that I'd find something missing in my own work. What was it? We speak a European language, but only when I started to draw from the landscape did I locate this dichotomy, these two strange worlds, and I knew then that in order to make sense of it I would have to go back to where it all started, which is why I decided to go to Europe.'

It was what Pacheco describes elsewhere as having 'completed the puzzle'.

§

With a nod, perhaps, in the direction of Goya's *The Burial of a Sardine* Pacheco produced a series of drypoints collectively titled *Misfortunes of a Sardine*, which may be read as an ironic commentary on her own journey. The danger is in making too close a reading of it for one's own purposes. Sardine's journey is not absolutely Pacheco's. (There is no clear evidence, for example, that the latter actually went to Hades.) And the journey she makes is not quite, although one might wish it to be, to this London of ours. The trajectory it follows is not just over the planet's surface, from continent to continent, or, for that matter, from ground level to subterranean, but it goes also into that verbally mushy zone we call our *inside.* (Already this journey is fraught with the danger that comes of employing words rather than images.) Words, though, are precisely what Pacheco's work invites. It is probably why poets are so attracted to her work, not only because of its narrative qualities but also because of its steady recourse to archetypes. Some of her pieces appear to be allegories almost, although, thank goodness, they bail out just in time. After all, it's the rare allegory that survives a single use. What her works do, rather, is to suggest or to tease a little. *Misfortunes of a Sardine* provides a structure upon which to hang certain particulars regarding Pacheco's post-Brazilian existence. It also serves to illumine the creative process, although here too one had better go equipped with a fishing net with very small holes. *Why Sardine?* Well, to be a sardine, she tells me, is to be a very small fish in a big pond and I rib her a little for being overly prosaic. After all, what's fuller than a tin of sardines? Sardine, and I speak here of the protagonist of the series rather than the species, is an anthropomorphic creature, but manages, just, to escape the cuteness that so often blights such strategies. If anything, she disturbs. As human, she is, snout aside, *almost all there*; as fish, she is too slippery to catch with words alone.

The five drypoints I have selected here, together with one sculptural aside, act as conversational touchstones, which is to say that through them we explored what they might contain with respect to a life transported elsewhere. The other thing, of course, and which is central to Pacheco's feelings with regard to biography, that it is a pit where we entangle ourselves in banalities, is that by employing these images as a backdrop to her life, they allow for a necessary distance.

'Who cares about what happened to me as a child? These things are irrelevant, but once they are put into images they begin to make sense because then it is no longer about myself. I am dealing with something bigger than me. Of course everything one does, whether it is writing a poem or making a sculpture, is inevitably about oneself – it is a folly to deny that – but when one gets in touch with this larger thing then there is no room left for the irrelevancies of one's daily life. You are connected to where you came from, which is not something you alone can determine. We might make all sorts of discussion but there is one bit we will never see and that's the other side of the cube. We live in the physical world, so with regard to that kind of omniscience we haven't got there yet. It is still the domain of the gods.'

We began with the first in the series, *Sardine Arrives*, when Pacheco aka Sardine parachutes her way to a new existence.

'Actually that's exactly how I felt, as if I had parachuted into totally unknown territory. I wasn't thinking about it as a friendly sport but rather as it was during the war, when they had to drop behind enemy lines. It must have been pretty frightening. You have first of all to get rid of your jumping gear and then try to blend into the landscape of the locals and there you have all these enemies waiting for you. Also it's like being born, which, when you think about it, is pretty horrendous. There you are in this cosy, watery place, being fed, and suddenly you are dropped – you have to breathe for yourself, and from then on things get worse by the minute.'

Cheeriness, though, rather than melancholy, is Pacheco's conversational keynote.

'It's not necessarily that I wanted to come to England. I came here only because I had a scholarship from the British Council, but with hindsight it was the best place to be. Well, it would be pretty disastrous if after all these years I was in the wrong one! Coming here made me aware of things that I might not have been able to accommodate had I remained at home, for example the vastness of the gap between cultures. There is a strong dislike in this culture for the kind of work I do, which is both narrative and figurative, with a touch of the Baroque – not that I make Baroque sculpture, that's nonsense, but that's what has been said about my work. It's worth remembering, though, that the Baroque evolved at a time when, with the religious wars and the Counter-Reformation, there was huge fragmentation in the culture. This was an attempt to glue together all these disparities. We now live in a time when, for different reasons, there is also huge fragmentation. The point I want to make is that being here has helped me enormously in that I have had to fight for my own identity. Also, being from such a different background and coming to where I have had to express myself in a language that is diametrically opposite to Portuguese – Portuguese is prolix and meandering whereas English, which has a richer vocabulary and structure, goes straight to the point – the combination of the two somehow helped me with regard to my own thinking processes. You think through language so the acquisition of another, especially one that is so different, opens up the mind a bit more. This has also made a huge difference in that it has made me more capable of making better judgements about my own work. When I was in Brazil I wanted to deal with our history but I couldn't because any such attempt would be overly melodramatic. I had to wait. Once I was here I was finally able to deal with this ambivalence in Brazilian culture.'

'Am I right in thinking that when you were first here you completely lost your bearings, artistic and otherwise?'

'Yes, I was working in the iconography of a former structure and suddenly I had come to a culture about which I knew nothing whatsoever. I had no experience that could connect me to anything here, so all the language that I had been using became completely redundant. Now considering I have always been a firm believer that one has to work *in and with* the world, here I was, not connected to anything. The experiences that had hitherto fed my work were no longer there. So I had to find a new vocabulary to deal with what I found here. It was all very subtle, and maybe I'm being a bit subjective, but it was real nevertheless, the idea that I had to change even my eating habits! At home I was always surrounded by people – a whole structure held me there, friends and family, and now here I was, totally on my own, and I mean *really* on my own. I had come to a country where the climate is different, the food atrocious, and the behaviour – well, people behaved so differently here! Of course I wasn't *really* surprised but there is a comical situation that illustrates exactly what I mean. When I first arrived here, this person from the Arts Council kindly took me to the Slade. There I was, at this great institution, being introduced to the Secretary of the Slade. I thought "secretary" meant something else. This man was actually in charge! As is the habit in Brazil, even with people you don't know, I kissed both his cheeks. He immediately withdrew and for a short time there was this comical situation with neither of us knowing any longer what the form was. And then I realised I had broken into the space between him and me. "Oh my God," I thought, "I haven't got a clue how to behave." I am telling you the funny side, but it was real enough and my having to start again from scratch, aged thirty, was very painful indeed. It couldn't have been more different in terms of behaviour.

'So there was the agony of finding my own way while at the same time being at a huge distance from origins I could not obliterate. This was the biggest conundrum. I had to allow myself to be open to new possibilities in an utterly different environment but at the same time, because I did not want to be completely swamped by everything that is *not* me, I had to be careful not to lose sight of who I was. I never intended to be English. I can't be. I am not English and I'm not exactly Brazilian either. On the other hand, I was never easily identifiable for the reasons I mentioned earlier. I had a different upbringing from most people, but despite all the enormous difficulties the one thing that sustained me here was an acquired independence. I could do things that if I were still in the country of my origin would be very difficult. I do not use the word "freedom", which is more complex and has other implications, but "independence". I suppose the drawback is that I have no place. I don't mind in one sense because in relation to the work it has been a very positive thing, but in terms of my own life I feel sometimes an enormous spiritual isolation. I mean you can also read the Sardine series as the description of an inner journey. The most potent aspect of leaving Brazil and coming to England was not necessarily the geographical position of the two countries. It had to do with the journey within myself, which is easier to make if you are in a foreign country simply because there you have no choice. You *have* to do the journey, otherwise you will not survive. I mean this spiritually – physical survival, by comparison, is quite easy. There is no support within the culture. You have to find the resources within yourself and only then will you find support from the outside. On the other hand, there are far more chances of failing here than if you were in your own country. The risks are much bigger.'

'Did you have to fight all sorts of monsters here?'

'Of course! Didn't you?'

'I just wanted to know whether your monsters were different from mine.'

'They have to be. It would be terrible if they were the same. I think the difficulty is in finding a language of your own, particularly with respect to your own work, and also – maybe this was my paranoia – there are all these clichés about South Americans, *mañana* and all that, although actually I have met quite a few who fit the cliché. Firstly, I think you have to prove you are serious. I have been away from Brazil for thirty-five years and obviously things have changed but when I was growing up there the country was deeply authoritarian but at the same time anarchic. The one thing you had to do in order to survive was to be serious. So I came to a country where it was the last thing to be, where people would say, "My God, you are *so* serious!" *Well, yes, shouldn't I be?* You have to understand just how complex this was. You are in a place that has leaders who are bandits, who rule by the gun, and then you come to where power is handled not only in a different way but one that is far more effective, where the idea of being serious makes no sense. Actually by being *unserious* you can erode this kind of power. It took me some time to understand that. It is not something you can understand intellectually – you have to dig much deeper. The other thing was that the language here could not resolve or reflect what I was over there. So how do you square this? You have to find a language that fulfils your deepest desires and aspirations while at the same time not make a mockery of what is here. What you have left behind, which is still inside, is far away in time and space, but on the other hand it's not that far because it is who you are. So it was rather like walking on moving sand although the monsters I had to fight were largely of my own making. They were real enough, however, and there could be no making compromises with them. Once you begin to compromise, you are finished.'

§

After a struggle, it's time for rest. The next image shows Sardine in repose, another day's work done, a knife in her hand as casually held as a closed fan, which she doesn't need because there is a breeze

coming in at the window, and there, stuck on a pole, the head of a giant. Something tells me she's done this before.

'Sardine has dealt with her own demons, and has won, but there is another point I want to make. The notion of the punishment of decapitation is a very ancient one. There is something so ultimate about it. Once the head is removed there is no chance of salvation in the future. What Christianity took from ancient cultures is that without a head you cannot go to the Last Judgement.'

Rest is also, of course, a time for reflection. It is when one considers what one has done.

'When you have finished a work only then can you lay back and start to read it and say to yourself, "Oh, *now* I have an idea of what it is about". One immense danger – and you will be the last to realise it – is that as you get older you begin to repeat yourself because to do so is comfortable. This happens when you have found a felicitous solution, one in terms of form and structure, for instance. You *know* it is going to work. Often, after achieving something, a terrible pride and vanity sets in. That is something you have to avoid, otherwise it's a disaster. Your work has to be a discovery all the time, but the older you get the more difficult it becomes. The hardest thing to do is to disengage and let things go because if you cling to the past you will not see what is coming next. You will be too heavy to jump into any new endeavour. You'll sink. One needs to refer to one's previous experiences but the thing to do is to try to make of them a kind of premise for the next one. I do not work like most sculptors. I do not embark on anything with a concept in advance. I start with just the vision and then things will take shape as I go along, at which point the work starts to inform me. What sometimes starts as a woman turns out to be a man or vice versa. The process of the journey changes the work and only then do I get closer to what I want although it is never what I first had in mind. You are disappointed because your vision is always better than that of which you are capable. Still, you have to listen to this other voice of the instinct. This, too, can be dubious because you can make mistakes but you have to listen to it nevertheless, amid this huge noise. This is how I imagine poets work in that they dig into something totally unknown. When I did *Dark Night of the Soul* at the National Gallery I knew I wanted to do a circular composition. With my next work I couldn't go and repeat this, I had to do something I hadn't done before, so I made *Land of No Return* where I went in the very opposite direction and did something symmetrical – three male figures here, three female figures opposite, and one in the middle. At the time I didn't realise the implication of what I'd done.

'Years later, I realised the female in the middle is the one who redeems those strong opposites. She is the hope of the three men who are so very strong in their deliberation – they have been fighting and are emotionally charged – whereas the three women opposite are seated, playing with these golden shells – this female notion of connection with the primeval world where fate is so stark there is no way one can change it. So what you have are these two opposing worlds, which are static, and then you have a new entity which is this woman and, because of the way the world has gone, it *has* to be a woman. Women have fewer things charged upon them whereas

men are charged with enormous expectation. The world is ruled not by men necessarily but by male thinking, so what you have is this woman in the middle as some kind of redeeming figure. What she may represent is a world of sensibilities where judgment is made without any rationalist notion. I can say that now, with hindsight, but I never thought of any of this while doing the work. Anyway in terms of composition, which is what concerns me ultimately, I didn't want to do anything even remotely close to the previous work. Art is not about concept, which is the domain of philosophy – it is visual, so it is all about effect and perception. Concept you bring later, when you are pondering what you've done, but if you begin to make a work based on an idea it becomes closed. Philosophy is what we know whereas art is what we do not know.'

'What you describe elsewhere "as breaking through to the invisible".'

'Yes, it is like poetry. It just evolves.'

§

Avernus is a real place, a lake near an Italian town called Cumae, which is of such depth it inspired the ancient belief that it was the entrance to Hades. It is there that Aeneas meets Sibyl and is warned by her, in terms that are psychologically sure, that although the way down is easy enough the coming back up is a bit of a chore. Dryden, in his translation of the *Aeneid*, puts it rather more eloquently:

> O goddess-born of great Anchises' line,
> The gates of hell are open night and day;
> Smooth the descent, and easy is the way:
> But to return, and view the cheerful skies,
> In this the task and mighty labour lies.

Surely, though, wherever one is, there may be found an entrance to Hades.

It may be that manhole cover I saw on the Old Kent Road.

It may be even closer to home.

'There is a tunnel to this other side of ourselves,' Pacheco continued, 'about which we know very little. You could call it the Unconscious or whatever. You enter there as if through a gate. You really do expect to see Sibyl, don't you? Why Virgil put her there is because she is a seer. She alone knows what's going to happen. What I love about her warning to Aeneas is that in artistic terms it is not so difficult to go to the Underworld – it doesn't require all that much effort – but making sense of it is hard. After all, we live up here, not down there. You have to go there because it is where all the images lie. This is where the intellect and critical judgement and individuality play such an important role because a selection has to be made of what one takes and what one leaves behind. When you get back to the surface that's when the real work starts, this dealing with the materials you've brought back from there. Of course this doesn't happen quite as clearly as all that. This is merely a way of communicating these things verbally, whereas, really, things are in total chaos. And I can only talk like this *after* a work is done, not before. I do not design a work and then make it. I go through an enormous process of investigations and of attempts, wrong and right. You do not start with an idea, but with a notion, or, in my case, with the vision of an image.

'Sibyl gives Sardine a mistletoe. As long as she carries it, the "Golden Bough", which most probably was mistletoe, she'll be safe. Remember, too, Sibyl is a female and has all the connections between ours and the underworld. It's where she belongs. That is why I made her numinous, brighter and taller. Another thing I love about the *Aeneid* is that when Aeneas arrives in Carthage he sees there, at the Temple of Juno, a work of art depicting the *Iliad*. Virgil does not say

whether it is sculpted or painted. In the context of Aeneas' marriage to Dido, his name was known before him. There are so many marvellous offshoots of the story. There is a lovely Mesopotamian text concerning the goddess Ishtar. What is so beautiful about this version is that during her descent to the Underworld she has to take off her clothes. She removes one layer at a time and each time she does so she goes through another gate. You have to arrive there with no clothes – you have to go there as you are. I love all these myths because they make sense. They make for a kind of reality that is not visible but which is as real as the sun.'

§

'Where, in that last image in the series, is Sardine going?'

'I don't know. That's my point. Clearly, though, she is going out to sea.'

'It is an image of death as well.'

'Absolutely, but it's not death as nihilism but rather as a process of renewal or rather that is what is implied. There is always death

in what one does because when you finish a work you have to let it go. I spent most of my life dealing with this and actually it is not so difficult any more.'

§

The big endeavour, Pacheco concludes, is to do the things that make sense to her. This attitude has made her one of the most refreshingly independent of artists and being here, in London, up against forces that might push her to be otherwise, has helped her immeasurably. She is also, where ignorance has come to be considered a virtue, the most literate of artists. She describes how, after reading Flaubert's *The Temptation of Saint Anthony*, she produced an image of a flying sphinx. The sphinx is quite a heavy creature. One art historian remarked to her that what she produced was surely not a sphinx but a harpy. After all, he reasoned, sphinxes can't fly. She did not seek to disabuse him of the notion. Also, she does not want to close anyone else's reading of her work. Actually, though, that sphinx of hers is not an Egyptian one. It's not Flaubert's male sphinx, which is clearly grounded, overweight, and sluggish with arcane knowledge, but the streamlined Late Archaic Greek model such as one finds at Delphi, a busty female, all body tone, smart although maybe just a bit *too* confident in her grasp of the new learning, and equipped with the wings of an eagle. Watch her move. A single-minded creature, she does not suffer fools gladly and woe to him who gives the wrong answer to her riddle – the Greek *sphingo* means 'to strangle'. The only escape from sure death, as Oedipus knows, is not by means of aerodynamics but through imagination, and he is just enough of an artist to understand that what a sharp mind gives admittance to it sets free.

A Metaphysical Shaggy Dog Tale

The Four Lives of Andrzej Michał Maria N. Borkowski

A small glass painting, a gift from my wife, hangs close to where I write. It depicts an angel or, rather, *an angel of sorts*, its character more secular than divine, whose face could be F. Scott Fitzgerald's, especially with the hair parted so close to the middle, although the red daubs on the cheeks suggest a more clownish demeanour, a touch of Fellini maybe. This man-angel, whose wings look like the insides of the two halves of a scallop shell, wears pink woolly pantaloons, clutches a magician's wand, and stands on a circular base of blue upon which is inscribed, in white, in a receding triangle, the letters ABRACADABRA. There's a complex, though not wholly proven, etymology here. Among the various interpretations ascribed to this ancient magical formula are the words 'I create as I speak' from the Aramaic אברא כדברא (*avra kedabra*), which has been taken to be a reference to God creating the universe. It's not a bad motto to have near as one struggles to make flesh of one's own scribbles, or, as in this case, another person's garbles.

I do not mean to be rude. The Wimbledon Pole who painted this image, Andrzej Maria Borkowski, speaks at such speed that when transcribing him from my little blue recorder onto the page it's all I can do to follow the wild leaps from phrase to phrase. The spaces in between are filled with despairing cries, verbal erasures – 'No, no, no, no!' or 'It's boring, boring!' (this usually at a point when I want him to continue) – and other sounds of a mostly zoological nature. I've never known a man who can take up so much sonic space. There's got to be a metaphysic here. I remove my earphones. The figure on the wall suggests an analogy, although not a wholly satisfactory one; and it is this: glass painting needs to be done in reverse, so when composing a face, for example, one begins by painting the pupils of the eyes. It is, in short, a medium that does not allow for any correction of mistakes. And so it is with Borkowski that spoken language is pulled inside out, its entrails the first thing to emerge.

There's no going back to any original grain of sense because sense has yet to arrive. There is only a forward charge – the Polish Cavalry is him alone. Maybe the solution is to translate him into Polish, which, sadly, is not a language I speak, and then back into English again. Joking aside, working his story into something approaching the comprehensible did at times involve my putting him at a double remove.

What is revealed, once spread flat on the table, is a singular intellect whose mode, if one were to translate this into visual terms, is cubist rather than representational. Of his diverse art he says it owes more to simultaneity than to sequentiality and likewise when he speaks all things come at once. There is no want of intelligence – it simply operates on a different plane. The words, though, they seem so very slow on the page. A kind of alchemical process seems to have taken place, a rendering of base materials into pure, and yet I have to ask myself whether this heavily edited, much reduced, portrait is at all true. The very fact that I have ironed out the crinkles seems to play Borkowski false. You'd really need to tear out these pages, crumple them, shove them in your pocket, and then, maybe a day or two later, try to flatten them out a little, to get some sense of what he's really like.

Soutine might have painted his face, Wyspiański his Piłsudski moustache.

The following is an autobiographical note:

> There are four people in me, hence the four names – Andrzej, Michał, Maria and 'N', all born in Warsaw out of the Teutonic Knights' and Tartars' blood of his Polish ancestors. Andrzej is an art historian and critic, graduated at Warsaw University (MA) and London (MA Courtauld Institute). He is a sceptical and sarcastic man, but his art can be fun. He teaches

in Brighton University in the School of Art. Michał is an angel and he hardly ever touches the ground. He flies. His is a mercurial nature. It is probably he who is the actor. He worked in theatre and dance and even did some films with Melanie Griffith and one with Sting. Maria is his third name. She is a woman, the Earth, and probably a better artist and poet than Andrzej, and through her I *feel.* 'N' is my fourth name. It might be an animal, wolf or ape. It is in me and plays with the other three.

And so, following on his own slightly madcap scheme, Andrzej Michał Maria N. Borkowski shall be here presented as the possessor of four lives. Admittedly the divisions between them are a bit arbitrary at times, and besides, I do not wish to put him, or, rather, *all four of him*, inside a verbal straitjacket. Anyway he moves faster than language. Also he has illustrated those lives of his with photographic shadow images, which he took mostly in Cappadocia, stark naked, away from the eyes of the populace. With a handheld camera he took pictures of his own shadow cast against rock and sand and trees. The trick is to keep the shadow of the camera out of the picture. The best time to photograph, he says, is between three and five in the afternoon when the sun is not too harsh because too much contrast spoils the effect. Those strange, haunting images reflect the multiplicity of one's existence. The incredible thing is that he should have thought of doing them in the first place.

'You project your inner story outside,' he says.

The ancient Greeks regarded shadow as a metaphor for Psyche, and that great myth-catcher Sir James Frazer writes of the primitive: 'Often he regards his shadow or reflection as his soul, or at all events as a vital part of himself, and as such it is necessarily a source of danger to him.' Jung, looking deeply into *his* shadow, maybe more deeply than he intended to, saw in it the instinctive and the irrational – 'the thing a person has no wish to be'. 'As the Sun is the light of the spirit,' writes J.E. Circot in his *Dictionary of Symbols*, 'so shadow is the negative "double" of the body, or the image of its evil and base side.' The general take on Shadow is that it's too dark a country to make one's abode. For Borkowski, on the other hand, smiling explorer of the mind's unlit places, it represents wondrous possibilities. Instantaneously, or, rather, simultaneously, as he flung phrases here and there, he drew on aboriginal art, the cave paintings at Lascaux, Plato's Cave, a Hopi legend concerning copulation with the earth, the physiognomist Johann Kaspar Lavater's silhouette-making machine, Adelbert von Chamisso's *Peter Schlemihl*, Athanasius Kircher's writings on the *Lanterna magica*, Cubism, *The Cabinet of Doctor Caligari*, animism, the early photographs of Stanisław Ignacy Witkiewicz, and finally his own childhood memories.

Andrzej

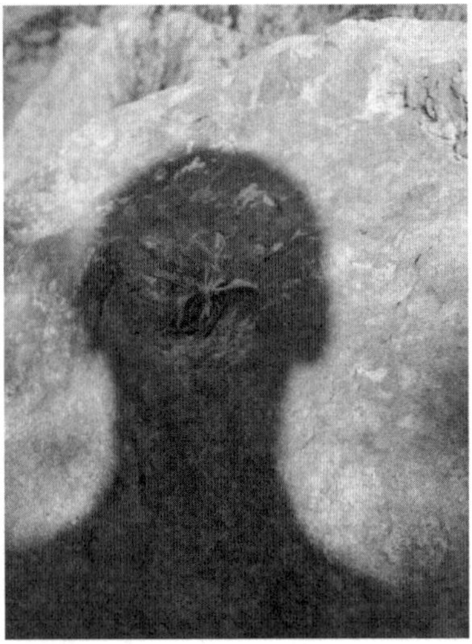

What's that growing out of the middle of his head? What life is this that clings to such a barren substance? Could it be analogous with all we attempt to do, when we wrest something from nothingness? Borkowski has as many professions as he has names – art historian, teacher, painter and actor. (I am tempted to add 'contortionist' because Guinness paid him £2,500, and a trip to Portugal, to do an advert posing as a *sadhu* after the original *sadhu*, that is to say, a genuine one, had failed to contort sufficiently.) Appropriately enough, given that he has many other guises as well, what first brought him to this country was the stage.

'I'm not sure to what degree I can be called an émigré because I was asked to join a theatre company here. So it wasn't the usual business of making one's way through a building site towards some idea of selfhood. In 1967, I applied to the Fine Arts Academy in Warsaw. There were only a limited number of places available, but although I was accepted on the basis of my work there wasn't a place for me in Warsaw. I'd have to go to Gdańsk, they'd said. My mum suggested I apply for art history instead so I applied to Warsaw University, thinking I wouldn't get in, and was accepted. So I became a bloody art historian, which I never wanted to be. That September, when I started my course, I checked out the student theatres to see if I could do set designs or costumes. I found one looking for set designers so I joined the queue. There was a nice girl in a neighbouring queue, applying for mime theatre. One thing I knew is that I could never be an actor. My uncle said that because I mumble and speak too quickly nobody understands me. Another thing I knew is that I liked girls. So I asked her, "What's mime?" She said it was theatre without words. "No words! *Really*? That's okay!" So I moved into her queue and that same evening I joined a mime troupe. That's how I became involved with theatre. It was not so much mime in the Marcel Marceau sense – it was more geometrical, more stylistic, and moving slowly towards performance art. I joined one group and then another and then finally, in 1971, a friend of mine, Wojciech ("Wojtek") Krukowski, now director of the Centre of Contemporary Art in Warsaw, formed a new group, *Akademia Ruchu* (the Academy of Movement), and asked me to join. This became one of the most important avant-garde groups at that time.

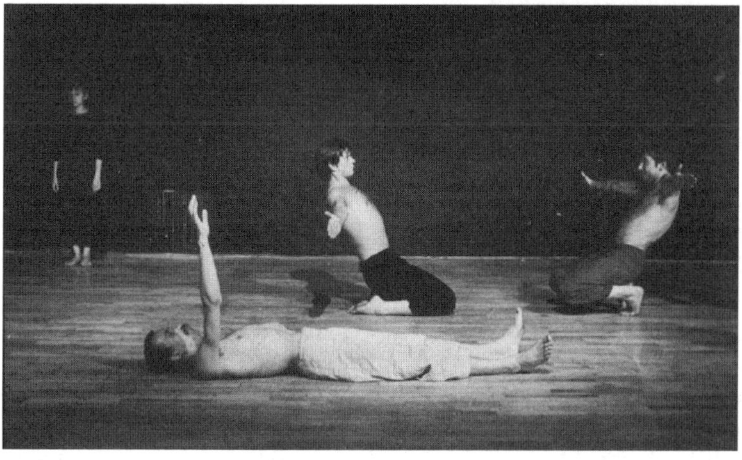

'We didn't use words except as written banners, these sometimes being lines of poetry, so the emphasis was more on fine arts than on literature. This was good for international contact because there wasn't any problem with language. Polish theatre was quite important in those days, mainly because of Jerzy Grotowski, and then there was Tadeusz Kantor with his Theatre of Death in Kraków, which was closer to some of our ideas. With Grotowski, on the other hand, there was a major difference in our attitudes towards theatre in that his approach was deeply psychological in nature whereas ours owed more to a formal neo-constructivist tradition, concentrating on body and image.'

A few years later, a young British director, Stephen Rumbelow, head of Triple Action Theatre, went to Poland seeking inspiration and actors. Poland was still very much a destination for the romantically inclined, especially with its added frisson of political menace, but, this said, or maybe even because of it, it also boasted some highly original theatre. The productions were often so concise that watching them reminded one of the workings of an immaculately constructed watch whose every movement is in perfect harmony with the whole. Student theatre was a particularly potent force and not to be confused with amateur theatre. Clearly Rumbelow did not go there in a haze. This was where major talent was to be found. At his invitation, Borkowski joined his company.

'I came here in that dry summer of 1976. Here I was, in London, for the first time, and I never got to see it! I arrived by train at four in the afternoon. They were waiting for me, and then we crossed the street from Victoria Station to a pizzeria where a Polish waitress served me. *What, already!* I was desperate to see Big Ben but instead this van zoomed through London to Newark which is one church, one library, one river and a castle. This was our base. It was spoken theatre, which was different from what I was doing in Poland, but really I came to England for the experience. *Why not?* The theatre was for me overly dramatic, a bit pretentious and overdone. We did *The Idiot* and I was Rogozhin. It was all rather alien to me because I had always felt like an independent artist. I had been the main member of *Akademia Ruchu* and, together with Wojtek, the creator of those performances, whereas here I was just an actor, which I never wanted to be. At Easter 1977, we decided to part company and I stayed on in England until the end of summer. Just before coming to England I had met my future wife, Gabriela. I felt badly about leaving her because I had only met her a few months earlier. She came to England and we tried to survive, God knows how. I taught some workshops and also did illustrations for the alternative magazine *International Times* but that, too, was difficult because they offered me hashish rather than money. What could I do with hash when I needed to pay my rent?'

Borkowski went back to Warsaw where he rejoined *Akademia Ruchu* and also he found a job giving lectures at the Fine Arts Academy in Gdańsk, the very school he was supposed to have gone to years before.

'Quite by chance, Gabriela, who I knew when she was still in school, was now a first-year student in my class. People said I was picking up students. No, I had picked up a schoolgirl! I lived in Gdańsk, three days with her, and then four days in Warsaw where I carried on with the theatre.'

'You must have been there when Solidarity started.'

'People always talk of Gdańsk but actually the strike began in Lublin. We had come back from a street theatre festival in Rimini, my wife something like six months pregnant, although still performing. Already there were rumours about strikes, and by the beginning of August Gdańsk had become a centre of growing tension. I went immediately to the gallery where I gave lectures. As soon as I arrived people began to shout at me, "Oh, Andrzej, we are going to strike!" The centre of the movement was in the shipyards and various groups, including ours, were joining it. "Are you with us?" they said. Half the people at the gallery were for the strike and the other half against. I was for it. We got into the car and went to the shipyard. This was a part of our history that could have been mine, but with Gabriela now seven months pregnant and my identification card a Warsaw one, I told them I'd rather stay with her. We returned to Warsaw. So that was the tense first year of Solidarity. An agreement was signed at the end of August 1980 and then the question dragged on and on as to which would be more powerful, the Communist Party or us. In March 1981, there were Warsaw Pact military manoeuvres, with our communist friends from different countries joining in. There were East German troops in Gdańsk and Szczecin. A few months later, we had martial law.'

Grotowski's assistant, Eugenio Barba, who had created his own theatre in Denmark, offered *Akademia Ruchu* a month's residence in Odense. It was there that Borkowski met Grotowski, one of the century's greatest exponents of avant-garde theatre, although by that point he had already quit the stage, at least in the public sense. He had begun to move beyond staged theatre into something which he coined 'paratheatre', which dispensed completely, or at least theoretically, with the idea of an audience.

'I met him a few times. I was invited to work with Stanisław Ścierski, one of Grotowski's main actors. All this anthropological theatre was definitely fascinating but I was suspicious of all the mysticism and charisma attached to it, that particular brand of seduction. Ścierski's workshops would begin at four in the morning and you'd have to come and wash the floor first. It may have been fascinating to observe, and there really was something pushing me in that direction, but I didn't like those group situations in which one lost all control of oneself. I found that building of a myth, which began with washing the bloody floor, rather scary, and although it might lead to shamanistic experiences, there was a fascistic element in it that I didn't like. It could be a way of getting into your soul but it wasn't for me. At that point Grotowski was doing these *święta* or "holy feasts" and was inviting people to a forest in the Polish mountains to work with him for a month, again beginning with physical work, all that hippie stuff. I felt a bit guilty that I hadn't seen more of his work. Obviously he was a legend but I couldn't really talk to him about theatre. I was afraid he would be deep into theory and all about reaching holiness and also, because I was suspicious of that charisma, I wanted to fight his influence as much as possible. I was therefore pleased to discover he was keenly interested in what was happening in Poland. So here he was, a normal man, caught up in that great moment of Solidarity, at a time when there was a real danger the Warsaw Pact would intervene. So rather than talk about theatre, Grotowski told me about the days he spent on trains in Poland, just talking to people, getting their thoughts on the situation. Also, because I had a short-wave radio, we listened together to the news from there. We discovered that, like it or not, we were both Poles and that as Poles we had a duty to, and responsibility for, our country. This was discomfiting for both of us because it blocked out any sense of normality, but at the same time it was a part of us that we couldn't allow ourselves to forget. This may sound deeply pretentious, or maybe even the building of another mythology, but because we were so deeply rooted in our history we had the sense of *taking responsibility for our peasants*! I met him again, when he came to the Cardiff Laboratory Theatre, and there I tried to put questions to him that had more to do with theatre and ethics. I have always been troubled by this problem of "Why should I ask anyone to be interested in my vision?" This is a question any artist must ask of himself.

'Meanwhile I had left Gabriela in Warsaw with a small child, in that hot situation. When still in Odense, I got a telephone call from England, from Richard Gough of the Cardiff Laboratory Theatre with whom I had already worked once, asking me if I'd be interested in joining his company for a festival in Leicester in the summer of 1981. This produced a major conflict in me, between carrying on with an old performance at another theatre festival and doing something completely new. Although working with *Akademia Ruchu* greatly satisfied me, I had been very much part of a collective and now I wanted more independence. I really respected Wojtek and he respected me, but there were some elements on which we were in disagreement. I felt a bit trapped, impatient to try something new, and so, for better or worse, after nine years with *Akademia Ruchu* I left. There were still a lot of practical problems such as my not having a private passport. I returned with the group to Poland, thinking I would go to England from there. Politically it was still a hot situation. I couldn't return my "group" passport because there wouldn't be enough time to apply for a private one, and, in any case, there wasn't any guarantee I'd get it. So I decided to do something a bit illegal and just not bother to return it. This was a bit unfair on Wojtek who was responsible for the group and all the officialdom involved, which, of course, included his having to return our passports. Anyway I held onto mine and then I negotiated with the authorities that I be allowed to take my wife and daughter. Two months later, I went to Cardiff and then to Leicester, and performed there with the street theatre. I didn't know what to do next. I still had my contract with the university in Gdańsk. After Cardiff we went to London and I reconnected with the people from *IT*. They were doing the final edition of the *Alternative London Guide*. I did illustrations for it, often slipping into them allusions to my love for Gabriela. I also did a workshop with Alex Mavrocordatos, who I knew from the days of Triple Action Theatre, and who was now with a company called Hesitate and Demonstrate run by Geraldine Pilgrim. They weren't very strong on movement so Alex asked me to do workshops with them. That was it. Summer was coming to an end. I couldn't keep a family on this, so it was time to go back to Poland. I had collected so many books, a whole trunkload, and because I knew Hesitate and Demonstrate would be performing in Wrocław in a few days' time, at the beginning of October, I asked them to put my trunk of books into their props. I flew with Gabriela back to Poland, on my birthday, which, as you'll see, was a nice coincidence, and returned my passport, which was dodgy because it was the wrong one. Wojtek was still furious.

'The following day, I got a train to Gdańsk in order to sign another year's contract for lectures and because there wasn't enough time to return to Warsaw I caught a train from there to Wrocław where I met up with Geraldine and Alex. Sweet Gerry, this English lady from London, she really was a fantastic artist, very much into B-movies, her performances strongly based on visuals but quite different from ours in *Akademia Ruchu*. She relied on props that were authentic objects, their purpose being to convey a sense of magic and nostalgia. She would go to scrap yards to get doors from old trains so as to make a collage of images. Her most successful show was *Goodnight Ladies!* She was in love with old tunes, men in Borsalino hats, and was very much into spy stories. A couple of weeks earlier, we had been talking about possible future cooperation. So here she was in Wrocław. I had just returned my passport, signed the contract in Gdańsk, and now she says to me, "I have thought a bit more about this and I'd really like you to join Hesitate and Demonstrate." *Oh, my God!* I said, "Gerry, only two days ago, I was with my wife, looking for a job, and there's no saying what might happen here. I'll do it, yes, but it will be at least half a year before I can begin to apply for my private passport and find a replacement for my lectures. I can't go just like that. Two days ago, I could have. After all, this is not a liberal democracy." A few months later, in January, 1982, I was supposed to have been in New York in *Goodnight Ladies!* but because of the introduction of martial law a month earlier I couldn't even phone my mother across the street. I was stuck. I couldn't call Gdańsk, *especially* Gdańsk, because there was no telephone communication. I decided that was it, I wouldn't be able to leave. Now, bearing in mind Gerry's passion for spy stories, here I was, badly needing to communicate with her. I had all these fantasies, and, after all, we knew the Russians could invade any minute. I remember going to my friend who was a pilot with Polish Airlines, and writing, somewhere in his notebook, a letter to Gerry, which later he would tear out, maybe in Athens, maybe in Stockholm, put into an envelope and send to her. I began to think it was hopeless, and that I'd never be able to join her company, but then I heard a Polish punk rock group was touring abroad. I thought well, maybe things are not so tight after all. I went to the Polish Artists' Agency. I had an official contract with Gerry so the only thing left for me was to get a passport. As I could no longer do it privately, I needed a sponsor to cover for me. I asked them for a passport for my wife as well. That took a long time, almost a year. In September, they finally organised a passport for me, but then the Gdańsk police told Gabriela they'd lost her passport so at the last moment she couldn't travel. Hoping she would be able to join me soon, I took a boat to England. I didn't think I'd be leaving forever.'

This was to be, although he did not quite realise it at the time, a major turning point in Borkowski's life. As any cinéaste knows, there's something deeply poetic in the way trains, boats and planes mark those divisions that exist not just in time but in the soul as well.

Michał

Are those not an angel's wings, such as one finds in mediaeval images of warrior saints? Are they not beginning to sag a little? And that hand pressed against tilted head, does it not suggest disquietude? A worried saint for worrying times? The trousered angel whom a trouserless Borkowski evokes is the archangel Saint Michael or, in Polish, Michał, Commander-in-Chief of the angels loyal to God, and he is also patron of police officers, mariners, paratroopers and grocers. If a serpent crawls upon that rock, he'll place his bare foot on it. This is inadvisable. Where's his unsheathed sword, though, and his scales of justice? Are they hidden inside his shadow? Where *is* justice, within or without? And where's the sword that aims true?

Borkowski continued.

'The story I'm about to tell you, which took place exactly one year later, is quite a different one. It has to do with the number "33". I haven't read much Jung but when I was in Odense I just happened to pick up one of his books, I can't remember which one, where he presents his ideas regarding the stages in human life and the process of individuation that is supposed to occur in the human personality round about one's thirty-third year, which is the age Jesus Christ was when he died. Symbolically, according to Jung, "33" represents the end of life, the point at which one is given the opportunity to die spiritually in order to be reborn in some higher embodiment. All I am saying is that I read this and for the longest time I panicked, as I still do, about the passing of time. I started making all these calculations, counting the days from the day of my birth onwards, and what I did was to create this inner myth that on my thirty-third birthday I would die. I didn't know what kind of death it would be, maybe symbolic, maybe real, but *something* would happen. I prepared myself for this, not consciously, but it was something I kept returning to, thinking I'd only so many days to go. I had been settled in England for about a year. In September 1983, I was in Rotterdam, at De Lantaren Venster Theatre, working on a new production called *Shangri La*. My birthday would be spent there. Our set was extremely complicated and we were terribly under pressure, working long days, sometimes twenty hours at a time. Some of us were doing coke, not so much for the effects but simply because of exhaustion. I never wanted to because I was already high enough without it. I was staying at a cheap hotel, the Central, with Alex Mavrocordatos, my old friend from Triple Action Theatre, and after a long day's work we returned there, absolutely exhausted. Alex had some really good grass, which we smoked, sharing music on a Walkman. I was just falling asleep when I had this vision. It was God's voice, coming to me in a most beautiful way. It's not something one can properly convey in words. It wasn't a person but a *voice*, or, rather, a *presence*. It said: "Well, that's it. This is your thirty-third year. You didn't notice because you've been working so hard, but today's the day you'll die. You've had a problem with asthma, you are exhausted, and on top of it all you've had that stupid grass which is too strong. I'm sorry, but that'll be it." It was so frightening. I was sweating. During those last moments of your life you think about those whom you'll be most sorry to leave. I thought about Gabriela and my daughter, Alicia. I took out my photos of them and set them on the pillow so they'd know they were in my thoughts before I died. It was my own little theatre, all this getting ready to die. And then it came, a dark wave, getting darker, darker, and just when I thought *that's it, I'm going to die*, suddenly there came this flash of enthusiasm, and, soon after, relief that I'd passed through it somehow. The music that had been so low and dark suddenly became ecstatic. It was just the joy of being alive. I understood now that my love for Gabriela and Alicia, and theirs for me, had rescued me. And I thought it wasn't meant to be a real death but that symbolic one about which Jung wrote.

'I prepared to go to sleep when once again this music started, this time even lower and darker than before, and the ironic voice of God returned, saying, although not in words exactly: "What are you talking about, *the love of your wife and child*? That's ridiculous. They won't miss you at all. Alicia, who is only a year old, won't remember you. She'll probably have another father. So you can't rely on her. It may be a nice idea, but what are you thinking? And Gabriela? Who are you kidding?" What He said was true. We'd had a serious problem because when I left for England she was having an affair with a fellow student, which got more and more serious and would eventually be the cause of our separation. And now God was saying to me: "All you did may be very nice and sentimental, but who cares? She will be free of her problem and, by the way, did you really think you'd die because you smoked a few cigarettes? Do you really think you have control over this? No way! This is nothing to do with you. There are bigger things than you. You'll die, yes, but not just because of a few puffs on a joint. You see, Rotterdam is a major port and, as it happens, there is an Arabic terrorist in the room upstairs with a bomb, which right now he is manipulating and which will accidentally explode. You will die not because of your little adventures, but rather because it's time to." All this sounded terribly logical to me. God was telling me to be humble, telling me what a small world mine was, and what a measly thing my idea of death. I was just a link in a network of things that cannot be influenced and which, in any case, I couldn't understand. And maybe because there was such a beautiful structure to this vision, I began to think again, along the same lines. "Who'll miss me, if not my wife and child?" So I thought about my mum. Again I prepared for death. The same thing again, going *down, down, down*, convinced that any moment now the bomb upstairs would explode. And then again – "Stop! Stop!" – I had the same message, the same light, the feeling I'd somehow got through this, and that thoughts of my mother had rescued me. I didn't even have time to reflect on what happened a few minutes before and because of the grass I was in a euphoric state, full of happiness and life. Then the situation repeated itself. I was just beginning to enjoy myself when once more everything started to wind down. God said: "No, your mum isn't a good choice. She is not happy that you'll die, but, c'mon, let's be frank, you are thirty-three years old, and you've done nothing with your life. You were always such a promising child – you'd be this, you'd be that – but really there was nothing ever there. So actually your death will be a solution for her. It will be really horrible, of course, but she will be conscious of the fact that you *could* have been somebody, or, rather, that you were just *about* to be someone. Oh yes, and the idea of the bomb, no, no, it is not like that. You can't understand the mind of God. It is above normal understanding so all that business was just *your* construction. This is a typical human notion, this seeking for causes, at the end of which all will be logically explained, but no, it's not like that at all. Alex who's sleeping in the bed next to yours will suddenly get up, open his brand new knife, which he showed you earlier today, and kill you, just like that. It'll be for no reason, nothing you can explain. He'll do it out of madness." I shook Alex awake, crying, "I'm really sorry, but you're going to kill me in a minute. I forgive you." "What are you talking about?" he groaned. "Have you smoked too much dope or what?" I pleaded with him. "I don't expect you to comprehend this, but it'll happen just like that." "Okay, okay," he said, "go back to sleep." So I thought again, "Who'll miss me?" I thought about my sister. The same thing: I was going *down, down, down*, about to die, and I don't remember the rest because either I fell asleep or died. The next morning I woke up.

"Shit, I'm alive!" I remember thinking God could do with me what he liked and that my looking for a reason was the wrong attitude. It was the same with Alex in that he was wholly free to do as he liked. He could have killed me if he wanted to. There came a moment when I thought maybe I really did die. And then I thought that it was because of my sister Eva's help that I survived.'

Andrzej paused for a rare moment, allowing me time to absorb what he'd just told me. Something in me began to subside. This simply wasn't good enough, these drug-fuelled hallucinations of someone who'd gone without sleep, a certain amount of Slavic histrionics tossed in for good measure, and in godforsaken Rotterdam of all places. Whichever way I looked at it, this was a pot-head's shaggy dog tale. Why dredge up all that Sixties moonshine, especially when its beams took almost two decades to arrive? I heard a voice in me, saying, 'This will not do, not at all. Thank you, but no thank you', and just as I was mentally packing away Andrzej's sorry case he continued.

'That would have been the end of the story except that while drinking coffee later that morning I thought again about all those earlier calculations of mine and I realised, "Oh, my God, I've made a mistake!" The date I was heading towards wasn't the 29th of September *yesterday*. It was the 29th of September one year *earlier*.'

This I could believe absolutely because the very same thing happened to me on my last birthday, when I discovered I was in fact a year younger than I thought, and, besides, there's something in me that thinks we've got it all wrong anyway. When we turn forty-nine, for example, we are in fact entering our fiftieth year, just as when Andrzej thought he was entering his thirty-third it was really his thirty-fourth year. If he was counting, as he said he was, the days from his birth, rather than from his first birthday, then his error becomes quite explicable. There is also the distinct possibility that, like me, he is innumerate.

'All I had been waiting for, this radical change in my life, or whatever form my death would take, took place exactly one year earlier. What was I doing then? Suddenly I remembered. One year before, on that precise date, September 29th, 1982, the boat which I'd caught in Gdańsk arrived at midnight, at Folkestone, on the coast of England. It was so obviously a closure, such a precise date, and a kind of a death. And when you think I'd gone back to Poland on the same date, a couple of years before! When, later, I thought about whether I'd ever move back to Poland I thought no, probably never. What makes me think all this was written in the stars is all that nonsense of the night before, with the grass, which was *so* obvious, *so* boring and *so* explicable. All that stuff was merely an introduction to something of real substance, a true story about a special day, and it had nothing to do with what I smoked. Also, and this is something I found in my diaries, earlier that day I had been reading the Polish Romantic poets. This bit of our history also explains my state of mind at the time. After the failure of the 1830 uprising against Russia there was a period when they all gave up art and waited for a sign from God. There was this mystical Towiański Movement under the spell of which Adam Mickiewicz gave up writing and Juliusz Słowacki started producing mystical poetry. They were trying to make sense of what happened. They were, most of them, strongly religious. They couldn't understand why they'd lost Poland and in their effort to ascribe meaning to this they decided it must have been a plan in God's head and so they began looking for signs. This waiting for signs can be pleasurable, especially when you are lost and trying to make sense of where you are. There is that fanciful, slightly mediaeval, concept that reality is a book of signs. This attitude has always fascinated me, and earlier, as an art historian, I'd read much on iconography, symbols and their attributes. I had stuffed my brain with these books on symbols which, more or less consciously, allowed me to look at something and build connections and make my own stories from it. There is always in me this hope for a message.

'All year I had been waiting for that major event, and, here again, this is in my diaries, it occurred to me that maybe it had already happened and I had just ignored it. And this actually was the case, except that I got my dates wrong. Some time later, I was asked to write a play about this, but it was too difficult because really one needs to be telling this to someone, face to face. On the page it would seem like I was patching together a nice story. It would be so easy to shift the dates a little so as to make it work, which is what one does when one writes, but this was not literature. It was all true. We look for those gaps in logic and the key thing for me, and I am speaking out of my deepest conviction, which isn't so deep in everyday life because there we are forced to think logically most of the time, that our knowledge of the world is nothing compared to what it will be in two hundred years' time. Things will be so different that one should recognise just how pointless one's current reasoning is. Actually that area of darkness allows for fantastic hope. I do believe it is a question of focusing our attention, of noticing those strange things, and that all our accommodation of the brain works towards ignoring them simply because they disturb us. My arrival here was on St Michael's Day or Michaelmas. Michał, the Polish form of Michael, is my second name.'

I told Andrzej that I first arrived in England on 29 September 1973, and that this also was the date of W.H. Auden's death, which I remember clearly because I was in a fish and chip shop in Dover, marvelling at the fact that fish and chips really did come wrapped in newspaper, and such was my wonderment at this simple fact of English existence that not even Auden's wrinkled face on the TV screen flickering above the counter, and the funereal tones of the newsreader, could entirely dispel my pleasure. And it was on that date, precisely twenty years later, that my first collection of poems was published, and when at the launch for the book I gave a reading from it one of the people in the audience was Auden's niece. And stranger still, for better or worse, Auden never really shone in my literary universe. I'm of another ilk altogether, closer to things that are not all close. When I told Borkowski this date also represented the closing of a chapter in my life, he cried, 'The angel's gaze!'

Maria

She is a troubling creature this one, at least to modern sensibilities, all hips and small brain, such as one finds in Venus figurines from the Palaeolithic Age. She has no purpose other than to be fertile. A pagan mother goddess, she's yet to be elevated to *Theotokos* ('God-bearer'), she who shall be Mary or Maria, Mother of God. For now, though, no virgin she, she's rooted in her sex. She aims to please. She's as primordial as a dinosaur egg omelette. She's got legs longer than Cyd Charisse's.

'Maybe I was being pretentious – I was fourteen or fifteen at the time – but I liked the idea of being given the name "Maria" at my confirmation. The usual male version is "Marian". I remember the bishop getting the slip of paper on which was written the name he was about to give me. "Maria?" he said. He thought for a moment. "Okay, then. *Maria.*" Now I've begun to treat "Maria" in a more obvious colloquial way, as an extra protector in my name, just in the same way you would give anyone a name that evoked the patronage of one of the holy apostles. Holy Mary is more important therefore gives more protection, but to begin with I wasn't especially thinking of "Maria" as the Mother of God even though all that Catholic background is important for me. The Polish writer, Artur Maria Swinarski, was probably responsible. I remember as a child reading a book of his satiric verses and thinking how fantastic it was that a man could call himself "Maria". Rainer Maria Rilke too. You want to know certain things are allowable and so there were these two examples. When I was still at school and trying to make sense of my life, I'd get these weird ideas. I had this French auntie who lived in Warsaw, Aunt Ella – she was really French, spoke no Polish – and when she died I inherited from her a *tricolore* ribbon and a thick *Petit Larousse*. I remember, aged fourteen, looking through it at all the small reproductions of the faces of great people to see if there was anyone who looked like me, so I could live *his* life. It was a rather Borgesian idea this choosing another person's life that would provide a map for mine. I didn't find anyone. Another reason I looked for another face was because when I was a teenager I was so sensitive about mine, which looked like a monkey's. As a child I sucked my thumb and, so the doctors say, developed a protruding mouth. I was called Titus, which is a nice Roman name, except that in those days it was the name of the monkey in a very popular Polish comic.'

'Do you consider yourself Catholic?'

'I *say* I'm Catholic and probably it's a lie because I don't practise. I haven't been to confession for thirty years. At the beginning of the 1990s, I was in Poznań and there was this small church, a kind of Romanesque, one of the oldest churches in the city. I noticed a priest in the darkness of the confessional and I thought this would be a fantastic place to talk. But then I realised it would be too difficult, the obvious problem being that I would be asked to confess as sins things I do not consider sins. If there was a written list of sins then maybe I could have a discussion with him, saying, "Look, I don't think this is a sin", but then it would be awkward for the priest too because I could not promise not to do it again. I wouldn't be able to say I'd avoid those love adventures because I can't really consider them as sins. If I were really sorry for something that *I* thought was wrong that would be great but I can't be forced to admit to things I don't believe are crimes. Obviously with an intelligent priest maybe I could get into some kind of agreement that yes, I am alone with my soul. But there is also something beautiful in the idea of confession, the humility of meeting another person who might be stupider than you. There again, like most Poles I am emotionally attached. I cherish the Catholic rootedness in pagan times, especially with the images and all those emotional elements which in Protestantism I find too much reduced to mere letters and words. With the cult of saints, and all the physicality, that part of the Mother Church is so much more sensual whereas for Protestants I think it is very much the religion of the Book. I think that the bridge between pagan cults and cults of saints and the usage of images and sculptures is more deeply rooted in the past and that the cleansing which came with the Renaissance and the Reformation made the Church all that much more controlling. I might have enormous respect for theological knowledge but for me the vagueness and physicality are more attractive. At the same time it is the very thing that irritates me when I go to a Polish church. There is all that theatricality, so much of it and not enough *thinking*, but those two elements do provide some strange emotional power. The relics, for example, are fantastic.'

'Would it be a mistake,' I asked him, 'to attribute your paintings and prints to "Andrzej" and the glass paintings to "Maria"? There is, in the latter, the iconography one associates with religiously inspired art.'

Borkowski seemed to leap at this. *Yes, yes, yes.*

'I really enjoyed making those glass paintings partly because I was really missing, and I still do, that fantastical world of iconography and legend. I did a few in Poland, mostly as presents for people. Those were not directly connected with religious subjects whereas the ones I did here are rather more so. The situation from which the glass paintings arose was that I'd booked a space in the POSK [*Polski Ośrodek Społeczno-Kulturalny*] Gallery in Hammersmith and I thought rather than show my prints wouldn't it be nice to have something that would directly address a mainly Polish audience. I really wanted to connect those paintings with literature, with scrolled texts hidden behind them. One of the big childhood inspirations for me was Kipling's *Just So Stories.* I loved the richness of that connection between word and image. I thought that maybe I, too, could try to manipulate the tradition, make adaptations to it, and find other stories behind those images, which is something contemporary art doesn't allow much space for. I was inspired by Islamic art, Mogul miniatures in particular. I concentrate mainly on contemporary art and so I really miss those lectures on mediaeval iconography and also those stories about the saints, the fantastic imagination you find in them. It's a pity it is so difficult to communicate this because already it has become lost knowledge. Also I really like those strong, vibrant Mexican colours, the way they clash, which is so joyful, so physical.'

And then there is Andrzej's other art that is much darker in tone, and which he attributes to a single letter.

'N'

This one's from a child's literature, some fable at which telling the poor mite is expected to sleep easy. Sweet dreams, then. It's no accident this creature has six fingers. What Borkowski needed to do was to find a rock that would split his image. What he had by way of inspiration was already shelved in his vast mental store. At one point in his career, inspired by a painted image on the wall of a caveman's cave, he adopted a six-fingered hand as his logo. It is what made him, *what*

makes any artist, an alien. Small wonder he finds beautiful the name that in others, especially those coming to this country for the first time, inspires a sense of grievance: Alien Registration Office (ARO). There, quite happy to be an alien, he applied for his resident's certificate. Did they ask for his fingerprints, all six of them? The most famous polydactyl was Goliath: 'And yet again there was war at Gath, where was a man of great stature, whose fingers and toes were four and twenty, six on each hand, and six on each foot and he also was the son of the giant' (1 Chronicles 20:6).

Hannibal Lecter had six fingers until he decided to remove one.

Borkowski appeared to have only five.

'I did a peculiar drawing of four monsters in a cave, in front of a gate. Only later did I think about it more. What did it mean? I then got the idea those four beings were all *me* inside in my mother's womb and that they would join together as one, as a single person, before going through that gate into the world outside.

'Andrzej is a man's name and Michał, that birdlike creature, is an angel's, and there, on the left of the picture, is Maria although she's pretty horrible. It was obvious to me there was something missing. Who was that fourth figure? So I kept thinking about the drawing and all that business about wholeness, those four elements in me which are like cardinal points – man, woman, angel … and then I realised I needed another identity, one that had to do with sex, earth, darkness, the body, maybe an animal of some kind, or even a devil

which in me would be the angel's opposite. I settled on the letter "N". Actually it came to me naturally. I didn't want it to be a full name because "N" is the Nameless One – Jules Verne's Captain Nemo, which in Latin means "no man" or "no-body", or Odysseus when he is asked by Polyphemus his name and he replies "Nobody". I have a passion for that letter. It's usually connected with water and fish and with the deeps. There is a beautiful chapter in a book [*Fundamental Symbols: The Universal Language of Sacred Science*] by the French writer, René Guénon, who was a convert to Islam. "N" is *noon* in both Hebrew (נ) and Arabic (ن). The Arabic with its open shape and dot above supposedly represents a seed in a cauldron, and also, according to him, it suggests Jonah in the whale, in that darkness before he returns as the human being he was before. Guénon, probably, is what most influenced my choice. And then there's all that cabbalistic speculation in which "N" equals 50 but it's too complicated to go into here. "N" is for me such a fantastic subject. You enjoy the possibilities! I like the idea of the Portuguese writer, Fernando Pessoa, creating several identities for himself and persisting with them. When I took on "N" I thought it would be a good idea to define more those genders and characters that are part of me. I could associate with this one or that one, and then more fully develop it. "N" is also an anarchic figure although I wonder how much I allow him to be. I made some pornographic, *on the edge of nearly disgusting*, drawings that could be easily attributed to him.'

'Your experience in Rotterdam belongs to which side?'

'I don't know! Who was talking? I really don't know. I think maybe all four were endangered there. My hope was to die in order to be reconstructed in some higher form, but I didn't go any further. I'm still immature.'

Immaturity is an obsession in modern Polish literature, especially in the work of Witold Gombrowicz, it being something one either rejects or embraces. Would this have been the case had it not been for the fact that all too often in Poland's history adulthood was rudely imposed upon childhood? Were its most beautiful martyrs not always children?

All Four into One Go

A crash in the Alps, a real one, marked the beginning of the end for Hesitate and Demonstrate. Another crash, a spurious one, was engineered by people without faces. An EEC dictate stipulated that the company would now have to seek *European* money rather than funds from individual countries. With this came other kinds of restrictions – having to employ local actors, for example – which would go against the artistic vision of a company that allowed for hardly any division between its creators and actors. Blandness is all. In 1985, the company went bankrupt and for Borkowski, apart from a brief spell elsewhere, this marked the end of his career in theatre. It was, of course, a certain kind of theatre. It would need to be in order to accommodate him. In 1986, he returned to London and went to the Courtauld Institute where he got a second MA in art history, which gradually led to a post at Brighton University where he still teaches.

I couldn't help but notice a faltering, an actual slowing down, in Borkowski's voice.

'Obviously I'm *nowhere*. The fact that I came to London so late in life probably did not allow me to ever be *completely* here. I was dragging behind me those thirty-three years and all those attitudes that had been much earlier created in me. On the other hand, I feel a sense of great freedom here and I can see all the possibilities – I see them, and yet I am not able to use them as much as I'd like to because I'm still haunted by the ghosts of the past. I really cut it when I first came here. I was doing another kind of theatre, and was successful at it. Obviously there were ups and downs such as any young person might have but the moment I entered this empty space, after the theatre collapsed, I was on my own. It was now up to me to find something else, and among the various options that presented themselves was finding this reconnection to Poland. I wrote some small articles for the *Polish Daily* (*Dziennik Polski*). At first I treated this as a small, quite unimportant, patriotic gesture but this, I soon discovered, was an umbilical cord that had never been cut. And so I continued to write short articles, mostly reviews of exhibitions. You feel there's an opening for a while and you think, yes, you've had a good response and you have found a place for yourself. You didn't fight for it, they invited you, but now it's become that big mother. You can be the most important Polish critic there, rather than try to be an important British one. You find those niches and suddenly you are sucked into what feels very much like a trap.'

'And so, what is the nature of this other place, this London within a London?'

'Very early on, whenever I met up with Poles, I felt there was a normal British society and then there was this copy of it which is Polish immigrant society recreated somewhere on the outskirts of the former. It bears no relation to the bigger one, but because it's small it's so much easier to manipulate. Meanwhile, you still see that other world in front of you, which is out there on the street. I keep returning to this painful metaphor of a Poland in miniature, as being a dangerous place to step into, because once you're inside you are seduced by it. You might have the same capabilities on the outside, but they're no longer as important because it's too big, this London where you are just one person standing next to millions. I'm terrified by how completely isolated I have become. Such articles as I write are mainly for the Polish press and even my exhibitions are for a mainly Polish audience. I do not have any part now in normal British cultural life. I never learned how to. That's really a problem of the will, however, and of not knowing what I want. I'm too much of a surfer. I enjoy the fact I'm on a wave. I never looked for work. Did I apply for that job in Brighton? *No*. One day somebody asked me to give a lecture. *Yes, why not.* Will you give another one? *Yes, why not.* It wasn't like I was choosing something. I was talking to my students about that Nietzschean will to power, which I probably despise, but then I think it's something missing in me. I have allowed myself to be swallowed by those huge cosmoses. I don't really get to make my point. My question to Grotowski was this: "Is it ethical to say, *I'm here*?" I want to be in total empathy with everything, but basically it's a kind of mirror in which I am not reflected at all because I'm everything and everybody. I think, "Why should they listen to *me*? I should be listening to *you*." I'm speaking out of the attitude that one shouldn't impose oneself. The things I do are the things that simply happen to me, that are dragged out of me, which are born of circumstance rather than of having to make decisions. People say, "Oh, would you like to do this?" and so I do it because it's another interesting adventure. You go with it because you are greedy and because you want to squeeze life to the maximum but squeezing is not just accepting – it is also *deciding* whether to take it or not. There is a frightening richness of possibilities.

'There was this famous figure in Poland, at the beginning of the last century, Franciszek Fiszer, a huge man with a beard and renowned for his *gourmandise* and his wit and humour. He would come like the seasons to Warsaw, to the Ziemiańska Café in spring, spend all day eating and drinking with writers and artists, and then, in late autumn, he would disappear into the residence of a wealthy cousin where during the winter months he'd do nothing but read. The thing about him is he didn't leave anything of his own behind but he was in everyone's diaries. Fiszer *lived*, his material was *life*, and I remember how for me he represented another option in life. Is it about solidifying, producing something for eternity, or is it about squeezing that life as much as possible? I'm pretty sure I didn't really squeeze it all but at least I have been greedy. I don't care so much about leaving something behind.

'*What is London to me?* Well, there is that Polish London, which is quite a strong presence. I never wanted to belong to it but I did in the end. I'm teaching in Brighton, and maybe I was tempted to move there, thinking it would be easier to handle, but I didn't do so because of that richness I recognise. I'm conscious of not having tasted enough of London. There are still Indian and Jewish areas to explore. I'm angry sometimes about being too much inside Polish London because I'd like to learn more about the other ones. It's also a London of the mind because I lived in different parts of it and had different experiences and so when I go through it now I find myself travelling in time. I go to a certain area and I remember this is where I had my asthma attack, I go somewhere else, Notting Hill, and this is where I was paid with hash for my drawings, and then I go to Camden Town, which was the base for Hesitate and Demonstrate, and then Charing Cross Road with all those amazing bookshops. It is travelling through your life. So obviously, in that respect, it is *my* London. I remember trying out this experiment with regard to its geometry, which is something I did in Poland once. When I fell in love with Gabriela I was living in Warsaw and she was living in Gdańsk and I remember taking a compass and making these circles and then I discovered that the points where I was, where I first met her, and where we spent our first holiday together, made a perfect triangle. I tried to do something similar with London, an art project involving a map of the city, finding all the places I lived in, marking them on transparent paper and then, choosing a centre, superimposing this on a map, trying to see if by doing so I could derive any possible poetic meanings from this. Once again, I was looking for signs. I had a problem, though, because I didn't know where London's centre was. Was it the City? Was it Piccadilly Circus? Was it Nelson's Column in Trafalgar Square?'

I will stop here. It is not where we stopped in our conversation but it's as good a place to stop as any because, as Ezra Pound writes, 'What is the use of talking, and there is no end of talking, / There is no end of things in the heart.' (Actually it's from the Chinese of Rihaku, or, rather, Li Bai or Li Po or even Li Bo, but it's Ezra all the same.) The sense one has of Borkowski is that with him one could go on forever, for such are the twists and turns of his remarkable mind. And then, of course, one trembles a little at the idea of *forever* because eternity comes at the expense of *shape*. Maybe, though, this is not really such a good place to leave Borkowski because when I last saw him he was in a black hole. I could see it in his face. I could hear it in his voice. It is no place to leave him, not when he dazzles the eye with his luminous images, and just when he seems to be on the verge of some fresh adventure. And so I shall settle where I began, on an image that is more a product of his thinking than I could have at first imagined, and which contains the signs he so fondly looks for in every place.

The man-angel clutching his magic wand comes to the rescue, reminding Andrzej and Michał and Maria and N that the future is not yet empty of things to be done and things to be made.

A Tree Grows in Brixton

Brian Chikwava's Dark Adventure in 'Harare North'

There stands in front of the Ritzy Cinema in Brixton one of London's mightiest trees. The sun can barely squeeze through its branches. All that surrounds it, even the buildings, seems to bow down in obeisance. Should I apologise for the hyperbole? I won't. A writer's business is to make a reader smell the leaves. Some trees, though, one simply can't ignore. This one, especially in summer, is a magnet for people who come and congregate there. They are mostly from elsewhere, which is to say they are, many of them, Africans who come here seeking other Africans. A man from Zaire waiting for a friend from Uganda might find himself eavesdropping on a conversation between two people from Namibia and Senegal. They all speak English or else some variant of it that sweetly rolls and bubbles. The language that shackled them once is that which now releases them from mutual incomprehension. There has been in recent decades a demographical shift in the borough, from West Indian to African: for evidence of this one need only step out of Brixton underground.

At the station entrance an African handed me a business card for a Mr Madiba ('from birth a gifted African spiritual healer and advisor') who deals with problems which *no matter how difficult* he can solve – 'no disappointment' – whether it be black magic, love voodoo, sexual impotence, business transactions, exams, relationships (both wanted and unwanted), gambling and court cases. The wording was suspiciously similar to another card I was given by someone else, also African, also at the tube entrance, for a Mr Sheikh Kabba, 'from birth a gifted African spiritual healer and advisor'. The cards, which are of an odd size, measure the same. Methinks there's a clear case of spirit theft here. And then I wandered through Brixton Market where I saw a sign for the African Shopping Centre where one may buy the makings for *egwusi*, *edikang-ikong* or *ogbono* soup, and there you can also obtain *fufu*, dried yellow *mystus* fish, *cocoyam* and *susumba* berries; then there are the various African fabric shops, the K Ace Afro Hair & Beauty Superstore, and, plastered to the wall of an Afro-Caribbean music and video shop, a movie poster displaying a buxom Princess Tyra in *Princess Tyra 3* (distributed by Venus Films, Accra, Ghana). Africa is everywhere. Sunday morning congregations at nearby St Matthew's Church are, so I'm told, almost wholly African. And where once one heard only reggae, these days one might hear *jùjú* from Nigeria, *kudoro* from Angola, *coupé décalé* from the Ivory Coast or even *sungura* from Zimbabwe.

The air particles jive upon fresh currents.

I figured I already knew what genus of tree it is, but because I am, at best, an uncertain botanist what I sought was an authoritative voice. I approached a policeman standing beside his bicycle. Surely he'd know, he who seemed so very much the custodian of that tree. Something about him struck me as a throwback to a sweeter period of Ealing comedies, when a bobby would enter upon the scene of a crime as timidly as a bride stepping for the first time into a bridal chamber. I asked him what kind of tree it was, and he started a little as if he had never seen it before.

'Why, it's … it's a *green* tree,' he replied. 'I've got one of them in front of my house. It leaves a sticky mess all over the ground.'

I didn't have the heart to tell him what he had at home was not one of these at all but a lime tree. I went into the public library, which is beside the Ritzy, and headed straight for the information desk, where a young woman sat at her computer. I asked her what kind of tree grew outside. She blushed a little, saying she really ought to know because, after all, she'd been working there for eight years but if I was prepared to wait a little she'd phone her father who is an arboriculturalist and knows every single tree in Brixton. Such moments as these make me feel like I'm one of the Famous Five. The answer came back first in Latin, *Platanus x acerifolia* and then, yes … it was indeed a London plane. I explained to her I was on my way to see a local writer who in his novel *Harare North* describes it as a chestnut tree.

I walked down Atlantic Road which becomes Railton, crossed Chaucer Road, Spenser Road, Shakespeare Road – a small poetic galaxy floating inside Brixton's prose universe – and then, after noting that their names had been set down in proper chronological order, turned right into Milton Road, which is where the Zimbabwean writer and musician Brian Chikwava lives. I knew I'd come to the right place when even before I'd spotted the house number I saw through the window, hanging on the wall, an African *batiki* textile.

§

Asking a man to reminisce when he has only recently departed the manufactory of his memories is not always the surest approach to making a verbal picture, not when there's not been time enough for him to assemble what truly has value. What he'll do, to steal an image from Chikwava's own page, is blink like a lost goat. It takes quite a while for there to be created in the brain a hierarchy of what's most important in one's life and when finally it is made, and in the auditorium the lights are switched on one by one, the result is, as with all good theatre, true bordering on false. Our biographies are, give or take a little, what we choose. The young, meanwhile, live in the realm of the immediate. An older man will keep his guitars, both of them, in their cases and not, as Chikwava does, on their stands ready for performance. This grappling with the here and now rather than with what's been and gone explains to some extent the inventiveness of youth. *Harare North* is rambunctiously inventive. It is a prose that simply loved being made.

While the book will not serve, thank goodness, as a blueprint for Chikwava's life it does contain many elements of direct experience. It draws to such a degree on people and places in Brixton that it comes as a surprise to learn that some of them are pure invention. Also it is a marvellous depiction of a certain species of émigré experience. The story is told, to great effect, in a kind of literary patois, maybe not quite what one finds in the townships but on the page it is most persuasive. When one first hears it – and one *hears* it rather than *reads* it – the immediate impulse is to laugh because of the speaker's accurate misuse of language. Soon enough, though, one sees what exactly one is laughing at – the tragedy that is a whole country's.

There's a bigger problem, though, which is not really a problem at all, and it's the narrator's voice, which is that of a Mugabe supporter. Aged twenty or thereabouts, he is one of 'them boys of the jackal breed', the infamous Green Bombers, the ZANU-PF youth organisation created by Border Gezi, the late Minister of Youth, and whose members are brainwashed in training camps or, if not brainwashed exactly, are offered the prospect of jobs in the army or with the police. The Green Bombers mete out justice, calling it 'forgiveness', which means breaking bones, murder sometimes. Often, 'lugging football-size eyes' they join up for no other reason than it is the easiest option in life available to them, but invariably the jobs they've been promised do not materialise. It is because our narrator goes overboard in his zeal for the cause that he gets himself into trouble in 'Zim' and has to flee to England in order to raise the US$5000 that will bail him out with the 'hyena' policemen back home. That Chikwava should have made the narrator's voice so attractive, so comical at times, is one of the dark marvels of this book. The speaker, thus humanised, is himself a victim of circumstance and yet just when you think redemption might be around the corner for him he finds it impossible to effect a real shift in his mentality:

> The president can come out to whip you with the truth. Truth is like snake because it is slippery when it move and make people flee in all directions whenever it slither into crowds ... Comrade Mugabe is powerful wind; he can blow snake out of tall grass like it is piece of paper – lift it up into wide blue sky for everyone to see. Then when he drop it, people's trousers rip as they scatter to they holes.

If this is the loud-mouthed talk of a bully 'spinning jazz numbers', it is also the literary invention of a man who is himself deeply gentle.

Brian Chikwava is modest, bashful even, a bit uncomfortable with the demands expected of him, speaking in public, for example, and is seemingly bemused by the attention his first book has received, all of it positive, and yet he is steely enough to be wary of the traps a little success can lead one into. When I tell him his biggest danger is in being thought of as an exotic African with dreadlocks in London and that this could put him inside a literary ghetto, although admittedly quite a nice one, he laughs wildly with something I take to be recognition. 'Writing,' he jokes, 'what a dubious career!' I wish I could reproduce his laughter in prose. It would take up a space

considerably bigger than this page. And whatever size that'll be, still it'll spill over the edges. It punctuates our conversations at regular intervals, a laugh that is like the breaking apart of a star, which is absolutely genuine, and just when you think it is over there comes a couple of salvoes more. It is, perhaps, the most delightful laugh I have ever encountered. When pressed further on the matter of being a writer Chikwava says that to describe himself so makes him feel like a charlatan, which, in a world where charlatanry rules, strikes me as evidence enough he is true.

§

'Harare North' is what people in Harare, Zimbabwe call London. ('Harare South' is Johannesburg.) The novel may be read as being about immigration and exile and the misfortune visited upon those who seek to relocate themselves without making the effort it requires to assimilate. The narrator may not yet know how to assimilate but at least he has got a hold of first principles:

> That kind of style we have to put inside bin, I tell Shingi. It important to pay big attention to some of them subtly things. I know how these things work. Also keep the native way down in the hole because if he jump out he can cause disorder and then no mother is safe in all of Harare North. Don't say, to them English people, 'How can I get to Animal Something?' when you want to say, 'How can I get to Elephant Castle?'

Note the skilfully missed ampersand.

That said, the book works on a whole other level which is, ultimately, more profound and goes straight to the darkness that enters the hearts of such people. *Mamhepo*, which translates as 'evil airs' or 'bad winds' or what we, in our infinitely superior wisdom, call 'mental illness', is what happens when we have angered the ancestral spirits (*mudzimu*). We who take our bearings from them must treat them with due reverence otherwise all hell breaks loose. *Mamhepo*, by the time we reach the final pages, seems to infect even the prose itself. There is no escaping the avenging spirits (*ngosi*) and, what's more, they can operate at a great distance.

I asked Chikwava to tell me about *mamhepo*.

'It's something that has become very much a part of our folklore but although one hears things I have never actually come across anyone with it. But then maybe I wouldn't have known if I had. What happens is that if a member of one family does something wrong to a member of another, such as killing him, even if it's an accident he has to make up for it somehow and if he doesn't the spirit of the one who was wronged will return and maybe take away members of his family one by one, sometimes until they are all gone. I think the belief still survives in our culture as a moral force or as a way of getting people not to do wrong to others. In the 1970s, during the war with Mozambique and Zambia, which was a horrible time, you heard a lot about guerrillas suffering from *mamhepo*. Of course you were never really sure if that's what it was. A modern psychoanalyst would probably describe it as Post-Traumatic Stress Disorder but the way it was seen then was that some of those guerrillas had done horrendous things, especially to civilians, people they would kill for no reason whatsoever, and as a result they would go loopy or be afflicted with this *mamhepo*. It was perceived as something that had come back to take revenge on those who had killed innocent people.'

'Can the *ngosi* follow one all the way to London, as they appear to do in the book?'

'Those avenging spirits will stop following you if you come here, re-imagine yourself and become a completely different animal, but as long as you remain within the Zimbabwean community and its culture, that is, inside its body of belief, then you are still within their reach.'

Another, less virulent, cause for *mamhepo* connects to the role of ancestral spirits in Ndebele and Shona belief systems: if a relative dies and one fails to perform the ritual of *umbuyiso* the spirit of the departed, normally a positive guiding force, will become irritable and will cause trouble. It can also operate on a wider scale in that being cut off from the influence of an ancestor can cause drought, floods, crop failure or problems of a tribal nature. It can even bring havoc to Brixton, where the narrator and his friend Shingi have failed to observe *umbuyiso* for their deceased mothers. The *umbuyiso* ritual, which involves slaughtering an animal – an ox for a male or a cow for a female – singing, dancing and drinking fermented *chibuku* beer made from sorghum, usually takes place about a year after the funeral. It signals what in Western culture is called 'closure'. At least, rather than resort to psychobabble, the Shona and the Ndebele beat the drums and celebrate.

They also beat the drums to summon forth the *mudzimu.*

'I remember being taken by my parents to my maternal grandparents' village of Monde near Victoria Falls. My mother spent a lot of time there, living with her parents. It is one of the family traditions in Zimbabwe that after getting married and having a child the wife goes and spends time with her parents to get them used to their new grandson. That village put me in touch with the old traditions. My grandfather who was called Mnkandla was what they call a *sangoma* or spirit medium. There were these ceremonies, which were quite moving and, at times, terrifying. They were always held at night, and the villagers would come, singing these songs in such a way, going on and on and on, without ever seeming to tire, until they hypnotised themselves. At about midnight my grandfather would move into the centre of the circle where he would dance. As he was Ndebele and descended from the Zulu he would be dressed in full Zulu attire – leopard skins, red and black fabric, some feathers. When you see it, it is frightening but rather mystical at the same time. This gentle old man who I had been so close to suddenly became someone I didn't recognise. There was this scary look in his eyes, and then he continued to dance for a while longer until in the middle of some song something took over and began to possess him. At the centre of my grandparents' homestead there was an old tree that had been cut down years before and all that remained of it was a stump. He would run to that stump and sit there and the people would follow him there, surround him again, by which point he had completely shifted into something else, and, depending on which of his ancestors entered him, he would begin to talk in his or her voice. It was freaky. When I saw this one of the female ancestors spoke through him in an old woman's voice. It is almost as if there was a psychological flip of some kind. Often I think about these things and because I am sceptical to the point of cynicism I think, okay, there must be some kind of trick here. Why I say this is because when an ancestral voice speaks through someone, people actually stop and listen and take it seriously. If my grandfather had said the same things when he was in a normal state nobody would have listened to him. Maybe what was said through him had to do with some problem in the family or within the community. So it would be like advice.'

'Would you look upon him as a creative spirit in your life?'

'Traditionally, of course, one is supposed to respect one's elders but now I wonder if this old man wasn't tricking us with this *sangoma* thing. It is a gift in a way, the ability to just flip into some other character, but I doubt he could have been really possessed. I look back on him now and think to myself, "So this old man had some tricks up his sleeve!"'

'If you believe in these things, though, don't they become real?'

'Maybe, but still I find it very hard to believe. The modern world gives me certain tools which I use in order to engage with that other culture. The real talent must surely lie in not having people see through you. My grandfather had this but those of the new generation are drawing from a different culture, which is very different from that which he drew from. Sometimes these people only pretend they are possessed. They get rumbled pretty quickly though. The younger ones, when they try it, end up falling flat on their faces because there is nothing in the culture to support them. You see them later on, looking sheepish because everyone else has seen through them. It has become commercialised. It used to be free, there was no exchange of money, whereas now they are like these *sangomas* for whom you get cards at the tube station. My grandfather, on the other hand, had experienced a lot more and, unlike the younger generation, knew the old traditions, and so he could play this thing to a lot of people.'

'This would suggest that in your own lifetime you have seen a split in your culture between old and new. Your grandfather was the last of his generation to be able to maintain this tradition. All this must have fed your poetic imagination.'

'Yes, but in a very scary way. Our culture and mythology are pretty terrifying. It scared me to see these things and to hear those stories. You also had these people who practised witchcraft and who could supposedly morph into owls, go and spy on people, and then fly back and float evil. There were a lot of owls back then and the moment it became dark and I saw them, I thought, "My God, we are surrounded!"'

Owl can call your name too.

'Was that your grandfather's main role in the village?'

'The *sangoma* thing he did only occasionally, maybe once or twice a year, otherwise he was a herbalist. He would take me out into the forest, showing me these different herbs and what you could do with them. I was young then and not so interested in this but he was so fond of me and he believed that I, too, would become a spirit medium.'

'But you *are* a spirit medium in that you write stories through which come all these voices.'

'Yes, in that way!'

§

A memory of Chikwava's grandfather informs one passage in particular, arguably the most sinister in the book because of what it takes in the culture and bends out of shape:

> The past always give you the tools to handle the present. Add small bit of crooked touch to what you do and everyone soon gets startled into silence and start paying proper attention and respect to you. Every jackal boy know that style; drop in crazy laughter in some crazy place during interrogation and any traitor will listen up. It's not accident that 'skill' and 'slaughter' start with a crooked letter. Every jackal boy know that too. Remove the crooked touch from each of them those two words and suddenly you kill laughter.

What is truly alarming is that the speaker is based on someone

Chikwava met, one of 'them immigrants that spend time mixing rhythm and politics under the chestnut tree'.

'I met this Ugandan outside the Ritzy. You get all sorts of different characters there, a mix of people that is normally hidden but you find them hanging out there. I became curious about those people. I think they go there for different reasons, maybe because they are lonely or because they don't know what to do with themselves at home. They come from all over Africa, all over the world. They spend a lot of time chatting and so I eavesdrop and listen to their conversations trying to work out what they are about. One day I found myself talking to this Ugandan, a perfectly normal figure, striped shirt, cap, quite handsome, and then he started telling me these stories which were quite incredible, about how he had been in Joseph Kony's Lord's Resistance Army in Uganda.'

A continent that has produced many a mad figure can have produced few madder than Joseph Kony, who, as self-styled prophet and spirit medium to the Holy Ghost, bases his campaign of terror on a reading of the Ten Commandments. *Mamhepo* seems to have claimed him whole. One story has it that each year he ascends a high hill where, covered with oil from the Yao plant, he lies in the sun for several days at a time, with red termites crawling all over him, lacerating his skin. Almost 20,000 children have been abducted by him, many of them forced to serve as child soldiers. Often they have been made to kill their own parents. They have been told that if they draw crosses in holy oil on their chests they will be made resistant to bullets. Any soldier who has ever fought for him will have committed atrocities.

'What happened is that this guy got captured by government forces and imprisoned for a while. Something went wrong with the trial. He did not go to prison but he had to leave the country and so he came here, claiming asylum. I suspect he made no mention of Joseph Kony. He still wanted to go back there but didn't know how to. Anyway, even after spending a whole year here, he had this strange yearning to be out there with Kony, carrying his AK47. Although he must have been a killer, he didn't talk about it. I remember at the time it got me thinking about how many other people like him had claimed asylum. I knew there were Rwandans somewhere about, and so I figured there must be Green Bombers as well.'

'Was he as comical as your narrator?'

'No, but what I found odd was that he did not see anything wrong with what he was saying. I wasn't sure whether he didn't know or was just putting on an act for me but I found it quite hilarious. I met him only the once. I went back, thinking I'd meet him again, but no, I never saw him again. This meeting stuck in my mind for a long time.'

There would seem to be only one possibility of redemption for the narrator and it resides in the memories he has of his mother, whose death a couple of years before is caught in a wonderful dream image: 'Knitting pins drop and go clink clink on cold concrete floor, Tanganda Tea spill everywhere.' *Your house is like your head*, says his mother in that same dream. *You have to keep sweeping it clean if you want to stay sane.* The narrator's inability to put this formula into reverse leads to disastrous consequences. So, too, does his failure to do *umbuyiso* for her.

'Yes, there is that aspect of him,' Chikwava continues, 'and in Zimbabwean culture this whole business of *umbuyiso* often gets people onto guilt trips. What people believe is that when someone dies his spirit goes to some indeterminate place and you have to perform *umbuyiso* to bring it back home.'

Where, though, is home? The narrator's friend Shingi needs to do *umbuyiso* for his mother as well but the very ground where she is buried has been subjected to Operation *Murambatsvina*, which translates as 'drive out trash', Mugabe's policy of sending in bulldozers to demolish the poorer communities. It is a peculiarly vicious campaign that has displaced approximately two and a half million people. And where the narrator's mother is buried is about to be requisitioned by an emerald mining company, with the Green Bombers making sure the inhabitants are removed in advance, growing news of which the narrator chooses not to countenance. Propaganda is what he calls it. There is a passage in the book where self-deception and self-awareness join forces:

> You always know more than you believe in but always choose what you believe in over what you know because what you know can be so big that sometimes it is useless weapon, you cannot wield it proper and, when you try, it can get your

> head out of gear and stop you focusing. Soon you lose the game and end up dying beyond your means in Harare North, leaving behind debts and shabby clothes.

The narrator's situation is further complicated by a terrible crime he committed in Zimbabwe. Whatever that crime was, there's something in the very prose itself that won't quite admit to it, except in only very brief glimpses. Clearly, though, he did something terrible to an opposition supporter. Why should there be such a fuss, he wonders, when 'the winds is blowing through the nation and making trees swing in every direction but the police only want to know how one leaf fall from tree'.

'Yes,' says Chikwava, 'for the narrator to admit to his crime would be to admit to a lot because really he doesn't want to change his ways and maybe it is also a fear of opening himself up to the truth. Once you admit to such crimes then you have to repudiate them for the whole of your life.'

Another thing about the narrator is his ability to keep a tab on finances such that with great ease, at any given moment, he can give the current exchange rate.

> Money is like termite. The more desire you have to catch it, the more you scare it down into its hole. You don't try to catch it by its head, but let it crawl out of the hole first. That's what I'm reasoning as I walk down Brixton Road. You have to have big patient style with these things.

The termite, at first a simile for money, becomes the thing itself: '£515 in my pocket; 515 termites in my pocket.'

'The image of the termite, where does that come from?'

'There is this flying termite which people in Zim catch and eat. In Ndebele they are called *inhlwa* and in Shona *shwa*. At first it flies a lot of the time and then at the end of its cycle it sheds off its wings and goes into the ground where people try to chase them from their holes.'

The soldier termites, often incorrectly referred to as flying ants, are a valuable source of protein and after they have been winnowed in order to remove their wings they are flash-fried with a pinch of salt and are said to make a tasty snack at beer parties. Also they serve as a relish for *sadza* porridge. Given the recent food shortages, though, they have become rather more than a treat. The best way to collect them is to insert reeds or blades of grass into the tunnels of their ant-like hills; the soldier termites grab at the reeds or grass with their mandibles. A multi-purpose simile, that termite: truth itself becomes like a termite. And then, what ho, even love.

§

'You describe life with your Ndebele grandparents but as you are Shona on your father's side I wonder if you feel one more than the other, or do you draw equally from both traditions?'

'I think from both but I never really felt at home in either. Where I grew up, in Bulawayo, with my surname people would say I was Shona and so I never quite belonged there and then when I moved to Harare, which is a very Shona place, they would hear my accent and say, "Ah, he is Ndebele". I am quite used to not belonging. Actually, though, for most of my life I was away from home. I spent a lot of time in boarding school. Things may have changed in Zimbabwe but back then if you wanted to give your children a good education you sent them to boarding school. It was quite traumatic, especially the first time my parents left me. There were all these kids crying for their mothers but what I missed most was my dog, Max, which I really felt belonged to me. I went to primary and secondary schools outside Bulawayo, and then to high school in Harare.'

The confusion Chikwava felt during his later education is the confusion of most young people when it comes to determining their futures. What his parents would have liked was for him to go into medicine. What he did instead was to follow his friends into engineering but, once there, he was, he says, insufficiently impassioned by the properties of concrete.

'I couldn't find among all those respectable people anyone I wanted to be.'

'Who, finally, did you seek to emulate?'

'There was this writer called Dambudzo Marechera who was a cultural icon really, so different from other writers, very popular among young people. The reason for this was he had in him these streaks of the unorthodox and the rebellious, and just didn't fit in anywhere. Marechera went to Oxford where he was kicked out after trying to burn down the college. I guess he was a character who you might describe as having *mamhepo*. They offered to take him back on condition he submit to psychiatric treatment, which he refused, and so he went his own direction, staying in England until 1982 and then he went back to Harare where he died in 1987. I never met him but he was one of my great inspirations. Many writers in Zimbabwe were trying to *be* him.'

Sometimes we admire outrageous people for doing what we dare not do ourselves. Dambudzo Marechera was the *enfant terrible* of modern African literature. After leaving Oxford, although to say he 'left' is a shade polite, he lived from hand to mouth in London's parks and squats, a ragged and crazed figure. Somehow during this period he managed to write his first book *The House of Hunger*, which was awarded the Guardian Fiction Prize. At the award ceremony Marechera showed his appreciation by hurling saucers at the chandeliers and throwing a chair at the then literary editor of the *Guardian*. When he went to the Africa Centre in London and took literally the director's invitation to make the place his home, one night, after being evicted by the caretaker, he smashed all the windows. Soon after, he showed up, shirtless and shoeless, at some dinner function and overturned all the tables. It is not a little ironic that recently there was a symposium in celebration of his life at Oxford University. Marechera wrote of himself: 'My whole life has been an attempt to make myself a skeleton in my own cupboard.' There can be little questioning the success with which he managed to do so, dying of AIDS, skeletal, at the age of only thirty-five.

The spirit of Dambudzo Marechera hangs over the Book Café upstairs at the Fife Avenue shopping centre in inner-city Harare. A Zim$10,000,000 note which a few months ago might have been enough to buy a chicken now barely covers the cost of a couple of eggs but even so, despite the food shortages, despite the constant surveillance, despite what goes on with the prostitutes on Fife Avenue, the Book Café remains the country's most vibrant centre for alternative culture. The brainchild of jazz musician Paul Brickhill and the Pamberi Trust, it is where one might hear traditional *mbira* music or the ravishing young diva, Hope Masike, or the 'Zimjazz' trio, Too Open, or the Zimbabwe College of Music performing Duke Ellington's *Sacred Concert*. It is home to the monthly 'House of Hunger' poetry slam, also to theatre groups and politically daring comedy routines. One may attend literary discussions and lectures by such well-known writers as Shimmer Chinodya and Tsitsi Dangarembga or one may just go there for beer or coffee, depending, of course, on whether you've got a few million dollars to spare. It is one of the few places in Zimbabwe, a country in which both black and white tend to be conservative, where the racial divide evaporates. The white poet and rapper Comrade Fatso reproduces the black lingo of the townships while young black writers and artists absorb white culture. It is also, sometimes with a little bit of help from friends in high places, relatively free from the prying eyes of the CIO, the Central Intelligence Organisation. Arrests, however, do from time to time follow performances. As Comrade Fatso says, 'One thing with the Book Café is that if you've got the guts to say what you want and spit it out in a poem you can do it, but you don't know what's going to come next. That's the joke. In Zimbabwe you've got freedom of expression, but you don't have freedom after expression.' Somehow the place manages to survive. It is also where, before coming to England, Chikwava played music and read his 'horrendous' early verses.

'A lot of arty types hung out there – poets, actors, musicians and visual artists. It was nice to be in that community. There was the Writers Association, but even though I was beginning to write short stories I never felt confident enough to join them. I thought I would be way out of my depth. So I kept my distance and played mostly music, doing writing on the side.'

'Was there a moment when you decided to be a writer?'

'It was not a sudden thing but more a yearning for change, to do something else with my life. I could see already that with the non-creative side of things I'd never get any satisfaction. There was this Association of Art Critics in Harare. I had friends who were painters and so I thought maybe I'd school myself, join the association, and that eventually I'd be able to write something for the newspapers or magazines. I gained enough confidence to write my first art review. I thought, "My God, they want to publish me! I can't believe it." This was my first writing and gradually I began to think maybe I could try something more creative. Without having any knowhow, I started writing short stories instead of poetry and this worked much better for me. I wrote all these short stories, a lot of them horrible and which will never see the light of day, and then getting the Caine Prize [for "Seventh Street Alchemy"] gave me confidence. So I thought maybe I should start doing it properly and invest more time in it. I'd just write and see what comes. Now people are reading my work and I fear maybe I'm writing rubbish and that I am going to have to continue to learn my craft in full view of the public.'

'What were things like for you under Mugabe? Did you ever come into conflict with the regime?'

'No, I was lucky. I was a nobody and so they didn't bother me. If you kept quiet, which is what they wanted, if you just kept to your place, they would not bother you but if you stepped out of line they would come down on you like a ton of bricks. There were some people brave enough to challenge him and they suffered in different ways for that. Writers, though, did not tend to get troubled much. I think it has to do with the fact that books are limited in their reach in Zimbabwe. The only writers who were closely watched were public figures like those who had columns in the independent papers. Often they had to leave the country. The moment you try to challenge the regime they play it in such a way that you are a proper Zimbabwean only until the moment you start to dissent and then you become *inauthentic*. You are not a Zimbabwean any more. Your thoughts are coming from elsewhere. If you don't agree with government policies it means you have become part of a whole imperialist plot.'

'What was it like for you growing up in this atmosphere? Did it put pressure on the brain?'

'Maybe I'm romanticising things a little but back then there wasn't that heavy presence. You didn't feel somebody was looking over your shoulder all the time. When I look back at the 1980s, the media was a lot freer than it has since become. All these cartoonists revelled in satirising government and a lot of newspapers exposed government scandals and corruption, producing articles that resulted in cabinet reshuffles. There were a few people who suffered for it of course. On the other hand, there was this editor who exposed a scandal that went as far as the president's wife and what they did was to promote him to the umbrella group controlling the newspapers. They pushed him up to a place where he had no editorial control! Also the thing about Mugabe at that time was that he still wanted to be seen as doing the right thing. He was worried about appearances. Already there was a problem in the early 1990s when you had a few opposition parties that were trying to do something else. Suddenly, during elections, you had all this violence which was perpetrated by the Central Intelligence Organisation. Even so, it was not what it has become in the past ten years. I have this musician friend who has a cousin in the CIO. One day they were driving from the funeral of a relative, chatting away in the car, when the CIO man thought he heard somebody say the word *chinja* which means "change". *Chinja* was the slogan of the opposition. Actually he had misheard. He pulled the car over, ordered everyone outside, saying he would not allow opposition talk in a car that belongs to the ZANU-PF. This is their paranoia in that they even hear things that are not said! So what you have now is a breakdown in family relationships. I don't think it was as bad as that in the 1970s when family members could be on either side of the divide, when the family bonds were still held together by things in the culture. The whole of African culture is disintegrating, with the emergence of a new hardcore attitude that produces characters like the Green Bombers who, stripped of any culture, become animals. They are vicious to an unimaginable extent – they dehumanise but are also dehumanised. Maybe this is our African modernity.'

'Were the Green Bombers already in existence? Or did you miss the terror?'

'Not quite. It was about 2001 when they came. Whenever Mugabe was pushed into a corner he would call up the war veterans, who were not really war veterans at all, people aged eighteen, and you would say to yourself, "Okay, *which* war?" Those were the ones who eventually became the Green Bombers. What they had was a certain, very terrifying, attitude. You had this also with the guerrillas during the war, when they would speak in such a way that you couldn't possibly engage with them. There was no saying, "Okay, let us have a debate or conversation and see who's right and who's wrong." You were simply told, in that terrifying voice, "You do this *or else*." There is an area of Harare called Avondale, which is quite an affluent part of the city with shopping centres, cinemas, et cetera, one of the nicer places to be, where you can go and meet other people. This was when we began to have all these shortages. I was in front of a shopping centre, standing in a long queue. Suddenly this young guy probably in his early twenties, rough looking, really aggressive, came and started ordering everybody about. "You people shouldn't be queueing here," he shouted. "What is your problem?" The regime's message was that there were no shortages, no problems, and so here was this young man ordering people about, saying, "Are you trying to embarrass the government? You are all sell-outs!" What made me realise that things had really changed was that in that whole queue nobody dared challenge him. That was the turning point. Before then, someone like him would not have tried to do that to a whole crowd of people. This character probably spent most of his life not knowing what to do with himself and then along comes this opportunity to be someone. The ruling party gives him this, and suddenly he feels alive for the first time. He has never wielded so much authority and it feels good. What's even more incredible is that he was just a conduit for something else, some bigger thing operating inside him, of which he himself was probably not aware. You think to yourself, "What do I do with this?" And you think if this attitude becomes prevalent then this place will become hell, not a place I'd like to live. Will this turn into another Cambodia?'

Punishment is the best forgiveness for a traitor. George Orwell's alive and well in Zim. *Making people think like you want them to think is one of them things you get teach first as Green Bomber.*

'It must be painful to watch at a distance.'

'Yes, but you've also got to distance yourself from it, and, maybe in a selfish way, try to switch off because if you try to keep an eye on it all the time and are too involved then it turns you into something really strange and you end up bitter. So you try to switch off and think of it in other terms and say, okay, look at all the other Africans who have come here. That's when you realise – this may be cynical – that the whole African post-colonial project is failing. You hope something else will come along, another generation with different ideas, but right now it is a complete disaster. Sometimes I think Zimbabweans should stop accusing Mugabe for their troubles because they really have themselves to blame. The country gets the leader it deserves. This may be harsh but I think maybe if they had stood up to him in a better way things would be different, but they didn't or else they didn't know how to. The tragic thing about this is that Zimbabweans fall into this kind of thinking. They say, "Yes, what's happening here is bad, and yes, okay, Mugabe is a problem. We acknowledge he is making life difficult for us, but we are not going to do anything about it ourselves because somebody else will fight this war for us." This is our tragic mentality. Zimbabweans at the helm of politics haven't much respect for tradition. When I look back on it, it's clear how politics and business are inextricably linked. The wealthy joined up with the politicians and the culture that has come out of that is not one that respects tradition. The people who are part of this are selfish and money-grabbing, respect nothing except getting more money, and they have this incredible disdain for other people. You see them with their big houses, with their millions, driving about in their flashy cars, and if you are anything less than what they are they look upon you as death or else as an imbecile. You have Zimbabweans escaping to South Africa, appearing in the media and saying "Will the international community do something about this?", but how are they going to help this democratic project if they are not willing to fight for it themselves? We had this opposition which had developed into a proper one, the MDC [Movement for Democratic Change], whose links were still with the trade unions and there was another organisation, the National Constitutional Assembly, which was trying to bring people together. They would call for people to demonstrate and stay away from work, but it never worked because people would then say, "I am not interested in politics. I will go to my job and look after my children." That's when I began to feel Zimbabweans were not really interested in their fate.'

'When you left, was it partly because of that situation?'

'There were a few times when there were high hopes things would change, but those hopes were dashed. It came to a point it almost felt like a kind of national depression, when I felt I really didn't want to be in this any more.'

'So you chose to become a "lapsed African".'

§

A few years ago, Chikwava's father died quite young of a stroke.

'I had a strange dream last night, which I am still trying to analyse. I dreamt he was in this room and he was selling wheat to me. I thought "Okay, then!" but really it was so strange. My father was very straight and would never approve of something like that. He was a policeman, very disciplinarian. He wanted his children to be straight and believed in people working hard and doing things properly. And here he was, selling wheat to me – quickly, surreptitiously, as if it was illegal to do so. Soon after, he picked up my coat from where I had put it down on the chair, saying to me, "This has been my coat all along. I just loaned it to you. I'm taking it back." And he started putting it on. I didn't expect it to fit because he was much bigger than me. Suddenly, though, the coat fitted and I was astonished.'

'How would he have felt about you being a writer?'

'Well, although he had ideas about how he'd like my life to turn out he would have kept his distance to see what came of this. There is this thing in Zimbabwean culture, especially among the Ndebele, and even with parents like mine, in that they never try to force you down a path.'

§

There is a sentence in *Harare North* that captures perfectly the disillusionment that sets in with people who come to London, thinking they will find there an escape from poverty and abuse: 'Yari yari yari yea when people is in Zimbabwe they fill the air with cries saying they want to come to the big lights but once they is here you find them blinking like lost goats, that's what she say to me.' She who tells him this is the wife of the narrator's cousin. It's not long before we know why she doesn't want him in the house, but even before she brings him home she is pegged by him for a 'lapsed African'. It is one of the drollest phrases in the book and yet it is also urgent with meaning. She has found her niche in English life and in doing so has forsaken her roots. She may get clobbered with scandal but never with *mamhepo*. One of the spookiest figures in *Harare North* is MaiMusindo, a practitioner of black magic who can 'wave death away like it is some nuisance fly'. I wondered whether there was such a figure.

'I made her up, but in one of the covered malls in Brixton Market there is this hair salon, with all these African women from different countries working there. I spent a lot of time at the café opposite, trying to figure who they were. I tried to make something from the people who work in that place.

'The girl Tsitsi, she works there as well. She's another one I made up but then I've come across quite a few people like her, who have relatives here who bring them over to become domestic servants almost. Their stories do not have happy endings. This happens a lot in Zim with people in urban areas getting their relatives to come from the countryside. It's a form of slavery but people there don't really acknowledge it. It is a young nation that doesn't yet know how to talk about difficult things unless they are hardcore, like beating up someone because he is from the opposition party. There are many such cases here, the difference with Tsitsi being that she runs away from that situation.'

She is Chikwava's favourite character. Tsitsi's fate is that of countless other Africans who come here. 'They carry bags full of things,' Chikwava writes, 'and heads that is full of wonders of new life, hustle some passage to Harare North, turn up without notice at some relative's door, only to have they dreams thrown back into they faces.' And then of course there are those who have already lived here for some time, 'lapsed Africans' who extend their invitations to people back home, knowing full well 'the British High Commission don't just give visa to any native who think he can flag down jet plane, jump on it and fly off to Harare North'.

The question, of course, is how people like Tsitsi and Shingi and Aleck and MaiMusindo, 'like many immigrant on whose face fate had drive one large peg and hang tall stories', survive.

> 'The fly that land on dollop of poo is the lucky one,' I tell Aleck. 'The one that land on honey is in big trouble. That's the tricky thing about living in Harare North. But some of us, we have to ask the question: you want to do something – what is better, to try doing it your own way and risk finding small success, or to do it in undignified pooful way and find big success?'

'Sometimes,' Chikwava continues, 'you think of that disjuncture between how people in Zim see England and how Zimbabweans here see it. They have this idea everyone in this first world country is having a great time and that this is where everything is. Meanwhile, you come across all these people struggling to survive, juggling three or four jobs at a time, sleeping for only three hours, but in that most Zimbabwean way people coming here choose not to talk about their difficulties. One person I met at the tree was a well-qualified banker in Nigeria and he threw everything away in order to do something menial here. It is quite hardcore. They keep quiet about their troubles because back home it would be seen as an admission of failure. They say everything is okay and they are getting on when the story is quite different. They are slowly dying inside. That is why among immigrants there's a high prevalence of depression and mental problems. The concept of depression is not appreciated within Zimbabwean culture – in both Shona and Ndebele there is no word for "depression".'

Whatever one chooses to call it – *mamhepo* or 'mental illness' – there's no escaping the fact that of all immigrant groups in London the highest incidence of people ending up on mental wards is among African males. Chikwava describes 'them eyes with the shine that come about only because of a reptile kind of life, that life or surviving big mutilation in the big city and living inside them holes'. Mental health problems are six times more prevalent in black Africans than they are in the white British population. According to a report produced in 2006 by the Royal Society of Psychiatrists only

23.1 per cent of Africans first seek help from their GPs. What is even more striking is that the majority of them go to their vicar first. One needn't go buzzing about the universe, seeking causes, not when the truth is there for all who care to see: quite simply they can't, or are not made to, feel at home.

'What about you? Did coming here require a big shift in your thinking?'

'I'm still going through that shift. I'm not through it yet. I feel almost like I'm in limbo, neither here nor there. I don't belong to Zimbabwe any more and I don't belong here. It's still a new place, and until I'm able to inhabit its culture, to find my way around it and read all its signifiers I won't be fully here. People have these conversations full of cultural references that don't mean anything to me.'

'When you first arrived here were there things you found upsetting?'

'Strangely not, or at least not in that way. Also I find it easy to just flow with things and probably because of that I miss quite a lot. The place itself was not really all that strange, but what struck me was the way people smiled. I thought, "I don't know, but there's a hell of a lot of fake smiles around here." I'd never seen them before, these smiles that simply flash and disappear. You don't have this in Zim. When they smile or laugh it is not meant as a kind of fantasy or just to be nice, which maybe is the case here, where you want to be seen to be making an effort and so you make a nice fake smile to show you have tried. It was as if people were trying to cheat me. "You can't cheat me," I thought. "I can see through that!" Maybe it's something that comes about because of the intensity of the social interaction here. You always have to interact with people, even when you are tired, and try to be as nice as possible.'

'I think each culture has its own set of reflexes,' I countered, 'and maybe they seem objectionable at first because they are the very things most difficult to decipher.'

'Yes, maybe. Also that flash smile in Zim is seen as rude because people over there have got lots of time. And because it's a sort of shorthand, it is unacceptable. You can't do shorthand over there. The pace of life is slower and people greet each other for twenty minutes at a time. What that smile means is that you haven't got time for me.'

'Was London hard for you in other ways?'

'It wasn't that difficult for me but probably the main obstacles were cultural ones, when, say, you interact with people and suddenly you discover the way you explain things is so different and it's because of where you come from or how you have been educated and so it takes a while for people to understand what you are saying and also what they say is not quite what you'd expect either. It can seem so fickle. Also it has got to do with the work ethos here. There is a great emphasis on presentation, which is not the case in Zimbabwe, and sometimes it is made at the expense of substance. That emphasis is so big that sometimes people don't give as much thought to whatever it is they are trying to present as to how they come across. It's as if it's all that matters. I suppose it is something that came with Tony Blair's "Cool Britannia".'

'You have come from a country where there is such tragedy and pain to an environment where that tragedy is only dimly registered. I wonder to what degree your audience understands that the things you describe, especially when they are couched in humour, come out of something truly terrible.'

'I find this particularly interesting when I give readings. You have all these lovely people listening to you but they do not know where exactly to position themselves in relation to what is being read to them. You read something which anywhere else people would laugh at but because here people are not quite sure whether they are supposed to laugh or empathise or because they are so worried about being politically incorrect with *this African type*, they just don't know what to do. There is that anxiety. Maybe there is such a big desire to empathise that they miss all the humour.'

'The picture you create of being here sounds a bit negative.'

'There is an incredible amount that is positive and just being here you get to do and see things you would never find anywhere else. You don't talk about the nice things because they don't present any problems. London has done a lot for me. It inspires a lot of ideas and I'm constantly brainstorming which is a good thing but this also has to do with the fact that when in limbo one becomes a complete outsider, *a complete observer*. You see things much clearer than you would if you were right in the midst of them. One of the most jarring things here, especially when I go into the underground, is the volume of visual noise, all these ads clamouring for your attention. I find it quite distressing. Go to Paris which has its metro system and it doesn't have all this clutter. Here, however, one is living in a society where the intention is always to trigger dissatisfaction. This is the masterstroke of capitalism in that it has made people feel permanently dissatisfied about their own condition so they always want to have something more. Everything around you solicits a response. It is really a kind of mental banditry. Maybe I'm more focused here, but also I have lost my peace of mind. Maybe that's what London does. It is like any big city in that it offers so many possibilities, but on the other hand it's a place that just grinds people down. You have to live with this awareness, always trying to figure at which end of the spectrum you are, and that can be quite terrifying at times. You begin to think, "What is happening to me?" It is an environment that demands that you go out there and be, at one level or another, quite aggressive. Otherwise you don't get anywhere because someone else is going to elbow you out of his way. This is just a bit *too* much sometimes.'

§

A tree grows in Brixton. I confess I stole the title. Actually I woke up with it on my tongue, as if during sleep the *br* sound of one place had been nobbled by the *br* sound of another, and I knew then that with such a handle I was well on the way to writing this piece. Brooklyn is where the original tree grows and although I never got around to reading Betty Smith's novel the movie made from it greatly impressed me. So too did Peggy Ann Garner. *At last* an American child actor that didn't make me want to puke. The tree that grows outside her grim tenement block is an *Ailanthus altissima* or Tree of Heaven, which the Chinese revere for its medicinal properties. Depending on which part of it one uses – root, bark or leaf – it is good for countless ailments, anything from balding to mental disturbance. Although I won't say *why* I drank it what I can say is that the tea made from it tastes foul, so foul in fact that I preferred the condition for which it was meant to be a cure. I don't know how much Chinese medicine is in Betty Smith's story but what is depicted there, and in the film, is the grinding poverty of immigrant life. My pilfering I therefore deem appropriate.

And so it was that one day, beneath that tree which grows in Brixton, Chikwava fell into conversation with a man absolutely crazed, who, later, transmogrified, would enter, indeed command, the pages of his book. It was also, if one wishes to take a more fatalistic view of the matter, an encounter that would transform his fortunes. That said, Chikwava is glad to be shot of that voice. And now he is troubled having to take it on tour.

There is an almost sickly pastoral quality to the passages regarding that tree:

> I go to the Ritzy Cinema. Under the big chestnut tree. There is heap of them laid-back liars, dog thieves in trench coats, pigeons, coarse runaway married men that have develop bad habits like spitting on pavement every minute, them the crazy ones and them the ex-pig keepers who have flee they crazy countrymen in hot climates; all of them funny types is gathered there on the grass or the benches … Then them homeless people start to trickle to the tree with they dogs, ready to start to put out the burning truths of they lives with buckets of brew and all.

'I think in a way the tree, and the people around it, saved the book at a point when I was stuck, not knowing which way to take it. The way the story was going I knew I needed to get out of that squat where most of it takes place. It would have been horrendous to be stuck in there.'

'You called it a chestnut tree.'

'Yes, I know! I know!' he laughed. 'It became one in my literary imagination but also I think it had to do with my liking of chestnut trees. When I was writing the book I spent a lot of time in the park sitting beneath one. That tree *moved*.'

Good enough, good enough.

A Ghostly Hum of Parallel Lines

Hamid Ismailov, Writer, and Razia Sultanova, Musician

An elderly Uzbek with a long white beard clings for dear life to the side of a moving train. The year is 1942. Why he is doing so is because a few minutes earlier an NKVD officer, carrying a copy of the Tashkent edition of *Pravda*, stepped into the compartment where he was. Also seated there were three Poles who had just been released from one of the Gulag concentration camps north of the Arctic Circle. They were on a journey of unlikelihood that would finally take them to England, that is if they did not first die of malnutrition or the typhus which had begun to claim thousands of lives. (There is a mass grave for Poles in Uzbekistan, near the village of Kirmine.) The old Uzbek was sitting with a basket of fruit and vegetables. The NKVD officer kept glaring at him from behind his newspaper, whose name ironically translates as *Truth*, and after a while, clearly taking exception to the Uzbek's presence, he opened the door of the compartment and ordered him out. The old man showed his ticket but to no avail and so resignedly he picked up his basket of fruit and vegetables and stepped out into the corridor. The officer slammed the door shut behind him and said to the three Poles, 'He stole these things from the collective farm and now he is taking them to the market to sell.' One of the Poles asked him how come he knew the goods were stolen and in any case how he could treat an elderly man like that. The officer replied, 'Who gave you the right to interfere? It's none of your business. We *know* how to treat them.' He then lit a cigarette and sat with a defiant air, the cheap rage of the bully swelling inside him. After a while, he got up and went outside. Suddenly there were sounds of cries and a scuffle. The officer opened the door of the moving train and pushed the Uzbek to what would have been certain death had not the old man managed somehow to grasp the door handle and hang there by one hand while still clutching the basket with the other. Just then, the train pulled into a station and stopped. The Poles saw from their window the old Uzbek on the platform, so lucky to be alive, clenching both fists at the departing train.

The above might have come from the pages of Hamid Ismailov's remarkable novel, *The Railway* (Harvill Secker, 2006), or *Zheleznaya doroga* to cite its original Russian title. The old Uzbek, though, comes from elsewhere. A story told well creates its own scene, a memory module which, if one's reception is clear and one's sympathies ripe, will pass down from generation to generation. Will my daughters one day see what I, who wasn't born at the time, and who have never been to Uzbekistan, can *still* see, that old Uzbek, white beard blowing, caught forever in the present tense? One of the three Poles sitting in that train compartment was my father, aged twenty-five, also lucky to be alive. The incident would haunt him for the rest of his life.

§

Hamid Ismailov's fictional Gilas is based on a real town in Uzbekistan, whose geographical coordinates, I shall reveal here, are latitude N 41° 24' 12" and longitude E 69° 12' 24". Why blow its cover? Go, traveller, with your GPS and you'll find it there. Anyway it hardly matters what its real name is because the town where Hamid grew up is barely recognisable any more, and, besides, a convincing fiction is made of sturdier material than the houses whose inhabitants scrape a living for themselves, sometimes procreate, and, with almost indecent regularity, expire. This is what great literature does: we find Troy alive, even in stone cavities. This is true even of Gilas where most of the houses are made of clay, a proverbially weak substance, subject to the whims of nature. Hamid describes how, with each succeeding generation, the houses of the town are resurfaced, often greatly altering their shapes, so all that remains of streets once familiar to him are their names. The apocalyptic mudslide with which the novel ends, which is based on a real one he witnessed in Kyzyl-Kiya in Kirghizstan, serves to demonstrate that *his* Gilas is not really there any more, likewise most of its inhabitants, who populate his novel in the thinnest of guises. 'How much less in them that dwell in houses of clay,' Job cries, 'whose foundation is in the dust, which are crushed before the moth?'

When I asked Hamid whether it was possible that the train on which my father was passed through Gilas, he said it had no alternative. All trains in Uzbekistan stop at Gilas. Gilas has no other reason to exist. I think, therefore, it is not *too* fanciful of me to suppose the old Uzbek with his fruit and vegetables might have found his feet there.

§

I have read *The Railway* twice, the first time with some bewilderment, the second time with unalloyed pleasure. My initial confusion stemmed mainly from the huge cast of characters, more in a mere 275 pages than in the multi-volume works of many other authors. I then discovered that the key to the book is not to worry too much about remembering who is who, but rather to surrender to them as one might in real life when, say, entering a town for the first time.

'Yes,' said Hamid, 'it's only then you'll become the boy who surrenders to this life and opens his eyes and ears to everything that happens around him.'

It will not be revealing too much here to say that the unnamed boy of the novel's italicised passages is the author himself or, more accurately, the author's roving historical eye. '*It was as if someone invisible were walking beside him and saying: "Tell me what this is! And this!" And with the ease with which you talk about your first home, about where you were born and where you lived your first years, he chatted away to this invisible figure.*' The boy shows up at different points in the country's history and seems never to age.

'Basically he represents my alienation. It is my way of making sense of all that happened around me. My mother was dead and I didn't meet my father until later. Life in Gilas was complete madness, so vulgar and so crude, and I was absolutely pure. I had come from a different world with different coordinates, and with different expectations of life.'

If, as Hamid says, the novel is folkloric, it is so to the extent that it becomes postmodern or maybe even a step or two beyond. It strikes as many registers of mood as there are people, dragging the reader between the pure and the obscene, the mystical and the profane, the tragic and the comic, the lyrical and the discordant, and it is also a testament to the extraordinary abilities of its translator, Robert Chandler, that the myriad characters become one's familiars within the space of a few lines. One walks and one talks with these people, even though for most readers they are people one would never encounter in ordinary life. The antipodean nature of the book is contained even in its physical dimensions: in translation it has been reduced by 20 per cent but in bulk it is about 20 per cent larger than the original.

'Does that mean,' I asked him, 'the Uzbek is more concise?'

'Uzbek is notoriously concise. I've got a theory Uzbeks are born fighters and so you can't say to them, "Follow me on the red horse and strike on the left". Instead, you have to put all this information into one word.'

Gilas may be seen as some oriental mirror image of the Wild West, an outpost, which, paradoxically, is only a whistle-stop away from Uzbekistan's capital, Tashkent. It does *feel* terribly remote, however, and, in some respects, nowhere is quite as removed as a major city's satellite. The novel covers the years, all of them tumultuous, between 1900 and 1980. It is banned in Uzbekistan and its author is said to have 'unacceptable democratic tendencies', which is odd given that his depiction of the Soviet period is not without affection. What may offend the authorities is the raucous laughter that at times is close to Rabelaisian. The intensely human never goes down well with regimes. A microcosm of Central Asia, the town's nationalities include Russians, Sarts, Uzbeks, Jews, Tadjiks, Tatars, Uighars, Kirghiz and gypsies, and maybe it has something to do with its being a train-stop that allows the reader to feel he is partaking of an archetype. As so many films and novels demonstrate, a train-stop is where human destinies are forged – a poetical truth which for those who have to endure it often feels like harsh prose.

The behaviour of the inhabitants of Gilas is outrageous in the extreme, their vices on display for all to see. The swearing is just terrible. One reason Hamid's people are so horribly attractive is because they are not hypocrites. And the goodly among them shine, though never *insipidly*. I had figured Hamid was much too sane to have survived such a madhouse and that therefore the characters that populate his novel were mostly exquisite inventions. When he assured me that they were all based on real people, I did not disbelieve him, but I assumed that at least some of them had been inflated to mythical size.

'Yes,' I said, 'but what about Mullah-Ulmas-Greeneyes?'

Mullah-Ulmas-Greeneyes is the book's most colourful rogue, a man who speaks many languages and has expertise in none, and who in the course of his picaresque adventures meets Camus ('this man seemed to be named after some cognac or other') and Sartre ('Sartre turned out to be truly a Sart in at least one respect: he proved treacherous') and Solzhenitsyn (who teaches him mathematics, in German); there are several others. And the journey he takes defies belief. I should have realised, of course, that only true journeys are incredible.

Smilingly Hamid reached for his address book and quickly leafed through it.

'He is not an invention! I can give you his telephone number and address. Yes, yes, here he is! Actually he is a mixture of two people. One is my wife's great-uncle, Ulmas, who had green eyes and always smiled – I added "Mullah" to his name because it alliterates. The other person I met in New York. Maybe he's still alive. I recorded him and he was so funny. He would listen to the radio and in a very satisfied manner say, "I know this word and that one and *that one.*"'

'And Mullah-Ulmas-Greeneyes met all those famous people?'

'Well, maybe not *all* but some of them.'

There was a sly wink in Hamid's voice.

So amazing are the stories regarding the originals of Hamid's characters that they alone could fill a supplementary volume. A mere glance through the book's *dramatis personae* will reveal the extent to which people's names reflect some aspect of their character, physique or vocation: Abubakir-Snuffsniffer, Adkham-Kukruz-Popcorn, Ashir-Beanpole, Asom-Paraff, Bakay-Croc, son of Mukum-Happy-Trigger, Basir-OrgCom, Bolta-Lightning, Djibladjibon-Bonu-Wagtail, *Fyo*kla-Whispertongue, Kuzi-Gundog, Lobar-Beauty, Mefody-Jurisprudence, *Nat*ka-Pothecary, Oktam-Humble-Russky, Ortik-Picture-Reels, Temir-Iul-Longline, Uchmah-Prophecies and Zumurad-Barrenwomb to name but a few of them. *Fyo*kla-Whispertongue is, of course, the local informer.

'Thanks to Robert Chandler who sent me two thousand questions, I understood the novel better. Suddenly I realised that names play a huge role. Take, for example, Kara-Musayev the Younger [the Gilas head of police], who gradually loses all his titles and finally even his name. And then there is Pyotr Mikhailovich Sholokh-Mayer who obtains different names – Pinkhas Shalomay, Pete Shelley May – he is flexible enough that in different situations he assumes different names although at root they are the same. There are different realities, different states of mind, with each name. The Soviet Union was not so much about changing the world as renaming it. Unconsciously I had reflected the reality that was all around me and how deeply it went into each one of us. There was a period in my own life when I created seven or eight heteronyms, some of whom became better known than me. Why did I create them? This renaming is deep in our mentality. That's one of the parallels between the book and my life. *The Railway* is not just about things on the event level. The relationship goes much deeper.'

'Is there anyone you particularly relate to?'

'I like the Jew, Yusuf Cobbler. I was quite afraid of him. We had these myths about Jews stealing and killing children. Yusuf was the *nicest* person you can imagine, so sweet, but because he was so sweet everyone suspected him. When the youth disappeared – '

'There really was a murder?'

'*There was, there was*,' Hamid whispered as though the news was not yet ready for release. 'And everyone claimed Yusuf was behind it. He went through hell. Our aunties told us not to go anywhere near him or his cobbler's shop. Uchmah the town's fortune-teller said Yusuf had nothing to do with it. As a mark of gratitude he came and repaired her family's shoes. When at last the murderer was caught, Yusuf was once again in favour but *poor man, poor man*! He was so sweet to all of us.'

Some of the most memorable passages in the novel are devoted to the poet Maike, who is based on another Maike from Hamid's childhood, a friend of his great-grandfather, and whose singing voice was said to be so fine that whenever he sang the sheep and the cattle multiplied. Hamid's description of his death, of which the following is an excerpt, is masterly:

> Suddenly Maike's voice shot up, far above the dust, into the heights where the steppe sun was listening entranced. No

> less suddenly his voice melted into blue smoke. The goats calmed down, the horses stood still, and the men arose from their prayers. Then Maike sang his last song about Gilas – a Gilas that was now a happy and barely attainable dream – and bloody saliva sprayed from his burnt and blackened mouth. And at sunset Maike stopped breathing and fell to the ground.

'Maike used to come, and in real life I must say he was always drunk, *really* drunk, and even in winter he would arrive half-naked on his horse. My great-granddad sitting on his horse would attach me to his belt, and there I'd be, only three years old, riding together with him and Maike. We would cross the so-called Satan's Bridge, which was just two ropes and a strip of wood. We rode at speed over that!'

One should never stereotype, of course, this being one of the gravest of contemporary vices, but Hamid, who is physically small but compact, warrior-like, alert to every nuance, does look as though he has just come from riding with a Mongol horde across the steppes.

§

There is another reason why Uzbekistan feels close to me. A woman's voice first took me there, if not in body then in spirit, that of the singer Monajat Yultchieva. She is the greatest living exponent of Uzbek traditional vocal music and it was my good fortune to have spent some hours with her, on the morning after her second London performance. There is something in the register of her voice that goes deep inside me, and where it makes its home, which is also a reservoir for my dreams, is beyond the reach of any common language. *Striking a chord* is a feeble phrase – she truly haunts me. She also brings to bear the old argument, which I'll never be able to resolve, about how it is that beauty and cruelty can come from the same place. Uzbekistan is one of the world's running sores. Our meeting, which was never once sullied by politics, was facilitated by the London-based Uzbek musician and ethnomusicologist, expert in Central Asian music, Razia Sultanova, who would later introduce me to her husband Hamid, spinner of incredible tales.

Razia plays the *dutar*, a lute-like instrument from Central Asia with only two strings, which makes it no less difficult to play, and whose soft dulcet tone has been compared to a wind blowing across the steppes. Some say *dead men's voices.*

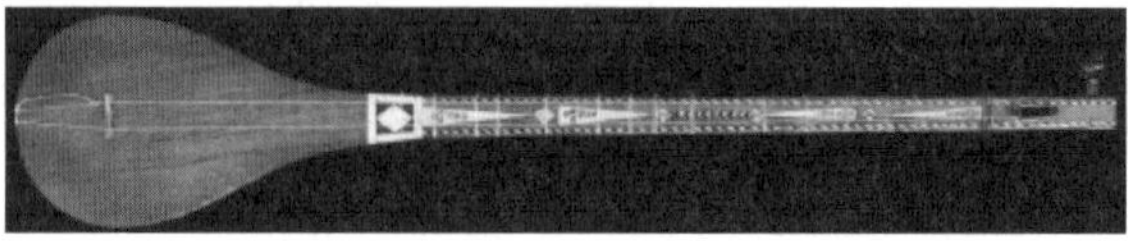

A *bakhshi* is a singer, instrumentalist and story-teller and his role has often been seen as shamanistic, something which the following passage by an unidentified Turkmen writer attests to.

> A hush fell on everyone. The *bakhshi* tuned the strings and, as though performing a solemn rite, tested them with strong supple fingers. He started playing slowly, uncertainly it seemed, then faster and faster until it was impossible to follow the movement of his fingers. A song poured forth, resonant and swift, long-drawn and melodious by turns. The *dutar* echoed it with an eagle's cry and the murmuring of streams, the whistle of arrows and the moaning of the wind in the steppes, with a war cry and the whispers of lovers, the cry of a new-born babe and the thunder of cavalry. These melodies took me back to the turbulent and ancient past.

Razia Sultanova grew up on the outskirts of Andijan, in the heart of the Ferghana Valley, which is surrounded by the high mountains of Pamir on one side and Tian Shan on the other. Its relative remoteness from the main centres of Tashkent and Samarqand enabled Ferghana to preserve much of its traditional culture, or, rather, a kind of Uzbek subculture. It is there that one finds Uzbekistan's literary tradition at its purest, and indeed it is one area in the Muslim world where women poets have flourished, such that even female members of the royal family were encouraged to compose poetry and set up literary competitions. It might be supposed that the young Razia absorbed what was around her, and packed it into a mental suitcase which she took later to London, but her story is not such an obvious one. It is, rather, about what time and distance, and an ache in the heart, brings close.

'I understood this special environment only later in life. At the time I thought things were the same the world over, this area where we had twenty different kinds of apples ripening at different times throughout the summer, and it was only when I read the diary of Zahiruddin Babur, founder of the great Mogul empire, who was born and lived in Andijan, that I realised the rest of the world was not like this. Babur had visited India and other places and was always remarking that their apples were not like ours but were good all the same. I didn't recognise just how special our culture was until I left the area, and later, when I went back to Uzbekistan, working as an ethnomusicologist, meeting musicians and singers, the big surprise for me was in discovering that the best of them came from the Ferghana Valley.'

'What kind of family background did you have?'

'My parents were very tough people, what we called "children of Stalin's time". My father was *deeply* of the Ferghana Valley, from a tiny village, near Andijan, called Asaka. He began to work aged eleven, when his father was killed in the war. This was because he had to take responsibility for his mother and younger brother. He was very gifted in languages, though, and made a career for himself in the army. It was the same hardship with my mother although she didn't have to start work so early in life. She is an Uzbek Tatar. Tatars are more like Russians really, with their white skin and pale eyes, and their own special ethnic style. The women are much more liberal than the Uzbeks, more mature, and, coming from outside, know more about life. My mother became a school teacher and then a headmistress. She told me the only adult she ever saw at home was her grandmother. Her mother worked fourteen hours a day in a textile factory. When your parents grow up without families, they become tough people. Soon I realised my friends had similar backgrounds. My closest friend was Jewish, another Armenian, and because we had parents of the same age we all suffered in the same way. We decided among ourselves there was something wrong with them because here was a generation whose god was Stalin. They knew everything Stalin said, and what he advised, such that their life programmes were set by him. I am not saying they *loved* Stalin, and maybe now they recognise they were completely brainwashed, but this was how they lived. Some of my relatives were leaders in local religious ceremonies, but my mother doesn't know any prayers. When I asked her about this, she replied, "It was forbidden in my time." There is no longer any Soviet ideology, but she is still on the outside of her culture. My father was a bit closer to the spiritual side of things, but he also was very critical of religion. I believe they were both victims of Soviet ideology.'

'And where do you come in?'

'When my parents married they were sent as a couple to Vladivostok and then to an island nearby simply called "Russian Island" where they had to spend the next three years. Stalin had just died and it was expected the next war would be with Japan. It was a dangerous time and forces were being mobilised to the borders. That was how my father, who had never seen the sea, suddenly found himself on an island. It was for them a difficult experience, cold, windy and wet. And that's where I was born, on that island. The only hospital there was for soldiers, so I was born in the wrong place, at the wrong time. Because my father had a higher rank they were able to live in barracks, but despite the better living conditions there were still insects, for example, bedbugs especially, and so they put me in a cradle hanging from the ceiling. After the situation between Japan and Russia eased we went back to Uzbekistan, which, by train, took eleven days and nights to get there. I went to the best school in Andijan and the walk from home, which was an hour, took me through ruins. Nobody told us these were the remains of a fortress built at the time of Babur. We used to climb up and down on them, not realising what they were. Finally, a main road was built through the middle of them.'

'It is another instance of your history and traditions being excised.'

'Absolutely, yes.'

Razia illustrated this divide between new and traditional with an anecdote from her childhood.

'One night, when I was about five or six, our next-door neighbours lost their father. For three days and three nights the women wept in the most terrible way, over and over and over, and I couldn't sleep. My mother who like all educated people was very reserved told me, "This is the traditional way to mourn but we do not behave like this." This was a consequence of our Soviet-style education, which ignored or neglected everything traditional in our lives. My granny, when she prayed, didn't want us to follow in her footsteps, saying it was better for us to remain on the safe side. The older people following their traditional cultures didn't want their children to experience their own difficulties. My granny told me how in the 1930s anyone caught at home with books written in the Arabic script would be sent to Siberia or the Gulag along with their families. So people either burned those books and manuscripts, some of which were poetry, or else they would bury them. All religiously educated people, especially those of high rank, were jailed or killed without trial or just sent somewhere. We never knew our grandfathers and this was true for most of my generation. If they were mysteries for us it was because they were either called to serve at the Front or were sent to prison. Very few survived. Mine, on both sides, were killed in the war. Stalin needed as many men as possible.

'My grandfather on my father's side had a high position in the police, which meant he was spared being called up for the army. His name was Ashur Mohammad but friends and family contracted it to "Ashurmat". Ashurmat saw someone at the local train station, taking bribes from families who were trying to leave. Those were difficult times, and with most of the men serving at the front, their families, often wives with seven or eight children, moved from one region to another looking for food. This man was charging them triple to leave. Ashurmak who was a very honest man and highly emotional went and shot this man dead in front of the people he had offended. As punishment he was sent to the Front where he was killed in 1942. I inherited from him his *dutar*. That instrument was for me the Asian voice, a link to the past, as well as being a sign of what was the right way for me to go.'

The handing down of that instrument also illustrates the Sufi doctrine of *sil-sila*, the chain of learning or transference of knowledge. Although usually applied to teaching, this can also refer to the transfer of memory from one generation to another.

'Was this instrument kept in the house?'

'Yes, but because the *dutar* is so delicate it does not last for more than twenty or twenty-five years. It was not playable any more, so it was more of a symbol for me.'

'When did you begin to feel this connection?'

'It was only *after* I left my country. It was like a pain. I wanted desperately to play it, to hold it, to hear it, and later it came together with my academic interests. Now I have more friends among instrument makers than I do among musicians. I visit them in the most remote parts of the country, in the high mountains or in the desert, and I listen to their stories. They tell me, for example, the best *ney* (flute) is made from reeds that grow in the desert or on the lake or in the cemeteries, especially from the cemeteries, which usually are in high places where there is more wind and sun. The making of those instruments is a geographically involved process. At the time we had no knowledge of such things. All we knew was that the *ney* was a reed with five stops. Also, with those instruments coming from the cemeteries, their makers said they were related to the souls of those who passed away, and so you had some kind of spiritual explanation for every single instrument. This was most extraordinary for me. It was my schooling, the discovery of my culture. What struck me on my several visits to Japan, China and Korea was that in those countries a musician's attitude towards his instrument is so closely related to our own. It is not just an instrument – it is a soul as well. The Ferghana Valley, being as it was, at the centre of the Great Silk Road, absorbed many features of the Silk Road cultures. The *dutar* is made from the wood of the mulberry tree and the strings are made from silk and, of course, silkworms feed upon mulberry leaves. So much comes from this richly symbolic tree. The instrument makers told me you should boil the silk thread for two hours, so that all the sweetness comes out of it, leaving only sadness in the sound, which is why it penetrates to your heart. You get all these stories from the instrument makers themselves. Each *dutar* takes twenty years to make. They have to find the right tree, and before cutting it down they pray of front of it, asking permission. They slice the wood, and then begins the process of drying it, which can take up to twenty years before it is sufficiently dry to shape into an instrument. The wood dries out in the courtyard and with its being there all that time, like a family member, what you get is a spiritual relationship. When the Soviets destroyed these instruments they destroyed the soul of the country.'

§

They destroyed not just the instruments but also the people who made them, and when they destroyed the latter, they all but obliterated the traditions which held together the idea of Uzbekness. What is to be marvelled at, though, is the resilience of a suppressed culture, whereas those that die quickest often do so in relative peace.

Hamid spoke to me of his ancestors, some of whom he has memorialised in his prose.

'Both my grandfathers, from my paternal *and* maternal side, were killed, but, to be absolutely honest, it was quite a while before this became a big factor in my life. As a child, and even later, when I was living in the Soviet Union, I never gave it much thought. It was only later, when I started thinking about who I am, that they became important to me. I started investigating this in the 1990s, at the beginning of *perestroika*. I wrote to the President of Kirghizstan and to all the KGB offices, asking for information about my paternal grandfather. All my family knew was that he had been arrested and put in Osh Prison. There was a rumour that he'd died but nothing definite as to *how* he died. The family were never given any documents. In 1992, I received a letter from the Kirghiz KGB, saying that they had now recorded his death. So for fifty years not even his death was recorded. They gave me a death certificate, dated 1992! They said he died in the prison hospital, but my grandmother Oyimcha had been told by those who were imprisoned with him that he was shot. She told me stories about how she would go there, and about how unfriendly the people were, treating her as a wife of "an enemy of the people". There was no chance of actually seeing him. She would go there, take him food, and then come home. Finally, in 2002, I obtained his file, together with all the interrogation papers.

What I discovered was that his behaviour had been very noble and that he said nothing against anyone. He admitted he was a mullah and taught the Qur'an simply because he believed in it, but there was never any blackmailing or slandering anyone. Apparently others gave so-called "evidence" against him. I inherited some books from him, which my grandmother buried in the cemetery.'

The Railway preserves an account of Hamid's grandparents' first meeting.

> Once, as [Oyimcha] and her little sister were washing clothes in the pool of spring water behind the white stone house her father had built after a trip to Skobelev, her little sister jumped up and sang out like a small bird alarmed by some animal, 'Sister, dear sister, you must hide. An accursed man is approaching. We mustn't be seen by him.'
>
> ...
>
> The sister looked up, saw a rider approaching and, not pausing in her work, said in a loud voice, 'Why should we hide? It's only a Kirghiz.'

This simple passage contains many of the complexities of Hamid's family history. The sixteen-year-old Oyimcha, whose name means 'Beautiful Moon', was of a noble family, descendants of the Prophet, *seyyeds*; and the Kirghiz rider, Obid-Kori, was a mullah who had spent twenty-three years studying in Bukhara. Despite the fact that his mother was Uzbek, and that with each generation, through the women's side, the Uzbek blood increases, Oyimcha didn't consider him a proper man. Clearly this only made him all the more determined to win her.

'Uzbeks are, by and large, a settled people, a civilised people, and they consider Kazakhs and Kirghiz second-class citizens. My granny was quite sarcastic about my grandfather. She said, "Firstly I was forced to marry him when I was only sixteen, this man who was forty and not even an Uzbek, and, secondly, he didn't even live with me properly because he was arrested and shot dead. He did not fulfil any of his manly obligations."'

'Surely this was a terrible judgement she made on him!'

'Yes, but it was a semi-sarcastic, even playful, judgement. She was in fact extremely loyal to him and after his death never remarried. She was only in her early thirties when he died. This Uzbek arrogance towards the Kirghiz side of my family survived through into my father's generation. I was the first to look into our genealogy and what I discovered was that in fact the Kirghiz were of even higher rank than the Uzbek side of my family who had always considered themselves the nobler of the two. My grandfather was of the family of Khudoyar Khan who was himself a descendant of Genghis Khan. When I discovered this I went to my father, saying to him, "Do you realise you are related to the last Khan of Kokand?" My father said to my stepmother, "Bring out the things I gave you, which are in the dowry chest." She brought two pillows that had been granted to my great-grandfather by the Khan himself. They were stuffed with quail feathers. To fill just one pillow with those feathers you would have had to have killed an awful lot of quails! Those pillows were kept in the family for a hundred years, and yet the Uzbek side of my family never admitted they had been given by Khudoyar Khan. What was interesting for me was that I could now put everything in the right perspective. Now I understood all the *seyyeds* were mocking my poor granddad. I suspect he was always on the defensive. The funny thing about him, and this would have tragic consequences, is that all his life, maybe because of all this family pressure, he wanted to become Uzbek. When he was arrested he was the only "Uzbek" in the village. As a pre-emptive measure all the real Uzbeks declared themselves Kirghiz because when the map of Central Asia was redrawn it would be safer for them to be so, and there was my grandfather, the only Kirghiz in the village, pretending to be Uzbek! Such was his loyalty and it says quite a bit too about his fight for his wife's heart, she who had been forced into marriage with him.

'In early childhood, I was brought up by my granny Oyimcha. She was the first person to tell me these stories. Every night, after telling me a story, she would recite a semi-religious spell against the Evil Eye, which contains the lines:

> We send greetings to the serpent of Quraysh.
> At the threshold to paradise there is a single tree.

Although the serpent terrified me, and as such was a moment of horror in my night, at the same time it made me see just how protective the tree was. All these elements – the serpent, the door of paradise, the single tree – would appear later in my poetry. They were so deep in me. It was interesting to discover where these poetic archetypes came from, my early childhood, and, more specifically, from Oyimcha. She did not write poetry as such but she made a belt, which actually was more like a shawl, in the middle of which she embroidered a quatrain of her own making. If I have anything poetic in me, it is mostly because of her.'

This ghostlike image is the only surviving photograph of Oyimcha. It dates from the 1960s but it looks like it might be a daguerreotype from the 1860s. It is hardly a photograph at all but rather a glimpse, a sliver of memory, of a world now wholly irretrievable, or maybe it's what the roving eye of *The Railway*'s ageless boy-narrator has smuggled into the future, the woman in the background stooped at her work, anchored in time, meanwhile, shuffling towards us, into the moment of this prose, Oyimcha and a gowned boy, who may be Hamid but he's not sure.

'After you were separated from your grandmother, presumably you were cut off from these traditions.'

'Yes, from five until I was twelve, when my mother died, I led a Europeanised life. I went to a Russian kindergarten and then to a Russian school. Then, aged twelve, I ended up in Gilas with my maternal granny whom I loved from the very start. It was a very traditional Uzbek family.'

§

'So, Razia, how did the Uzbek traditions first present themselves to you?'

'It was the usual kind of granny school experience. I would go to visit my father's mother in the village of Asaka. I thought it was a wonderful place. I remember the village houses and their seemingly endless gardens that stretched far into the distance. Also, because of the hot climate, we would sleep outside in the courtyard, which had this local furniture called *supa*, a kind of high bed which was extended like a room, on one side of which there were pillows and blankets. We would sit there during the day, eating our meals off a carpet set in the middle. When night came everything was removed and it was turned into a huge bed where all the women, grandmothers and granddaughters, would sleep. I remember looking up at the Milky Way, which was fantastic in those dark country skies, listening to the sounds of cicadas. Also there were all kinds of local, traditional cures. If someone wasn't well they'd call for one of the grannies. If one of the girls had a sore throat, her granny would take an axe and behead a chicken and with her fingers immediately dab blood on her granddaughter's sore throat. This was our traditional life.'

'What about the music?'

'I played piano at that time, and I looked down on the village children because they couldn't play Western classical music. Later, when I became a musicologist and returned to the village, my great-aunt said to me, "We are so happy you have now discovered Uzbek music, whereas before you used to just look through us." They had these simple but deeply penetrating songs, sometimes with words written by Sufi poets. This music was never studied or documented. It was forbidden to do so. Uzbeks weren't even allowed to study *shash maqam*, which is the crown of our musical tradition, until 1953 when Stalin died, and even then we could only mention it and nothing more.'

'The religious songs, were they disguised?'

'They were openly performed but nobody took them seriously. It was thought we were merely singing songs from our youth. Interestingly enough, this attitude came mostly from the males in our society whereas the females took the music much more seriously. At important events, birthdays, for example, or when someone had recovered from illness or had safely returned from a Soviet camp, they'd invite a local female religious leader called an *otin-oy* and she would read *sura* from the Qur'an or Sufi poetry. This was their way of marking those occasions.'

'So it was the women who preserved the traditions?'

'Yes, but I was in a strange situation. I stopped going to the village when I became a teenager, and then, when my father was promoted, we went to Tashkent, which was a period of great unhappiness for me. It was such a change from the authentic, close community I'd been accustomed to, but even in Andijan I didn't pay attention to all this religious stuff. Later, when I went to Moscow to do a PhD on classical *shash maqam* a Russian publisher asked me if I'd do a tiny book, written in a popular style, on the religious musical tradition in Uzbekistan. What an irony! So I went back to Uzbekistan and in Tashkent I asked people about this music and nobody knew anything about it. It was like asking if there was life on Mars. Then I went to Andijan, which was my city, and there a friend told me her neighbour was the leader of one of these female religious groups. It was the 1990s and the Soviet Union was about to collapse. If I said I'd come from Moscow, this woman wouldn't want to know me. When I asked her if I could make a recording I knew immediately I had touched a difficult area. "Will you tell others?" she said. "Will you write about us in the newspapers?" She then asked me where I was from. When I said from Andijan, she asked from what family. We discovered one of my female ancestors was also a religious leader, so now there was a connection between our two families. She said, "Look, tomorrow we are gathering to mark the end of Ramadan."

'The following day I went and I was so impressed. There were these women wearing white clothes, sitting around in a circle, some of them with strong voices, others with weaker ones, one after another, each giving a fantastic performance. They knew everything. If you asked them to perform works of the Sufi poets Ahmad Yassavi or Mashrab they could do it. They sang and sang and I lost all sense of time, exactly as if my mind had been taken elsewhere. Some of the women were from a religious background. Others were the bearers of difficult destinies, widows some of them, others high-ranking ladies whose husbands were imprisoned. They couldn't do *zikr* (prayer) openly around the mosque or on the banks of rivers, so they prayed at home, which meant these closed female societies had their own cultural and physical space, where they could continue with their worship. This was how it all survived. At the surface nothing was happening, there were no Sufi gatherings or brotherhoods because there was a ban on everything associated with male religious activities, but the women who'd witnessed these kinds of rituals were able to continue in their private spaces.'

'And what about the book you were going to write?'

'What happened is that not only the Soviet Union collapsed but the publishing house too!'

Razia laughed, and then I asked much too soon the question that should have been allowed to ripen on the vine.

'So why did you leave Uzbekistan?'

'You must ask Hamid.'

§

'We made our first move to Moscow in 1984 and we adapted well there. I was the representative for Uzbek literature in the Union of Soviet Writers. Also I started to publish my books there. Magazines contacted me for articles on Uzbekistan. I did not have to move very far to find work. Later, things got more complicated. We created a foundation in Moscow for the support of democracy in Central Asia. All the members of this foundation were arrested, beaten up, or had cases filed against them. We were betrayed by the very person who set it up. The whole thing was created in order to trap us. We were too naïve, but with what was happening in the Baltic States and elsewhere it was a time when everyone was full of hope. Life in Moscow got increasingly messy and so we went back to Uzbekistan, but there our problems worsened. It was 1992, the early days of Uzbek independence, and anyone who represented Russia was considered an enemy of the state. I was a correspondent for *Literaturnaya Gazeta* and with every article I published they would invite me to the Ministry of Justice or the Prosecutor's Office or the police. They filed a case against me, saying I was among those who were preparing demonstrations. I said to them, "You know me. I am not an enemy of the people. What I do is journalism." They said, "Yes, yes. You have to be patient. When the forest burns, every tree burns. It could touch you too, but don't worry too much."'

'Was there a particular moment when you realised you had to escape?'

'Yes, one day I was sitting at home after work when there was a knock at the door. There was a policeman. He said, "I know you. I used to go to your poetry readings in Moscow. I respect you, but you must come with me." While he was driving he confessed his love for me and at the same time, so as to prepare me, he cautiously told me what I was about to be charged with. Out of loyalty he was alerting me to the seriousness of the situation. He was playing a good game. At the same time he wouldn't allow me to escape. At the police station the heads of two units, one from the Prosecutor's Office and the other from the Tashkent State Police, started to interrogate me. I bluffed, saying "Do you understand that as a correspondent I can record everything you say?" So they took my recorder and broke it in front of me. This was so as to put everything in the right perspective. They meant a different business. They interrogated me for maybe an hour or more. Then they allowed me to go. When I walked out of the building I saw them slip into a car and go somewhere. I discovered the next day they'd gone to interrogate the leader of the opposition party, Abdurahim Pulatov, and in front of them he was beaten with steel pipes by four people. When I went to see Pulatov next day, it was breaking news. I went to the hospital and he was in intensive care. The same people who interrogated me had gone to interrogate him, so I knew what was in store for me. That same night we decided to leave. Next morning we set off on the train. They were not quick enough to react. Our daughter was left behind and I still keep the letter she sent to France, written when she was twelve, saying that if I came to pick her up that I should go not to Tashkent but to Moscow because every day the Prosecutor's Office was calling after me.'

'Many of your friends were arrested. This must sit heavily on your heart.'

'Yes, but on the other hand I wouldn't wish any of those people to lead my life either. We went through hell. They created these gangs who attacked people like me. Several people were beaten up. When we left Uzbekistan, we came to Moscow. We lived in hiding, leading the life of Salman Rushdie. The lady who'd taken my place as representative for Uzbek literature invited my wife over and she said to her, "Apparently you are planning to go to France." Apart from a couple of people in the Union of Soviet Writers who were preparing our documents, nobody knew about this. "They will get you even there," she said. "Your husband has already been sentenced to death by the Uzbek authorities. A very high-ranking person told me." I tried to blackmail this woman, saying that unless she revealed who said this I'd expose her, but she wouldn't tell me. I sent letters to friends and members of the Writers' Union, saying, "If I am killed, this person will provide some clues." We stayed at Razia's professor's house. She had gone to Beijing. Every night we barricaded the door with our bicycles. On the street we would look around at every car, wondering if whoever was inside was coming to kill us. There weren't any mobile phones, so wherever I went I'd phone Razia, telling her I'd be moving from this point to that point and if she did not hear from me she'd know I'd disappeared. We spent three or four months hiding and changing places. I wouldn't wish this life on others.'

'Your relationship must have been put under such pressure.'

'I am extremely grateful to my wife, starting with our voluntary moves and then ending with this forced one, and all the while she never protested or accused me. She led a harder life than me, being exposed to all these difficulties. We went to France. I got a scholarship for three months, which we were efficient enough to spread over six months. Then luckily Razia got a scholarship in Germany. For a while, we lived as a family in three countries. I was in France, Razia was in Germany and our daughter was still in Uzbekistan. We succeeded in getting her out with the help of friends who put her down in their passport as their daughter and brought her to Germany. We had excellent friends everywhere. A Turk who'd use any excuse to give me a job got me work translating from Russian into Uzbek just so as to be able to pay me some cash, but I couldn't accept money for nothing. He said, "I don't know how your faith will go with this, but I found a church that is giving free lunches." With my poetic imagination every day I pushed my shadow in front of me, thinking, "When will I get a proper job?"'

Hamid is presently Head of the BBC Central Asian Service.

'You brought all this *with* you from Uzbekistan whereas Razia seems to have found it here, the music in particular. You moved in different directions, yet they join up in an interesting way. What about your children? Which world will be theirs? Will it be the English one?'

'We speak Russian and Uzbek with them at home. And speaking

of Razia and me, I used to take so many things for granted. Maybe it was because of my traditional Uzbek upbringing. I didn't make much fuss about Uzbekness or whatever because it was already within me whereas in Razia's case it was *obtained.* Therefore she is much more respectful towards that side of herself. She loves it more than I do. Sometimes I am overcritical of Uzbekness and sometimes she is the one who opens my eyes to it. For instance, I didn't bother much about Uzbek prosody, about the metrics, about *barmak*, which is traditionally Uzbek and tonal, and *aruz* which comes from Arabic culture and is more about syllabic metres. I knew the basics already whereas Razia went professionally into this. Her example made me more interested in it, so I started to go into it deeper and deeper, and to take more seriously the system of Uzbek metrics. Now I probably know it better than other Uzbeks because, like me, they took it for granted, thinking to themselves, "Why should we care about these metrics when we already write in them?"'

'This is something, then, that has happened to you in exile.'

'Yes, I began by treating rationally what I already knew in the blood but now, thanks to Razia, I know it both by head and heart.'

'Do you still write in Uzbek?'

'It depends on what I am writing. Poetry, although I haven't written any for five years, is exclusively Uzbek, but with prose it depends. One thing I write in Uzbek, another in Russian. It depends on which part of my life I am telling or thinking about.'

'You seem not to be getting this big, magnetic pull from Uzbekistan whereas with Razia I sense it is still very much there.'

'Kirghizstan makes me more nostalgic, sadder, but in Uzbekistan I have to force myself to be nostalgic. Kirghizstan is much more unsettled, more slum-like, so there is a space there for your nostalgia, whereas in Uzbekistan every generation settles down and wipes out what belongs to you. While there are differences between my wife and me, at the same time we are very similar. We are adaptable. We have this nomadic attitude. The first great adaptation is that which I describe in *The Railway*, when I moved from a mountainous area where the relationships were pure, where people were open-hearted and simple, into a land of crooks, the hell of the railway station, but because the latter was so diverse, in all manner of goodness and badness, it gave me the resilience with which to adapt to different situations. When I came here once again it was a matter of adapting to another mode of life. I arrived with a Soviet mentality in which obedience to the law is no great thing; laws are there in order to be broken, or, rather, there is a conventional law which everyone agrees to break, and then carry on with their parallel lives. One thing you *say*, the second thing you *think*, the third thing you *do*. They are completely separate things. When we were first here, I made a painful discovery. We invited an Uzbek singer to give a performance in London. I went to pick him up at the hotel where he was staying in Bayswater. I thought why spend money for the tube when I have the car, and so I went there and parked on a single yellow line. I went into the hotel to collect him but he was praying at the time, which took roughly twenty minutes, and later, when I came out, I saw my car being towed away. I said to the man, "Look, this is a famous singer. There is a party we have to get to. I am ready to pay whatever you ask me." "No, you must release your car at the pound." This incident turned me into a law-abiding person. This was the first great adaptation, moving from this Soviet loose cannon mode into a very strict sort of Englishman in my dealings with the authorities. The Soviets were an ideological empire, a system where everything was about concepts and theories, whereas here it is about experience and pragmatism. So I became more down to earth here. That was the biggest change in my mentality. When I lived in the Soviet Union I used to think that was the only reality, the only way of thinking, whereas here all of a sudden I realised there are many ways of thinking about the same thing.'

'So where is your audience?'

'Though I indulge myself with the thought that what I wrote in Uzbekistan was for an Uzbek audience, what I wrote in Russia was for a Russian audience and what I write here is for an English one, I go with myself as the ultimate reader. With all these changes that occurred in me, my adopting an Uzbek way of thinking, then a Russian way of thinking, and finally an English one, they have produced a mêlée. If I am ten out of ten with myself and I am satisfied, then this mix is the right one, but I am not dragged by this or that or by topicality.'

'Are you still able to go to Uzbekistan?'

'Only on my British and Russian passports. I am still on the list of one hundred public enemies of Uzbekistan, whom President Karimov considers as *personal* enemies. It doesn't create any problems for me because of the BBC. I am afraid, of course. I take all precautions. Usually I go with my colleagues. Once, however, I was coming back on my own. At the airport, after I passed through passport control and checked in my luggage, there was an announcement: "Passenger Ismailov, flying to London, please come to the luggage compartment on the lower ground level." I was really scared. There had been a couple of disappearances, a mullah flying to Moscow, for example, who was similarly paged. We know that he is in prison, but they have never admitted this. There were other cases. Anyway I frantically looked around and there was a student. I asked him: "Are you flying to London? Here is my business card. If I don't appear on the plane, please ring this number and tell them I was invited to the luggage compartment." So I went there. Three policemen, two of them plainclothes, were waiting for me. They asked, "What do you have in your suitcase?" I told them I had this and I had that. "No, there is something else." I was trembling because usually they place fifteen grams of drugs in your baggage and that's it, you are finished. Unfortunately I wasn't cautious enough to put a lock on my suitcase. So, trembling, I opened it. There were two cartons of cigarettes, which my colleague's wife had given me. "Do you understand you are breaking regulations? You can't take two cartons. You are allowed only one." I was *so happy* to be fined, but I was really, really scared. It is always like that. When I go to my sister's flat I am always aware that someone could find me on the stairs as was the case with Anna Politkovskaya. When I sleep in the hotel and there is another closed door seemingly going nowhere, I put a chair in front of that door. They could, of course, come through the main door. So it's always nerve-wracking. You try to think nothing will happen, but the fear is always there. Nothing can stop them from arresting you and to be absolutely cynical I know that three days of shouting here in London won't make any difference.'

Hamid recently had good cause to shout. His friend Mark Weil, director of the world-famous Ilkhom ('Inspiration') Theatre, was murdered a month before, on 6 September 2007. He was entering his apartment in Tashkent when two people stabbed him to death. He had just returned from the final dress rehearsal for Aeschylus'

Oresteia, which was due to open the next day, and his dying words in hospital were, 'I'll open the new season tomorrow, no matter what.' The performance went ahead as scheduled. When Weil came to London the year before to stage a play at the Barbican, he took away a copy of *The Railway*, intending to do a stage version of it. Weil, who had a high profile in Tashkent, where he was born, considered himself immune to attack. His death went unreported in the Uzbek press.

'They are not afraid of anything. If they decide to kill, they'll kill anyone. They will claim it was a criminal case, drug addicts or whatever. In a totalitarian state everything is controlled by structures and for every single act you have to be held to account. It is exactly the same in the criminal world. Nothing is ever done in a random way. They get criminals to do the dirty work so that they are not held responsible themselves.'

When I expressed my worries to Hamid, about his putting himself in danger, he shrugged.

'If it happens, it happens. It has nothing to do with me. If you do not raise these issues, nothing will ever change.'

'Do you see hope?'

'Not immediately, but nobody lives without hope.'

'Somehow I think your grandmother's spells protected you all your life.'

'Shall I tell you a story concerning her spiritual power? I was at military school in Kaliningrad and my battalion commander was doing a university correspondence course. This rather dim character used to invite me into "Lenin's Room" and while all the others were doing dirty jobs, cleaning the kitchens, et cetera, I'd write his essays for him. One day he said to me, "Look, your colleagues are now going to have to work in the forest, cutting wood, preparing for the winter, but because you finished your job you can go on summer holiday, with your friend, Slava, who helped you. Off you go, two weeks of additional leave for you." He signed the order and my friend and I flew to Moscow and from there to Tashkent where we had to register ourselves. We had time on our hands and so we went to the art gallery. There I saw a painting called *Autumn in the Mountains* by an Armenian Uzbek artist called Nikolaj Karahan. It made me so nostalgic for the mountainous area in Kirghizstan where my

granny lived, and where I spent my childhood before going to Gilas. My father also lives there with my stepmother.

'I said to my friend Slava, "We're going to Eski-Naukat!" That same evening we took a train to Andijan in the Ferghana Valley and in the morning we took a bus to Osh, 30 kilometres from Andijan, and then another 37 kilometres to my native village in the mountains. We arrived and immediately went to my granny's house. I didn't really like going to my father's house because he was remarried and had a new family. My granny's house was closed and the courtyard locked. We went through the clay fence and inside everything was ripe, the apricots, the pomegranates. We spent a couple of hours in the garden, eating fruit and talking. I told Slava my granny must be at my father's house, maybe for a wedding or circumcision party. Everything there told us she'd be gone for a while. So although I didn't really want to, we decided to go. At least we'd get the keys to my granny's house. When we turned into the street where my father lives there was a crowd in front of the house. I said to Slava, "You see, I was right. There are some festivities." When we went inside the house, everyone said, "Allah Akhbar" and took my grandmother's coffin outside. I joined the procession and they asked me to put the first handful of soil into the grave. Afterwards my father repeated to me her last words: "I won't feel comfortable if Hamid doesn't come and put soil over me."'

§

Razia poured tea, saying that in Uzbekistan when one's host pours just a little bit at a time it means he or she respects the guest and is prepared to do it over and over with pleasure, whereas in Russia it's quite the opposite – it signifies a lack of respect.

'So, Razia, what about your time in London and what has it meant to you?'

'Coming here opened my eyes. I understood how many fresh opportunities there are. While I am still some distance away from saying what an exciting country this is or what a glamorous people, it was, as we say, "a sign of the universe" that God brought me here. I am much happier from the standpoint of my interests and academic possibilities. Also the practicality that I see as a part of "Britishness" enables me to do my research while at the same time teaching and playing music. Although people here are interested in Uzbek music and its structures, very little is ever said about the *soul* of that music. It is important not only that one plays those instruments and speaks about them, but also that one knows about the people who make them. My Uzbek music teacher before returning her instrument to its case would kiss it every time as if it were her baby. There is, in the relationship between player and instrument, so much that remains outside our knowledge, and being a scholar here enables one to pursue those matters not just from a historical point of view but also from an anthropological or even a purely biological one. I will give you an example. After a lengthy music session, when the musicians' fingers are actually *supposed* to bleed, they heal their sores by dipping them in their own urine! These things you learn in the field. We are so far away from our culture however. I don't want to say it was really bad over there because, as we say, "black comes from both hands" – there were bad *and* good sides – but these comparatively limitless opportunities we obtained only by cutting ties with our country, by moving away from there. This is partly because in this country each scholar is allowed to create his own path – whether it is studying music, the society from which it comes, or the actual sound the instruments make – and to follow it in a personal way, without, as we were forced to do, having to continually quote earlier sources. With our system in Uzbekistan, although it had its good sides, if you obtained a degree in musicology it meant you should put a full stop to your career as a musician. This was one of many such artificially created limitations. You had to be one thing or another, whereas here there is more choice. We are given wings to fly in the direction we choose.'

'What about this question of who or what or where your audience is? You go on stage, play the *dutar*, this exotic instrument with only two strings, and then maybe you'll sing in a language nobody understands. What happens in this space between where the audience is and where you are? Where are you? Does performing here in some sense take you back to Ferghana?'

'I am *there* with my teachers, my family, and with all my childhood pictures, but at the same time I must be present on the stage otherwise I will lose the thread of my performance. People are so curious to know more about my country, more about my music, about who plays it and for whom, and about how it is played, and in that respect answering all these questions makes me happy just to know people here are interested in knowing more about that life. So I come as a kind of ambassador, presenting this culture. The really interesting thing, however, is that I am representing the "wrong" side of that culture, one which, during Soviet times especially, was never taken seriously by academics, by the media, and, because Uzbekistan is a predominantly male culture, even by the men there. So I'm doing all this in an upside-down way, but the more I do so the more people learn more about the deepest layers of my culture. And then I also learn something new every day. Very often people ask me things for which I have not prepared answers in advance. "If this is a wedding song," someone asks me, "why is it so sad?" And I think, "Yes, *why*?" and because people from outside ask these questions you begin to ask more questions about your own culture. I explain that it is because the bride is leaving her home, her family, maybe to go to another village. And then recently I had to prepare a lecture based on this wonderful exhibition I went to, which was on Uzbek *suzanis*, which are these wonderful cotton cloths richly embroidered with silk. It was then that I made the most amazing discovery. Many of the lyrics in those wedding songs contain references to the number 8. The bride will sing, for example, "I will miss you, my eight flowers" and then somebody else will sing in response, "Don't worry because tonight you'll look to the skies, and there you will see eight stars." I discovered that the dominant pattern in these *suzanis* is the octagon, which often comes in the shape of eight-cornered stars, and then I learned that this was the shamanic symbol of the universe. When placed in the middle of the *suzani* the family will be protected against the Evil Eye. And then, of course, these *suzanis* were made to be given as dowries to protect families against difficulties in the future. So here is something that comes from pre-Islamic, shamanic, culture. And later it shows up as one of the main symbols of Sufism, this mystical development in Islam. You can see how symbols move from millennium to millennium. Now, thanks to this exhibition, and the connections I was able to make between it and music, I have learned something about my own culture. I am also, in a way, a product of this search for a past, for my culture. If it wasn't for the English audience who pushed me to do it, I would never have done it myself.'

'It strikes me as ironic that you reinvented your life in the direction of your roots, that is, the very thing you had to leave.'

'I think many people do this. When they leave their country they are immediately taken back there through memory or culture or homesickness. It is like looking in the mirror. You see nothing's the same any more, so you are doing your fieldwork every single minute, and whether you like it or not, consciously or unconsciously, with your experience, your interests, your style and your habits you go somewhere, you see something, and you immediately put everything into parallel. It's some kind of non-stop process. It's like a virus in your computer. You go out, see the weather, and you think, "There's no sun", and then you are taken back to your childhood when the sun shone. Everything becomes a comparison. Everything in your reception works this way. It is a kind of inertia. It's not *you*, it's something outside yourself.'

'You spoke very well on the outward shifts in your life, but coming here must have produced some internal ones as well.'

'In physics, remember, there is this law, Archimedes' Principle of Floatation. If you take a piece of wood and push it into water there will be an equal reaction, an upward pushing force. It is as if that piece of wood does not want to go into that other material. It is the same with life. Sometimes I am so unhappy there is nothing left for me but to cry, but then sometimes I'm so happy too. It means a balance has been reached – the whole picture comes together. The more you are pushed into this fresh environment, this country with its new language, new circle of friends, new weather, the more you are pushed out of it by your internal genetic code. Those internal forces inside one come from one's childhood and one's culture. You should feel as much force from inside as from outside because only then will you achieve harmony. If we are here it means it was in our destiny to be so, and we should be grateful because, really, I like this country and its people, but at the same time our past experience in life is just as important.'

We drank to the dregs our green tea in a yellow room redolent of Uzbek sunshine.

'Thank you for not filling our cups.'

§

The search for patterns in people's lives can take one to silly places, but it does occur to me that where Hamid and Razia live, in New Barnet, which is as remote to central London as Gilas is to Tashkent, owes its existence to the construction, in 1850, of the Great Northern Railway. Like Gilas, New Barnet is a station. One can hear the rumble of passing trains from their house. Although Hamid admits maybe there was something to it, that maybe in some area of his unconscious he'd gone back to Gilas, albeit a rather tame version of it, it's an argument which, if too strenuously pursued, can take one into the regions of psychobabble. The chief reason for moving there, he says, was because of the surrounding verdancy.

'We people of the steppes go after green places. We see two trees somewhere and we think it's Paradise.'

The nomad allows his horse to graze.

And the Uzbek lady strums a gentle tune.

Staring down the fretted neck of Razia's *dutar*, at those two strings that catch just enough of the surrounding light to deceive one, for just a second or two, into thinking their glint is metallic, and not at all silken, one may glimpse, too, a visual echo of the rails that run through Gilas, and maybe, in some parallel universe, all the way from there to New Barnet, that iron road upon which so many destinies are forged, or at the very least the ghostly hum of one and the ghostly hum of another.

Tehran in Stoke Newington

Mimi Khalvati, Vuillard and the Stone of Patience

The day before I went to interrogate Mimi Khalvati in her cave of silence I read again her 'Interiors', a work that had always given me trouble. A lovely poem to observe, its constituent parts would seem to drift apart from each other until there'd be no more seeing them together in the same space. This time, however, sunlight dappling the pages, something clicked inside me. All made perfect sense. One could lean all day against that poem and it wouldn't give. Also I was reminded of an experience I had had in a carpet shop in Damascus. What might have sparked this memory were the lines:

> Take a motif from a carpet,
> the intimacy that kneels
> at the foot of something larger,
> too large to fit the frame

The seller spread out for me a highly ornate Persian carpet, which sometimes I fancy I can still see, although, in truth, there was too much going on in it to be able to absorb. Whoever made this had arithmetic in the soul. Although I could appreciate the workmanship, and said as much, privately I knew my tastes ran towards the simplicity of the nomadic. (The small rug I craved, and which I really *do* still see, was a strange one, humming with desert sonorities, with the images of the sun and moon on it, and quite unlike anything even the carpet seller had seen before. Its price was astronomical as well.) Angrily he whisked the Persian away from me, rolled it up, tossed in the corner of the room, and began to direct his attentions elsewhere. 'But I haven't finished!' I protested. And he replied, 'I can see from your eyes that you were looking *at* it whereas really you should have been looking *through* it.'

I'm pleased for the sake of this prose that it was a Persian carpet and not some other. Also I had been given a wonderful lesson in aesthetics. What he meant by *seeing through* was that with a carpet as complex as this one it can only be properly gauged when seen as a three-dimensional object through whose many layers the eye passes. When the mind has been dulled, and everything in everyday life conspires to keep it so, all it can ever apprehend are surface values. Sometimes, though, when the brain is shorn of its prosaic growth, and the soul of its scar tissue, what one gets is an epiphany or revelation – one sees *through* a work of art. Although I saw through that poem, or so it seemed to me, I wonder if I'll ever understand it as well again. What stays with me, however, is a sense of being submerged in its light, and the light, I swear, although nowhere do the words say so, is Persian.

This would seem to go against the grain of what its author said several times, that she is rooted firmly in the English tradition. She has always written in English and she has lived only fleetingly in Iran, Tehran to be precise. I have no cause to argue with her other than to suggest that there is continual seepage from her mother culture. After all, she is the author of a number of *ghazals*, an Arabic form adopted by the Persians, which she brings most convincingly into English verse. The *ghazal*, she tells me, gives her permission to be rhapsodic or sweet in a way she wouldn't dare attempt otherwise and as such it enlarges her range of linguistic expression. It is the form that interests her, she says, even more so than the culture from which it comes. I will accept this, but only on condition she'll be my representative of all things Persian.

§

I first met her in 1991, when I worked at Bernard Stone's Turret Bookshop. I had arranged a launch for her first collection of poems, *In White Ink*, and no sooner had she begun to read in that womanly girlish voice of hers than I was entranced. She writes beautifully without falling into the traps beauty makes. Soon after, we published a broadside by her, on dusty pink paper, 'That Night, at the Jazz Café', a mother's deeply felt lines to a daughter about to set out into the world with 'fluorescence on her cheekbones'. Over the years we would see each other infrequently, mostly at literary events, and once at closer range, when she and the poet Archie Markham invited me to read for them at Lumb Bank in Yorkshire. (Archie was for many years the man she was romantically attached to, and, at the time of writing, had only recently died: Easter Day, 2008. Sorrow, when we spoke, was therefore in attendance. Archie I remember well, which is not to say I knew him, but his was a character in which one felt at home. As Mimi told me, everyone has something to say about Archie, which probably means he was quite unknowable. Originally from Montserrat, he had lived in England since 1956 and was renowned not only for what he wrote but also for the voices in which he chose to write, which included an urbanised Caribbean, Paul St Vincent, and, may she rest in peace, Sally Goodman, a Welsh feminist.)

Some years later, shortly after I had made a journey to Iran, I saw Mimi at the Poetry Café in Betterton Street. She wanted to talk to me about Hafez and I was in a hurry to get somewhere. I don't know what species of stupidity operated on me that I didn't arrange to see her immediately after, because my experience of visiting Hafez's tomb in Shiraz had been such a deeply moving one. A year later, when finally I raised the subject with her, it was too late: Hafez had settled into her psyche. There was no need to discuss him any more.

When Mimi speaks she stretches in the patch of sunlight her thought makes. Although as a poet she's pretty steely, as these days one has to be, she is just as liable to pronounce a triumph a failure. I learned fairly early on not to accept this curious line of defence. Where she lives, in Stoke Newington, really is a cave of silence. (It's no accident, surely, that in Persian her surname means 'seclusion', at least in the sense understood by Sufi orders.) Although her home is crowded with books, pictures and textiles, each thing is in its place. This is order of a kind that keeps a troubled soul sane. She cannot bear to see anything aslant, including her family photographs which she adjusted while I was there, and truly, in the manner of the tidy obsessive, she frets more than she needs to. The walls on both sides of the stairwell are covered with pieces of needlework, dozens of them, all framed, some of them awful, others exquisite, but their value is not in what they are but in the fact that she feels she has rescued from extinction the work of 'little old ladies'. The presence of these products of spare time in a busy age is just one of many keys to Mimi's character. Covering almost the whole of one wall of her living room is a ruby red cloth, embroidered with silver thread at the corners, which was the top cover of her grandmother's *korsi*, the name given to the system that comprises a low table, covered with quilts, beneath which is a charcoal brazier for keeping warm the legs of the people seated there. An expensive cloth such as this would probably have been brought out for special occasions such as the pagan Mithraic celebration of the winter solstice (*shab-e Yalda*) when people sit up late, often reciting Hafez's verses. The letters of her grandmother's name TALAT SALTANE are evenly distributed over its four sides. The 'N' of SALTANE, which is actually an honorary title, is sewn in reverse, an error such as a child might make. What is perhaps even more remarkable is that it should be in Roman rather than Persian lettering, which is a fair indication of the direction in which the country was looking when this cloth (*ru-korsi*) was given to Mimi's grandmother as a wedding dowry some time at the beginning of the twentieth century. That cloth, in the context of all that follows, seems imbued with symbolic value.

Where Mimi lives is a lovely place to be, as is, of course, the interior her poem makes.

Between the saucer and the lip,
the needle and the cloth,
the closing of a cupboard door
and the reassertion of a room,

in those pauses of the eye
when the head lifts and time stands still

what gesture flees its epoch
to evoke a crowded continent?
What household conjures household

in the heterogeneity of furniture,
rituals that find their choirs
in morning light, evening lamps,
in cloths and clothes and screens?

As it turned out, she would be its most perfect guide.

'Telajune', the name she gives her grandmother, is a contraction, the *june* of which denotes affection.

'I spent ages reading about, and looking at, the work of Edouard Vuillard. I did so for months, and, you know how it is, I got completely obsessive. I went back to the poem and, reading it again, I thought, "What *was* I talking about? I don't quite get it." It is the sort of poem during the writing of which you know what you are trying to do, everything's crystal clear, but later you realise the poem hasn't really done it. Still it encapsulates a whole world for me and I think one day I'll go back and write something completely different but drawing on the same source. It's funny your saying you looked *through* it because I think that poem is like a veil. I couldn't write like that now and it's something I've lost which is quite precious, a kind of daring that I don't have any more. On the other hand, I have achieved a sort of clarity. What you lose here, you gain there. I have finally developed a reader's eye, which took me years to do. At the time of writing "Interiors" I don't think I had that eye at all.

'I'll tell you where that poem came from. I've had two happy dreams that have stayed with me. One was this dream in which I was swimming underwater. It was like I was tripping – everything was in psychedelic colours. There were these trees growing down there in luminous purples, pinks, greens and reds and also, at the bottom of this ocean, there was a massive painting in an ornate gilt frame. That dream – or *film* as I call it – had something to do with feminism. In my other dream, and this is where this poem originates, I was back in my grandmother Telajune's house in Tehran. I was seventeen when I went there in the 1960s. Emotionally it was terribly confusing for me because it was the first time I had lived in Iran since coming to England aged six. I never had a childhood home that I could remember – I'd been in boarding school on the Isle of Wight and didn't even carry inside me any image of home – so when I found myself, for the first time in years, in the heart of a family it felt like a completely new experience. It was as if I were eight or nine again. First I lived with my mother who had this minuscule apartment, which was a bit awkward, so then I went and lived with grandmother Telajune for about three years. All these memories come really from that time.'

Mimi pointed to a small oil of part of her grandmother's house, which she had asked her mother to paint for her.

'She made it look much prettier than it actually was. It's not really the house, but the *iwan*, and the little pond on the left has been made to look more like a swimming pool. There was nothing glamorous or beautiful about it. It was a conventional, walled-in courtyard with a little pool at the centre, where the washerwoman would scrub the sheets and my grandmother would do her ablutions before prayer. In one corner there were pots of mint and jasmine and a huge white mulberry tree. The paving stones would be littered with squashed white mulberries that were really sticky and attracted wasps. Trays of herbs or berries would be laid out to dry in the sun. Also it was where the carpets were spread out to dry after they were cleaned and where the washing was hung out on the lines. This purely functional space became one of those images that stay with me always. Anyway in my dream I was back there – it was midsummer, I was all thin and brown and summery, wearing flip-flops and one of those little cotton house dresses. I was walking between the washing lines, and, as usual, my grandmother was somewhere inside, in the shade, probably sewing or cleaning herbs.

'And probably Akhtar Khanum was there too. She was the seamstress. She used to come every day and was very much part of the life of the household. Akhtar Khanum had white, thinning hair that was hennaed, that strange orange colour, and her skin was very pale, quite shiny, and rather sweaty. I remember her as being wound round with cloths, probably the things she was working on. She'd throw a cloth over one shoulder and have pins stuck in her mouth, and she'd give me these big sweaty hugs. Now, my Farsi is such that when the radio's on, especially if it's the news, I can't understand a word. I speak colloquial Persian only. Anyway in the dream the radio was on and I understood every single word! Otherwise it was exactly like it was when I lived there. I was so happy I awoke from that dream crying. I said to myself, "My God, my mind recreated that Farsi, both created *and* understood it." I was convinced it was real Farsi, although when I awoke I couldn't duplicate a single sentence of it. I was so happy to think that maybe, somewhere in my brain – this was my myth – the Farsi language had been preserved. The rooms I can remember in any case, but this business of the radio really did astonish me. It was a very simple dream, but, for me, enormously wonderful. I tried to write a poem about it, which didn't work at all … and I *knew* it wouldn't. And then, after having forgotten about him, I reconnected to Vuillard and suddenly everything went clickety-click because his world seemed to parallel the world of my grandmother's house. Vuillard adored his mother and lived with her throughout her life and had his studio in the same house. His mother was a seamstress with her own workroom. He has many paintings of seamstresses, and their materials – the textiles, the different colours of threads – inform all his work. There was no artist in my grandmother's house but there was the seamstress's room. The poem conflates Vuillard's world, or what I knew of it, with my grandmother's world. So it was, in a sense, a double vision.'

This image of Telajune was taken well before Mimi was born but it is one to which she returns, and which I visit, with pleasure, maybe because it represents an age when one might strike such a pose. It is of a world in which one dressed to the nines to do so. A photograph, or, rather, the taking of it, was still an event rippling into the future. (Who is that sliver of a man who stands off to one side? If a husband, it is very much a husband in attendance. Maybe for him, whoever he is, she was, even then, in those pre-Revolutionary days, something marvellous to behold, and, as her honorary title suggests, sultaness of all she beholds.) One can almost hear, across the decades, a rustle of cloth.

'I remember her mainly from the 1960s when, aged seventeen to nineteen, I lived with her and again, between 1970 and 1973, when I was in my twenties and married to Paul. It's weird how short the time was because in my mind it seems so massive. Yes, she is a central figure in my poetry such that at one time I was convinced she was my Muse. The first *real* poem I wrote, "Rubaiyat", was about her and

I'm sure it's *because* it was about her that it became a real poem, and then of course she informs totally "Interiors". She comes into other poems as well, either tangentially or centrally. At first we couldn't communicate because she spoke no English and I no Persian. She had one English word and that word was "*luverly*". She used to say to me, "Mimijune *luverly*" like in *My Fair Lady*. I had the feeling always that my grandmother knew me in a way that other people didn't. She was very protective of me, and she always used to say, "Mimi is very *mazloom*", which is a difficult word to translate. It can mean "quiet", "passive", "uncomplaining" or "unassertive" and even all those things together. That seemed a very key word to me. Other people saw more obvious qualities – I don't go round like a timid, unassertive person and I laugh quite loudly and I don't think I'm some little thing in the corner – but my grandmother knew that's what I'm *really* like.'

I suggested to Mimi that extraordinary Oriental quality, which I experienced in Damascus, of being able, sometimes, to communicate beyond language. It was, rather, a species of divination. Then Mimi seemingly entered the very space she was about to describe, recreating it, as it were, and because she did so, hesitantly, as if her voice were on tiptoe, I, too, was ushered there.

'We communicated in the same sort of space that poetry comes from. It was so silent there. My poems certainly come from a sense of everything being silent, extremely calm, so still that things shine there. There'd be a strong sense of shadow as well as light. And then the small gesture. She would suddenly place a glass and a jug of freshly squeezed grape juice in front of me. It all had a sort of purity. The sensation was of *pure* space, uncluttered with language. She would go about her daily tasks and the whole house was like a beautifully oiled machine. Every day was the same, the same rituals and routines … clockwork … so beautiful. I think it felt to me also like the turning of the seasons in Iran, the four seasons always just where they were supposed to be, with everything happening at the same time of day. It was a very balanced – I am tempted to say almost *sacred* – little universe within the larger universe. It gave me a sense of a great harmony and I think because we didn't have a common language there was nothing to shatter it … to spoil it. She would go quietly about her things and I'd go quietly about mine. We met usually over food. She'd give me grapes, at eleven it would be some morning treat, and then there'd be lunch obviously. I connect that kind of feeling with what happens before you write a lyric poem, when you enter a similar sort of space. An image comes floating out of it and then you put words to it but really it is all rather beautifully *wordless*. I do mutter things to myself but I don't fully vocalise them. And every sensation I have of her is very aesthetic in nature, well, the qualities I like in lyric poetry. She never seemed to walk – she sort of *glided* so that her presence was like something on hidden wheels. She would glide silently from this part of the room to that part of the room. She was very quiet and very rounded, nothing angular or jarring, and also somehow *sad*. I don't think she was a happy person, but she kept her own counsel. It was all inside her, and then there was a sense of great love which came by way of little kindnesses, like the freshly squeezed grape juice. In that poem "Rubaiyat" I talk about her breaking up the sugar loaf. I was so struck by the fact that the last thing she did in life was to *sweeten* things. She died in her sleep, during her siesta, very peacefully. People say you die as you live – I don't quite believe that, but I think, in her case, she did.'

My grandmother would rise and take my arm,
then sifting through the petals in her palm
would place in mine the whitest of them all:
'Salaam, dokhtaré-mahé-man, salaam!'

'Salaam, my daughter-lovely-as-the-moon!'
Would that the world could see me, Telajune,
through your eyes! Or that I could see a world
that takes such care to tend what fades so soon.
(from 'Rubaiyat')

'Vuillard's best paintings are always those where the figure of the mother is there somewhere, and even if it isn't a portrait of her she's there in the room. In his later work, where she is nowhere to be seen, he really lost his magic. I always had this notion that he had abandoned his Muse or that she had abandoned him. I worry because I haven't written about my grandmother for a very long time now. "Oh God," I think, "I've used her up. I'll never write as well again."'

'On the other hand, it could be argued,' I said, 'that she was the springboard who set you on your poetic trajectory.'

'I think so. She gave me the qualities that my own sensibility instinctively goes towards anyway. I like things to be calm and peaceful.'

§

'Tell me about the Quilt Man.'

Lahaf-Doozee! My backbone is an alley,
a pin-thin alley, cobblestoned
with hawkers' cries, a saddlebag of ribs.
The Quilt Man comes. He squats, he stoops, he spreads
his flattened bale, unslings his bow of heartwood
and plucks the string: *dang dang tok tok* and cotton
rising, rising, is snared around his thread,
snaking, swells in a cobra-head of fleece.
(from 'The Bowl')

'Oh, the Quilt Man!' Mimi cried, as if some long-lost friend had just stepped into the room. 'He was great! He'd go about the streets – there were these various hawkers, melon sellers, et cetera – and he would come, crying "*Lahaf-Doozee! Lahaf-Doozee!*", which translates as "quilt" and "sewer". I remember that because we'd hear him in the distance. We thought he was saying "I love Suzie!" *Why was he saying this?* It had to do with the accent because when Iranians say the English "love" it comes out sounding like *lahaf.* Anyway he'd come and people would give him their old quilts that had gone flat and what he'd do was unstitch them, take out all the cotton stuffing and then – I don't quite remember the instrument, which was a piece of wood, like a primitive musical instrument, with a piece of string attached to it – and somehow, while twanging the string, the cotton would be spun through it and refluffed and then he'd shove it all back inside the quilt and sew it up again. I remember distinctly the sound it made – *dang dang tok tok* – but I don't think we ever used him so probably it is an aural memory rather than a visual one.'

'I like the way you capitalise him, as if he were some great symbolic figure.'

'Yes, and really all he was doing was going about the backstreets of Tehran, proclaiming his love for Suzie.'

'Something you do twice in a big way, first in "Interiors", where you have the sewing machine, and then again in "The Bowl", is to take an object and make it the conduit through which everything passes. Was that an actual bowl?'

'No, it was an imaginary one. It was more like a vision. I don't know where it came from. I was sitting at my desk and I saw this bowl floating about in space. I wrote down, "The bowl is big and blue" and really I wrote the poem in order to discover what that object was. I think "Interiors" came from inside me whereas "The Bowl", except for the originating image, came from outside. It wasn't the memory of an object. I didn't actually *see* those details. What I saw was too vague to describe. It was quite big and all I knew was that it was a Persian turquoise blue.'

'It's as if you were decorating that bowl with memories of images.'

'They *were* specific images – "*Lahaf-Doozee*" is in that poem – and there were a few memories but then much of it came out of my reading of travel writers in Iran, Curzon and others. That is my only poem that is, if you like, rather researched.'

My bowl has cauled my memories. My bowl
has buried me. Hoofprints where Ali's horse
baulked at the glint of cutlasses have thrummed
against my eyelids. Caves where tribal women
stooped to place tin sconces, their tapers lit,
have scaffolded my skin. Limpet-pools
have scooped my gums, raising weals and the blue
of morning-glory furled around my limbs.

My bowl has smashed my boundaries: harebell
and hawthorn mingling in my thickened waist
of jasmine; catkin and *chenar*, dwarf-oak
and hazel hanging over torrents, deltas,
my seasons' arteries … *Lahaf-Doozee!* …
My retina is scarred with shadow-dances

and echoes run like hessian blinds across
my sleep; my ears are niches, prayer-rug arches.

'Yes, the bowl becomes my body, the landscape, and then a lake. Maybe it was an attempt, that poem, to claim ownership of a country that wasn't really mine. Also it comes out of a sense of shame and loss that I don't know my culture, its history and language.'

'There is, on the other hand, that line in "Rubaiyat": "I don't mind that the lilac's roots aren't mine." You are still getting its flowers.'

'Yes, that is what that poem says and to my amazement "The Bowl" ends up yet again with my grandmother. I had no idea it would go there. Maryam is my real name. When I was born my mother and grandmother did a deal in that officially I'd be called "Maryam" but everyone would actually call me Mimi. *Maryam* means "tuberose" in Persian and *talat*, my grandmother's name, means "gold". The poem ends up with me being the flower in the bowl. Tuberose, which is very common in Iran, has the most astonishing perfume and every visitor comes with these great whacking bouquets of it. If you take jasmine, multiply it by a hundred, you get tuberose.

... scent whose name
I owe to *Talat*, *gold* for grandmother:
Maryam, *tuberose*, for bowl, for daughter.

'A lot of those early poems were written at the time of the Iran hostage crisis. There was such virulent anti-Iran feeling, and here we are again with Hillary Clinton saying she will obliterate the country. I was terribly aware of feeling a responsibility, or at least a wish, to present positive images of Iran. I have these feelings of loyalty and you really do feel the pain of all the horrendous images you get of Iran and its people. And so with the negative things, deeply reprehensible though they are, you don't want to put the focus on them because then you are just confirming all the prejudices and stereotypes. If, on the other hand, you focus on the positive then you are evading issues. A lot of people are stuck in this position, while, at the same time, they want to say neither one nor the other presents the whole picture. So those were either personal poems about ordinary human beings or else to do with aesthetics. I remember having a political, even polemical, motive. I wanted to represent the country as *not* being all raving fundamentalists. I wanted to show something other than the violence and primitivism, that there are other dimensions to this culture and these people, something holistic even, there again that cyclical thing, "the tree holding the sky in its arms, the earth in its bowels" [from "Amanuensis"]. And then, too, there is the question of how does one write a political poem. I wrote "Ghazal: The Servant" some years later, during the invasion of Iraq. Oddly enough, though, it goes back, yet *again*, to my grandmother's house. We had a servant called Ma'mad who was really "the man of the house", who looked after my grandfather in his final years when he had Parkinson's. Supposedly the poem is in my grandmother's voice, although in no way is it an attempt to recreate it – it is, rather, a symbolic voice – and, although it is not overt, it's *her* talking to the servant. It is difficult to write a political poem, but I think the *ghazal* suggested to me a way by which it might be done. It has the simple refrain "out in the rain", this also being the rain of bombs, and the insistence of that refrain and the simplicity of the form and language of the *ghazal* gave me a doorway into writing an anti-war poem.'

Ma'mad, hurry, water the rose.
Blessed is the English one that grows
out in the rain.

Water is scarce, blood not so.
Blood is the open drain that flows
out in the rain.

Bring in the lamp, the olive's flame.
Pity the crippled flame that blows
out in the rain.

Where are the children? What is the time?
Time is the terror curfew throws
out in the rain.

Hurry, Ma'mad, home to your child.

Wherever my namesake, Maryam, goes
out in the rain.

§

'My mother's family, the Samii's, were very aristocratic on both sides. In Iran, they had this thing about "the thousand families" and if you were from one of them everyone else had to bow and scrape. We were quite Westernised, going back to my grandfather who was schooled in Belgium – aristocratic, but fallen on hard times. My grandmother had gone from having vast estates, orchards, houses with many rooms, courtyards and pools and servants to a single rented house, with just one servant, in the middle of Tehran. It was all very Chekhovian.'

'It doesn't sound like a particularly religious atmosphere.'

'Not at all. The only contact I ever had with religion was at boarding school on the Isle of Wight, Church of England – Sunday chapel, singing hymns. When I lived in Iran, during the heyday of the Shah, I had no sense of being in a religious country. My grandmother was a practising Muslim in that she said her prayers five times a day, but generally speaking religion was something of which you were only dimly aware. This was partly because the gulf between the classes was so huge. There was the educated middle class, whether they were wealthy or not, the sort of people I would know, who were all pretty much Westernised, spoke another language, and were into avant-garde theatre, and then there was the working class, like our seamstress, Akhtar Khanum, who were religious. Although we loved her and she was part of our lifestyle there was no *real* connection. It was appalling, the gulf between the privileged and the mass of people. The Shah was happy to keep the whole nation under his thumb *and* illiterate. At the same time there was much discontent with the oppression and the secret police. You couldn't make any criticism of the Shah. When we went to Iran the second time, Paul and I got jobs at a tatty little language school, teaching English to mostly underprivileged fifteen- to seventeen-year-olds. Now, in that class were two or three kids who we all knew belonged to SAVAK, the secret police. It was the same with my theatre group. They were just poor Iranian kids from working-class homes. Sex and alcohol, on the other hand, my God, there was much more of it there than here. It was rampant – bottles of whiskey, nightclubs, Saturday gambling tables, everybody divorcing, sleeping with each other – it was party time!'

'So Hafez's taverns were real. What about the Revolution, was your family caught up in it?'

'Some of them, not close relatives, were executed or imprisoned. Obviously everybody was affected, but my mother and her family were anti-Shah, not pro-mullah but more like Western liberal thinkers. My father was more conservative, more royalist, this, of course, being the paradox of being a working-class boy made good. As a young man he had been sent on a scholarship to Germany. He became an engineer, gradually made more and more money, and then was Deputy Minister for Transport in the Shah's government. With the Revolution he lost a lot of property and fled to America. My parents divorced at some point and only gradually did I grow into some kind of knowledge of it. I never had contact with my father during the years I grew up and only got to know him as an adult. My mother, I love her dearly, but I'm so *not* like her it's unbelievable. She is like one of those elegant, moderated Italian ladies who wear silk scarves. I spoke of tuberose earlier. She, too, is hugely associated with flowers. After training at Saint Martin's School of Art she went into fashion and design and made these fabulous silk flowers, hence my poem, as seen through the eyes of a ten-year-old, "Overblown Roses":

> She held one up, twirling it in her hand
> as if to show me how the world began
> and ended in perfection. I was stunned.
> How could she make a rose so woebegone,
> couldn't silk stand stiff? And how could a child,
> otherwise convinced of her mother's taste,
> know what to think? *It's overblown*, she smiled,
> *I love roses when they're past their best.*
>
> 'Overblown roses', the words rang in my head,
> making sense as I suddenly saw afresh
> the rose now, the rose ahead: where a petal

clings to a last breath; where my mother's flesh
and mine, going the same way, may still
be seen as beautiful, if these words are said.

'When she went back to Iran she did interior decoration, posh stuff, like the Shah's villa on the Caspian. And then she built this house in Tehran on the street level of which she ran this business doing exotic flower arrangements for weddings and parties. When she retired she came to London, bought a little place in Hampstead, thinking she would spend half her life here and half in Tehran, but after the Revolution her life over there went up in smoke. She has lived here ever since.'

§

Whose face is this, staring out through young Mimi's, but Telajune's?

'Do you have any memories of your earliest years? You were six when you left Iran.'

'Virtually nothing. And six isn't really *that* young. Well, I can remember the colours, their precise shades, of my childhood furniture, pink and yellow, a very particular, rather weird, pink and a

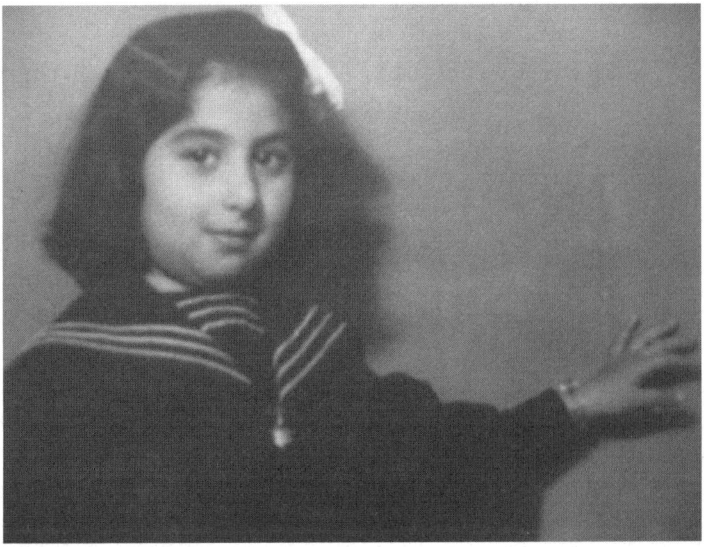

creamy yellow. I used them in "The Meanest Flower" – "Colours keep the line to memory open." Actually I think I had a rather spoiled childhood. I was the first grandchild, a pretty doll for everyone to play with, with idiotic bows all over me, and *hugely* loved. It was a big extended family, with grandmothers, aunts and cousins. I was an only child. I remember my sixth birthday which was shortly before I came to England and being, even at that age, obsessed with my looks. I was sulky because my mother wasn't there but in Switzerland and *she* was the one in charge of my appearance. My whole relationship with my mother is based on clothes. My dress was too long and I thought it didn't look cute. My hair was parted in the wrong place. I was so upset because my grandmother did it all wrong. I don't remember missing my mum but being really upset this was my sixth birthday and I looked horrible. So I remember that but not anything much.'

'Obviously it was a major decision sending you to a boarding school in England. Did you come here alone?'

'I might have had a guardian who came with me but I can't remember. This, along with childhood – not *remembered* childhood but, rather, the *sensation* of it – is one of the central themes of my life and poetry, the absence of memory. My work may give the impression of coming from lots of memories but actually it comes from the *lack* of them. I think this whole question of not being interested in one's own story, of not having had much of a memory for the whole of one's life, not just those first six years, or of not having curiosity for anything that comprises a life story, *that's* what fascinates me, the absence of those things rather than the things themselves. What happens to memory? How does one write if one can't remember anything? I think endlessly about whether I might one day write a long poem. I have written sequences, but really they are small things strung together. I don't know if I could actually sustain anything at length and also I do *so* love the short lyric and you know why: it's because in order to write a short lyric you don't have to have any memory or narrative. You can have some fleeting sensation just like now with that fly going in its crooked little path. That's all you need. That's why I love the short lyric because I can *do it*. Narrative I can't do because I have no sense of having lived a narrative. My whole history is made of these *I don't know's* which I call *holes*. One hole is tenuously connected to another hole. I even have a line, "For what was mine but a hole in the sky?" [from "Childhood Books"]. When I try to tell my life to myself and ask "Did I come to England on my own?" the answer is "I don't know." There's the first hole. "Was it traumatic?" "I don't know." There's a second hole. "What was it like coming to a country where you couldn't speak the language?" "I don't know." *Another* hole! "When and why did my parents get divorced?" The other thing that obsesses me, the more so as I get older, is not that I forget things but that I never knew them in the first place. All these significant events or markers in a life are just like particles in air, vaguely sifted through somewhere in the back of my consciousness. It's as if nothing ever happened. So yes, writing at length, how do I do so when my life is not a long piece of string holding real memories but rather a series of holes strung on an invisible one?'

§

'I studied poetry at school, the Romantics in particular, which is where my great love of Wordsworth comes from and to this day he remains my favourite poet. After I left school my connections were not with poetry, however, but with theatre, which is where I did a lot of verse drama and Shakespeare. Without realising it I was always imbibing poetry although at the time I thought of it as drama. You learn a lot of skills that later you use as a poet. You are alive to nuance, tone and inflection – the spaces between what's *there* and what is *not* there. My first acting was in Glasgow at the Citizens' Theatre. I never wanted to act though. When I was at school, aged fourteen – a senior – someone roped me into directing the junior play. I took Hans Christian Andersen's *The Nightingale* – ironic, isn't it? So Eastern, so lyrical – and adapted it into a play. It was *gorgeous*. My best friend was from Thailand and she had seven sisters who had lots of silk pyjamas, all different sizes, which I borrowed for costumes for the little courtiers. It was that experience that made me decide I wanted to be a theatre director. When I look back I see that all these things led to poetry or, rather, the kind of lyric poetry that I write.

'So later I went to drama school. One either went to university to do drama, followed that route, or to drama school and learned acting which I didn't want to do. There were no directing courses, so I had to do an acting course instead. I hated performing although I loved the rehearsal process. Actually the training was just amazing with all kinds of unexpected aspects. After the Citizens' Theatre I did a film with, of all the awful people in the world, Ken Russell. I was one of the nuns in *The Devils*. I was the one who kept my clothes on. Blink and you'd miss me. It was the most obscene process, the filming of that thing. A woman got raped by the extras. A girl got thrown so violently she ended up in hospital with stitches. A friend of mine could go into a trance. She said to Ken, "I'll do it, but I can manage it only once. It will have to be done in one take." She did it and then he told her there was no film in the camera and that she would have to do it again. She did it again and became really ill. It was a series of nightmares. Equity got called in and there was a lot of fuss but people who could have spoken up didn't because they wanted parts in his next film, *The Boyfriend*. The whole experience disgusted me. When I first went into theatre, I was tremendously naïve and idealistic, thinking it was great art and all that. A dreadful man, Ken Russell really turned me off the whole business, and I'd only been in it for two years. I was with Paul at the time. We dropped out and went to live in the little village of Alte in Portugal for a year. There I painted and wrote a bit, no poetry though. And then we went to Iran in 1970, originally for a summer holiday. When we got there we met up with a friend from London who was also in theatre. He said, "I've a job at the language school. Do you want a job?" Somebody said there was a lovely flat going so we got that and then somebody else said, "Do you want to work with some actors?" What began as a summer holiday ended up with us staying there for three years. I said all right to the Theatre Workshop, which consisted of three or four different companies and was the main theatre base in Tehran. One theatre group was experimental and another was traditional Persian theatre connected to folk styles. I got these mostly young men who had no training and very little education but after working with them for three months, although we didn't have a common language, I formed one of the companies there. I put on a few productions, mostly translations, a couple of Edward Bond plays, or else adaptations such as the one I did of John Steinbeck's

The Pearl. At that time, even with the political censorship, one could do allegories. They didn't *get* them!

'I also worked with the American experimental director, Robert Wilson. In 1972, I was his assistant director at the Shiraz Festival. Wilson performed this thing called *KA MOUNTain and GUARDenia Terrace*. He took over this sacred mountain near Shiraz, called Haft Tan ("Seven Bodies") after seven Sufi poets buried at its foot, and decided he'd put on a show that would last seven days and seven nights non-stop. It wasn't really a show, more a human installation. The mountain, which he renamed KA, was divided into seven stages, the bottom one being this massive wooden platform, and he positioned different people doing different things on different levels of the mountain. I remember this woman, a quite well-known actress, who did nothing but peel an onion very slowly on stage three of the mountain. Andy, who was Wilson's partner, did a whirling dervish dance elsewhere, going round and round in circles for hours on end. My job was glorified prop manager and the list of things I had to get would include things like two hundred live pink rabbits, well, not rabbits maybe, but *something* we had to dye pink. Everything he ordered came in hundreds – one hundred of this, one hundred of that – the maddest list of things you could imagine. He did have a brilliant designer's eye, though, and he could create the most amazing *tableaux vivants*. This, I think, was his main genius but the things he wanted were always things that had to be flown in, orchids, for example. At one point he wanted to blow up the top of the mountain and excavate some massive hole in which he'd place "the lamb of God". And this was a sacred mountain! He was used to getting his own way but of course it was a complete fiasco. It was supposed to go on all day and night and theatre-goers do *not*, at the height of summer, in the middle of the day, go up and down mountains. Most people just went to the evening show on the platform but because it was so slow they walked out. There were all these installations – a whale, Noah's Ark, the Trojan horse, the Acropolis surrounded by missiles, a skyline of New York City, a dinosaur – and on the final evening some of these were set on fire. One good thing I remember is that with all the days spent going up and down that flipping mountain, it was the thinnest I have ever been. Otherwise I learned nothing from this other than to marvel at how reputations are made.'

(I read later in an article about the production that at one point Wilson took to the stage and asked people why they were leaving in droves, to which a Scotsman answered, 'To *gi' ye* an action!')

'We left shortly after I gave birth to my daughter, came back to London where Paul was able to pick up his acting career. Soon after, my son was born.'

Several years later, Mimi and Paul separated.

§

The patience-stone – *sang-é saboor* in Persian – makes its appearance in folk tales from places as far apart as Libya, Turkey, Afghanistan, Israel and Iran. The patience-stone, which can be any stone one chooses, is what one addresses in one's pain and solitude, and when it reaches the point at which it has absorbed all the sorrow it can take then either it or the person who grieves will explode. What determines the choice of stone remains something of a mystery to me. It could be, say, this one.

This stone, which resides on the window-ledge where I live, might be aping the man in the moon. Could that be a gag over his mouth? Could it be there in order that he *not* let go all his pent-up sorrows?

According to legend, or at least one of its many variants, and which I here greatly abbreviate, a girl called Fatemeh falls in love with a handsome young man whom she's been promised in a prophecy. A trusted servant tricks her, takes him away from her, marries him, and, in a cruel reversal of roles, Fatemeh ends up slaving a proverbial seven years in the young man's house where, as one might expect, she is constantly abused by her former servant. One day the man goes on a journey to town and asks Fatemeh whether there is anything she'd like him to bring back for her. She asks for a patience-stone. After much searching, he finally obtains one from an old man who warns him that whoever seeks the stone is filled with sorrow and that unless she is closely watched its employment could have fatal consequences. Later that evening, she tells her sorrows to the stone and just as she is about to explode, she cries:

> Patience-stone, patience-stone
> You are patient, I am patient.
> Either you burst, or I will burst.

The young man, who has been listening behind a door, rushes in, orders the stone to explode, which it does, embraces her, and then, as tends to be the case in moral tales, she is restored to him and he to her and they live happily ever after. The imagination, though, craves darkness as well as light. According to novelist Sadeq Hedayat's retelling of the story the stone secretes a single drop of blood and the young man orders that the servant – a gypsy girl in this version – be tied by the hair to the tail of a mule and sent into the desert where, presumably, they become fodder for the vultures. I wonder, though, *why the mule*? What had he done?

In Sadeq Chubak's great modernist novel, *Sang-é Saboor*, there is no escape, only death and destruction for everyone, and indeed, considering Iran's history, from the Arab conquests to the Revolution of 1979, and the sense of defeat that is so much a part of the Persian psyche, there could not be a more appropriate object upon which to rest the country's case. My own experience of Iran is that of a sorrowful place where one can almost smell the tears on the breeze.

'*Melancholy* is the word they use,' Mimi corrected me, 'that Eastern melancholy which is something I have. I think here, in the West, it is seen as a negative thing whereas in the East, close to the end of its spectrum, you find romantic longing, beauty and separation. So much of Persian poetry is about separation, which means it is also about union. What others might call sorrow, I see as something very close to desire. That sweetness is not something you'd necessarily want to be robbed of, whereas here it is often allied to depression. Another word for it comes from Elizabeth Bishop who speaks of "homesickness", a *metaphysical* homesickness that you feel even when you're at home.'

Patience-stone: I much prefer Mimi's triangularly phrased 'stone of patience'. She wrote, early on, a poem of that title.

'That's my grandmother again. She always said of herself, "I am a stone of patience". A person, too, can be a stone of patience, but really the locus of that poem is the house where I lived in Highgate. I was stuck at home, a single mother with two children. A lot of my early poems – I have to use the dreaded "F"-word here – come from a feminist position and my own experience of the different ways in which one engages with men and women … and with lovers – I suppose I've had my fair share of them and with always the same shortcomings. Why is it that with women you can effortlessly empathise and with lovers it is such a struggle? The "stone of patience" – I have never actually seen one – comes from a time when I was torn between stoic patience and going where one might risk rupture. I was trying to work out, both pragmatically and morally, which route to follow. And because I have difficulties in my relationships with men very often I feel I have to be a stone of patience. *Stone of patience, sang-é saboor.*

'Anyway I couldn't do theatre work any more, I had no money, and so my neighbour said, "Why don't you go on an Arvon writing course?" I'd always had a horror of being a writer. I could think of nothing I wanted less. The word was always *writer* – never *poet*. It never entered my mind that one could be a poet. As for being a writer, I had images of Hemingway with a horrible old typewriter and a bottle of whiskey. So I went on an Arvon course for script-writing *and poetry*. I was interested in the first. At that point I was desperate to work in theatre again. I'd written a half-baked radio play called *Stone of Patience*. This is almost the very first thing I wrote. I took that script with me. They were not interested in it and Archie Markham, who was one of the tutors, said "Go and write some poems." And so, being very *mazloom*, I said "Okay". The first poem I ever wrote, aged forty-two, was "The Black and White Cows". I looked out of the window and saw some black and white cows. I wrote, "The black and white cows hold centuries of use like china." The radio script, of which I have no recollection whatsoever except that it was somehow connected to my grandmother, went into the bin. Soon after, I wrote that poem "Rubaiyat", which in my mind is somehow connected to *Stone of Patience* and then, later, I wrote the poem of that title which bore no resemblance to the original radio script. What interested me was that something I'd been unable to write in another genre could suddenly become a poem.'

'And so you began to write poetry at a time of turmoil in your life.'

'My life is endless turmoil except on the surface it is quite calm and quiet and orderly. It has always been so – calm *and* turmoil. It has never been one thing or the other but both together. If I have a terrible row with someone it has to be in an extremely tidy room.'

'So Archie entered your life and inspired you to write.'

'I don't think he *inspired* me to write – he *told* me to go and write some poems. So I did. And he said they were really good and ought to be published. It all happened so quickly. I went on that course in 1986. My first book came out in 1991.'

'If Archie didn't actually inspire you, he would seem to have been the still point in your life.'

'God no! Every single one of my relationships was fraught apart from my second marriage, to Paul, the father of my children, which lasted for about fifteen years. I was happily married to him until things started to go wrong. My relationship with Archie, on the other hand, was the most intractable and difficult of my life, also the longest. It lasted twenty-two years but if you add up all the time we were together I don't think it would amount to even a year.'

'Maybe that's why it lasted a long time.'

'You put it in a nutshell. We were sort of together and *not* together but we would speak on the phone four or five times a week, for an hour at a time. I think of him as family, as more than just a partner. He was someone who'd been in my life for a long time, in a very close way, and knew me very well. We were never really able to build what I think of as a relationship. He would never physically stay in one place long enough.'

Will anger shift
the boulder, buy her freedom, and the earth's? Or patience,
like the earth's, be abused?

(from 'Stone of Patience')

'I can't remember which man I had in mind when I wrote the

poem – they have all merged into one! – some line there about a lover grabbing for his shoes – but I think maybe it was Archie. Yes, it was. In that relationship in particular, I felt a great pressure not to open up, not to complain and not to express any needs – to be a "stone of patience" in other words. And yet at the same time, with my background and sensibilities, I knew I was not really like that. So I was pulled in two directions at once and then my grandmother came to mind as a kind of model, as someone from whom I could learn, take on board some of her patience, which I had never done in my life. Maybe I was paying too high a price for being, if you like, my feminist self. I feel more and more that life is pushing me in the direction of being a stone of patience. I think this is what happens to a great many women, especially as they get older.'

'And now, with Archie gone, it must seem the stone is still being filled.'

'Yes, a large stone, very probably a boulder.'

A silence fell upon the room where silence is already the rule.

'I think poetry itself is like that stone. It's like when you can't express things in life or make things work out. Whether you like it or not, you are in a silent space. You write from out of that space, which is quite different to writing out of angst or trauma, when the pressure of the emotions is such that they pour out all over the page. I have never written like that. With me it has more to do with silence, when the pressure of that silence becomes so intense, so unbearable, the words come out of the air just in order to alleviate it. When I write it is either out of a sense of intense beauty or else a void, when the emptiness is so large, the skin of it so tense, you feel it should break although it never does, it never changes its stone shape.'

§

There would seem to be a neat metaphysical shift in Mimi's poem 'Eden' where the two geographical realities of her life, the dryness of Iran and the verdancy of England, meet up, making this, at first appearance, a poem bridging two cultures. What I could not have anticipated was her response.

'Actually this poem comes out of the fact I get sick to death of all the green in England. I get a feeling of deep depression because I can't stand the green, the endless grey and green, the only two colours I ever see, especially on train journeys going through the English countryside. I have to read because I can't bear this non-stop display of little green fields. It makes me feel so claustrophobic. I long for those great tracts of dusty ground where you might get the bright orange of a nasturtium whereas here, with all this greenness, all you get, if you're lucky, are some bits of white meadowsweet. If I still lived in a dry country I would hardly be praising dust, so politically it's not on, but aesthetically … *aesthetically* all this green depresses me. Also behind this there may be a kind of resentment: why are some countries lucky to have all this rain and water? Don't they know how lucky they are? I remember once my father coming to England, and we were standing on a high terrace at the South Bank Centre overlooking the Thames and just when I expected him to say "How wonderful!" he said, very bitterly, "It is all very well for a country which has water." I was so struck by that.'

'And London, what about London?'

'I have often wondered why I have never written about London although I am drawn to the natural life in this city, its flowers and trees. I do not have the vocabulary for inorganic things. I'll look at something, trying to decide whether it is a winch or a crane. I will look at drainpipes, wondering if they're not in fact some other kind of pipe. When I walk about, which is a lot, I don't ever notice buildings. There is a huge, bright red, fire station nearby which, until someone recently mentioned it to me, I never noticed. London, though, is where I became a mother – the whole of my life with the children has been here. Also all my later schooling – secretarial college, the Drama Centre, and then, of course, there is the Poetry School that ate up ten years of my life. My whole working life has had something to do with schooling, but the situation I'm happiest with is when I'm in the pupil role.'

'Are you an outsider here? Do you feel a separateness and, if so, do you appreciate it?'

'I think it depends on whether you see yourself from the outside, which is partly how one sees oneself anyway, or whether you see yourself from the inside. If the former, then I would probably use words like "outsider" or even "exile", but as I tend to look at myself

from the inside I don't really think in those terms. It's been observed that I write from the margins or as an outsider. Although I'm not particularly aware of that it's a valid thing to say but its validity is neither here nor there because it doesn't interest me.'

'Maybe separateness is more to the point, a separate place.'

'I do feel a sense of slight isolation in that I don't fall into any group or camp or shared platform and there are times when I have felt the lack of that. You wonder about whether you *have* a readership. I just assume any readership I have is an English one, but at the same time I do not particularly want people to read me as an Iranian *anything*. Those matters are a bit awkward at times but they don't really connect with any sense of where my writing comes from or what interests me or what ideas are circling round in my own mind. Those things only come up when I wonder how I present myself, or how I'm read, or when I wince at something said in a review. Sometimes people comment on my Persian childhood memories when there aren't any or on my being influenced by Persian syntax, which is laughable, given I can't even read the language.

'As to this question of separateness, I wrote a *ghazal* recently and in the signature couplet came up with the line, "I've searched for sameness all my life / but Mimi, nothing's the same despite the candles of the chestnut trees." *I have searched for sameness*: I realise that even in relationships that's my difficulty with men. Maybe I should have been lesbian. It would have been the answer to all my prayers. Sadly I'm only lesbian in spirit. I have difficulty with *difference*. I am most comfortable when I am with people with whom I feel kinship or a connectedness to. I am not someone attracted to opposites. Are they two sides of the same coin, sameness and separateness? I don't think so. There is something quite appealing about separateness as there is about solitude or even *aloneness* as opposed to loneliness. It also connects to the idea of wholeness. When something is separate, it is also whole. It has its own integrity and is not muddled up with other things.

'There came a time when suddenly I realised I'm British. I accepted that to be British incorporates this whole thing of multiculturalism. In that respect, I can claim to be as British as anyone else. I also feel, for the same reason, that I am a Londoner. But just look where I live. There aren't any white English people here. This stretch of the road is a very Caribbean bit of Stoke Newington. To be honest, though, ever since I started writing I have been plagued with questions, observations and comments about identity and exile and multicultural this or that and, quite frankly, the language has got to a point where I just can't stand it any more. That's probably *now* whereas next week I might feel slightly differently but at the moment I'm feeling so jaded and so tired of all that. "Am I this?", "Am I that or the other?", and at the end of the day I feel like saying, "Oh, I don't know. All I've done is to write some poems about flowers and I was thinking about Wordsworth at the time. Make of it what you will." Sometimes I just want to escape all those frames of reference, and of course I can't escape them because even the things that really do interest me are somehow connected with all those issues. But they connect through different doors, through back doors, rather than the "here I am, coming in the front door" approach to questions of identity.'

'What you are saying is music to my ears because nothing bores me more than multiculturalism. I relish *difference*. Difference is the thing that needs to be preserved and not dissolved in some kind of cultural gumbo soup.'

'I totally agree with you. I think that's the important thing, the ethical thing, the politically *right* thing, but *emotionally* it makes me profoundly uncomfortable. Maybe that's because when I arrived here in 1950, so very different and with everything so different around me, and so young as well, like all young children I wanted to be assimilated. I feel still that sense of being *different*, not culturally or racially, but temperamentally. It's difficult for me at times. I had it in my relationship with Archie too, that sense of never having been so different from anyone I was ever with. I just couldn't deal with it. I have an innate longing, almost a lyric desire, for *sameness* … for *mirroring*. One of my favourite things in the English language is that little phrase *me too*. I love it when you say something and someone else says yes, *me too*. I find that so exciting, even with the small things whereas if I say "Oh, I really love this" and the other person says "I don't" then I immediately feel depressed. I am disappointed and I think it's that sense of feeling *all wrong*, which probably goes back to my childhood. I did feel *all wrong* but only if I looked at myself as a physical being … if I allowed myself to be aware of what I looked like, the colour of my hair and my skin and all the physical, racial characteristics. And so I grew up living much more in the things that are invisible, such as language or how you relate to people, whole areas where everything is without material, physical existence, and that to me also connects with poetry. This goes very much against what everyone says about writing *from the body* and all that. I may be able to take it in intellectually, agree with it, or else just go along with it and say "Yes, yes, that's great!" but really I write from *bodilessness*.'

'You're not really much of a feminist!'

'I know! I know! All that *écriture féminine*! I have betrayed the cause!'

I suggested to Mimi that maybe we'd had enough of all the *isms*.

'Of course I profited from them because, to be honest, I would never have been published so quickly and in so many magazines. I would not have had all those readings had I not been "ethnic". *No way!* You wouldn't be talking to me if I were Sarah Smith from Wolverhampton.'

The Burning of a Thread

Rajan Khosa, Film Director

When I first met Rajan Khosa in 1998 he was working in a second-hand bookshop on Gloucester Road. The antiquarian book trade is a floating world for people meant to be elsewhere. You'll find there writers, singers, musicians, actors, painters, photographers, dancers, mathematicians, campanologists, ichthyologists, all of them waiting for the call, which for many never comes. It is one of the few jobs in which, although penurious, one might preserve one's face. Certainly Rajan kept his. Aristocratic in bearing, bearded, a Brahmin to the core, he might have stepped out of an Indian miniature. I saw him once a week over a period of two or three months during which time our chat slowly blossomed into dialogue. One day I happened to mention that my father, who was suffering from Alzheimer's, watched *Gladiator* and at the point in the movie when the crowd at the Roman Coliseum stands up to support its hero, shouting 'Maximus! Maximus!', he stood up in front of the TV set, thrusting his closed fist into the air, chanting along with them 'Maximus! Maximus!' The anecdote delighted Rajan, who said it was his dream to have an audience so completely *inside* any film he'd made. I might have said that in the case of my father such aesthetic involvement came at a huge expense. This was not, however, some quip he made but rather the expression of a deeper purpose.

I asked him what kind of films he made.

'Art-house,' he replied.

The answer set off alarm bells in me. More often than not, *art-house* points to the absolute worst in terms of pretentiousness and self-indulgence. I made the right noises, asking where one might get to see one of his films. Rajan told me his first full-length feature was available at a video shop down the street. I had no excuse not to see it.

§

I've watched it three times. It is a quiet masterpiece. One of the best films ever made on the subject of music, *Dance of the Wind* concerns a female classical singer, Pallavi, who, after her mother and teacher Karuna Devi dies, undergoes a spiritual and artistic crisis. Suddenly, on stage, she is unable to sing another note. Will she or will she not recover her voice? There is a striking parallel here with the career of one of India's most famous classical singers, Kishori Amonkar, who in the late 1950s lost her voice for two years. Rajan learned of this only after he made the film, which serves to demonstrate the existence of those invisible currents upon which imagination rides before conscious mind does. The film is also about the transfer of knowledge from guru to disciple (*shishya*), which in the North Indian classical tradition (*khyal*), a modal system with no standard notation, is absolutely vital for its continuance.

Karuna Devi is played in the film by the great Indian scholar, Dr Kapila Vatsyayan, who on occasion has played a significant role in Rajan's life. The role of Pallavi is played, against type, by the Bollywood and soap opera star Kitu Gidwani whose ability to act in serious roles is too often overshadowed by how well she looks in

a negligee. The elderly guru is played by B.C. Sanyal, a well-known painter and a friend of the Khosa family. The street girl is played most hauntingly by Roshan Bano who really does come from the slums.

The loss of voice Pallavi has to endure might be that of any artist in any medium whether it be the empty stave, the white canvas or the blank page. It might also be said to presage Rajan's own artistic silence, although this would be imposed upon him from outside. Karuna's death coincides with the mysterious appearance of the young girl from the streets, Tara, and an elderly man who stands silently by her side.

Rajan wrote the song Tara sings:

> Neither stars there, nor the night,
> O departing one, you ride the winds,
> You leave no trace behind.
> Neither moon there, nor the night owl,
> If you find the lasting friend,
> O departing one, I wish to fly,
> Give me desire in my wings.

We learn later that the old man was once Karuna's guru, Munir Baba, and that when Karuna started to perform in public, mortified by the sacrifice of her divinely inspired talent to the masses, Munir undertook a vow of silence.

I hope it will not be revealing too much of the plot if I say that when she hears Tara sing Karuna removes the thread she wears about her wrist and sets it on the window ledge from where, at the moment of her death, it is blown away and picked up by the young girl below. After the thread is returned to Pallavi, Munir Baba takes it and throws it in the fire. As we shall see, the symbol of the burning thread is one central to Rajan's own thought and spiritual experience.

Although the film garnered awards and had excellent notices, rather than mark the beginning of an illustrious career it did precisely the opposite. Despite a wealth of projects, which included a documentary about literary pilgrimages to places such as Hafez's tomb in Shiraz and Rumi's in Konya, Rajan was unable to obtain funding for another film. It is a mark of shame that, in an industry where most of what is made is absolute tripe, for the next few years, during which time he returned to India, he was in an artistic wilderness. The reasons for this I suspect have to do at least partly with his being out of step with the times. *Dance of the Wind* bears comparison with the films of the great master, Satyajit Ray, but when even the latter's films rarely get a screening in his native country it is not a matter of surprise that a film as thoughtful as Rajan's cannot reach a public glutted on junk culture. Happily for Rajan there has been a reversal in his fortunes with the recent commission to make a multi-media museum, containing film installations and holography, devoted to the memory of one of India's best-known spiritual leaders, Sadhu Vaswani. Also he is making another feature film on the subject of street children, which I suspect will be a home-grown, and perhaps necessary, response to Danny Boyle's *Slumdog Millionaire*.

The death of a close friend was to be the occasion of Rajan's return to London. Stored in the attic of the deceased's house were twenty trunks of belongings left behind from his years here, which now he had to remove. A bit older, his beard gone, and perhaps even more intense than before, he mulled over the vicissitudes of life, death for him not quite the tragedy it is for most people here.

'Time and space is such that here you are,' he said, 'doing this piece on me, and I'm thinking, "My God, how strange this is. I have been spending my time in an attic, looking back at fifteen years of my life." There is an Indian saying, "Anything more than five years is a dream."'

It was an apt opportunity to peel away the phases of a life that seemed, just then, as if they belonged to someone else.

§

'I was a happy child,' he began, 'a participant in my parents' years of growing. My mother had me when she was nineteen. My dad was only two years older. So in a sense they themselves were still developing. My mother was deeply into yoga and spirituality. A voracious reader of philosophy, she taught us the Sanskrit scriptures, which we started reciting at the age of three. She is a very graceful, dignified woman with an attention-seeking husband and son. She will keep them at the front but really she is their backbone. I love women like that. My dad had his bohemian salon with all these painters, poets, playwrights and musicians. As I was not considered a burden, they took me everywhere. What I loved as a kid were all the poetry sessions at home. My dad was part of the so-called "anti-poetry" movement. It was really poetry, of course. He went through all these phases. As there wasn't that much age difference between us, we were more like friends. One of the gang, I was called "the little man". I remember them being excited about the gramophone, the joy on their faces when listening to LPs of the people they loved. And then there were the spool tape recorders. In India these things arrived a bit later than in the West. So that is how Indian classical music came down to me, from my parents and their friends, both on record and in concert.'

'You seem to be an aristocrat of the senses!'

'If one is lucky enough to be born into that artistic milieu, yes, it was a kind of aristocracy. My origins are Kashmiri but I was brought up in Delhi. Actually I was born in Bhopal. My mother went to visit her brother there and gave birth to me. After twenty days we went back to Delhi, which is where I spent my childhood. We would go up to Kashmir for our holidays, where all my aunts and uncles and extended family lived.'

'Did they suffer because of the insurgency?'

'Tremendously so. Everything got wiped out. It is a complex issue. Obviously the needs of the Muslim majority had not been addressed over time. The Muslims did the menial jobs while the Hindus were comparatively well-off. Ethnic cleansing took place in 1989. I remember all these slogans, graffiti everywhere, asking Hindus to leave. If there was a row of houses, they would put petrol around all the Hindu homes, many of them separated from their Muslim neighbours by only a few feet. You could walk down any street and see all the gutted houses. Some Muslims who liked their Hindu neighbours would warn them the night before, saying that on the following day they would burn down their homes and kill them. After they were forced to leave many of my relatives died of psychological disorders. The Kashmiri Hindus had been a settled people. They lived in old houses overlooking Dal Lake, in which their families had lived for six or seven generations. It is possible to continue only when your ancestral wealth stays in one place, but when you are uprooted again and again it is no longer possible. The government has been trying to rehabilitate the Hindus but nobody has had the courage to go back. My father is a painter and he had a lot of artist friends there. I have seen from up close what all this did to their psyches.'

'Was your father born in Kashmir?'

'No, in Lahore, in Pakistan. My mother was born and brought up in Kashmir, my grandfather too. My father was seven in 1947 when the Partition of British India took place. His family had to flee overnight. He has memories of burning streets and of being taken out of Lahore in an army jeep. My grandmother never stopped talking about all the jewellery and precious things they left behind. They had to start all over again. Some twelve million people had to move and they all carry those scars.'

'So you grew up with the pain your parents had to endure.'

'I left home when I was sixteen but it was inescapable. I still don't understand what any of it means. I understand to the extent that it was painful for my parents who had to go through these things twice, firstly when they were children during Partition and then again, in their fifties, with Kashmir. They are liberated, progressive people but I think education can do very little to remove the scars.'

'Your father Kashmiri Khosa is a distinguished painter, as was his father before him.'

'My grandfather, Somnath Khosa, died when I was twenty-two. I was very close to him. In the early days he did lovely landscapes, which he'd been taught to do by the British, and then he got his start doing cinema hoardings in Lahore.'

'So there is some kind of cultural transference there!'

'I hadn't thought of that. He was the one who took me to see my first films. He loved film.'

'You said he knew Gandhi.'

'Mahatma Gandhi, Nehru and all these politicians would come to the house. This, of course, was before I was born. A passionate man, my grandfather used to drink, smoke and womanise but after Gandhi he changed and started wearing the *khadi*, simple clothes made of hand-woven cotton. This Gandhi thing changed a lot of people. My grandfather was involved in the freedom struggle and then, for the next thirty or forty years, he painted the life of Gandhi.

'After Gandhi was killed the politicians encouraged him to

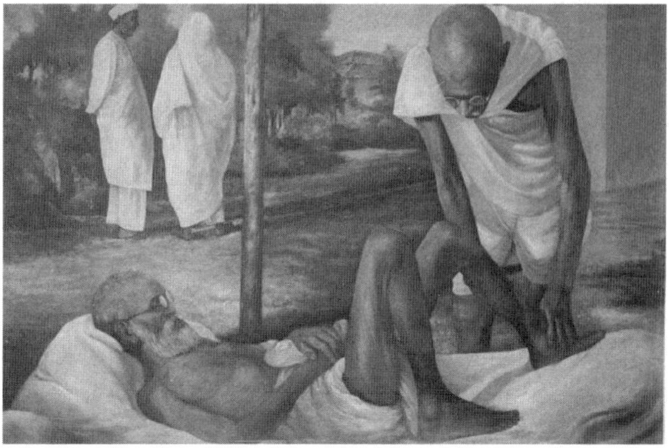

continue painting various episodes from his life – the non-violent *satyagraha* movement, the Dandi salt march, the burning of foreign clothes, et cetera. It was in the interest of the Congress Party which came into power after Independence to harp upon the Gandhi legacy. My grandfather used to work through the night. As a child I would lie on the sofa watching him, then fall asleep, and wake up in the morning and one whole portion of the painting would be done.'

'Did your father hope you would become a painter as well?'

'My father struggled as an artist. Only in his early forties did he begin to get noticed and started receiving various national awards. He is selling well now, and divides his time between the mountains and Delhi, so livelihood is not a problem any more. But earlier in his life he understood how difficult it is for a painter to establish himself and he did not wish to see me struggle. So I went to design school which I left after a few years. When I moved into film he understood it was an art form and thought it was better than being a painter. So he was supportive.'

'I would have said that you are still a painter in your films.'

'Visual language gets embedded in you when you grow up with painters. My father would show me a painting and then ask me, "Why isn't the composition working?" "What is negative space?" "What is balance?" "What do these colours do?" As there was this dialogue going on all the time I was taught these things early in life. Painting was therefore always in my blood. It was the first thing I did as a kid. I went to my father's studio when I was sixteen or seventeen, learned still life, and was very good at it. It helped me later on when unconsciously I would translate these things into film, drawing frames, for example.'

'And then there was this great-grandfather of yours, Swami Shambhu Nath, who lived in a cave.'

'That's another film I should make. There is so much room for the imagination there. My great-grandfather was a treasurer in the court of Hari Singh who was the last maharajah of Jammu and Kashmir before Partition. He had a stunningly gorgeous wife called Badaur Ded. I remember a painting my grandfather did of her, which hung above the fireplace in our house. The story goes this man lived happily enough until one day he was accused of stealing from the treasury. He fled Srinagar and the police chased him down to the bottom end of the country where he was caught near Hampi, tried and jailed there. While in prison he wrote a philosophical treatise on Kashmir Shaivism that my father still possesses and which has the stamp of Hospit prison on it. After he was released, rather than go back to Kashmir, to his beautiful wife and family, he chose to live in a cave in the ancient ruins of Hampi. There, living among monkeys and cows, he meditated and became known as a saint and a healer.

'On a normal day maybe three or four hundred people, many of them coming from great distances, would queue up at the entrance to the cave where he'd have a log burning twenty-four hours a day.

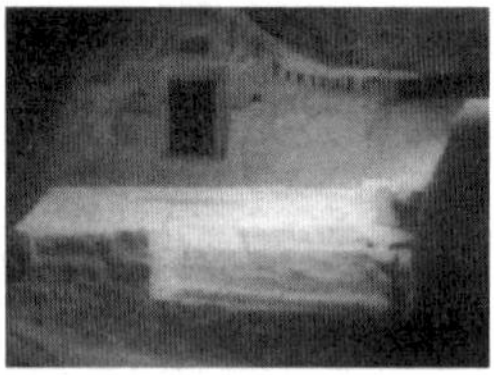

It was something like a sacrificial fire, and he would give ashes from it to people who then became healed. Today there is a temple in that cave with a sculpture of his bust and local believers still go there to worship. I haven't yet been there. Things have their own time. I don't know for sure what happened in his personal and professional life that made him decide never to go home again but I have this idea that here was this beautiful woman, this sexual being who was very domineering and flirtatious, and my very calm, very stoical great-grandfather who simply couldn't handle her. I suspect he used the accusation of theft as a justifiable way of running away from his personal life. Sometimes mystics are irresponsible. It was probably why my grandfather became an alcoholic, chain-smoker and womaniser. This said, in the Vedic belief system there are four ashrams in life, of twenty-five years each. The last one, *Sanyasa*, is when you walk away from your family in order to reconnect yourself with the godhead, when you practise detachment. Sometimes we use things in life. The world thinks one thing and we allow it to while we make our spiritual escape. Why else would he run away from there? As a child, when we went on holiday to Kashmir, I stayed in that house. My grandfather had an inter-caste marriage around 1938 and being a Kashmiri he wasn't allowed to marry a Punjabi so he went to his father in the south and got married in his cave. This is when he took pictures of my great-grandfather, which I saw as a child, and which later were destroyed by damp. Years later, my dad went there and made a video document of the place. People there touched his feet because he was the grandson of this man. Obviously there is a wonderful film there.'

§

While still a student at the Film and TV Institute of India, in Pune, Rajan made a short black-and-white film called *Wisdom Tree*. It was nominated for the Indian entry at the Oscars and it won international awards in Oberhausen and other places. The film has all the faults and virtues of an early work – a callowness that verges on naivety, a certain roughness which in itself is attractive. A minimal budget allows for an imagination unfettered by the constraints of having to pay its way home. If the setting is India, or, more specifically, a dilapidated interior somewhere in India, the mechanical sounds coming from outside might have been added by David Lynch. A poetic monologue, *Wisdom Tree* depicts graphically the indignities of old age, in the person of an elderly lady, and how they are met with through the interiorised voice of the young woman, presumably the daughter, who looks after her. At one point in the film, in what I suspect is an imaginary or dream sequence, the young woman disrobes, showing the old one the beauty of her body, and then spits in her direction. This may occur in the mind of the younger woman or the older one. Whichever it is, it is as unsparing as any mediaeval woodcut on the theme of mutability. It is not, perhaps, quite the stuff for a modern world in which decay is either shoved inside a cupboard or dabbed with cosmetics, but it goes down well as art-house. The film's relative success enabled Rajan, aged twenty-five, to travel to Europe and to see for himself what was happening elsewhere with film, but little did he realise this would engender, at square one, a loss of faith in what the medium can do.

'I went back to India, thinking cinema was not dealing with answers to the meaning of life. So I stepped into Indian philosophy. I started studying Sanskrit and reading the scriptures. My mentor in Delhi, Dr Kapila Vatsyayan, who later played the role of Pallavi's mother in *Dance of the Wind*, directed me to go to Varanasi, Orissa and Calcutta and to various centres of learning to see what areas of Indian philosophy might interest me. India is a big place. Once you start to explore, it is an inexhaustible treasure. At first I slept on the streets of Varanasi. It was great to experience this, to lead the life of a mendicant, although I remember once waking up in the middle of the night and seeing rats in front of me. At the time I thought to myself these ideas may be good but in reality they're not so hygienic. I couldn't tell my parents any of this of course. They would have come and taken me home. As a young man I already knew what they shouldn't know. I led a very basic existence. You know how *sadhus* live. They wear a *dhoti*, a single Y-shaped piece of thin cotton cloth with a string that ties. It is a beautiful object. They bathe in the river, washing the *dhoti* at the same time, which dries in ten minutes, and then they put it back on and wander from place to place. They never take public transport. It is basically like a pilgrimage. While walking one remembers the name of the Lord with each step. Every act is one of worship, in each of them a whole mythology, a subtext and a meaning, and by merely repeating them over and over you connect to that cosmic energy or godhead or whatever.'

'Was this something you did because you could afford to?'

'Money was never a concern. I do not really remember *how* I lived. I had got some money in awards. I realised I could just go. I didn't need very much. Most of these ashrams feed you and give you shelter, which is why they get so many devotees. I spent three years wandering about in Bengal, Orissa and Varanasi, making contact with people who lived the spiritual life. I read a lot on the subject. Ultimately, though, everyone needs food, shelter and security. When you look at all these *sadhus* they too live within structures. They have the same problems as everyone else. It was not so much a matter of disillusionment for me as of realising they were as human as I was. I had put them on a pedestal and then I expected them to give me answers which not even they themselves had. Also I realised they were rife with academia of the same kind you find in film theory. There were fights over stupid things which did not amount to much and when, after three years of this, I went back to Delhi, Kapila told me that there was one more man I should go to, someone in my own tradition, who lived in Kashmir. "Go and stand at his door," she said. "If he accepts you, he accepts you – if he doesn't, he doesn't. It's a matter of luck. He is eighty-four and the tradition will die with him." I was born into Kashmir Shaivism. Seven generations of my family practised it, and from it came the prayers and ceremonies I learned as a child, and so although I did not live by, or practise, Shaivism, it was quite easy for me to see where it was coming from. When I look back at that phase in my life it was in those final two years in Kashmir that everything crystallised for me. I had a living master and I could see and learn through his eyes, his vision.'

The famous mystic, Swami Lakshman Joo (1907–91), may be said to have been born a saint. Swami Ram gave a single almond to his mother and nine months later Lakshman Joo was born. The tenets of Kashmir Shaivism are too complex to go into here, but suffice to say it is a school of Hindu philosophy deeply rooted in the Tantras and which began during the eighth or ninth century C.E. Lakshman Joo was its last teacher. It was his belief that intellectual understanding needed to be tested with personal experience. Unlike many religious figures he did not seek recompense.

'Swami Lakshman Joo was an absolutely wonderful man, with such energy about him and intensity in his eyes. When he ate a piece of bread the birds would settle on his shoulders and eat with him. They would not come near me but after a month or so, maybe because I had some of his influence on me, they began to trust me. Gurus can initiate you even by their gaze. If you believe the intangible can work through those energies then it'll come. I took a lot of battering. It is the familiar

story of an old man breaking a young man's ego. Swami Lakshman did not accept people easily. A very unconventional man, he was not one of those *sadhus* who wear saffron, as they tend to do in India, and whoever he met, whether it was a bread seller or milkman or the prime minister, he treated him exactly the same. Sunday was "open day" when maybe two or three hundred devotees would be allowed into his house, otherwise from Monday to Saturday nobody was given admittance. The only other day would be on his birthday when about four to six thousand people turned up from all over. The huge wooden house where he lived overlooked Dal Lake in Kashmir. It had beautiful surroundings – orchards, a garden – and he had a temple of his own. There were two sisters who lived in that house, who looked after it. A lot of Americans went there and documented him and his commentaries on the *Bhagavad Gita* and on the meaning of Kashmiri Shaiva texts but he actively shunned academic intellectual pursuits. The mind, he taught us, wants always to be master. It wants to know which direction you are taking, how significant it is, what you are achieving or not achieving. When enlightenment or whatever you may call it occurs you do not realise it. What's most important is for recognition to occur like a flash of lightning and for it to get into your system. Once you abandon mind, then the path opens for this other which is the source of creation. That sense of a greater presence comes though faculties other than the mind so first and foremost one is taught to obliterate mind. Meditation is good for this. Once you manage this, then what does it matter where you are going or what you achieve. All we need to do is go back to the source from which we came, by which I mean we connect to the source of creation – we become *it*, so to speak. When I met Swami Lakshman he was in a different zone altogether … he was like this beam of light. He was ruthless about his fire ceremonies, which were elaborate. In the Vedic ceremonies they would have grains, mustard seeds, all kinds of raisins, almonds, cashew nuts and so forth, and all I did was spend the whole day counting them, making mounds of them. I was focused on this alone. So he had his own ways of obliterating mind.'

'I understand you were not accorded the welcome you had hoped for.'

'First of all, I arrived on the wrong day. It was not a Sunday.

Secondly I was alone. I remember him opening the door and looking at me questioningly. I had always heard that a teacher waits for his best disciple to arrive. Also I knew he had not found anyone worthy of carrying on the tradition and so I announced to him, “I have come!” I thought *I'd* be the one. He looked at me as if to say, “Who the hell are you? Get out of here.” It was winter and it was snowing and I sat outside. Kashmir is very cold, minus 10 at times. Day after day, I went back. It made no difference to him. All he did was look at me. One day, after the fire sacrifice or *yagna*, when they distribute sweetmeats among the devotees, he told someone to give me some. I was still sitting outside. It was a long and tedious process getting his acceptance. It was several months before he let me inside and before he would let me press his feet, which is what we do for old people in India, the practice of *seva*, massaging them and helping them to relax. *Wisdom Tree* is about that, about caring for the old. Actually he didn't like people doing things for him. He did the daily chores himself. He was so particular about pruning a tree so I was taught how to prune a tree.'

'So he made you a good film editor!'

'Probably! Also he taught me to see how the water flows and how I should obtain the edges, which is to say he taught me to focus, to concentrate and to pay attention to details. It was the first time I understood what is meant by being completely in the moment, by which I mean 100 per cent in the moment, focused in such a way that any separation between my being the subject and the other the object was erased.'

'And I believe it was there you had the initiation ceremony.'

'That was when they tied that thread the image of which I use in *Dance of the Wind*. As in all Indian tradition they would tie the thread at that time. It is tied in various other contexts as well, at the *Raksha Bandhan* festival, for example, when sisters tie it to their brothers. Historically, when men went to war, it was a thread of protection. Basically, though, the thread is tied when you do prayers or fire sacrifices. At initiation its meaning is, “I take spiritual responsibility for you, I shall guide you” and then they give you meditation techniques or mantras and a schedule is made, when to combine this with yoga and other practices. When you are formally accepted this gives you a rank in the circle around the teacher so you might get the benefit of being able to sit next to him or to wash his feet. I was there for two years, one year with him in his house and the rest of the time I was living nearby and coming and going, up and down.'

'Why did you leave him?'

'What I realised, and it really was the saddest thing for me, is that his world was no different from any other. Whether it is the world of publishing or cinema it's all about who has how much significance or how one obtains that significance or whether it is ascribed to one by other people. There are systems for it, whether it is in initiation rites or in other ceremonies. You can be at the Kumbh Mela pilgrimage beside the Ganges where once every twelve years twelve or fifteen thousand *sadhus* turn up. There is a good stock of *sadhus*! They all come with their symbols which vary according to which sect they belong to and what their position within that sect is. It is all highly regulated and elaborate. It was not so much the case around Swami Lakshman because he was very unconventional but in the rest of India it is. At least in India you can have these questions, the addressing of fundamental questions which I had never seen film do. So that for me was the attraction of Indian philosophy and religion. If they did not have the answers then at least they have the questions. All I am saying is that whether it is the world of spirituality or the world of cinema a human being is the same everywhere and because I had this gift I realised I must utilise it in order to say something about life. At first I thought I had exhausted all that cinema could do for me. Cinema could not provide me with answers to the fundamental questions about existence. At that age I thought there *were* answers to things, which was a nice belief – that this life had a meaning and there were answers and there was an ultimate reality and if cinema and art weren't the way to get me there then philosophy and spirituality were. I would not have minded *not* coming back to cinema. I thought being an artist was not *quite there*. I knew about my great-grandfather, how he lived, I had seen the pictures of him, and so I knew the spiritual life was an option for me. So when I said to Swami Lakshman "I have come" I was serious. I would have embraced that tradition. I would have learned to live like a *sadhu*, but it was only after five years that I realised no one had answers, let alone them. They all pretend they do. If that really were the case, then one could merely use art in order to explore life. Life, though, is one big scary hole. I finally realised that art is as good a way as any because really there are no answers at the end of the day. I could not accept this until I was thirty. I fought and fought and fought. I would have given anything for someone to take me closer to the truth until I realised people who were supposedly taking me closer to it didn't know it themselves.'

'Was it a shattering realisation for you?'

'Of course! I remember standing in front of this lake, howling and crying, and seeing the moon and the stars reflected in it. I was crying because I could not understand this reality. I did not understand where I was. I had been taken to a place I knew nothing about. Why should anyone do this to me? I thought my teacher had the answers but not even he did. I read the *Upanishads* which is a poetry of great wonderment, which is about the same moon and the same stars, and the same man gazing and marvelling at them. One of the things I learnt is that there is no *why* in nature. The first thing I learned from my swami is that only the human mind says *why*. There is no straight line in nature. The tree doesn't ask, "Why a tree?" So this obsession with *why* is ridiculous – it is an illness of man's mind. I suppose my time with him did help. No one else would have told me or made me realise these things, nobody else would have given me the techniques.'

'Would you say you were disappointed with that phase in your life?'

'I was probably more disappointed with cinema, which was beset with commercial factors and did not address the fundamental questions of life such as "Who am I?", "Why am I here?", "What is the purpose of life?", "What is morality?", "What should I be doing?" The *Upanishads* address these questions. They address man finding himself on this planet earth, watching the sun rise, asking himself, "So what do I do now?" We have to come to terms with the fact there will never be any answers. You can call this a prison or you can call it a blessing. It depends on your vision. If you call it a blessing then enjoy life. If it's a prison then why not commit suicide? You are driven to that edge of darkness where you can take your own life. Or you can part with that whole question and call it a blessing and then you start enjoying a life of the senses.'

'So you consider it a blessing in the end?'

'If I am living that is the only way to see it. It is a good enough reason to wake up and start your day.'

§

> But my old lover was beckoning me again. I was convinced I wanted to return to art. I was convinced there was no ulterior meaning to life, it was only my youthful idealism that searched for certainty, a direct result of my haphazard growing up, an oppression of various tunnels which had landed me in this desperate state of mind. If life was *maya* – a dream, a play – then all I could do was to use cinema as a way of bringing self-awareness to the contents of my life.
>
> (from Rajan Khosa's 'Biography of a Colonised Heart')

'What brought you here?'

'Accident! A complete accident. I was up in the mountains of Kashmir and my parents were getting worried about me. So, without telling me, they came there on the pretext of a holiday and found me in a sleeping bag. Soon they realised I'd been living like this for the previous eight months. I didn't have a bed so they bought me a mattress. They were increasingly worried about me. I was already in my fifth year of doing nothing, when all my classmates were in professions and getting married. One day I got a telegram from my dad saying I had been invited for an interview in Delhi. I did not know what this was about but I went there immediately and learned I had been recommended for a British Council fellowship. Later I learned that it was Kapila who recommended me. They were all trying to get me out of a spiritual trap. I thought to myself, "This is enough. I really need to make a film." I went to the British Council and there was a whole queue of people who had been recommended for just the one fellowship. All these people had brought their portfolios and I went empty-handed. I didn't care a damn. There was this man Robert Cavaliero who interviewed me, who told me that if I got the fellowship, which was £16,000 at the time, I would get to make a film. I said, "Sure, I'll make a film". I was told I'd have to go to England to make it. "Sure, anywhere." I would have to be attached to an institution and so they found this programme at the Royal College of Art. The money was routed through the college and with cash in my hand and equipment I made *The Moth and the Flame*. The poet Kathleen Raine read the script. The film was shown at one of her gatherings. She read all ten drafts of *Dance of the Wind*, painstakingly one after the after. The very first ones were poetry literally, which slowly I turned into drama. Someone recently gifted me the very early first draft of *Dance of the Wind*. It was bound like a book of poetry … it wasn't written like a screenplay. She had read it from that stage onwards, over a period of five years, and then it was taken over by Robin Mukherjee who wrote the final screenplay. I had already written one but he did a more dramatic version of it. I knew Kathleen Raine from when she used to come to India. She was very kind to me in London, compassionate and loving, and I would spend time at her place and she introduced me to a lot of people. I had read a lot of poets, mostly Indian and a few in the English language, but I think what I loved most about her writing was its tremendous simplicity and directness of heart, and the spirituality that was there. The sacred and the profane were together somehow and yet it all seemed sacred to me.'

'If I have one criticism of her,' I said, 'it is that too often she elevated beauty above truth.'

'I used to tell her this to her face! I would say to her, "You go on and on about it." She *did* repeat herself. Over a period of time, however, I realised she was so very alone in this world, not, as I first believed, in the mainstream, and that a lonely artistic voice like hers had to scream over and over again in order to be heard. She did things so doggedly, the way she managed, for example, to publish *Temenos* from her room. One of those issues, which I found in the attic, contains a piece on my father.'

'It is ironic that you had to come to England to make Indian films.'

'At that time and in that particular space there were a lot of things happening in Europe. There was respect for the arts, which wasn't the case in India. If you were bright and wanting exposure or starving for knowledge, India was quite a stifling place. The economy hadn't yet opened up. It was still a socialist country, not exactly communist but socialist, and everything, whatever came into the country, was controlled.'

'There is probably not a place in the world without its own set of controls. What about those which you found here?'

'The economic scenario in the West is quite pathetic actually. My good friends here, some of them highly accomplished artists and writers, when you see how patient they have been and then how they have had to embrace the reality of feeding their stomachs … I never knew about these things. It was the most bizarre, excruciatingly painful, experience to discover that this is what one had to do in order to be able to follow one's art. Here, no one will pay you for it. I saw my friends get stuck in this double life. I don't know if it was the economic structure or whether their minds would not allow them to challenge this structure, but I think their very acceptance of it was a first submission to the hypocrisy of the system. That kind of duality does not exist in India. There I will ask for alms and someone will feed me. India is so chaotic, you don't know how you will get fed and yet somehow you do, whereas in England you do not feel you can claim anything. Over there, you wouldn't think twice. Also life is so cheap and there are various ways you can live. The system here indoctrinates you right from the beginning … you are a struggler and then one day you might make the transition. I think it kills people. It doesn't allow for the space and distance in which they can observe what is happening to themselves. You have to *buy* creative time, and so half your energies are focused on how many hours in the week you can purchase. I had already had some artistic success and so I felt they should feed me. I didn't think I should be in an environment where everyone around me thinks that first I have to earn my artistic space. I always thought it was my birthright, the condition I was born into. All those assumptions were challenged here. It was a severe shock. I don't think I handled it well.'

'And yet within this system you were able to make *Dance of the Wind* …'

'Actually it was *after* making that film, not before, that I started living this dichotomy. That's when I ended up working in the bookshop where we met. It is the only regular job I've ever had. It was like being told this is how grown-ups live. When you are not yet grown up you believe it is your birthright to be an artist and then when finally you *do* grow up you learn it is not your birthright! That is where the system here has got it so very wrong.'

'You were still living here when you made the film?'

'I shot the film in India and edited it here. I had already made short films that were financed by people who wanted European art-house. Somehow, at the Royal College of Art, I came across these people. It wasn't much money but at least I didn't have to live two lives. I was hugely privileged. It was only later, when I first met you, that I realised there is this small matter of economics. There is the world of business and what I had done was art-house cinema. When your box office figures come back you are made to realise what you have done. Only then did I learn there is mainstream cinema, independent cinema and art-house cinema. That also was a rite of passage. As an artist you are necessarily sensitive, that is the price one pays for being one, and because I was *extremely* sensitive I didn't handle it all that well. Everything came to me as a shock. I had taken certain things for granted. That innocence is the strength of an artist because how otherwise do you believe in an idea that is intangible? You sense it, you feel it, you trust it, and that trust feeds the idea until it becomes reality. If you do not have innocence, you can't feed it. Innocence is your strength really but it also makes you susceptible to a lot of worldly things that hurt. So that's the price you pay, but today I'm happier in terms of knowing this is how life is going to be.'

'Would you say that coming here actually gave you an artistic focus? It sounds like you were lost for quite a while.'

'No. My artistic focus had already come back after those five years of spiritual meandering during which time I experimented with being a celibate and living a monk's life. So I had already come back to film. It was just that I was waiting for *any* opportunity and it happened to be this one. The moment I came to England I was over with all that dabbling in various philosophies. And then I met my English wife who used to go to India and stay with close friends of mine. She was like an adopted daughter of theirs and so it was like everything fell into place. I started a whole new life, artistically and otherwise.'

> So when I think of my creative experiences, I see tunnels, only tunnels. I walk through the passage of these tunnels. After some darkness there is light, but darkness again. I am

> not allowed to go back or to stop. And what do I hold in my hands? – Two hearts. One is centuries old, a collective yearning of my ancestors where meditation and work were synonymous. The other heart is colonised, first by the Mogul and then by the British. After all, I am an Indian and the various tunnels which lead me from the Third World to the First have been full of propaganda. And I have been the choiceless sucker.
>
> (from 'Biography of a Colonised Heart')

'Do you think that being here increased your sense of the value of your culture?'

'Absolutely! It really was like coming to the mother country. India had been colonised for three hundred years and to come here and realise all the things that I thought were Indian – the institutions where I studied, the judiciary – I suddenly saw it was the British who had made those things. I have been to Calcutta. If you put Calcutta in a washing machine, you get London. They actually made better buildings there. They made their mistakes here and then corrected them there. Victoria Station in Bombay is better than Victoria Station here – it is a beautiful piece of architecture. It made me realise what *was* Indian, what was there before the English came, and how India was changed by their imprint. So that was one aspect. There was also the realisation that I was in a country almost a hundred years ahead in its processes of development and growth. What came shockingly home, on the other hand, is that if you take the pursuit of materiality to such an extent what happens to humanity? What happens to human relationships? That was quite incredible to observe.'

'It seems to me you do not feel, as so many Indians do, resentment towards the British. You seem to see the positive side.'

'I don't see any reason for bitterness. What kind of bitterness do those people carry? When you talk about three hundred years of colonisation all you are talking about is four or five generations out of many. When you consider the Mughals, for example, India was already heavily colonised. After a point you no longer know what is *you* and what is *them*. If you take my love of tantra, which is close to Aztec culture, you will see just how far back Indian culture goes. You begin to see the roots of what is truly Indian.'

'When you enter another culture something happens inside.'

'Yes, completely. It was probably like shock treatment. I was in the Royal College of Art, which was almost entirely upper-class white. There was only one other Pakistani girl in the film department. It couldn't have been better in terms of one's connecting with the artistic tradition of another country but their ignorance of India baffled me. My head of department said, "You speak very good English!" It wasn't quite right. Indians couldn't be *that* bright and knowledgeable. It was interesting to observe how they dealt with me. And then there was my insistence on doing poetical, metaphysical work while they were doing this socialist realist stuff. I found my support in Germany and France before I ever found it here. And then there was my personal life. Before Partition my wife's father was in the British Air Force, based in Pakistan – there is a hangar named after him – and at the time of Partition he was dropping bombs on my ancestors. My wife was deeply into India and the role of her family there. So this country was happening to me on all levels, professional and personal, and all these questions about ancestral hatred and love for each other made me see just how deeply this Indian/British dynamic goes. I wasn't accepted easily by her family. You do not take away your master's daughter. I can understand why people become economic migrants. I didn't have much reason to live here because I was never one. If anything, I was a cultural migrant. I had a good relationship with painting and conceptual art and so just to be able to trace the artistic tradition in this country, to see how it all happened, was a valuable experience. You have good museums. It shows the kind of *mind* this culture has. It is of such a different make and this artistic mind is not separate from the political one. So it was interesting for me to see what this culture deems of importance, what its values are and how they are expressed in art. The two countries are distinctly different.'

'How would you quantify that difference?'

'India is changing as well, and is becoming more Western, but I would also say that mystical values persist. The final goal of life is to surrender to that presence and to constantly reaffirm its value in a material world. It is such an intangible thing and of course intangibility does not have much place in Western culture. Only what is verifiable, quantifiable or tangible has a place and is given a value.'

'Could it be that this actually drove you deeper into your Indian culture?'

'Yes, you can say that. At the same time the challenge is to make it identifiable, quantifiable and tangible. So you go deeper into the intangible, but the only way it will be understood or communicated is through the tangible. *That* is the demand of the world today. If you don't do it, *they* will do it. They will push you aside, obliterate you, and if you scream too loudly they will classify you and put you on a shelf. By "they" I mean the Western world, the forces of consumerism, the free-market economy. It is all about staying in circulation, being talked about, being relevant, and this significance only comes with what is relevant to *them*.'

'I wonder to what extent your own notions of art have altered since making *Dance of the Wind*.'

'My idea of poetry has changed over time. Recently I saw *City of God* again. I think that is poetry. I no longer have to see Tarkovsky to feel the poetry. There are films that have tremendous poetry in them because they go deep in terms of questioning humanity and what people do to each other. When one touches that thing deeply enough the poetry comes. I was much too attached to form and to experiencing a certain kind of silence, or, rather, the epiphany that comes though a certain kind of formal approach. I began to find it too limiting. I don't want to make good-looking images any more. They are what distract us from what really matters. Once you know your skills, what you are able to shape and ornament, it becomes too easy to lend yourself to them. There is no rigour left in your enquiry. It is an easy trap. For a young artist the world is a terrible place and he is trying to protect this flame but as he grows older he is *in* that flame. So much of art is coming to terms with pain through understanding. Once you understand a thing the pain dissolves. When a poem comes to you it dissolves what is locked inside and you become free.'

'So how do you pursue your vision in India as it has now become, with all its crass commercialism, the "dumbing down" much the same as we have had here?'

'I see it as more of a challenge. I think that to make sense to people who are not cultured is more of a challenge than trying to do so with people who already are. *Dance of the Wind* was recently given a limited release in India. Upper-class intellectuals went to see it but not the people I really wanted to reach. I was very depressed after that. I fell into a mould of blaming myself. People told me not to undermine what I had done, that I had achieved something that will spread slowly. It is good to understand that things have their time and place. Sometimes you see the results in front of you, sometimes you don't, or they may come after your death. I think artistic activity is really one of surrender and prayer. These days I have little notion of what art is or what form it should take. All I know is that there are subjects that need to be told with some directness and simplicity and which need to be aimed at the people who are listening. You have to speak to them and know their language. If it means you have to simplify things, then you do so. Every art form is a product of its time, space and audience. I am now working for a certain kind of audience. I know this audience and that it has been spoiled rotten by a great deal of rubbish but I also know it still has a heart. The question is how to do so. Once you kill off the arrogance that comes of a certain sanctity of form and thought, so to speak, and you start respecting people and not blaming them for their ignorance, then it becomes a matter of communication. I have to use a language they will understand. With those *sadhus*, for example, ten thousand people will come to listen to just one man. These are villagers, farmers, rickshaw wallahs, household maids, and here this man is speaking to them of deep things – about values, about spirituality, about intangible presence. How does he manage this, tell me? *He* succeeds. So why can't *I*? This man is speaking their language.

'What I need to do is to give up my attachment to what art is and what my ideas of it are, and only when I have cut through it will I find something. The fact is I need first to respect those people and to know they feel the same things I feel and that they are looking to understand. It is an altogether new challenge. After production of my second film failed last year I had ten months of doing nothing. It's amazing that I survived. I had to shut down a whole office, sell everything from the tables to the stationery. There is no time to do your sums. It takes time to recover financially. The world is not going to change. *We* have to change. You cannot *not* practise your art. Something changed in me. I decided I needed to practise my craft and I was no longer going to make any differentiation. I was not going to judge anything any more. I just wanted to work again.'

'But surely as an artist you have to judge!'

'You stop a lot coming towards you by being overly discriminatory in advance. You become too protective of your territory. A lot of energy gets lost there. It is a complete waste, it should go elsewhere. This should not be your concern. I wasted a lot of time sticking to my vision and not bowing down to what finances would demand of me and it hasn't really helped me. Today I think that those people who actually get their vision across and who send certain messages into the world have accepted compromise with grace. I was never able to do that. I bruise easily and I walk out. It hasn't helped, walking out of meetings just because they didn't understand what I was trying to do. These financiers have their own problems. They may love you but their hands are tied. They have to give money under some charter. They do want to help you. One senior filmmaker told me, "Do you not think, Rajan, everyone here wants to help you realise your film? It is only *you* who does not want to realise it." That really shifted a gear in my head. So even these people whom I accuse of lacking integrity, within their means they admire my work but are having to move five different things to make life possible for me. I never spent any time looking at things from their side. It all has to do with the ego. The standards you have set become so high you cannot see yourself as anything less than those standards. It is the preoccupation of the ego to constantly judge. This is an obstacle to addressing something truly, simply and directly. The day I lost my attachment to form, the idea of the kind of film I wanted to make,

suddenly I became free. The strange thing is that because of this all of a sudden projects started coming my way and they are the films I want to make. I know they will be different, how exactly I don't know, but that is what is exciting. What's the point of knowing something ahead of time?'

'I have a sense that you are constantly returning to your culture while running away from it.'

'At that time, ten years ago, I think I was running away from my artistic lineage, from my father … from *his* territory. I needed a different territory in which to prove myself. At home I was acknowledged merely because they couldn't separate me from who I was or where I came from. I was too privileged in some senses. Whatever recognition I'd get there, it would never feel as if I had achieved anything. Another thing I ran away from was the lack of opportunity. I wanted to be in a place where I had access and exposure to everything. I didn't want it to be limited because of my passport or my nationality or my culture. These were issues of equality. Meanwhile the world was telling me, "You are not equal. You were born in a shitty place and that is never going to change. You may have some privileges, you might boast about your culture, you may even pull a few things from your pocket and say these are unique, yes, sure, but I'm sorry, you are out of money and your nation is in debt." I think every migrant goes through these issues of equality, and of seeking acknowledgement in a territory that is not his own.'

'And ironically you sought this in a territory which was that of the great coloniser.'

'When I went to the British Museum and saw all the things that have been stolen from my country I felt humiliated. "What right do you have to it?" I asked. "Who says you should have it?" Kapila Vatsyayan, who was Minister of State for Culture at the time, a custodian of Indian culture, would go to the British Museum and shout at them. I have seen her fight those battles. These are volatile issues. *What* battles was she fighting though? What do you do with a philosophy, such as you have in my culture, which says tradition needs to keep changing its clothes? When, in order to welcome the new, it needs to destroy the old, and not to preserve or archive it? It *welcomes* destruction because that is the only way to ensure what is of lasting value. What is permanent and sustains will stay and from it a new form will emerge. *That* is the true Indian tradition. The truth is not in materiality … it is not in worshipping the physical … it is deeper than that. This *other*, the making of museums and archives, is what we have gathered from the British. That is my fight with this remarkable woman who has founded so many institutions, including the Indira Gandhi National Centre for the Arts in Delhi, amongst others. She struggles to preserve our traditions, and I tell her she is doing so against her own philosophy. Her response is: "But look at what the British are doing. If we don't preserve these things, they will steal them from us." We didn't really mind when the Mughals came and razed our temples. If our philosophy is strong and alive it will find a new form and so it did and so it will continue to do. That is how Hinduism has survived over the centuries.'

'So in a way those who stole cared about what they stole.'

'So is that really stealing? You dump something outside your home and I come along and pick it up and when I say I like it your response is "No, no, no, why did you take it away from me!" That's why it is important to understand evolution and historical processes because it is the only way one will be able to dissolve this anger. There are moments in history when you are weak and moments when you are strong. When I spoke earlier of the ruins of Hampi, where my great-grandfather lived in a cave, they are from a golden period of Indian civilisation. And then came the Mughal invasions, the ethnic cleansing, the systematic razing of the temples. It can't have left people with much self-esteem. If I were a Hindu child at that time I might have willingly embraced Islam. It would give me food and power. I would deny my roots. I might have done all those things.'

'What finally made you go back?'

'My marriage was a big reason to be here and when that dissolved my staying on didn't make much sense. I still couldn't see England through my own eyes. I saw it through Kathleen Raine's eyes and I saw it through my wife's eyes. I don't know how else to put it. You can't really penetrate a culture. You get a very different view of it when you are an outsider. You can admire it, you can love it, you may embrace it, but you will never get to know its nuances. The rituals of any one culture are tied to emotions and feelings. When I was given my Brahmanical thread there was a ceremony for it. I went around and touched the feet of the two hundred-odd people who were there. You wear this thread and an orange garment. The colour orange signifies the burning of the ego, the sunset … the Upanishadic poems are all about walking into the sunset. It is symbolic of twenty thousand different things, which your mother or grandparents had told you about in your folklore. You can never really leave your culture and you can never communicate it. A person from another culture may be fascinated by it, make an attempt to understand it. With my wife it was a great exchange in the sense that as we moved deeper into each other's cultures we also realised it was essential to go back to our own roots. It was like surrender. Finally it is a circle. People have to go back. After all, man's mind is conditioned by a certain set of cultural and social apparatuses by which means he is able to persevere. You need to go back to those tools and to understand them and *be* them.

'I feel at ease in both worlds because I have spent so much time in them. Earlier today, I thought I could forget I am not living here. I thought everything makes sense and I can deal with everyday life. But really they are two different worlds. When you are on a street in Bombay there is no comparison. There's another reason why I went back to India. Some of my friends, whom I had known since I was fifteen or sixteen, and with whom I later went to college, came here. They started saying things like, "You are changing." They did not like what was happening to me. I had become more formal, more English. I said "please" before every sentence. They didn't like that. They felt I didn't take them for granted in the way I had before. I realised that to take someone for granted is to show a kind of love, which is to say he has a place in my life. I couldn't just turn up at their places any more. I would ask five times if it was okay to do so, how they were placed, at what time they were free. I had learned and imbibed all these things in this culture, thinking I was getting better, but for a set of people very close to me I had become estranged.

'All this has to do with our Asian culture. What Fawzi Karim says about the precision of language here is so true of English culture. I learned that in screenwriting one must be like an architect, absolutely precise. We express a lot through our hands and head movements. You don't see English people doing that. They appear to be cold and withdrawn at times, but they don't need to express themselves that much because they use precise words. There is something about our excessive passion that fuzzes things … it limits itself to passion alone … there is no progress there … there is too much noise … not enough clarity. You win a war through organisation, clear thinking, clear markers. That's the kind of mind that went behind colonising most of the world. They knew their power.

'What is curious is that I find the same "Asianness" in upper-class English people here. They are the only people who are wacky, who are twisted, and who can't be bothered with decorum. It is the middle and lower classes that have been crushed. It is still a very class-ridden society in some ways. You discover this ease of relationship in the most surprising of places, irrespective of class or where people come from, but I realised I was losing something and that people emotionally close to me noticed. I was wasting myself. It was a strange equation I got into. The fact that I was sitting in a bookshop when I wanted to do art was incomprehensible to them. Why had I isolated myself into this strange space and with this obsession that I had to suffer in order to achieve certain things? Indian friends are like family. They kept telling me, "Our wealth is your wealth. Why would you kick on that wealth and treat us as if we were strangers?" I think they were right. I didn't need to do that. I didn't have to behave as if I were a pauper because I wasn't one. I'm not saying I haven't experienced similar generosity here but people on this island have become too isolated trying to secure their personal futures. They have lost generosity in this material world. Already there are enough products in the free-market economy to constantly make them feel they're alone. What I am trying to say is that in developing or third world cultures, because people are used to suffering it makes them generous, it allows them to give, whereas in the developed world people have become intolerant. It hurts them to suffer even a little bit. The whole culture is geared to make you suffering-proof. So it has become strangely selfish and that I think is a sad thing that has happened. People are being programmed to cover themselves. This is a strange paranoia. It is like an infection that spreads.'

'It sounds to me that what your friends said about you being lost or disenfranchised from your culture here had already happened to you when you went to Kashmir. Maybe this is something in your own nature.'

'I think you are probably right because some of them visited me there as well. When you are emotionally close to people they feel threatened if you don't live a life like them or at least what is taken to be a healthy or normal one. But that's okay because I realised going back to India also meant that I did not want to lose the emotional bonds I had formed with so many of my family and friends – they need to be valued, integrated and responded to all through my life. I feel the same for my Western friends. After all, it was a long life in England as well. And when I come back here I feel I'll never lose these people. As my ex-wife says, "Only the arrangements change, the love never dies." You are formed by all these people so you need to continue to nurture them. I am at a point in my life when I realise all these different parts of me have to live. They are like your children and as I grow older, whether I have physical children or not, I need to fulfil a fatherly role to all these parts in me. You can't cut something off within yourself because of not understanding it or because of bad experiences. You might think these are cancerous bits and you can get rid of them but it doesn't quite work that way. At the same time, some things you will never understand. That is the mystery and magic of life.'

'So the burning of the thread at the end of *Dance of the Wind* was emblematic of much in your life?'

'Yes, in the sense of getting myself free, of there not being just one way to find answers and that life has to be lived directly, so to speak, and that in one's own way one will find the truth. All those methods you learned need to be abandoned. There is no such thing as originality – this I strongly believe – because our consciousness is formed of all the things we have learned or imbibed but nevertheless with each attempt we hope to come up with something fresh, which belongs to us alone, that does not subscribe to any known system of thinking. We have to get out of the security zones of all these threads and traditions ... all those value systems need to be abandoned for the pursuit of truth and so in that context the burning of the thread was something I did in my life and it is what I wanted for my character in the film.'

When asked by Pallavi to sing, the guru Munir Baba replies with a written note, 'Only if I remain silent, can you sing.' And then, just before he burns the thread, he writes another note, 'Give up searching, only then will music find you.' It could well be that the same will hold true for Rajan: now that he has stopped searching for the kind of film he'd most like to make the offers come to him.

'Would you ever contemplate coming back to England?'

'I don't think I will ever give up India. You would have to give up five thousand years at the same time. There you can still be in places where time hasn't left its imprint. And you can be there quickly ... you find yourself in a physical space, which is just like a verse from the *Upanishads*, in which you can read about a man finding himself alone on earth or touching a tree. Where my father has his studio, in the mountains, you can go for a walk and find the area dotted with ancient temples. When you walk among them you enter these zones of concentrated energy. I can't explain this. You will find the ancient symbols of fertility, the vagina and the phallus, and then you realise people have been going there for thousands of years. They are not crowded places and whoever goes there connects with that mystical force behind all this. Those things can be found just around a corner. Your acknowledgement of the mystery and your celebration of it are far greater than anything you would find living here in London. It's a good enough reason to go back.'

Three Chinese Characters

Liu Hongbin, Word Conjurer, Smuggler of Nightmares

Such news as I have, which is to say within the time of this prose, is that the poet Liu Hongbin has gone into seclusion. Whether for spiritual exercises or in order to write or to further immerse himself in two thousand years of Chinese literature he won't say, but it is perfectly conceivable that it's a combination of all three.

Soon after he arrived here, in 1989, swinging wildly between despair and hope, he declared that what the contemporary Chinese poet must seek to do is build 'a historical bridge between the glory of Chinese classical poetry and the ruins of modern Chinese language'. An older, humbler, Hongbin finds such words, when mirrored back at him, pompous in the extreme and yet they do not come out of nowhere. As a child during the Cultural Revolution he witnessed the most extreme self-desecration of any single culture, when the great classics were thrown to the flames, temples destroyed, antiquities smashed, teachers beaten to death, often by their own students, and censorship so extreme as to be barely censorship at all but rather a monitoring of the flickering of one's neighbour's eyelashes. All this was at a time when elsewhere in the world university students clutching their translations of Mao's Little Red Book *spoke blithely of its author as having done what needed to be done.*

The day before we spoke, Hongbin walked to a nearby internet café in order to check his messages when a well-dressed woman, clearly troubled, sat down opposite him, asked him who he was, and when he smiled back at her she said, 'Do you think I'm rubbish?' Hongbin pointed to a vase of flowers on his table and told her how beautiful they were. She moved to another table where there sat another man before a similar arrangement of flowers, took the vase and smashed it down hard on his table and walked out.

A few hours later, Hongbin got on the Underground where a man clutching a bottle of whiskey moved aside for him.

'I am impressed by your holy water.'

'Do you want some?' the man said, and then, 'Are you a monk from Tibet?'

These days Hongbin shaves his head.
'Closer,' he replied.
'Are you holy?'
'Everyone is holy.'

There is something in Hongbin's observations of everyday life that have about them the quality of Buddhist fable. It's there even in his name, the first syllable of which means 'spacious water' and the second 'scholarly' or, in the Confucian understanding of the word, 'form'. As he seemed to be in full monkish throttle, I asked him whether he had managed yet to conquer vanity, which is when I got a first dose of his delicious humour.

'I try to preserve some for occasional use.'

§

The story which follows is that of a perennial struggle between the conjuror of words and those who fear the power those words release. The conflict goes back to ancient times. An image, if sturdy enough, rattles thrones. A poet whose chief love is words, who is mostly hidden from the world's gaze, yet admired by those whom he most admires, who include writers as diverse as John Ashbery, Peter Porter, Stephen Spender, Doris Lessing and Arthur Miller, Hongbin via his testimony bespeaks the continuance of that struggle. It is most vividly expressed in his incantatory poem 'Who Are You?' which he wrote on his birthday in 1987. When, in the summer of 1990, Peter Porter introduced him to Stephen Spender, it was the poem Hongbin chose to recite, in Chinese, while the latter followed it, word by word, in the English version. (When the poem was republished in *Agenda* the acting editor, Anita Money, asked Hongbin whether he might dedicate it, belatedly, to Stephen Spender and this he agreed to do.) Apart from its obvious images of 'a devoted son now abandoned' the poem may be read as the statement of a still greater dispossession.

> I am a frayed rope, cursed by people who used it to tow their boat.
> I am a piece of wreckage on the beach to which the drowning clung.

I am a mast broken by the sail's need.
I am the conversation between the sailors and tidal wave.
I am the conch shell, innards scooped out, now blowing a
fisherman's song.

Although a thing that stands proudly on its own, the poem appreciates in value when placed in the context of Hongbin's early life. There is a date in his passport that serves to approximate when his birth *might* have taken place – 19 June 1962 by the solar calendar or 18 May 1962 by the lunar one. When he was thirteen he asked his mother the date of his birth and she could not remember. She asked her colleagues who gave birth to their children at approximately the same time, thinking someone among them might know, but nobody could tell her. All she could say for sure is that he was born at daybreak, in the early summer of 1962. What might at first seem callous to our ears will be, when one learns more of the circumstances of her life, more a cause for our compassion. This most devoted of mothers had quite the most difficult time. It could be that the events of that period of her life rendered it a horrible blur. Or did she simply forget? After half a century, Hongbin's response is that it would be more honest to leave these questions unanswered. 'I accept my birth as a blessing', he says, adding that what he must do now is to prepare for his own death. Such words coming from a man not yet fifty may seem alarming but he does not intend them to be. Actually there might well be a correlation between what he says and what I hazard to guess are his spiritual exercises of late.

'When I was a few months old,' Hongbin began, 'I was sent to live with my grandparents, many miles from home, in a small village in the countryside called Shi bà lí tūn. I spent, on and off, five years there. That poem suggests I was an abandoned child but really I do not have any resentment towards my parents, both of whom had to work all day. Actually I was lucky. If I hadn't stayed with my grandparents who would have looked after me? How would I have survived? When I started school back in Qingdao everyone, even my mother, was a stranger to me. When I saw her again and she tried to cuddle me I slapped her, saying I wanted to go home. I did not recognise her. This was while my grandfather still held me in his arms. My mother told me this. The village was home to me. I can still remember the landscape, the small hamlet, the lake behind the house, a stone for grinding beans, the smell of cucumbers and tomatoes, and the sound of donkeys braying. Many of the images you find in my poetry were formed then.'

'The Hunting Song in the Forest' in particular sets the primordial world against the city and its problems. It is also a statement of poetic intent.

> My immortal soul contemplates:
> The hunt for prey,
> Aren't sharp eyes all that are needed?
> For the chase,
> Isn't reckless courage all that is needed?
> For the capture,
> Isn't a momentary impulse all that is needed?

'I wrote that poem when I was nineteen or twenty, when my social consciousness was awakened. There is no political allegory as such, but it was a young man's wish for a world of social justice and also to prepare himself for the possible sacrifice he would have to make. It does, of course, owe much to a very important period of my life, which represents a kind of innocence, and what I seek to achieve in my writing is the mental state of childhood.'

'To what degree,' I asked, 'does your ancestry influence that mental state?'

'Years later, I went back to see my great-grandparents' house, which was a magnificent place. When I visited my great-uncle in Taiwan he told me something of my family's historical background, of how, for example, when they counted money it was done with a length of bamboo. You would break through the separations inside, put the money in the bamboo and count it that way. The coins had a square hole, which symbolised the ancient Chinese view of the world: the sky is round, the earth square. My maternal grandmother, who was from quite a wealthy family, divorced my bookish grandfather because of the Japanese war. He worked in Qingdao and was not able to keep contact with his wife and two daughters and could not even send money home. In old China, girls, especially after they got married, were not important. Whatever the case, her family would not support her. My grandmother had to survive so she divorced my blood grandfather and later remarried. The main impact my grandparents had on me was, quite simply, their love.'

'Was your family bookish? Where did your love of books come from?'

'My maternal grandfather was college-educated, which was quite rare in those days. I can still remember books in sewn bindings, which we inherited from my paternal grandfather. Our family used to have a *siheyuan*, which, in its most direct translation from the Chinese, is a courtyard surrounded by buildings on all four sides. As they were a symbol of social status many of these *siheyuans* have long since been demolished. This earlier part of our family history became a terrible taboo during the Cultural Revolution. When the Communists took over the educated people became underdogs whereas those of the new ruling class were mostly peasants or farmers. When it came to my parents' generation they couldn't write and I was a potential illiterate.'

'Do you have memories of your father from that early age?'

'One of the reasons I love him so much is because I never got to enjoy him for any length of time. A love such as this lasts all one's life. I do have some memories of him. One is of when I was ill and with his very strong hands he fed me medicine. I remember a long scar on his chest where he had an operation. Also, when I was four, I went out on my own to the school which my brothers and sister went to and came back home at midnight. It was at the height of the Cultural Revolution and students were fighting one another for mimeograph machines and loudspeakers that they'd use for propaganda purposes. I picked up a packet of the red colour with which they wrote their slogans and tucked it into my pocket. My father, who was clean and industrious, would often wash our clothes, soaking them first in a wooden basin. On that occasion the whole lot, including his white shirts, turned bright red. In the middle of the night he summoned the five of us, my brothers and sisters. "Who did this?" he asked. "Did *you* do this?" "No," I said. I had really forgotten about picking up the red colour. "Go back to sleep!" he told me. My brothers and sisters who'd been made to stand for a long time were later invited to do the same.'

'It is ironic that the clothes should have been stained revolutionary red!'

'Yes, absurd, disastrous too. I also remember the annual traditional Chinese Spring Festival when my father led the whole family to bow before Mao's portrait. This was utterly against Chinese tradition as it was the time when normally one would pay respect to one's ancestors. He did *that* and still he didn't survive the Cultural Revolution!'

In 1968, the year Mao initiated the policy of sending urban youth to the countryside to be re-educated, Hongbin, aged five, returned home from his grandparents' village.

'As nobody in Qingdao had time to look after me, my father took me to his place of work – he was a railway administrator – and there he found me a spot where I might have a siesta. When I woke up he was gone. I looked for him everywhere, his office, even the European-style toilet. Many years later, in 2004, when I made a trip back to Qingdao, I went to see the place and everything, even the toilet, was exactly the same. What it confirmed for me was that my memory of that day is accurate. I was taken home by one of my father's colleagues. Mother had prepared dinner and because my father liked wine she had a bottle ready for him. The man who took me home said my father had been arrested by the Red Guards.'

Was there ever another time in history when an entire populace fell prey to teenagers on a rampage? The Cultural Revolution was initiated by Chairman Mao in 1966 when he called upon China's youth to root out those liberal bourgeois elements which he claimed had begun to permeate the Party and society at large. They were free to do so by whatever means they chose and without the impediment of judicial rule. The Red Guards were the result and soon they acted without even the say-so of the Party, freely entering schools, temples, museums, factories and people's homes. Mao, no stranger to ignorance, praised them, saying, 'The more knowledge you have, the more reactionary you are.'

'My father remained in prison for two years. It didn't end there, though. The police would come to our home, ask my mother and the children to write things against him. This was the regime's masterpiece, calling upon people to denounce their own families. They completely destroyed family life. This is very hard to forgive. After his death, because of the stigma my father's name would have on the family, we had to change our surname to my mother's maiden name, Liu.'

'Did they ever give a reason for his arrest? Was he accused of being a "counter-revolutionary"?'

'When my schoolmates bullied me that was the term they would use. You know how boys fight sometimes. They would stop me, crying, "Down with Wang Huaiyi", which was my father's name, and then they'd hit me on the face and run away. In order to talk about this properly I'd have to provide a detailed historical background otherwise a story told in isolation will be difficult for people here to understand. What happened between my parents was a personal thing that became political. Also there was a lot of fighting between different factions. My father was a party loyalist and on the other side were the so-called revolutionaries. Actually they did not know *what* they were loyal to. When one looks back and analyses this, their loyalty meant nothing at all. The "Great Leader" stirred up conflict between people. I wrote about this in my long poem "A Day Within Days":

China, you could not cleanse these wounds
With the river of your tears.

Alive, you force man to fight man, man to trample man.
Dead, you command one to press down on another, one to
    pile up upon another.
Why have you produced so much hatred?

'My father, who was very direct, offended members of the opposite faction and so they seized the opportunity for revenge. One thing I want to say is that I am now older than my father was when he died in his early forties. A father to five children, at the same time he supported the parents from both sides of the marriage.

Something else I want to emphasise is that he was half Manchurian. While I don't want to dwell on parentage, as I grow older and as within me the gulf between China and the West increases I realise how different I am from my fellow countrymen. This includes my behaviour. I realise there is something different about me, which has been passed down through my Manchurian genes. My mother is Han Chinese. When the Communists came to power two of my paternal great-uncles slit their wrists because they knew life would be intolerable. During the Cultural Revolution many people perished simply because they spoke a "wrong" word or because a neighbour reported that so-and-so said he'd prefer to a buy a snack than use the money to purchase Mao's *Little Red Book*. When they victimised you they also made you feel ashamed to talk about it later. This was the genius of their evil. I will talk about the trumped-up charge against my father when the time comes. And then there were the humiliation parades when people were stood on trucks and made to wear big placards stating their crimes. One day there was such a parade and I rushed from the house to see if my father was among them. At primary school there were denunciation meetings from time to time, when people had to stand on the stage, wearing placards, their heads lowered. Whenever this happened my teacher would say to me, "Liu Hongbin, you can go home." She knew what I was feeling. I am so grateful to her.'

At that time the judicial system was a complete shambles. There was no law to speak of.

There is only one photograph of Hongbin as a child, aged six, taken before he started school and when his father was still in prison, incommunicado. Pinned onto his jacket is the obligatory Mao

badge. At the lower right-hand corner is printed the name of the photography studio and the legend 'The East is Red' (*Dongfang Hong*), which was the opening phrase of a song eulogising Mao and which during the Cultural Revolution became a popular anthem. The child averts his eyes. He looks as though he has been forced into the frame. Already he seems serious beyond his years. The photograph, a little spotted and creased, is commemorated in Hongbin's prose poem 'The Unfamiliar Customs House', in which he writes, 'In another place, Mother, through her glasses, fixes her eyes on the only photo of myself as a child, expecting my mischievous footsteps.'

In April 1970 came the event that would shape the whole of Hongbin's life.

'When I left school I saw in the distance a gathering of people. On the wall in front of them there were posters, including one with a photograph showing my father in the execution ground with a gun at his head. There were copies posted everywhere. According to my brother, there was also one opposite the entrance to our house. After my father was executed, we were kept under surveillance. I remember lying in bed, in the moonlight, and seeing human shadows on the white curtain. They would try to listen in on the family conversations. I couldn't really believe my father had died. One summer evening, when people sat outside in circles, cooling off, I saw among them someone who looked exactly like him. I went and put my arm around his neck. And then I realised it wasn't him. He comes back in dreams still. On 11 September 2001, when nobody dared fly, I flew to Venice, taking with me a copy of Joseph Brodsky's *Watermark* as a guide. I stayed in a youth hostel on a small island beside a beautiful lagoon. Maybe it was the Venice air that reminded me of Qingdao, which is also a lovely city beside the sea, with all styles of architecture – memories are easy to evoke with our senses. There I had this wonderful dream in which my father was still alive. He had just been released from prison and was now without money or credit card in the south of France where I often go and there we were beside this blue lagoon, whether in Venice or Qingdao I couldn't tell. Forty years prior to this, my father was killed and now, all those years later, I had this absolutely beautiful dream. I don't know whether poets have an ability to deceive themselves or whether in their poetry they create another reality or what you might call poetic justice, but I have never stopped searching for him.'

Most gruellingly, that search is not only a mental or spiritual one.

'When I was nineteen or twenty I met a girl, a student of

medicine at Qingdao Medical College, who invited me to visit her at the college. On the way there I imagined I would see my father's skeleton in the anatomical lab. The reason for this was because we were not allowed to retrieve his remains and even now we don't know where they are. The bodies of those who were executed were usually taken away by medical institutions and without the permission of the relatives. A few years ago, on the internet, I read an article in one of the local Qingdao papers about a crematorium where there were unclaimed ashes. Thinking my father's might be among them, I immediately phoned the crematorium. I was informed that the ashes dated from *after* the Cultural Revolution and that nothing at all survives from before that date. But to tell you the truth, recently, over the past few years, these things have to begun to recede. I do not want to live with any kind of bitterness.'

Hongbin's father is the ghost at the centre of his most famous poem, 'A Day Within Days', written in 1990, a six-page work of dream images and satirical bites, in which he calls up cultural figures from the past, even Mao Zedong and Deng Xiaoping, upon whom he exacts, if not revenge exactly, then justice. Sartre and de Beauvoir – supremos of the existential, apologists for so many of the horrors of their time – get married in Tiananmen Square; invitations to the wedding party are extended to Chinese students but the Ministry of Security, fearful that the newlyweds might be kidnapped, advise them to take their honeymoon in Hong Kong; meanwhile, Confucius enrols at the Open University, Li Po drinks Mao-tai, the famous – and some say undrinkable – Chinese liquor which President Nixon was offered when he came to China in 1972, and Tu Fu dies of exposure to the cold, the papers for his rehousing still in his pocket. This is exactly what is happening now, with the forceful demolition of people's homes and their former occupants not yet being given places to move into.

The breathing of the wind blows out the lamps.
Dreams settle,
The island of white bones looms.
I would go to the execution ground where my father was
    killed twenty years ago.
He was sending his ideals wrapped in those transparent
    gunshots –

Three bullets pelted through his head –
And I inherited his suffering.

On this day, I lean against the head of the wind.
White bones beneath my feet are turned to pebbles.
Crows are flocking in my thinning hair.

Peter Porter writes of the poem as being 'a kind of last look back, a version of Lot's grief at the destruction of the Cities of the Plain', and continues, 'It's as if the prophetic utterance of Allen Ginsberg's *Howl* was being shaped by a real and not merely a symbolic terror.' There's nothing of the luxury of intellectual despair in the poem.

'The only politically explicit poem of mine, it is based entirely on my personal experiences. True, my father is a leitmotif. It was not a poem of revenge, however. There is anger, naturally, but I think there is more satire.'

The year Hongbin's father was executed, China's first satellite was sent into orbit and it broadcast the song 'The East is Red' back to earth. There could be no escaping it, not even in outer space. One day Hongbin's mother, for whom life had come close to intolerable, came home and said to him, 'My son, you are so little. Were it not for you I would have thrown myself under a train.'

There is something almost unbearably expressive in her face and yet for all that is revealed much else remains hidden, not least the terrible paradoxes with which she permitted herself to live. As a teenager, a fervent believer in the Communist cause, she tried several times to run away from home in order to join the People's Liberation Army. Her mother kept her locked up. She later appeared fleetingly in a popular film of the time, *Nan Zheng Bei Zhan*, which translates variously as *Conquer South, Victory North, From Victory to Victory* or, somewhat more cumbersomely, *Conquest in the South*

and Battles in the North. Set in 1947, it depicts the civil war between the Nationalists and the Communists; Hongbin's mother plays a member of Mao's paramilitary forces. Hongbin still remembers being taken to the film by his father, who pointed her out to him, saying, 'Look, that's your mother!' Absurdly, given the context, Hongbin's father had served as a conscript in the Nationalist army, which later would be one of the accusations brought against him.

'She was starry-eyed about the Communists,' Hongbin continued. 'There is also a story that my grandmother, finding it difficult to feed her children, wanted to give her away to a foster family; either that or to give her away as a child bride. My mother escaped both fates. The circumstances behind my parents' marriage are that my grandmother met my paternal grandparents on a train and they started to chat, one of them saying, "I have a son of a certain age" and she saying, "I have a daughter." My mother, although she was impressed by my father's family, believed in freedom of choice. And with my grandmother being of an aristocratic Manchurian family, she never got over the fact of it being an arranged marriage. This has remained a problem for her all her life.'

'And yet for all her desire to be free,' I said, 'she put her faith in something as absolute, as confining, as Communism.'

'If you live in that kind of society very soon everyone speaks in the same voice and wears the same clothes. There is no independent thinking, no choice whatsoever. Either you go with the flow or you become extinct. My parents' relationship didn't go well, her explanation being that my father suffered from a tumour of the liver and had to go for an operation. At that time medical treatment in China was not as advanced as it is now, even with respect to anaesthetics, and so he went through all the pain of an operation and afterwards, according to my mother, he became another person. At the same time she was not a good-tempered lady, so the conflict between them escalated. After speaking to people who were close to my father, one thing I'm sure of is that she played a very important role in his death.'

'You mean she denounced him after his arrest?'

'I think even *before*.'

'Would you say she was a victim of history?'

'If we want to explain or defend such behaviour in a time of inhumanity I'm not sure what the answer is, and it remains a problem for all the children, but this was not just an isolated case. It was widespread throughout China. The regime broke up families. When I was sixteen I went on my own to the law courts, seeking to renounce my relationship with my mother. I told her what I'd done and this, I'm sure, deeply hurt her.'

'Was this because you came to believe she'd been responsible for his death?'

'It is not that simple. The fact of my father's execution was a stigma, one that has remained with me all my life. She was the mother of five children, all of whom would suffer from persecution, and for whom she felt huge responsibility and obligation. She went to the municipal government offices to petition them on the matter of my brother's job applications being continually turned down. In that respect she was extraordinary. Sometimes, after her day's work, climbing the long staircase of the German-style municipal government building, she fainted and would be taken to hospital by ambulance. She made less than fifty *yuan* a month. A whole family had to depend on this. We would keep a ledger, recording the amounts spent on rice or salt. She could be marvellous. Sometimes she would even manage to buy us chocolates or roasted chestnuts.'

'So how does she look back on those times now?'

'The Chinese are not like Western people. If they regret, they do so in private. She claims she has become a Christian, reads the Bible every day and goes to church. I asked her once, "Have you ever prayed for my father?"'

'So how does she square all this?'

'She did once admit to me that my father treated her well in the early years of their marriage. She was indoctrinated, however. She rejected many of the Chinese traditions such as observing the memory of one's ancestors, but then family life more or less disappeared under the regime. When I was a child of seven or eight, at the dinner table she would talk only political philosophy, Marx and Lenin. At least I started my study in philosophy early in life. It was a good starting point from which to get to another side of that philosophy. The only time she ever spoke of these things critically was after I was expelled from China in 1997, after my first visit back there. Most of the Hong Kong newspapers, both English and Chinese, and Reuters, BBC TV and World Service, reported my expulsion. I faxed the press cuttings to my sister, who showed them to our mother, whose response was that I had done the right thing in giving a press conference. It was the only time I had ever heard her say anything like this. Even now, with China supposedly opening up, when I phone her and get angry at how the government continues to harass her or how it will not allow me home she simply hangs up on me. The telephone is bugged twenty-four hours a day, of course, and for her merely to listen to me would imply she is taking my side. The fear is still there, deeply rooted in her consciousness. This said, she is a very talented woman, a good fashion designer and tailor. We were the most nicely dressed children in the school and even the neighbours would ask her to make clothes for their children, for the Spring Festival. She could make something simple from very little and even my first pair of leather shoes were made by her. One morning I woke up, snow on the ground, and there was a pair of newly knitted gloves on the pillow beside me. I'm sure she worked the whole night on them. She was, despite her judgement of the political and personal situation, a great mother.'

The year 1970 continued to be for Hongbin, aged seven, one of terrors.

'I had just started school and our first lesson in Chinese was "Long live Chairman Mao" and the second "Down with Liu Shaoqi". Liu was the disgraced state chairman. I went to the public toilet and, reversing the wording of the slogans, wrote on the wall "Down with Chairman Mao".'

'So you are a born dissident!'

'Absolutely not! The psychology was simply that of a boy seeking adventure, doing something untoward just to see what would happen next. At that age you didn't know or estimate the risk. The police came, photographed the graffiti, and started an investigation. I was terrified. I had a cousin at least ten years older than me, who was visiting us at the time. She would cuddle me or take me out for a while. All I could do was sleep. I didn't dare wake up for fear of what would happen when I did. When I went back to school… to my shame… even now I feel very sorry about it… "Who wrote this?" the teacher asked everyone. We each had to say something. I stood up and said it *might* be an older student in the upper class. I gave them a name. The only reason my denunciation did not do him much damage was that his family was very Red. Nevertheless he was labelled "a little reactionary". Soon, though, everyone forgot about it. If I had been found out my whole family could have been sent to the countryside – "education through labour". And, besides, our background was already bad. I still feel guilty about this.

'At that time, I started visiting bookshops. Whatever pocket money my mother gave me, which she wanted me to spend on food, I set aside for books. The first friends I made were booksellers, many of them old ladies whose daughters would take over after they retired. Sometimes, when I got home, my mother would search me. I would hide the book on my back beneath my T-shirt with a belt tied around it. So this, perhaps, is the beginning of my relationship with books.'

'As something forbidden…'

'Not just forbidden! Good books were a luxury. This was during the Cultural Revolution when there were virtually no serious books at all, only Communist propaganda.'

The ferociousness of the Red Guards with respect to books and works of art was such that frequently their owners would destroy them rather than risk death or imprisonment. Mao himself stated that the 'Four Olds' – old customs, old culture, old habits and old ideas – were to be swept away.

'What about when Mao called for all young people to be re-educated in the countryside?'

'I escaped that. I started to prepare for it when I was eight. My mother said to me, "You are so frail. If you are sent to the countryside you will not be able to survive." She introduced me to a doctor and from him I began to learn about Chinese herbal medicine and acupuncture. I started to memorise some of the classical texts, most of which were originally written in verse or song. Whereas, before, I couldn't tell *yin* from *yang* suddenly it all began to make sense.'

It is most telling that in recent years Hongbin has become an accredited practitioner of Chinese medicine and that, in keeping with Taoist tradition, wherever he goes he treats patients and friends alike. The whole of Chinese civilisation has its roots in Taoism and so, too, does its medicine. So close is the relationship between Chinese medicine and humanities, and such is its beauty, it is hardly surprising that many doctors are also men of letters. Actually that relationship is universal: Apollo, it should be remembered, was the god of poetry and medicine. 'Medicine is my lawful, wedded wife,' writes Anton Chekhov, 'and literature is my mistress.' And, as another medical practitioner puts it, 'The clinical gaze has much in common with the artist's eye.' A poet inserts a needle; the flesh surrenders its ills. Among Hongbin's patients the film producer Richard D. Zanuck spoke of his 'masterly acupuncture treatment which is of the highest order'. It would seem that the man who cures is himself cured; as Hongbin observes, the process of making a diagnosis is itself akin to philosophical speculation and as such it provides one with the ultimate intellectual gratification.

'With my family,' he continued, 'things turned out to be different than for most people. My eldest brother had to quit school, aged sixteen, in order to help my mother raise the family. Although he had been one of the best students nobody would take him on and so he ended up working in a kiln for many years, breaking down and burning building materials. My second brother, when it came time for him to go to the countryside, was rejected. He was not eligible even for that! He wrote a letter to the army representatives, asking to be sent to Inner Mongolia, but because they were worried he would defect to Russia his application was refused. For almost ten years, he worked as a carpenter, making furniture for people he knew because nobody else would take him on. All this was because of our family history. The reason I did not go for re-education was because by the time I finished high school the political situation had changed. One no longer had to go, and yet I was made to suffer for that all the same. Aged eighteen, I wanted independence. I didn't want to go to university because I was the youngest and also because in a family of five children relationships could be rather tense. My brother said I wasted too much money on books. So I decided I would get a job. In 1980, I sat for the civil service examinations. Most of the candidates were over thirty and with university degrees, while I was the youngest one there. I passed the examination, came sixth, and then I was interviewed. The two interviewers asked me whether I would like to be a teacher. I said, "Yes, sure, whatever". But then they rejected me on the grounds that I hadn't been for re-education in the countryside even though it had already been stopped. The real reason was my family background.'

In 1981, Hongbin became a student in the Shandong Foreign Trade School in Qingdao. This is the school where he should have been given a job as a teacher but ended up as a student instead. Subsequently his relationship with the teachers was tense, especially as some of them had sat the same examination as Hongbin and had become teachers although their marks were lower than his. He sat alone at the back of the class, often slept there, and for this was punished. If business was not his forte, poetry was already very much so.

I asked Hongbin whether his family respected the fact that he was a poet, at which point he laughed incredulously.

'I'm sorry, but a poet was a pathetic thing to be. You could not win the approval of your family with poetry. I was sixteen when I began to write in earnest. My second brother said, "If you continue to write these counter-revolutionary poems I will send you to the police."'

'Was he serious?'

'Of course! He didn't want me to get into trouble or to create problems for the family. I had already been a difficult high school student, even playing truant for two or three months once. I got away with it. When I sat for the examinations I still passed with a first. One day the teachers came to my home without notice, pushed the door of my room open. They saw books and papers lying about the floor. I had been seriously reading the works of Karl Marx and other communist literature. They could not imagine I'd be doing this! So yes, my brother was worried by my poetic activities. On the other hand, when one of my early poems was broadcast by local Qingdao radio we all sat and listened to the radio. I looked at him and there was relief on his face that I ended up on the radio rather than in prison. Years later, I wrote a poem to my mother, which was broadcast from Paris over Radio France Internationale. She was pleased to hear it.'

'There is a poem of yours, "You Predicted My Destiny", which draws on those years and which seems to be one of poetic intent. In it you appear to be setting your stamp upon the world.'

> You predicted my destiny,
> That I would become a poet.
> Since then your name has echoed in my blood.
>
> I chose the black and cold volcano.
> The crowded city bequeathed my space to others,
> A man came who would reclaim
> The mountainous wild manuscripts.

'When I was in high school I knew this girl whose calligraphy was better than mine. Sometimes after I finished a poem I would give it to her to write out in her beautiful hand. One day she returned a poem to me with a note, which simply read, "You will become a good poet." Many years later, I met her in the street. We hurriedly exchanged a few words and then, as I mention in the poem, I saw her off at a tram station in Qingdao.'

> You turn around and wave to me.
> The doors close like a camera shutter,
> The tram moves on.
>
> You image surges in my mind,
> A statue.

'Afterwards I went back and wrote the poem. That line "I chose the black and cold volcano" is symbolic of the knowledge that I'd have to choose a solitary life and that I would not be interested in the rivalry of the crowd or in participating in any kind of jungle activities. That kind of life was not what I aspired to, but I knew I would lead a very lonely existence.'

'Did she ever find out about the poem?'

'No, and it is best she doesn't. I have been through many different stages in my life and at each one I'm different. All I have is the same name. Sometimes it is impossible for Liu Hongbin at one stage to talk objectively or accurately about Liu Hongbin at another stage.'

1983 was the year of the Campaign against Spiritual Pollution, which, according to the Communist Party Propaganda Chief, Deng Liqun, would root out 'obscene, barbarous or reactionary materials, vulgar taste in artistic performances [and] indulgence in individualism'. This doubtless added to Hongbin's misfortunes. At this point he was in his final year at Shandong Foreign Trade School in Qingdao.

'A visiting American professor from Berkeley, Professor Oakes, who was one of the editors of *The Norton Anthology of Poetry*, came to China to run a class for university teachers. She gave me a precious typewritten course-book she had edited on American poetry. She had a minder, an agent posing as a teacher, and one day I phoned to tell her I'd be at her lecture. The minder picked up the phone, asked who it was, and informed me that I would have to apply at the Foreign Affairs office for permission. I said I didn't think they would be of assistance. Soon after, I received notification of my expulsion. The accusation was that I had spoken words that disgraced China. This effectively put an end to my future prospects. So I went with something like five *yuan* to Jinan, the capital of Shandong province, in order to petition the authorities. I said to them, "Look, in all the newspapers Party Secretary Deng Xiaoping says, 'We should select talent without any prejudice, regardless of family or political background.'" I thought I would surely be accepted. I even wrote a letter to Deng Xiaoping to ask him to intervene. Of course I did not receive a reply. Years later, I conceived the plot of a short story about this episode. In the story the letter is returned with a stamp on it saying, "No such person. Your letter is hereby returned."'

At Shandong University Hongbin met two people who would help him to keep in touch with the academic world, both at home and abroad. Professor Wu Fuheng, at that point president of the Society of American Literature, was a student of I.A. Richards when he was in China and then later again in Harvard, and when he went back to China he was a colleague of the poet William Empson. Professor Wu and his wife, Professor Lu Fan, took Hongbin on as their protégé, giving him books on American literature and encouraging him to write. They would watch over Hongbin even in later years when, prior to leaving China, he worked for the China National Arts and Crafts Import and Export Company.

'My experience there put me off business for life. I was assigned to that company where I experienced great resentment. First of all, given that the main way of promoting their business was to have exhibitions abroad – in Frankfurt, Las Vegas, Hong Kong – they never sent me anywhere. They knew I would defect. After all, I was a poet and trouble-maker. On the other hand they did not want to irritate me too much because when one is *that* bad one is like a mad dog. You leave him alone and he will leave you alone. They didn't mind giving me a bit of money just to keep me quiet. Still I did get into trouble while there. Yet again Professor Wu in his capacity as President of Shandong University and his wife came to my rescue. It just happened my director was a graduate of the same university. "Look at this miserable and silly guy," they said to him, "He is a good man but he doesn't know how to deal with life."'

The inability to 'deal with life' was not a little exacerbated by the fact that Hongbin was already an object of suspicion with the authorities and was kept under constant surveillance. It was a period of student unrest which probably led to the downfall of the sympathetic General Secretary of the Party, Hu Yaobang, whose death a couple of years later would be one of the factors leading to the Tiananmen Square Massacre. In 1987, Hongbin was caught up in the student activism. One symptom of the period was that the literary magazine *Literary Messenger*, to which Hongbin contributed a column devoted to translations of Western poetry, was closed down by the authorities.

The fact that he was watched was cause for yet another literary struggle.

'One day I met an English sailor. Qingdao is a large seaport, ships of all nationalities calling there. Because I spoke English he wanted to talk to me, to someone friendly in this strange place. I asked him whether he had a library on his ship. When he said yes I asked, "Do you have any Shakespeare?" "Yes." "Can you give me a copy?" Without any hesitation he said he would bring me the volume of Shakespeare at three o'clock the next day if I would meet him at a certain place. After that conversation I had a struggle within myself and in the end I didn't go. I was sure I'd be followed by the secret police. I was already a problem for the authorities. And if I had gone for that book I might have been in trouble again.'

'You must feel that that book is still waiting for you.'

§

In 1989 the asteroid Asclepius, named after the Greek god of medicine, came perilously close to earth, missing it by a mere 700,000 kilometres. What cure might it have carried for ossified regimes? A man sympathetic to the Tibetan cause, the aforementioned Hu Yaobang, died of heart failure. What began as a public expression of grief over the death of the man who might have reformed China had he not been forced to resign escalated into protest and after a few weeks, during which time a million lovely faces beamed with hope, the event known to the world as the Tiananmen Square Massacre took place.

'I was travelling between Qingdao and Beijing during the pro-Democracy movement, more or less in order to observe and incite. I made speeches in both places. I told a friend that I might post my poems at Qingdao Ocean University, which was a main centre of protest. My friend, a kind of official, told me I had to be very cautious. So I went with my poems to a typesetter, the wife of a professor at the university, and said to her, "Would you set these for me?" "What for?" she replied. I laughed. She knew immediately what I was going to do with them. These typesetting machines are an ancient system with separate printing blocks for every word. To own one you had to have a licence from the police, the reason for this being that if anti-establishment slogans appeared the police would be able to trace whoever printed them. The professor's wife set the four poems – "Sparrow", "The Spirit of the Sea", "On the Way" and "Rhapsody" – and mimeographed them, and armed with copies I went to Beijing and posted them in Tiananmen Square.'

'The Spirit of the Sea' contained now for the first time the line, 'The blind man tears the sun apart', which in the poem's original magazine appearance had been removed by the censors. We need hardly be told who the blind man is. Certainly the authorities did not require recourse to literary exegetes. Why, though, did they ignore, after lines bidding farewell to an earlier romantic voice, the line 'I want to build a new life'? Was this not also at odds with the *vita nuova* offered by the regime? It was written at a time when, Hongbin says, his body was bursting with hormones and he could produce several poems a day. One of Hongbin's loveliest poems, it is

a powerful evocation of the sea beside which he spent half his life. So closely does he identify himself with it that he writes, 'I am a demented wave thrown down on a reef, / instantly torn apart to reveal the explosion of light.' Only rarely does that light come on demand. Youth makes it shine all the more. Maybe it's this very poem before which the man in Tiananmen Square holds up his hand as if in a gesture of surprise.

'Were you an actual member of the pro-democracy movement?'

'No. I made trouble as an individual – I appeared, I disappeared – but I am not comfortable with, nor did I ever join, any political organisation. I am glad to have participated in the movement and posting my poems was a natural response. When you look back at Chinese history, in order to pass their examinations everyone had to be able to write a poem. I was merely honouring the Chinese tradition, making a poetic response to a social event. That is all I have ever done. I never wished to be a professional activist. I'd prefer a quiet life because, after all, I have suffered enough. There are times when I want to *burn* myself in Tiananmen Square. Although I couldn't help but get involved in social and political activities poetry was always my first love. The point I want to make is that people choose to see me as a political dissident. A year later, I was asked to go on the BBC TV *People Today* programme in Manchester. I stayed in a hotel there, feeling absolutely desolate. It was Chinese New Year, which overlapped with Valentine's Day. I started to make phone calls to Qingdao. The next day the people at the BBC asked me if there were certain areas where they ought not to intrude, and yet when the programme started, which was live, the questions were along the lines of "How did you manage to get out of the country?" The presenter asked another man, the head of some Chinese exile organisation, who was being interviewed alongside me, "How would you help refugees like Hongbin?" I was happy enough to go on the show, but what I am trying to say is that for the past twenty years or so I have been introduced as a dissident rather than as a poet. I'm not sure this is good for me or for my hosts or for my adopted country.'

'So do you feel some ambivalence about your role in Tiananmen Square?'

'No, I have no regrets whatsoever. It was a defining moment in my life. I am very happy to have risked myself in order to participate, to incite, to mobilise. When I stood in Tiananmen Square for the first time ever I felt I had dignity, that at last I was a human being. There was no crime whatsoever. Even the thieves were on strike. In the early morning, students would play flutes and sing. I was young and had a sense of justice. You can't expect me to have been obedient.'

The elation of victory is clearly written in Hongbin's pose. The ghostly obelisk behind him is that of the Monument to the People's Heroes. On the back of it are inscribed words drafted by Mao and polished by Zhou Enlai: 'Eternal glory to the heroes of the people who laid down their lives in the people's war of liberation and the people's revolution in the past three years! Eternal glory to the heroes of the people who laid down their lives in the people's war of liberation and the people's revolution in the past thirty years! Eternal glory to the heroes of the people who from 1840 laid down their lives in the many struggles against domestic and foreign enemies and for national independence and the freedom and well-being of the people!' Soon the tents in the picture would be flattened, the figures camped out beside them either dead or dispersed. Will the day come when there is added to the obelisk another line in memory of them?

'You must have been afraid.'

'The fear came *after* the massacre, not before. I left the night before the tanks rolled in. It was not because I knew a bloodbath would happen. It's just that I got tired. It seemed nothing was happening and I couldn't stay there indefinitely. So I went back to Qingdao and from there I phoned Zhang Hanzhi. She was a writer whose second husband Qiao Guanhua was a literary critic and was also the foreign minister who headed the delegation to the UN when China was admitted as a member in 1971. A very beautiful lady, she taught Mao English. She implied in her book that she had been raped by him and that afterwards he sent her a basket of apples which had been given to him by Kim Il-sung, the North Korean dictator. I called her "Auntie Zhang". When I visited her earlier, during my ten days in Tiananmen Square, and showed her the poems she said I should be prepared to leave the country as soon as possible. And now, on the phone, which was bugged, of course, I asked her how she was. She replied, "I'm fine. My young colleagues are with me. Can you hear the gunshots in the lane? Look at those counter-revolutionary gangsters out there! I behave so well. The mayor should give me an award for being a law-abiding citizen." This was her way of letting me know what was happening. And then I saw the images in the newspapers that had been faxed to our company by clients in Hong Kong, which I then photocopied and distributed. China has since become much cleverer at controlling communications and websites, but at that time even the telephones were still working. After the massacre, I acted as if nothing had happened. I continued to give public lectures and open forums in English at the city's best-known place, the German-built pier. Sooner or later, though, I knew they would find me. "The Spirit of the Sea" had already been published with that one missing line in a magazine and because the Writers' Association had asked poets to send lists of all their published poems they would be able to trace me. At first I wanted to go south and try to get into Macau or Hong Kong. Some people swam. Although I was born by the sea I can't swim at all.'

'How did you get out of China?'

'Zhang Hanzhi told me that as far as she knew the American embassies were giving out visas. First, though, I needed an exit visa. You had to get permission from your company. At the time I was working for a newspaper affiliated with the provincial writers' association and also at the China National Arts and Crafts Import Export Company, which does not exist any more. I told them I wanted to visit England. The boss summoned me for a meeting. I have to admit he was quite nice. He asked me, "Are you leaving for good?" I said I'd return. And then he said, "If you do, I advise you to be careful with what you say." I told my mother I'd have to go otherwise I would end up in prison or in a labour camp. The problem with Chinese mothers is that they regard their children as part of themselves. They sacrifice their lives for them and they love them. She resisted. Finally I said to her, "Mother, if you do not allow me to leave, I will commit suicide." This was the deal I struck with her. It was hard, very hard. My girlfriend went with me to the airport. I knew her for only three months. This was *after* the massacre. She was very intelligent, finished university, aged nineteen, with a degree in mathematics! The police harassed her over me. She suffered much although her parents were very Red, both of them party secretaries. They didn't like me. She learned from them there would be arrests and searches and so she warned me to stay outside the city. I was very grateful to her. After I arrived in England I asked a friend to invite her to come, but the Chinese authorities would not give her a passport, saying she was too young. I didn't want the police to continue to harass her and if she couldn't leave China what was the point? After two years, I told her we had better finish things. I still feel sorry about this. I understand she is now an American citizen living in Washington, DC. I could not be a better boyfriend to her and because of my infatuation with poetry I was not responsible either. I simply don't live like other people.'

'So then you got onto the plane…'

'A group of uniformed officers boarded the plane. They said, "All Chinese citizens show your passports." There were quite a few Japanese tourists around me. One of the officers said, "Are you from Tokyo as well?" I nodded but said nothing. And he walked past. Sometimes you can't tell Chinese from Japanese. This is exactly what happened. And then the plane was half an hour late. What else would happen? When it took off at 5.45 in the afternoon, the 9th of September, I wrote in my diary "Goodbye, China".'

§

When Hongbin first came through UK customs he had to have an X-ray. The plane he was on had made stop-overs in Islamabad and Istanbul and presumably they were looking for drugs. When, later, he was summoned before an immigration officer with a stern face he asked, in all innocence, whether he had to go through another screening. Amusingly, or perhaps not so amusingly, the man's gruff reply was, 'Don't spill blood on the carpet.' That experience, transmogrified, would work its way into Hongbin's prose poem, 'The Unfamiliar Customs House':

> Nightmares waylaid me. I could hardly make a declaration to the customs officer. I had become a smuggler, dealing in nightmares. I was once again in exile.
>
> When I took up my pen for the first time to write poetry I felt exiled from the ordinary world; then I was only a teenager. My exile was a voluntary one.
>
> The night in London became damper. Sound flutters its wings hovering in the air. The lighted cigarette in my hand is like a sleepless eye.
>
> The sky of the square in my mind seems to me still like a bloody, messy wound.
>
> My frozen tongue has come alive. I want to speak.

'After I arrived here, a local support group protesting the massacre already knew about me and had prepared everything – a free immigration lawyer, et cetera. Many of the Chinese who came here were not involved in the demonstrations but it was a chance for them to stay, whereas although I was actually there, in Tiananmen Square, and had given speeches and so forth, I didn't want to claim asylum at all. I wanted to go home. A poet is destined to have a feeling of exile. At the beginning this may be a horrifying experience but at least it helps one, as an onlooker, to gain a perspective. Of course one pays a price. When I was in China I read a lot of Western literature,

American and English poetry in particular, and I longed for the world outside. In fact the first of my poems in English translation had been published in *China Now* in 1988. Without hesitation I'd have defected to just about *any* other country. And yet after I arrived here I had a very different attitude. I had no choice. I clung to my Chinese passport until maybe two days before my visa expired in September 1990, at which point I gave it to a lawyer who put in my application. That was a painful moment. Within a week I got notice that I had been granted *indefinite leave to remain*.'

A near loss of balance in the physical world, a coin dropped into the slot of a payphone, would bring Hongbin some kind of redress in the literary one.

'Soon after arriving here, I got a job helping a Chinese Malaysian decorate a flat in Norwood. I took buckets of mixed cement up a high ladder. One day my legs were trembling so badly I might have fallen from that high roof. I can still remember when later that day, on the platform of Kennington Station, I got on the payphone to the Poetry Society and asked them to put me in touch with Elaine Feinstein, whose poems I had translated in China. She and her husband took me to a party, the first I attended in London. Many people there questioned me about Tiananmen Square. I must say I was still full of fear. I asked Elaine whether there were any other poets I could talk to. She introduced me to Peter Porter who in turn said I should meet Stephen Spender. I remember the first time I went to see Peter Porter at his flat and he took out an atlas, located Brisbane, which is where he comes from, and then looked to see where Qingdao stood in relation to it.'

The *Independent on Sunday* marked the first anniversary of the Tiananmen Square Massacre by publishing Hongbin's poem 'Consultation' together with a photograph of him in the Square. The poem, one of his darkest, is based on his visit to an English psychiatrist at St Mary's Hospital who spoke some Mandarin Chinese. What the doctor says in the poem, which may not be quite the same as what he said across the table, is that there is no cure for the darkness in his patient's eyes.

> Terror had broken into my eyes,
> My memory is ransacked by thieves

and howls through my teeth with pain.
Those crooks are swinging from my every nerve.
It seems to me that eyes are envelopes
and make good cells – I seal mine tightly shut
and tell the doctor, 'Please let me sleep.'
I ask him to write out a prescription for death.

'There is something bad in this poem because psychologically it represents a kind of revenge. Although now I can disavow the negative mentality in that poem, when I first arrived here my thoughts, my consciousness, my spirit were more pervasive than my physical presence. It is a young man's poem. We can forgive him. I mean he really had become a smuggler of nightmares. It was a difficult time, however. When the poem appeared in the paper the caption beside the photograph of me sitting in a tent in Tiananmen Square said I was washing dishes in a Chinese restaurant. Blake Morrison was then literary editor at the *Independent on Sunday* and prior to publication I went to see him in his editorial office where he asked me to look over the proofs. When I saw the line about washing dishes, I was upset. "Well, isn't it true?" Blake replied. I like Blake. Talk about vanity! I was a bit vain. I mean how *could* I have ended up as a dishwasher? It was the lowest kind of job you could have because everyone else could bully you; although, in truth, I was happy in a way because I could feed myself and also because my imagination was free. Soon afterwards, I went to Bristol to give a poetry reading and talk arranged by Amnesty International. A number of students came, some of whom asked which Chinese restaurant I worked in and whether they could come to visit me there. "I work in the basement," I replied. "You will not be able to see me." When I met Joseph Brodsky for the first time, he asked me, "What are you doing?" I told him I was washing dishes. "Do you need money?" I said no. Later, I learned he did in fact give money to fellow writers. Hard times, indeed. In my second year in London, on Christmas Eve, I was evicted from my home. It was raining. The old landlady asked me, "Why don't you spend more time in the park rather than stay at home?" All I had with me was a suitcase. I became homeless.'

'Were you disappointed with your earlier idea of freedom after you came here?'

'It's not like you cross a border and then you are free. It takes a long time, even years, for the idea of freedom to settle into the consciousness, and that's because freedom is a subjective feeling. I'm not sure many people living here feel they are free.'

'Did coming here enlarge your life as a poet? Surely it must have done.'

'Quite the contrary! When I first stood in Leicester Square, in the sunshine, it seemed to me that my shadow thrown on the ground was shorter than my own life. I was naïve and young and I had ambition and yet when I walked about the British Museum I felt terribly depressed. And when I passed the blue plaques displayed all around London I knew I could not compete with all those dead souls as the dead are more powerful – they are giants of thought, not just in literature, but thought in general. I didn't write poetry in English. I didn't have any audience here. So I did not feel my life was enlarged at all, and yet this kind of adversity became an advantage. I started to write for myself. I wasn't an established figure in China nor was I chosen by the authorities there for "direct export" to sinologists overseas. I was just an obscure boy with a passion for poetry. What else did I have? The driving force in me was so immense and yet I was not quite sure about what I had. According to many people's standards my life is a total failure. I am almost fifty and *still* I am unrealistic. All I had in China was one disaster after another, and here, one accident after another. Who else would want my life? On the other hand, when looking back on one's existence, one should not complain about suffering or humiliation. It is exactly those things that make what you are. You should not have any resentment, despite the humiliation you undergo in life. Also this has nothing to do with how you write… the greater the humiliation, the more you grow mentally and spiritually as a writer. It gives you the strength to continue and also it will enlarge your presence in the world of your art. I'm lucky to have met people here otherwise I don't know where my dark thoughts would have led me.'

As to the matter of what it is to be an exile, Hongbin writes in his autobiographical essay 'Out of Exile: Language, Memory and Imagination':

> I took with me only my mother tongue, perhaps also my unscathed imagination. If I survived, it would be on account

of them. I would claim my life back one day. If my memory serves me well in return, I will serve my own imagination. Memory and imagination are one. Language is imagination's playground, but at the same time, it is also the battleground of one's own ideas. Every word forms the fabric of the world we inhabit. For most of the time, a poet lives within language – and by it. I smuggled my language, imagination and memory out of China… In exile, I still felt drawn towards a form of celestial reality that is the reality of imagination. This seemed a higher form of reality. Every day, through living and writing, we are convinced of the existence of different levels of reality, visible and invisible. I feel the constant desire to be raised to that higher level, to see the invisible and to hear the inaudible in the doom and gloom of exile – although isolation, homelessness, loneliness and despair have almost driven me to self-destruction. If I died, I have died many times.

In 1993, Jiang Zemin became President of the People's Republic of China. Soon afterwards, China conducted a nuclear test which in effect brought an end to a worldwide moratorium on such activities. That same year Hongbin was diagnosed with cancer.

'I stayed in my flat for a week and then I phoned Elaine Feinstein and told her. "Hongbin," she said, "open the window." I opened it. "See," she said, "how lovely the sunshine is." Then I went to the Chinese Embassy and told them I wanted to go back to China, either for treatment or to die. They refused me four times. I was in despair. That is when I wrote "Valediction", which I dedicated to my nieces and nephew in the hope that they would grow to love poetry.

At daybreak my bloodstream becomes a fire
burning, I am rainbow-hued and drained to nothing.

Words are a gleaming river in the night,
an elegy.

All children who read poetry are my own dear children.
Their voices are like dawn breaking over darkness.

Children I am back with you.

'When a Buddhist or Taoist monk dies he does not want to leave anything behind on earth. All those monks who achieve Buddhahood or immortality burn themselves like a rainbow hue. You start an inner fire and then you are gone. There is an element of this in the poem but I think what I created above all is an atmosphere of solitude. It is important sometimes for a poet to achieve a sense of detachment, sufficiently so that reading his poem is like reading someone else's. I cannot help but be moved by this poet, this pathetic guy who genuinely loves poetry. A friend who practised Tibetan meditation kindly sent me books and tapes, which helped me to relax and get into a tranquil mood. Later, the doctor told me I didn't have cancer at all. They had made a mistake!'

§

Hongbin, carrying a British passport, made his first return visit to China in 1997. When he arrived at his mother's house six police officers broke in and, after telling him he was not welcome in the country, put him under house arrest. Although he was later free to go, which is to say they henceforth followed his every move, by the time he got to Shanghai he was re-arrested, this time in broad daylight, and at the police station was offered the choice of keeping either his Chinese ID card or his British passport. When he chose the latter the chief of police informed him that he had been performing activities incompatible with his tourist status.

'They tried immediately to deport me to Hong Kong. On the way to the airport I told them it was a disgrace for China to expel a poet. They replied, "You are not *worth* deportation!" Hong Kong Dragon Airlines refused to take me. So the police put me in a hotel for the night. I slept on one bed, two policemen in another bed, another on the floor. They ordered a meal but in order to protest my expulsion I refused to eat. A senior official came and said to me, "Do you know how much *my* family suffered during the Cultural Revolution?" The next day they escorted me – one of them was an attractive woman in plain clothes – to the airport. They changed my surname on the boarding pass, which I still have, to "Wu". They did not want me to be known to my fellow passengers. When I boarded the plane two of them followed me. I said, "Can I give you something?" They exchanged looks. I gave them my book. I said to one of them "What is your name?" And he replied, "Zhong", which, as well as being a surname, is also the first character of the Chinese for China, *Zhōngguó*, the implication being that he *was* China or that *he* was loyal to China. It was so pathetic, this individual so engulfed by the state he did not have even an identity of his own. I said to them, "I will return through my poetry." After I sat down, another person arrived who I assumed was with the secret police. He accompanied me to Hong Kong.'

Man is born unto trouble, says Eliphaz the Temanite, *as the sparks fly upward*. The second half of the sentence from the Book of Job has baffled commentators for centuries, and yet, like certain lines of poetry that resist paraphrase, when taken neat it makes perfect sense. As sparks fly upward, just as surely affliction comes. Our mistake is to attribute it to fortune. The Taoist perspective on this is that misfortune comes from having a body and as such it should be accepted as the human condition. Trouble seems to follow Hongbin wherever he goes. After his expulsion from China, he returned to England only to discover he'd been evicted from his home. He moved into a place for homeless people where the manager, an old man, attacked him with an axe. What's the full story here? Well, let's just say Hongbin is still alive.

In 2004, in Taiwan, a decomposing sperm whale was transported through Tainan City to the university where a necropsy was to be performed when suddenly it exploded, splattering hundreds of onlookers with blood, entrails and stuff even more unmentionable. There is in this image, surely, an analogy for the fate of all regimes. Also that year, thousands of people in Hong Kong took to the streets to commemorate the fifteenth anniversary of the Tiananmen Square Massacre. In October of that same year, Hongbin, together with his young daughter, went to China to visit his ailing mother. A piece he wrote for the *Index on Censorship* describes one episode from that journey, which took place on his mother's birthday:

> All I hoped was that the police would not harass me this time. When we arrived, we were driven to a detention centre, and I was interrogated by the police. My daughter was three years old at the time and asthmatic, and started crying. But she put

> her hands across my mouth in an attempt to prevent me from answering the police's questions. A woman police officer was called in. I knew she wanted to take my daughter away from me. I took out the puffer to help relieve her wheezing. My daughter was crying and said in English: 'I don't like them,' and again put her little hands across my mouth to stop me from talking to the police. In the end, they didn't take her away. We were locked up in cell 308 – a small bare room, with a bed, a few dirty white quilts and a bloody handprint on the wall. The window had triple iron bars.

They were finally released, Hongbin's daughter covered with insect bites, and they made it to Qingdao where his mother still lives. One sad consequence of this journey is that the ban on his returning to China, issued on his first return visit in 1997, was renewed, this time indefinitely. Hongbin has not been back since.

On 9 November 2005 Chinese President Hu Jintao visited London at the invitation of Queen Elizabeth, who wore red for the occasion. Was this an ironic gesture on her part? When President Hu was approached by the BBC's *Newsnight* for an interview he declined. Hongbin went on the programme instead to speak about the human rights situation in China, with the consequence that within hours a UK-based Chinese website posted over ninety pages of complaints, mostly from Chinese students and scholars residing here, accusing him of being a traitor to his country. Some of the messages screamed, 'Let him die in England!' and others, more worryingly, 'Let's get rid of this scum!' China is not opening up in the way its apologists assume. Indeed, recently – as with, for example, the arrest of the artist Ai Weiwei – repression in China has been on the increase again. These are matters Hongbin would like to put behind him.

I began by saying I found him in monkish mode. In 2000, Hongbin had been invited to visit the Dalai Lama in Dharamshala to see the refugee camps and the S.O.S. Children's Village, and when he spoke to him of his own plight His Holiness, sensing Hongbin was on a fruitless course, which is to say he was seeking justice for his father where there could be none, replied, 'Let it go.' When Hongbin went on to tell him he wanted to learn more about Tibetan Buddhism, which he had already practised for eight years, the reply was, 'If I were you, I would be more interested in the Chinese root and its form.' It was a response that was to have serious repercussions for Hongbin, one that put him back on a course that he had begun to explore many years earlier and of which he spoke with something like spiritual yearning in his voice.

'When I was twenty, I went to a mountain above Qingdao called Laoshan, which was famed for its Taoist practice. It is the second heavenly court of the Quanzhen Longmen sect. The Chinese poet Li Po visited there. There, at Shangqing Palace, one of the very few temples to have survived the Cultural Revolution, I met a Taoist monk and told him I wanted to join the order. He said I would need to get permission first of all from my mother because I wouldn't be able to marry. I told him she had four sons, three of whom were marriageable. Then he told me I'd require permission from the Qingdao Municipal Administration of Religious Affairs. I applied and was refused. One consequence of this rejection is that I was motivated to know more about what it was I had not been allowed to learn.'

'Are you about to retreat into a monastic space of your own?'

'It is not that concrete. As the twenty-second generation heir of the Quanzhen Longmen sect ideally I should have retreated to the deep forest mountains, but then the state of my mind is more important than my whereabouts… clear tranquillity of mind. That monastic space contains perhaps five thousand years of Chinese civilisation and whether it's on the mainland or in Taiwan or in any other part of the world the Chinese people have never really abandoned their cultural heritage. So it is not as if I am erecting a barricade between my poetry and the space of my thought but rather it's that they might marvellously combine there.

'I have been studying the *I Ching* for more than twenty-five years and by doing so I have come to a better understanding of human fate and the soul's landscape. All natural phenomena are contained within its hexagrams, which begin as eight, then become sixty-four, and, eventually, millions. It is a poet's mission to interpret symbols and images. If you are born in an inauspicious time you are going to have a troubled life and yet the suffering enables you to experience that life to the full. You may count on one hand the writers who have had a happy existence. Their experiences are what made them great. So it is difficult to say whether someone has a better or worse fate than other people or if he is lucky or unlucky. There is, ultimately, no such interpretation and as soon as one realises this the easier it is to live and to die. You will have no complaints. It's not that I seek to evade real questions. It is up to you how you perceive your life, whether you are happy or sad, rich or poor, creative or uncreative, loved or unloved. You are blessed with all those tribulations, disappointments, sufferings, human tragedies. It is what helps me to survive and also it enables me to understand other people.

'When I began to learn about Tibetan Buddhism I recognised a relationship between it and Taoism. Taoism is the earliest native Chinese religion. Without Taoism the introduction and translation in China of the Buddhist scriptures would have been impossible because so much of their terminology was borrowed from Taoism. The whole of Chinese culture is based upon Taoism – its philosophy, medicine, astronomy, mathematics… even the invention of the compass and gunpowder. It is difficult to say whether I foresee a monastic existence for myself. I went to a temple in Taiwan and stayed there for quite a long time. I got up at 5.30 and went to bed at 10.30. It was a hard life. Also I went to a Tibetan monastery here in London. I was terribly depressed and the teacher-in-residence or *geshi* was very kind to me. He knew I was an exile and said to me, "I, too, have lost my country." There are people who have suffered so much, who have lost everything, yet this man could maintain his peace of mind. When the Dalai Lama said I should consider my Chinese roots I went back to Lao Tse whose *Tao Te Ching* is the classic of all classics, written in only five thousand Chinese characters. My life might finish tomorrow but Taoist philosophy values and respects life. There is a Taoist saying: "The span of my life depends on me and not on the heavens." One of the Taoist practices is to achieve long life. Managing one's physical health is like governing a country. Tao finds its law in nature.

'I'm sure Taoism could be a think-tank for contemporary

ecologists and also for those yearning for a better politics. On the other hand I could say the life process is a journey from ego to no ego. Have I conquered vanity? If you decide to give it up it is not so difficult. Sometimes you will have difficulties without it or because vanity has been made to equal dignity. Many people mistake dignity for vanity. The most important thing is the life *within*. What other people say or think will not have an impact on you if you are liberated from yourself.

'Poetry has helped me. I owe so much to poetry. If there is an aim or purpose in life I want to give it all the more credit for that. As a poet you can certainly believe in a life of the soul. But who could measure that kind of life? I know I am just a passerby and that I will perish here with gratitude. That is my fate. And yet when I first arrived here I was angry, full of indignation for a life lost. The thing about totalitarian regimes is that they stir up hatred between people and then they try to keep that hatred alive. With that kind of hatred, however, I don't think I would have been able to make a fresh start to my life here. I have many friends in this country and I love them, which is why I like to start my story in the middle, with my past at one end and with my unknown future at the other. All this seems so simple now that my life is drawing to a close, when I might be reduced to three Chinese characters.'

'Which ones?'

'I don't know,' Hongbin concluded. 'Maybe the ones that make up my name.'

刘 洪 彬

Or might it be, when it was still a name one could use with impunity, Wang Hongbin?

王 洪 彬

Maybe, though, they're three characters, as yet unknown, for a monk bearing that name.

The Happiest of All Stories

Coleridge Goode, Jazz Bassist

'The century will soon be upon me.'

'There will be centenary celebrations galore!'

'Well, I'd like to enjoy what time is left to me.'

'You'll make the century, I'm sure.'

'Well, I'd *like* to make it.'

Coleridge George Emerson Goode made a couple of mental calculations and then chuckled quietly. 'Yeah, I'll do what I can!' He continued, 'At 95, the business of looking reasonably well, at least in social circles, is half the battle otherwise people will cease to take notice of me.'

So jests, seriously enough, a man who has rarely escaped the music world's notice. Often dubbed the best jazz bassist in Europe, for over six decades he moved through almost every musical style – from swing to Django Reinhardt's 'jazz *manouche*', from bebop to free-form, and from Indo-Jazz fusion to Michael Garrick's religious 'jazz praises'. The spaces between are adorned with the names of musical accomplices such as Andy Hamilton and the Blue Notes; the Caribbean Trio; big band leader Eric Winstone, who suffered from a nervous affliction that caused him to thump his chest from time to time; singer Julie Dawn, whose real name was Juliana Rosalba Maria Theresa Mostosi; Jamaican trumpeter Leslie 'Jiver' Hutchinson, father of singer Elaine Delmar who has also, on occasion, been accompanied by Coleridge; accordionist Tito Burns, born Nehemiah Bernstein; 'the little giant of the tenor' saxophonist Tubby Hayes; Ray Ellington, whose rendition of 'The Maharajah of Magador' is a favourite of mine, although 'Little Bop Beep' is a serious contender; singer Ray Nance, on occasional loan to Ray Ellington from Duke; and Guyanese pianist Iggy Quail, born Cuthbert Ignatius Quail. There are plenty more. The discography is equally impressive. A year ago, Coleridge was still playing Sunday afternoons with the Laurie Morgan Trio at the King's Head in Crouch End, but feeling he was no longer up to his best, which is just about the best any jazz musician has ever done, he retired. 'It was forced upon me,' he said, without any trace of self-pity, 'when I couldn't play any more.' It was not that he couldn't play but that he had begun to suffer from the gout which made standing for any length of time prohibitive. The double bass that has accompanied him throughout his performing life, which during the Blitz he lugged about on the tube, and which is covered with scars from other kinds of battles, stands monolithically at one end of the room where he sits and listens to music. ('A life without music,' he says, 'is not life.') That instrument, born in the small town of Mittenwalde, Germany, in 1860, seems a living creature, an extension of its owner, and, equally, when Coleridge speaks, he becomes, so I fancy, its deep sonorous voice. They are quite inextricable.

When I first visited him, the autumnal air already beginning to bite, opera was playing on the radio and when I next went to see him, a week later, the chill a bit sharper, he was blanketed over, listening to a recording of Glenn Gould playing Bach. Bach is Coleridge's musical god. There can be few who can speak of Bach solely in terms of his bass lines.

§

The happiest of all stories begins on 29 September 1914, in Saint Andrew Parish, Jamaica, about six miles' distance from Kingston. The parish, small though it is, has been associated with a plethora of musicians and popular musical styles – jazz pianist Monty Alexander, reggae singers Bob Marley and Peter Tosh among them. Musically Coleridge was born into a rather different milieu, one reflecting an altogether more genteel age. His father, George Goode, secretary to the Director of the Department of Agriculture, was also choir master and organist in a church in Kingston, a position he occupied for over fifty years. Hilda Goode, Coleridge's mother, had a good soprano voice. The music that was played at home was remote from anything one might term 'island music': it was all classical. When I invited Coleridge to name pieces of music he associates with different periods of his life, Tchaikovsky's Symphony No. 6, the *Pathétique*, was his childhood favourite. The original Russian title *Patetičeskaja* means 'passionate' or 'emotional', this being the quality in music that Coleridge rates above all others.

'What are your memories of Jamaica?'

'I had a very sheltered life. My parents were very strict although they also liked the better things in life. They wanted their children to be respectable, well, at least not *too* much of a problem. Because of the pressures on my father, the amount of work he had to do, I didn't actually see that much of him. His office was close to where we lived, in this complex called Hope Gardens, which included a school for teaching young farmers. Constantly busy, he worked all day, came home, and would then disappear into his study to attend to the musical side of things. The only time I remember him occasionally taking time off was when he would go down to the grounds attached to the school and play cricket, bowl a ball or two, and even then not for very long. As well as music he loved literature, poetry, Emerson's in particular, which is how I got one of my names. My first name was not because of the poet. At the time of my birth my father was performing work by the black composer, Samuel Coleridge-Taylor. That was a really lovely thing to have done, to name me after him.'

'Did he have aspirations for you to become a musician?'

'He may have done but he wouldn't have put pressure on me. What happened, happened naturally. At one of my father's concerts I was inspired by the performance by one of the people in the orchestra who played cello. I went home, got some bits of wood from an orange crate, and tried to make one. My father saw this and so he bought me a violin which is what started me off in music.'

'So you began violin dreaming of cello.'

'I suppose string music in general was what I most liked, anything strummed, plucked or bowed. It was obviously the right thing for me. I took to the violin and did well in my exams for it, getting a gold medal.'

'Did you see yourself becoming a classical musician?'

'I did not see myself as *any* kind of musician. Nobody in Jamaica played music for a living. My father would cover his expenses, only just, but then for him it was mostly voluntary. He simply loved music and had to perform it somehow. Also, Jamaica was not at all classically minded. There was this popular style, but I never heard anything of it when I was a child. I didn't go to parties. I stayed home most of the time, listening only to classical music. Obviously as I grew older I began to think about what I would do with my future. My father had bought me a bicycle to go to school and then he got me a motorbike and that prompted me to become interested in mechanics. I used to take the motorbike to pieces, clean and paint it. Jamaica was late in getting electricity. We had paraffin. I figured that Jamaica would need engineers who could deal with this newly arrived thing and so the best thing for me would be to go to England to study electrical engineering and then come back home.'

In August 1934, aged nineteen, Coleridge stepped onto the Elders & Fyffes weekly banana boat, a steamship destined for Avonmouth.

> Away across the sparkling waters mangroves and palm trees are seen rising from low shores, above which great purple banks of forest tower four thousand feet in the air. To the west are lofty mountain ridges of a rich dark blue, throwing out buttresses almost to the water's edge, on which nestle here and there trim houses of bright colour. These mountains give an impression of such nobility and grandeur, that it is almost with reluctance that one sees them giving way to a long low spit of land behind which the buildings of Kingston become visible, backed by well-treed slopes which lead to encircling hills. The mountains are the Jamaican Blue Mountains, and the spit is a submerged coral reef covered with shingle, called the Palisades, behind which lies the great lagoon of Kingston Harbour.

This is the scene George F. Timpson describes in his *Jamaican Interlude* (1938), and, although all memory of that departure has been erased from Coleridge's mind, it must have been pretty much what he saw when he looked back on the island he did not at the time realise he was leaving forever.

§

In his autobiography *Bass Lines – A Life in Jazz* (2002), which he co-wrote with the jazz critic Roger Cotterrell, Coleridge describes the shock of arriving in Avonmouth and finding things not quite as he had expected them:

> When the boat docked and we disembarked down the gang-plank the first thing my feet touched were cobblestones. Cobbles! That was a terrible shock. You didn't expect to be coming to the mother country from Jamaica and landing on rough cobbles. I thought there should have been a lovely landing stage, a proper welcome for the ship and all that sort of thing. But those ruddy cobbles were the first bit of Britain to make contact with. I hobbled about on them, trying to walk on the uneven surface, carrying my luggage, feeling confused.

'Shortly after I arrived I went up a mountain and saw snow and ice for the first time. That was an experience one doesn't get everywhere. I wondered how one could lead one's life in these conditions. Down in the lowland it was not as cold as all that and anyway I had not yet really experienced the extremities of cold. I always feel it. I can't bear being cold. I suppose I was born and made to be comfortable in heat. Cold affects how I feel about things. I can't function the way I'd like to. It withers me. As I was going to be here for some time I was going to have to learn how to deal with it. I just wear more clothes and keep the heat on, but it takes getting used to, and I'm still uncomfortable with it. I'm generally miserable. Give me sunshine and warmth and I'm fine.'

'So you chose to spend the greater part of your life in misery?'

'Well, it chose me! The way things turned out I never expected … well, what *does* one expect as a youngster other than to make enough to get oneself a good meal and to sleep comfortably at night and that's about it. As far as music is concerned, that to me is life. So I enjoy myself and every now and then forget about the cold.'

The studio photograph of Coleridge, aged twenty, was taken in Glasgow where he enrolled first at the Royal Technical College and then, after completing a preparatory course there, at Glasgow University.

'As I travelled through Glasgow for the first time in a taxi I wondered "Where do the people live?" There were all these huge blocks of concrete. At university I studied violin under William Whittaker who was a friend of the composer Ralph Vaughan Williams and played second violin in the university orchestra. My engineering professor who also played violin sat beside me. I used to go to his house on Sundays to play chamber music. His wife played piano and there was an oboist too.'

It was during this period that currents other than electrical moved through him.

'At home, in Jamaica, I never heard a note of jazz. My father would not allow any other music in the house so I never heard anything until I came here. I got myself a radio and I started to hear jazz from the USA. Also visiting musicians like Art Tatum would come on tour and play locally.'

It was in Glasgow that Coleridge acquired the bass which, at least for purposes of this prose, he has so come to resemble. A visiting musician left it too close to the fireplace. Seeing that its back was scorched, the musician lost faith in its capabilities and Coleridge, always one ready to believe, discovered that while its looks may have been impaired its sound was not, and so he made an offer for it. Soon he neglected his studies in order to practise as much as eight hours a day. Within a year, although his hands hurt because they hadn't yet had time to set, he was doing local gigs, which was when his instrument was to endure yet another blow, this much more serious and expensive. One day it was swept off a tramcar onto the street where its neck got broken. That instrument was accident-prone.

'Was there any specific piece of music that made you think yes, this is it, *this* is what I want?'

'My love of music has always centred on J.S. Bach, the *way* he wrote his music, and the bass lines that ran through it. When I first heard Count Basie, in 1936, he had a bassist, Walter Page, who played what was then newly called "walking bass", which, instead of the notes jumping about, moved along as one might walk. That really impressed me. Page was the only musician who played that way and I thought that was what I would like to do. One piece I remember in particular is "Oh, Lady Be Good". It wasn't just the one song though – it was how Page played through all the music.'

'So we move from Tchaikovsky to Bach to Count Basie!'

'Later, there was another bass player, Jimmy Blanton, who played with Duke Ellington. Blanton was the only jazz bassist at the time who used a bow. And then, later, there was Slam Stewart who also used a bow and at the same time sang an octave above what he was playing. So I developed my style on that basis, playing solos with the bow and using my voice. As far as I know, I was the only one here who did that.'

After seven years in Glasgow, Coleridge set his sights on London.

'Was there an English jazz scene already there?'

'It wasn't very strong. There was a group called Ken Johnson and his Rhythm Swingers, the only black band of any consequence. I heard them on the radio and when I heard they were about to change their bass player I wrote to Johnson, offering him my services. I never got a reply.'

It was most fortuitous he didn't. On Saturday, 8 March 1941, Ken 'Snake-Hips' Johnson was drinking with friends at the Embassy Club on Bond Street. At 9.30 he realised he had to be at the Café de Paris on Coventry Street where he was due to start performing at 9.45. The Blitz was at its height and Johnson's friends urged him not to chance it. A conscientious man, determined not to disappoint his employer, and very dark-skinned, Johnson joked, 'I will run there, nobody will notice me in the dark.' He ran all the way, arriving just in time to strike up with one of the club favourites 'Oh, Johnnie'. A young woman, executing a step, cried, 'Wow, Johnnie!' at which precise moment, at 9.50, a bomb fell through the roof, instantly killing Johnson and several members of his band. Over eighty people died, the freakishness of the blast being such that while one woman merely had her stockings blown off the woman beside her lost all her fingers. Charles Graves, who wrote a history of the club, describes it as having resembled a slaughterhouse.

'Somebody was looking after you!' I said. 'Are you a fatalist?'

Coleridge hesitated a little.

'I think one's life could well be guided by external forces. After all, the force that created this universe is so enormous and so powerful it is beyond our human imagination and knowledge. Nobody knows how this world was formed and I can't see anyone finding out soon but something *this* vast could not just happen – it had to have been ordered by some fantastic thing outside our knowledge.'

§

In 1941, the worst of the Blitz over, Coleridge ventured down to London where he was offered a job at the Panama Club with trumpeter Johnny Claes and the Claepigeons, and they were later joined by one of the most dynamic guitarists of the period, the Trinidadian Lauderic Caton, who was also one of the very first musicians to go electric. Glasgow and college were now behind him forever. The Claepigeons made a tour of American army bases, during which time Coleridge had to endure some of the worst prejudice he has experienced in this country. The British, whatever prejudices they themselves may have harboured, accepted black American soldiers as Americans pure and simple, whereas the white American troops brought with them the racial patterns that had been so much a part of life back home. Often this resulted in violent street clashes. The army authorities, in order to reduce contact between the two sides, went so far as to designate pubs 'black' or 'white'. The British were scandalised by the intrusion of American racial mores into their own daily existence. In *Bass Lines*, Coleridge writes:

> I saw plenty of that kind of racism from the American forces

> during the war. Fights would often break out when black servicemen tried to dance or talk with English girls in clubs or dance halls. The white GIs would start a brawl when they saw the black servicemen with the girls. I saw all that kind of nastiness. Those poor guys were humiliated so often.

'I remember one specific occasion, when we played at an army base not far from London. Lauderic and I were the only two black people in the group. It came to refreshment time. They put the white members of the band in one room and us in a separate one. Lauderic was incensed and immediately went home. Another occasion was when we gave a concert in Bristol. A hotel had been booked for us. After the concert we all turned up there and were told the white members could stay and we couldn't. The hotel did not want to offend the American servicemen who used the place. So the whole band left and slept in the concert hall where we had played earlier. It was the British this time. So these things did happen.'

§

The Caribbean Trio of which Coleridge was a founding member was formed together with Lauderic Caton and Dick Katz in 1944 and probably represents one of the happiest periods of his musical career. It seems, though, that good fortune was already on his side. In 1943, an Austrian Jewish refugee, Gertrude Selmeczi, went to visit her old school friend from Vienna who was now living in London, in the house where Coleridge lived, and her friend, thinking Coleridge was away, offered her his bed for the night.

'The way things turned out, I think she was sent to me. Yes, I've been very lucky. I never even had a girlfriend at home. I had no experience with girls at all. Somehow it was ordained. At the time I was a jobbing musician. I was out on a gig, and I came home – or to what I *called* home at the time – and found that my bed had been slept in. Gertrude was presented to me as the person who slept in the bed. We got talking and from thereon … ah, well … we are *still* talking. We have been married sixty-five years. I always wondered whether I'd ever get a partner who had intellectual graces and a love of music and the things I like. Amongst the black population there were very few women in London at the time. Anyway I've always thought people segregate themselves too much. The world could do with being more mixed up. There'd be fewer factions to fight against, of whatever colour or race.'

As if on cue Gertrude entered the room and I told her that we had just been discussing the fact she had been ordained.

'*Ordained?*' she said, with irony in her voice. 'Oh, I think everything is an accident. Do you *really* believe that, Cole? I don't.'

'Yeah, I do. I do, I do! Very much!'

'Well, you *would*,' she replied, and, turning to me, quipped, 'He is very gullible.'

'So it was just by accident you met him?'

'I think so. I might have been staying somewhere else.'

'Ultimately,' I said, 'I think men are the romantics and women are …'

'Cold-blooded!' interjected Coleridge.

'I meant to say the more level-headed of the species.'

'I suffered from a Hungarian surname that no one could pronounce,' Gertrude explained, 'which is why I married Mr Goode in order to simplify matters.'

'She wanted a good surname, you see,' joked Coleridge.

Gertrude's Story

'My father's father, who was Hungarian, started a textile factory in Austria, which was bombed in World War I. My father rebuilt it. There was a post-war boom, during which time everyone made money, so I remember relatively high living until the Crash of 1929. My father had a chauffeur who had been his batman during the war and who also shaved him every morning. We had a posh car, a Daimler with a flower vase inside. After the Crash they had to economise. The Daimler was exchanged for a Fiat which I remember was a convertible with celluloid windows. We didn't stay in hotels any more, but spent our holidays in a cottage. The cook and the maid stayed on probably because they had no choice, the younger one, the maid, being a very clever, spirited woman with a baby she saw only once a fortnight. She must have had a tough life. On the other hand there was great familiarity, and, apart from the hard work, we had fun. My maternal grandmother was a hoity-toity, rather pretentious, lady who had a thing about being beautiful. None of her grandchildren ever came up to her expectations. I had freckles, so something was wrong with me. We all lived together in a huge flat but there was enough space for everyone to have his or her own quarters.'

'You witnessed the rise of Hitler.'

'I suppose I did. I was a teenager living in this kind of semi-fascist Austria. They called themselves Christian Democrats but it was a relatively liberal fascism such as they had in Italy. A Catholic party, they were anti-Nazi and put quite a few local Nazis in jail, although as Hitler became ever more threatening they tried to make last-minute concessions to him. It didn't do them any good.'

'Did you have a sense of something awful about to happen?'

'I was too young to think of it quite like that and, besides, we didn't know how terrible it would become. My parents had one or two literary friends who came from Berlin to Vienna because they thought it was a safe haven, and who told them stories of what went on in Germany, about concentration camps for political people. I think Hitler was still more a figure of contempt or fun or even ludicrousness. Some people were probably much more politically aware than we were, but as for me when one is young one is not so scared of life.'

'Your parents must have had sufficient foresight to want to get you out of there.'

'They definitely felt we had to go once the Germans arrived in force with their tanks, their swastikas, rounding up people in the street if they didn't wear Nazi armbands. The Viennese fell over backwards and wore them from one day to the next. They all became Nazis. Even the German officers were disgusted with them, shocked at how slavish and compliant they were. They really were a shocking lot. I remember I had a hysterical outburst with my parents who were cogitating on whether to stay or leave. I couldn't bear it any more. I cried, "For Christ's sake, let's go." My parents, although they were still bickering about where to go and what to do, wanted my sister and me out of the country. My mother had a friend who owned a palazzo in Florence, which she didn't use in winter because it was too lonely and too cold. Eventually she let us live there. It was freezing cold. We spent about nine months in Florence and then came to

London in April 1939. War broke out in September. We came here as domestic servants. The average woman was only allowed in as a domestic whereas with the men they took those with a profession or trade. A cousin of mine came here as a gardener's apprentice. I felt it was poetic justice that we ended up as parlour maids because we had grown up with them. I was living outside London in Berkshire, in a weekend house that belonged to a managing director of Decca Records. It was like a 1930s drawing-room comedy. They entertained showbiz people. I was in domestic service for four years, from 1939 to 1943. I left there and then went back when the Decca man went to America leaving his mother in charge of the house. It was filled with a very odd assortment of people. With one thing or another I got fed up. The place got flooded every year. We were cut off for a fortnight and you had to row your way to the station in order to get away for a bit.'

'Did your parents get out of Vienna?'

'Initially, yes. They went to France and in the summer of 1939 my sister and I went over to visit them. We could actually afford to go to France on our parlour maids' wages which were quite good at the time. War was imminent. I had a cousin who was with them, who was two or three years younger than me. My mother and her sister and their two husbands and this boy of seventeen lived in a little channel port near Boulogne. They were not allowed to live in Paris. They shoved everybody who wasn't French out of there. My cousin, who later on became a journalist and writer, described what it was like. They were overrun by the German army and of course the Pétain government complied with the Germans who asked them to round up Jews, foreign or otherwise. My parents were caught in one of these raids. My mother survived but my father didn't.'

She sank into a silence in which that small word 'didn't' grew larger and larger. When finally it reached full size, it could no longer be addressed.

'Meanwhile, stuck in Berkshire, I wanted to be in the auxiliary air force. When they first interviewed me they said that because I spoke German I would be a great thing, a special duties clerk. I envisaged myself in some hush-hush job that never materialised. By then they had sufficient people and then I decided I'd had enough of hanging around waiting to be called up. Somebody told me I could be employed in catering in London. They opened something called British Restaurants which were the only places where city workers could have meals fairly cheaply. I decided to go on a catering course and I jumped straight to being manager of one of these improvised restaurants, telling them what to do, dishing out rations, and keeping accounts. I had written to a friend of mine who was living here, asking if I could come to stay with her, which was where I met *him*.'

'By accident?'

'*Sheer* accident.'

'She took my bed,' Coleridge laughed. 'She has paid for it ever since.'

After they got married, the owner of the Caribbean Club where Coleridge played tipped them off about the house where they still live. Coleridge was only the second Jamaican to live in Notting Hill, the owner of the club being the first. It was a smart purchase.

'At the time how did mixed marriage go down?'

'You know as well as I do,' Coleridge replied, 'that a lot of people look down on such ideas and that they do not treat people of my colour as normal human beings. If you share your life with somebody it has got to be someone who understands all that and who can deal with things unpleasant.'

'You felt this country was a much kinder place than America.'

'Obviously as far as a black person was concerned it was.'

'Not everyone would agree with you,' Gertrude said. 'We had black American friends who said they would rather know where they were rather than have people not say what they thought or else in a roundabout way not give you jobs or housing. I think they are wrong, however. We're talking about the 1940s and 1950s when over there you couldn't go into certain places whereas here at least theoretically you could go anywhere. Whether waiters snubbed you is another matter but you could still go. Anyway we never experienced full-force prejudice because the people we moved among were those whom we could choose or else they chose us. Among artists and free-thinking intellectuals there was not the same amount of prejudice. So we didn't have to cope with job or housing discrimination.'

All in all, though, Coleridge seemed unwilling to speak of racism here or of black empowerment, his geniality doubtless owing much to his Victorian attitude of loyalty with regard to the 'Mother Country', a sentiment that vanished with black and white alike, when in the 1970s and 1980s such notions had all but died.

§

'What about Django Reinhardt?'

'The French violinist Stéphane Grappelli and Django had both been here before the war with their group. Django then went back to France and Stéphane stayed on. During the war Stéphane was given the job of broadcasting and he picked me as his bass player as well as choosing a great blind pianist, George Shearing, who later went to the United States. We did regular broadcasts from underground studios. The way Stéphane and Shearing worked together was remarkable. If Shearing had something he wanted to play he would perform it at the piano while Stéphane copied the notes down on a piece of paper and then we would do it. It was quite something to play with those two and later on, when Stéphane was asked to do the music for a film, we were joined by a drummer called Ray Ellington. Ray had already sung and done broadcasts. Later, when I got the opportunity, I asked him if he would join the Caribbean Trio, which he did. That's the way things happened in those days.'

On the evening of 26 January 1946, Django, his wife, Naguine, and their son arrived at Stéphane's flat at the Athenaeum overlooking Green Park. They had just come in on the ferry from France. Grappelli, who was performing that night, which also happened to be his birthday, did not arrive home until after midnight. When they saw each other, the war years having separated them, they were so moved they couldn't speak. Stéphane took out his violin and began to play the *Marseillaise* and Django immediately joined in. As Django's biographer Charles Delaunay notes, 'Without a moment's forethought it was the national anthem, solemn and impassioned, that they had chosen to play. In a foreign country these two reprobates had given vent to the kind of patriotic gesture one would never have thought them capable of!' All night they played, songs both new and old, and, some bottles of gin and whiskey later, they were still playing when dawn broke.

'A day or so later, Django came into the Caribbean Club where I was playing. It was as if he had come down from a mountain. He had these big boots on. Quite a spectacle he was. Fortunately our guitarist Lauderic Caton had a guitar with a specially widened neck, which was like the one Django had. Django couldn't play an ordinary guitar because of his injury, but what he could do with those two fingers, which were all he could use after his accident, was extraordinary.'

That accident took place on 2 November 1928 when Django, aged eighteen, returned to the gypsy caravan where he lived together with his young pregnant wife. While investigating a noise, possibly a mouse, he accidentally dropped a candle onto a pile of artificial flowers which exploded into flames. Within seconds the place was an inferno. While only barely conscious he heard distant cries, 'Django's inside!', and with death hovering close he struggled into the open, his burns so severe he almost lost a leg and his left hand in such a state that the older men of the tribe wept to think this great musician would never play again. Happily he proved them wrong.

A few days after the emotional reunion, a recording session was set up with some of Grappelli's colleagues, including Coleridge and guitarists Jack Llewelyn, who is sitting at the right in this picture, and Allan Hodgkiss, who is hidden from view. It was basically the same instrumental line-up as the pre-war quintet of the Hot Club

de France. When interviewed by Grappelli's biographer, Geoffrey Smith, Coleridge Goode spoke of the allowances that had to be made for one of Django's gypsy temperament: 'Once you got Django to the studio you were all right, but times had to be a little fluid to accommodate him. The session had to be pretty businesslike, because you had to get on with it while he was sort of in the mood … But it certainly was a great session, and it went extremely well.' Over two nights they recorded eight pieces, among them one of Coleridge's favourites, a piece that captures for him the essence of those times, 'Nuages' ('Clouds'). A few days later, Django was taken ill and went to hospital where he had an operation. All further concerts, both at the BBC and throughout the British Isles, had to be cancelled and as soon as he began to recover Django returned to France.

'A few years later, in 1951, Gertrude and I went to see him in Paris where he was staying in this hotel across from the nightclub where he was working at the time. When he was well enough he would go downstairs, cross the street, into the club and then go back upstairs back to bed. That was his routine. We found him in bed – this was not long before he died – his wife was there. Gertrude spoke French with them. I couldn't speak French so I watched their reactions. He was a bit fragile, was Django. It was a shame he went when he did.'

The venue was the Club Saint-Germain and Django, whose only true home was the open road, lived in the Hôtel Crystal. 'Every night his playing was a source of joy and amazement to enthusiasts and musicians alike,' writes Delaunay. 'And, as in bygone days, his fellow gypsies used to hang about outside the club, kneeling down by the ventilator to listen to the sounds of his guitar that came up from the famous cellar.' I asked Gertrude what her impressions of him were.

'He was conceited but very attractive.'

'*Rightly* conceited,' said Coleridge. 'Nobody else could do what he did.'

'It was part of his naivety,' Gertrude continued. 'He didn't hide it like other people brought up differently would. He was *openly* conceited, even endearingly so. What you got with him was what he was.'

The legendary Django Reinhardt died of a stroke two years later, on 15 May 1953.

§

In 1946, Coleridge, employing the electronics skills he picked up at university, devised a pickup which he attached to his bass. The newly amplified instrument was first used on a BBC session with Stéphane Grappelli and marked an end to a long struggle against overbearingly loud drums. One may go a step further and say that he pioneered the use of electric bass in jazz. It was around this time that the bass suffered another shock. A small newspaper clipping, brittle with age, describes what happened.

> May 4th 1946, famous bass stylist Coleridge Goode of the Lauderic Caton Trio had an amazing escape from injury when last Friday night his car was involved with a head-on collision with another car on Edgware Road when on the way to the BBC studios. Although the car was badly damaged, Coleridge's bass escaped comparatively lightly with light concussion and bruises. He put up a splendid performance but was obviously unwell and fans who spoke to him afterwards found him suffering from memory loss and general effects after incurring a slight touch of concussion.

I asked Gertrude about her memories of the jazz club scene. 'They were what clubs should be, a mixture of all kinds of people.

This doesn't exist any more. The atmosphere was free, but then life was freer. People tried to make the best of things in a wartime atmosphere, and it went on right through to the 1960s. The Caribbean Club on Denman Street in Piccadilly was run by the Jamaican who got us this house. He was the black sheep of his family, who were all professional people. I remember Lucian Freud who was then aged about twenty-one and the worst dancer you ever saw, just terrible, so awkward and tortured. A lot of good artists went there, as well as wide boys and gangsters, a real mixture, the black ones mostly gangsters and wide boys. There were literary people like Tambimuttu and, later, Michael Horovitz and Christopher Logue. There is one expression we still use. One night I was dancing with a chap wearing a zoot suit.' (The zoot suit, which became popular in the Harlem jazz culture of the late 1930s, comprised high-waisted, wide-legged, tight-cuffed, pegged trousers and a long coat with wide lapels and padded shoulders. The young Malcolm X, as troubled then as he was at any point in his life, bought his, aged 15, describing it as 'a killer-diller coat with a drape shape, reet pleats and shoulders padded like a lunatic's cell'.) 'I said to him, rather unkindly, "Where did you get that *thing*? My husband would like one." This was just to show him I had a husband. He replied, "*Him* had it." In other words there was no chance he was going to give away the source of his suit. "Him had it", it's an expression we use all the time. Anyway that was a great club. It was all a matter of economics. These clubs never made a lot of money and when their rents were put up they were no longer viable. The people who went to them didn't have a lot of money either. So back then it was affordable. That whole world is gone.'

'Coming to England,' I said to Coleridge, 'must have effected a revolution in your life, more so than just going from sunshine to grey skies. Do you remember the thrill of discovering a new world, an opening up within of something hitherto unknown to you?'

'One's horizons were widened, of course, and if one worked hard there were possibilities here that one could not get at home, and fortunately having a lovely companion and wife enabled me to put up with whatever was thrown at me. One could make one's life worth living and be healthy enough to be able to stay and see if some changes could be made.'

'I wonder to what extent the fact you became a jazz musician here rather than in America might have determined your musical style.'

'America would have been impossible. I couldn't have put up with the apartheid. I would have been killed. I love their music but never wanted to be part of their society. It was dreadful what happened to black musicians over there.'

'How, though, would you quantify the difference in the music?'

'Obviously the difference in background has an influence. There is a different way of living over here, different values, and so one *thinks* differently. You learn to appreciate things in different way. Music is part of how you express yourself. The way you produce it comes from inside you.'

§

The most innovative British jazz group of the late 1950s and early 1960s, only distantly remembered except by those who were, or still are, 'informed', was the Joe Harriott Quintet, which at the height of its powers had its Jamaican-born leader on alto saxophone, the St Vincent poet Shake Keane on trumpet and flugelhorn, Pat Smythe on piano, Bobby Orr and Phil Seamen alternatively on drums, and Coleridge on bass. They were all at the top of their game. Shake Keane was considered by many to be the best jazz trumpeter in Europe; unruly, drug-addled, superb Phil Seamen was mentor to a future generation of drummers, Ginger Baker among them; and classically trained Pat Smythe with his steady lyricism was the perfect foil to Harriott with his musically abstract departures. Whether this country was ready for the music they played is another matter. A style we have since grown accustomed to, which our ears have shaped themselves to, was first met with bafflement in some quarters, derision in others, but with admiration by those few with a wetted finger to the breeze. What is certain is that Joe Harriott's brand of 'free form' was arrived at independently of Ornette Coleman's American. The legend is that early in 1960 he was recuperating from tuberculosis in hospital and there had a vision of the shape his new music would take. As he wrote in the sleeve notes to the *Free Form* album, 'In this form of music we're not using any particular set harmonic structure. We're attempting to paint sound colours and effects.' Clearly, though, he had already been exploring these ideas a couple of years before. The pity of it was that once they were put into practice he was taken to be a mere imitator of Coleman. The truth is rather different. Whereas with Coleman the new style was largely manifested in the virtuoso playing of one man, with the Joe Harriott Quintet what mattered most, notwithstanding its leader's apparent inability to acknowledge his colleagues, was in how it worked as an ensemble. Coleridge writes, 'The idea was to try to see where our collective imagination would lead the piece.' The quintet's first album was recorded before Coleman's *Free Jazz* was released. Curmudgeonly Philip Larkin, even he who had no sympathy for innovation in his most beloved music, who detested Coleman, was able to write: 'Personally I relegate free form along with action painting to a limbo of absurdity, but Harriott and the plump, smudgy tone of Shake Keane's flugelhorn make agreeable music that can be enjoyed in any mode.' The American musicologist Hilary Moore, in her perceptive book *Inside British Jazz: Crossing Borders of Race, Nation and Class* (2007), writes: 'the quintet was to dismantle the existing jazz language and construct an approach to musical sound that was entirely unknown on the British jazz scene'.

This photograph, surely one of the great jazz images, depicts a somewhat earlier line-up, probably that of 1959, with Harry South on piano, Hank Shaw on trumpet, Bobby Orr on drums, and, of course, Coleridge on bass.

'Which recording captures for you one of the best moments with the quintet?'

'There was one in particular, "Modal", which came at the end of a very exacting session, when we recorded *Free Form*. Our drummer, Phil Seamen, was very tired and started to undo his kit. Joe had gone upstairs to listen to the playback. Smythe was doodling about on piano. Shake was wandering about the studio with a brandy glass. At some point Phil picked up his cowbell and struck it. Then Shake hit his glass with a pencil and a miracle happened because that note was exactly one octave above the one the cowbell made. That signalled something was about to happen so I told Pat to keep playing and I called over the microphone system to the recording engineer, "Run the tape. We are going to play something." We made the recording just like that. It was a magic moment. It was the most lovely thing. There can't be anything freer than that, which was simply manufactured from what was happening at the time. It's all there on the record.'

Joe Harriott's biographer, Alan Robertson, writes: 'A performance like "Modal" showed the incredible level of empathy which the members of the quintet had reached by this time.'

'How would you define that musical language?' I asked Coleridge. 'Otherworldly?'

'Definitely! It depends on how sensitive you are. It brings out some kind of reaction in you. You realise you are dealing with somebody with unusual talent but who probably does not know how to control it. Joe, although a very difficult person to get to know, was sure of what he could do and he was not afraid to tell you what he wanted.'

Coleridge spoke of this at the Joe Harriott Tribute held at the Purcell Room on 23 November 2003:

> If you know the people you're playing with you have a fellow feeling musically … I think it's only possible under those conditions – you have to have a very strong fellow feeling, so that whatever ideas one musician puts on, the others will also respond to this in whatever way it comes to them … it's a matter of tossing ideas around and being appreciated by the other members of the group and they add their version to it, which makes a whole.

Making a whole is at the very heart of Coleridge's musical thinking.

'And yet you found Joe Harriott difficult.'

'*Very* difficult. His background was hard. The Alpha School he went to in Kingston, Jamaica was for delinquents, more or less, but they taught the youngsters to play their instruments very well. Joe could play his like anything but it didn't teach him much about living. It was difficult for him to fit into life here and to communicate with people. As regards personal feelings it was not easy to discover how he really felt about anything. He gave the impression of being very distant and so probably people thought he was conceited but it's simply because as a child he never had a chance to grow up among decent people. He was a bit out of things, which was a great shame.'

'You have been protected in your life, not just during the war but also when working among musicians who destroyed themselves.'

'I have seen it happen so many times. Thank God I was brought up as I was. It was quite some time before I tasted any alcohol and I'd seen what drugs do to people. They were soon dead. There was no future in that at all. They may have enjoyed life for a very short time but I preferred to enjoy my life *all my life*. So I did things in moderation. I realised the necessity of exercise, of keeping in good shape, so I adopted a game which not many musicians took part in, tennis.'

'Was it also a matter of you occupying a separate mental space?'

'I had to. If you let yourself get tied up in that atmosphere you got swept away. That is what happened to a lot of nice young people. They did not want to be left out and I suppose they did not have much to look forward to and so with the excitement of being with all that was happening they got sucked in and once that happened they couldn't escape. That was the end of them. Fortunately I had a lovely family and so I had more to lose.'

There is an interesting verbal snapshot of Coleridge from this period of his life, which was related to Alan Robertson by Colin Barnes, a drummer who was fleetingly with the group: 'Cole was someone that when you looked at him, you couldn't imagine him being young. It was something about the dignity and the authority he carried.'

I asked Gertrude how she felt about Coleridge's association with the quintet.

'I was very happy about it. It was more interesting than anything he had ever done before.'

'What were your impressions of Harriott?'

'He was impossible to get close to. You couldn't get to grips with him. He was like an armadillo, armour-plated. Things happened to him early in life that made him defensive. He was permanently dismissive, sneery and non-committal. You could not really penetrate him, yet the feelings came out in his music. He was not somebody I could say I knew at all. And Cole didn't either. He knew, though, his reactions to things musically.'

Turning to Coleridge, she asked him, 'Did you have any feelings for him?'

'He didn't engender any,' he replied, although quite without rancour.

'And yet,' she said, 'you could communicate with him on a musical level.'

Joe Harriott was one of the most enigmatic figures on the jazz scene, known to everyone, a friend to none. Difficult he most certainly was. 'Joe doesn't have a chip on his shoulder,' Phil Seamen jibed, 'he's got a bloody telegraph pole!' A man apart, his relationships with women were seemingly perfunctory, and yet the fact of his being able to communicate happily with young children suggests depths rarely probed. Coleridge puts it most poignantly when he writes:

> Because he had not been given that warmth as a child he could not produce it himself. He must have grown up longing to be appreciated for what he could do and, because he could play an instrument, he channelled all that longing through his music. You can hear it on the records. Sometimes his playing has a desperate cry. He's striving, almost fighting the music and dying to play it.

After recording three albums, the most revolutionary in British jazz, disappointed by the poor reception they received, not so much from the public as from critics and other musicians, Harriott turned his back on the bold experiments of the 1960s. Shake Keane's departure from the group also made for a gap that could not be easily filled, and indeed there are those who argue that he was the greater musician. Coleridge followed Harriott into Indo-Jazz fusion but, groundbreaking though this was, the musicianship superb, the blend of musical traditions seems more than a little dated now. After this, Harriott went into a state of perpetual drift, often sleeping on people's floors, eating poorly, playing in pubs for a pittance. Coleridge writes, 'In the last years he was not at all the same chap who started out. All of us involved in his projects felt his pain.' Only rarely does Coleridge speak in terms of race, but with Harriott he lays the blame for his lack of critical success on his not being white. Whether or not this is true, Harriott had also abandoned any ties he had with his Jamaican past. Absolutely rootless, he became a Rosicrucian but only to occupy an area even more remote.

Joe Harriott died as he lived, alone. His last years were a steady decline in spirit and health, and he drank heavily in order to mask the pain from the spinal cancer that finally took his life on 2 January 1973. He was only forty-four. At his funeral a lone black woman, Jamaican, attended, not because she knew him – she didn't know him or his music – but because she had heard about a fellow Jamaican dying alone and felt she ought to be there for his, or maybe even *their*, sake.

All he owned went into a single suitcase.

The whereabouts of his alto sax is unknown.

§

'After the Joe Harriott Quintet broke up were you lost for a while?'

I might have guessed that Coleridge, so embracing of the continuum that is the jazz century, would never be at a loose end.

'No. Fortunately there was Michael Garrick who had a really lovely quartet that played downstairs in the Marquee on Oxford Street, which is also where the Joe Harriott Quintet performed, so we had already heard each other. After I finished with Joe, Michael immediately invited me to join him. He wrote all the music we played, much of it religiously inspired. When we did the *Jazz Praises* with choir in St Paul's Cathedral I organised a recording with only one microphone suspended from the dome. The acoustics were so fantastic it worked.'

The jazz pianist and composer Michael Garrick, as much a maverick in his way as Joe Harriott was in his, has, over the years, developed a jazz idiom which although informed by the American is uniquely of these isles, at times drawing on its folk and classical traditions. There are other currents as well. One hears, at times, cadences more oriental than occidental. Jazz critic Dennis Harrison describes him as 'a true representative of the diasporic spirit of jazz' and also speaks of *Jazz Praises* as having been written 'under an English heaven'. (It is worth noting that it pre-dates Duke Ellington's *Sacred Concerts* by almost six months.) The music is of a man endlessly inventive. Garrick was also, in the 1960s, musical director of the popular "Poetry and Jazz in Concert" series, organised by Jeremy Robson, which included poets Dannie Abse, Laurie Lee, Spike Milligan, Adrian Mitchell, Vernon Scannell and John Smith. It was of the time, a Dionysian decade clad in purple, which is to say it was not for all time, and yet, whatever the contrivances, the doubtful cocktails, jazz and poetry were taken to new audiences. One could at least move on from there, shedding the paisley as one went.

I asked Michael Garrick whether he would care to submit any thoughts on his relationship with Coleridge and he did so with a composer's immaculate sense of timing, producing a paragraph on New Year's Eve, 2009:

> I was attracted to Coleridge by his professionalism, good spirits, reliability and dignity. Any performance he was engaged in was lifted and lit up by his good-humoured and melodically inventive bowed/sung bass solos. So well constructed was his solo on 'Morning Blue' [recorded by the BBC at University College School, Hampstead] that I was able to transcribe and translate it into a feature for my jazz orchestra. [*Big Band Harriott*, JAZA 10]. He has that excellent ability to smile when playing! He proved the ideal participant in our *Jazz Praises*. Decades later, he told me he took to the genre because of physically pumping the church organ bellows for his father

in Jamaica when a boy and drinking deep of the European choral classics which Goode Senior conducted. He said *Jazz Praises* came 'just at the right time' for him though he 'didn't know how he did it'. Many were the hours I spent sharing the back seat with his bass while he drove me to Scotland, Wales and wherever else for poetry and jazz gigs as well as the *Praises*. He was a calculated-risk-taking driver – only once did I genuinely feel we'd had it! You could never, ever, separate him from his bulky and somewhat Heath-Robinson homemade amplifier which was his pride and joy and notoriously prone to howl with feedback at the least appropriate moments. His contribution to our music [beginning with *October Woman*, 1964] has been pivotal and, as Duke Ellington used to put it when inviting applause for his soloists, 'Thank You [i.e. God] for Coleridge Goode.'

When I visited him on that second occasion, Coleridge, whose first language is always music, was very much in the mood for playing me some recordings not readily available. They included a splendid 1968 BBC broadcast of Michael Garrick's music. What I experienced in his company was strikingly similar to that which Hilary Moore describes, when she too spent such an afternoon with him:

> We listened together, speaking little, but moving, drawing in breath, sometimes delighting in a particularly delicious turn of phrase or tantalizing delay in the placing of a note. It is difficult to index the effect of this kind of shared musical experience.

I watched him, his fingers playing along to the music, moving over the neck of an imagined bass, its original only a few feet away, so monolithic in a white room, and Coleridge, blanketed against the autumn bite, his head bobbing up and down, his eyes closed, completely inside the music, quietly laughing at the phrases he liked most, and it struck me that what was happening with Coleridge was not so much a memory of performing that music as of reinserting himself, note for note, into the moment of its making.

'I've been watching you,' I told him, when he opened his eyes, 'and it is like you are actually *there*, playing with the group.'

'Well, that is how it feels sometimes.'

It was getting late, and I felt I should go, but he asked me to wait just a little. There was something special he wanted me to hear, singer Norma Winstone performing Michael Garrick's setting of the Beatitudes. It was not like anything I'd ever heard before, words of old, so simply put we hardly ever pause to consider just how complex their meaning is, pushed into an unfamiliar soundscape. *Blessed are the poor in spirit, for theirs is the kingdom of heaven.* Who but those sufficiently humble in their art, and yet with just enough arrogance to say this is how the world is, will make their heaven with pen, brush or stave? *Blessed are the meek, for they shall inherit the earth.* Small wonder the speaker of such inflammatory words was put to death. *Blessed are the pure in heart, for they shall see God.*

'Would you consider yourself a religious man?'

Coleridge, purity his credo, both in mind and body, pondered this for a while.

'As far as heaven goes I'm not too sure about all that but I think one's heaven comes according to how one has lived one's life. It's a reward almost. The spirit, I should think, lives on. I believe all is not completely lost but that somewhere, for those who have led a decent life, there is the freedom of the spirit to roam and enjoy what there is left for it.'

'It sounds like heaven to me.'

'Yes,' he said, 'I think that's what heaven is.'

The Goat that Stood upon the Bull's Spine

Zahed Tajeddin, Sculptor

The blind mediaeval poet Abul 'Ala al-Ma'arri (973–1058), who lived in the village of Maarrat al-Numan, a few miles southwest of Aleppo, wrote: 'Take care where you walk because you walk upon the dead.' So inclusive have those words become we forget sometimes that he was writing on the death of a close relative. The Syrian dead are everywhere. They have been piling up for centuries. As of late there's been a fresh surge of bodies. Al-Ma'arri also wrote: 'The inhabitants of the earth are of two sorts – those with brains but no religion, and those with religion but no brains.' The sightless head that housed the unruly tongue was removed, although, luckily for its owner, not until 11 February 2013, when jihadists opposed to the regime decapitated the statue of him that stood in the front of the museum dedicated to his memory. It is probable that they were 'outsiders' and, in any event, ignorant of his blasphemous verses. 'And, beauty dead,' Shakespeare writes, 'black chaos comes again.' Chaos is everywhere. The maps are in shreds, unreadable. There are those who claim it was actually the regime which vandalised the statue in order to discredit the opposition. This I doubt. There is no end to the twists and turns of Arabic opinion: what enters the bazaar as one thing leaves it as quite another. Syria is no exception to the rule although it is, or was, a most exceptional place.

The beloved scene of my earlier adventures has become rubble.

Some months ago, during the conflict that continues to rage as I write, fire swept through the ancient souq of Aleppo, destroying most of it. Each side blames the other. It was like having a tooth pulled, so familiar had it become to me. One could walk seemingly forever through its maze of alleyways, dust particles hanging in the sunlight falling through open shafts in the mediaeval arches. Where now are the seven plump brothers with their fake silk scarves? Where now the elderly beggar who when I gave her a coin raised her veil and with a toothless laugh cackled, in English, *I love you*? Where now the boys cross-legged on their mules, swearing their way through the belching tuk-tuks at closing time? I had a debate with a friend from Damascus who said that the destruction of this magnificent souq was not equal to the taking of a single child's life. What I said to him, after begging to disagree, was that the destruction of a country's heritage makes the taking of that same child's life all the easier. These are, ultimately, mental games. The gods deserve better although, when bored, they will settle for blood sacrifice. When I put this argument to my friend Zahed Tajeddin, keen antiquary, he spoke of what can never be replaced. When it came to talk of lives lost the Aleppine disagreed with the Damascene and his voice trailed away into the distance.

Admittedly I could never get beneath the skin of Aleppo, whereas Damascus, by contrast, almost flung open its arms to me. I would find the former's soul later, in London, in a shop just around the corner from where I worked. Zahed *my Aleppo*: all the aristocratic airs, the merchant's stratagem, the manners and culture of that legendary place are invested in him. Zahed, as I like to remind him, has Phoenician eyes. They hide as much as they disclose. I've been with him in Aleppo twice, in happier times, once when he rescued me from an accidental drug overdose, the second time when his dentist provided me with a hundred-dollar bridge. Zahed, irrepressible joker, photographed me in the dentist's chair with my mouth open wide. Worse still, after my parry with the Fates, he photographed me in bed, the very image of a deathly tussle, in a very bright pink room. We could still jolly our way through the country's many bitter intricacies. There was little sign of what was to come.

Zahed has become a sadder man than when I first knew him, when he was proprietor of a small shop/gallery close to the British Museum, devoted to antiquities and tasteful reproductions on one side and Egyptian souvenirs of doubtful value on the other. A good many of the latter were made in China. One time, as I entered the shop, he gave me a security body scan with an ankh the size of a ping-pong bat. I would visit him regularly during my lunch breaks and we would confabulate, gossip, chuckle, console, indulge in sometimes philosophical, sometimes nonsensical, reverie. 'Where's the wisdom?' he'd exclaim in all semantic innocence. There were the women who came into his shop, one by one, lured there by the

Egyptiana, all of them nutty as fruitcakes. They were reincarnations of ancient royals or deities (never slaves, of course), among their number a woman with teeth that jutted every which way, dishevelled hair, thick-framed glasses, who shambled into the shop on crutches that swung wildly like a geometric compass unscrewed at the hinge. She claimed to be Meritaten, daughter of Akhenaton and Nefertiti. There must have been, in her mind, quite a battle of resemblances. Meritaten's beauty, if the sculpture of her is to be believed, outshone even her mother's. And then there was Nefertiti herself, who spent over £200,000 on plastic surgery so that she might more closely resemble the famous bust in the Altes Museum in Berlin, but whose lips were just a bit too large, her eyes too small, her nose too blunt. And then came the lady who every Saturday went first to the British Museum, where she placed a rose at the statue of the Egyptian lion-goddess Sekhmet, and then to the shop with another rose that she placed beside a reproduction of the same. And what about Zahed's Egyptian colleague, Ahmad, who, reared in the Cairo bazaar, brought his bazaar mentality with him, together with the banter which in Arabic is called *'fi al-harikay barikay* and which translates rather splendidly as 'There is blessing in the movement'. (What kind of movement, I wonder.) The growing tensions between Zahed the purveyor of antiquities and Ahmad the flogger of Upper Nile kitsch were worthy of a TV comedy series. It was Ahmad who one day, seeing I was grey with fatigue, offered me a pick-me-up that comprised a single drop of a gooey, blackish substance that he put in my cup of tea. 'Drink it,' he said. I obeyed. The taste was so rancid I could not rid myself of it for a couple of days. I gargled. I chewed gum. All to no avail. 'What's *in* that stuff?' I asked him three days later. Ahmad hesitated. 'Ambergris,' he said, 'and something else maybe it's better you don't know what it is.' I pressed him. Ahmad blushed. I pressed him a bit more. 'Semen of crocodile,' he whispered. Well, then, brave the man who procured it in the first place.

The shop is long gone. Zahed, never one to stay put, has in recent times devoted himself to his first love, sculpture, and is making a decent fist of it. Also he has studied and practised archaeology. I visited him at his studio where he wore a green apron stolen from Starbucks, its logo covered with a small label saying TOXIC. As he worked, casting clay bulls that might have detached themselves from the walls of the caves at Lascaux and gone for a bullish adventure, he spoke of his shattered dream, the late Mamluk house in the Jdeide quarter of Aleppo, which he had bought and lovingly restored.

'It is a typical Arabic house where the life is around the courtyard and you are completely sealed from outside. You sit there beneath the open sky and whether you want to call it God, nature or whatever it is your own private space. The house dates from 1560 and it takes me back to that time. I could be in that courtyard and just look at and admire the stone. After two earthquakes they rebuilt the damaged parts of the house and you can tell from the architecture where they cut, added, joined walls to other walls, and, from the style of the masonry, the size of the stones, the way they used the metalwork and the shape of the lattice in the windows, in which period these changes were made. The joy of it for me was that the house was a kind of biography whereby I might link myself to different historical times. Do you want to hear the story of how I came to buy it? When I visited Andalucía in the 1990s I rediscovered the magnificent Arabic culture, and just how beautiful those wonderful gardens and architectural jewels are, and then I realised many of the people who made this came from Syria. They had recreated their lives there. Three months later, I went to Syria and as usual I was looking about in the antique shops when someone offered me a small intaglio in carnelian. It bore the motto of the last Arabic dynasty of Andalucía, the Nasrid: *Wa lā ghāliba illā-llāh* ("There is no conqueror but God"), and it is even inscribed in the Andalucian calligraphic style. I wear it all the time.

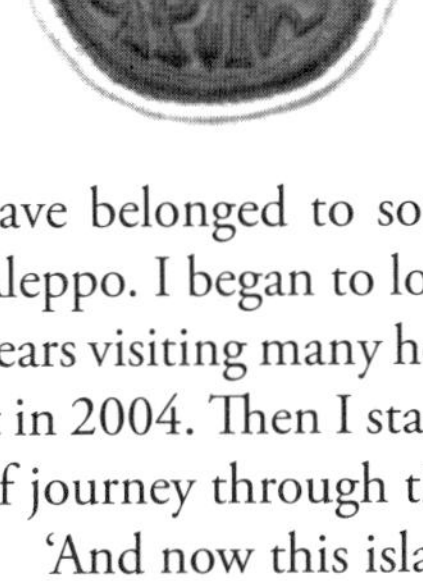

'This for me was a sign. That stone must have belonged to someone who left Andalucía and went back to Aleppo. I began to look for an old house there. After spending nine years visiting many houses I settled for the first one I saw and bought it in 2004. Then I started on its renovation, which for me was a kind of journey through time.'

'And now this island is lost to you.'

'Yesterday I was looking at a documentary film about Aleppo and there was my house. It made my heart weep. I was last there two years, nine months ago, the longest ever I have been outside Syria. You could see the damage in the streets around. I can show you videos of fighting on my very doorstep, people throwing grenades. It was just around the corner from my house that they bombed the bakery. This became a trend. Whenever there was a queue at the bakery they would come in their helicopters and shoot. It hits you most when you know the people. All the residents moved from that quarter to the other side of the city where they were re-housed in schools, mosques and people's homes. Maryam, who often helped me at my house, went and lived with her four children in a school for almost four months. She decided it was too horrible, sharing toilets with hundreds of people and so forth, and so, despite everything, she decided to move back home. A week later, at six in the morning, she sent two of her children, a boy and a girl, aged twelve and fourteen, to queue for bread. They were both killed. Maryam has lost her mind. She can't work any more.'

'And then there was the terrifying business with your father.'

'Well before the conflict began, my father went to the house every single day. He'd water the jasmine and honeysuckle, sit and read in the courtyard, and then visit the nearby mosque. The atmosphere was so relaxed, the old way of life. His parents had left their Ottoman house, one of the most beautiful in Aleppo, in order to move into one of the fashionable modern flats the French built in the 1920s and 30s. And so for him it was a return to childhood. Then the war started and he would risk his life to go there, crossing regime and Free Syrian Army checkpoints, sometimes taking cups of tea with him as bribes. On one occasion he was trapped in crossfire and had to hide in a small alleyway for two hours. The shelling was so heavy he has now permanently lost his hearing.'

'I remember you were almost relieved when he was caught up in the battle.'

'Yes, in order to teach him a lesson! I discovered later that he had been lying to me, saying he wasn't going there any more. Obsessed, and against my pleas to him not to go, he kept returning because he did not want anyone to contaminate that space. One of the stories that haunted me at the time was that of an old man who was on his way back to his house in the Salahadin area of Aleppo. He was hit by a sniper and lay dead in the middle of a traffic junction. This is what the snipers do, they create a trap. Anyone attempting to remove the body is shot. Only with the help of the Red Cross and after long negotiations were they able to remove his body after it lay there for a few weeks. I said to my father, "I don't want that to happen to you," and he replied, "I'll die on my own time." And I argued back, "Yes, but I do not want you to die in *that* way. It is not any way to die. Please give us peace, even if you don't care." On one of his last visits he threw buckets of water over my doorstep to wash away the blood. It reached a point it became impossible to go there. By then most of the neighbours had fled the area but there was one who remained and contacted him, saying there'd been a big explosion. It destroyed two of the rooms and the massive wooden door with its hammered metal was blown wide open. The high pressure of the explosion was such that even the electric sockets flew out of the walls. Once again, my father took a massive risk and in order to get to the liberated zone first travelled outside Aleppo and then re-entered the town from the other side. He reached the house, did some repair work, and on the way back the little bus in which he and his friend were travelling was shot at by a helicopter. My father was okay but his friend was badly wounded and rushed to hospital. After seeing what happened to his friend he finally accepted just how bad things had become.'

Zahed's voice got quieter and slower, the words he spoke hanging together by only the slenderest of threads.

'With all that I've seen and heard… I don't care about what happens in the town any more. It is beyond repair, at least in my lifetime. My main concern is for my parents. I feel so sad that after long lives, after working so hard, they have to spend their last days in such hardship. They don't deserve it. *What can you do?* My father is on the stubborn side. He does not want to leave and would prefer to die in his own house. *I can't do anything.* I'm a prisoner in a way and at the same time I know what I'm going through is nothing compared to what they have to endure. My parents now sit on the balcony and say, "Oh, they are bombing there, look, there's a helicopter coming from that side." It's strange how people adapt. Sometimes, though, my father coughs it out and says how terrible things are, that he could never have imagined this would happen to them. So mostly he is hiding it, which hurts me, knowing they are in pain. And then they deny it, saying, "We have some bread and water, we shower in a bucket." This has become their way of life. That line of al-Ma'arri's you quote, it's the history of Syria. *It's not the first time.* This is what people keeping saying to me. *Hulagu destroyed Aleppo.* Maybe it is true but Aleppo will never be the same. Maybe my little island can be repaired but outside everything's in ruins. There is no life, no culture. *So much death.* The people are traumatised. I don't think I'll ever be able to go back. I am really desperate to. I want to see and document what has happened to my city but before any of that I wish to see my parents again. My nightmare now is that something will happen to them. They are old… I would not be able to go to their funerals. Imagine that! This is my nightmare. I *promised* them… I am their only son… I promised them when I left Syria that I would never leave them alone. You know this oriental thing we have, that the first son, especially if he is the *only* son, will take care of his parents. And they agreed to my going. My mother said recently, "We are happy, we thank God every day a thousand times, that you are out of here because we don't want you to be here. This is our fate but we know you are safe, you have your family, and this is our pride. We have *had* our lives. We will die the way God wants us to die." So they are at peace, they forgive me, or at least they say so, but in my conscience I don't want to let them down. I want to be there for them when they need me. You met my mother. She is one of the most beautiful creatures ever… she is 82 now… she is not going to live forever and at this rate, the way things are going, I am not going to be able to see them again. Sometimes I think I'll go there and risk it all but then if something happened to me they would be in even more pain. I am beginning to lose hope for Syria. I am almost fifty now. It will be decades before any of this is put back together again.'

At Zahed's house in Aleppo there is a family tree, a scroll a metre and a half in length, which dates from Ottoman times. The family line goes all the way back to the Prophet and indeed the name Tajeddin means 'the throne of religion'. One of his ancestors lived in Mar'ash in Turkey and there is a mosque there, home to one of the Sufi schools, called the Tajeddin shrine. And because he is in the line of the family of the Prophet Muhammad, when he went to Iran and visited shrines dedicated to his ancestors he was seen almost as a walking saint. The Shi'a refer to descendants of the Prophet as *sayed*. ('Sayed Zahed', I shall have to look at him with different eyes.) Zahed is Sunni, though, and the honorific carries not quite as much weight at home. So not only is he twenty-ninth in the line to the Prophet but also on his paternal grandmother's side, through the Hariri-Rifai branch, one of the old families, he is a descendant of the great Sufi, Mustapha al-Hariri-Rifai, founder of the order that still bears his name. Zahed's mother's family is of Turkish origin with a military branch and there exists a photograph of Mustafa Kemal Atatürk and Zahed's maternal grandfather in military uniform. Zahed showed me a photograph of his father as a child in 1938, in the courtyard of his family's Ottoman house.

'My grandmother, look at what she is wearing. No headscarf! A very proud and cultured woman, an aristocratic lady in every sense, in the way she moved and dressed, full of dignity and grace, I loved her. I remember as a child going to her house. She had grand furniture, chandeliers from Bohemia, tango records. This was already the last of the money. When her father died they had already lost a lot of money – they had been wealthy aristocrats and controlled the pistachio trade in northern Syria and Aintab in Turkey – and then came the nationalisation of land and factories and that was the end of their fortune. They were not like average Syrians. They travelled and spoke languages. And beside my grandmother in the photo, the man with the bicycle, is her brother… my uncle Wahbi. My family say I have his genes. Wahbi al-Hariri was an interesting character.'

Indeed he was. At the time of the French Mandate there was a reception put on at his school to welcome the new French governor of Aleppo. Al-Hariri was aged seventeen at the time. As a protest against the French occupation he and two other colleagues hid in a canopy overlooking the tree-lined alleyway leading into the school and as the French governor passed below, making his symbolic entry to Aleppo, they pissed on him. They caught al-Hariri, expelled him, and banned him from all Syrian schools. As it was a rich family, his father sent him, aged eighteen, to the Reale Accademia di Belle Arti in Rome. Wahbi was the first Arab to study fine arts there. When he returned to Aleppo he was now a fêted figure, a sculptor and artist with a strong cultural and social presence. After independence, in 1948, the French, who admired his work, invited him to study art and architecture at the École nationale supérieure des Beaux-Arts, after which he came back to Syria to become an architect and designed many buildings there. Then he became increasingly involved in archaeology and became chief architect of the Directorate-General of Antiquities and Museums. After the Ba'ath Party took over in 1963 he left Syria to go to Saudi Arabia where he worked for King Faisal, documenting all the archaeological sites there. He wrote massive books which he also illustrated. Wahbi al-Hariri (1914–94) is remembered as 'the last of the classicists'. A couple of streets in Aleppo bear his name.

'Uncle Wahbi gave me my first watercolours. I always related to him or, rather, he identified himself in me, and whenever he visited in the summer he would bring me Matchbox aeroplanes, models, art equipment, et cetera.'

'Would you consider him a major influence?'

'I would say more in terms of aspiration than influence. Certainly he encouraged me. I inherited from him the same problem he had, which I didn't know about until after he died. I am colour-blind. I only learned that from one of his old colleagues. That is why he never used colours, only pencil, and became a sculptor.'

'Somewhere, though, there must be the germ of your artistic future.'

'Plasticine.'

'*Plasticine?*'

'Plasticine. At school, when I was seven, a new student came and sat next to me. A very cute boy, I remember his face. I lost contact with him ages ago. His mother was German so he was different, even in the way he dressed. I remember going to his house and that, too, was so different from our crowded houses, each child with a room of his own and his own desk. I remember going into his older brother's room where – I remember it precisely – there was this L-shaped shelf to the left of his desk with all these figures displayed there. "What are *those*?" I asked him. "Did *you* make them? *How*?" This was a big experience for me, a moment of revelation. I went out and bought a pack of plasticine that wasn't like his, which was

German and very nice and clean. Mine was Chinese and stinky and it stained the fingers but from then on I played with this plasticine. My teachers told my mother I was a nice child, very quiet, but that I was always playing with plasticine beneath the table. The quality of the plasticine was so poor I had to keep the figures I made in the fridge so they'd keep their shape. My mother liked them, and was always showing them off to guests – cowboys and Indians, horses, and even, yes! a head of Nefertiti.'

Zahed's father, Ghassan, was a policeman. A difficult person to deal with, in other words not a 'yes' man – like father, like son – he was punished by being put in posts outside Aleppo where he worked as a border control policeman. When Zahed was born, in the winter of 1965, Ghassan was at al Salama outpost near the Turkish border. When he received news of Zahed's birth he walked for ten kilometres through a snow-covered minefield. Good thing he knew the route. When Zahed, aged five, said to him on one of his weekends home, 'What kind of life is it when we do not have a father?', Ghassan promptly resigned his post and became a tax inspector in the council, the main focus of his work being parties, restaurants and cultural activities. At concerts he would have to oversee the ticketing and the accounts, and declare the revenue, and because of this he was given tickets for himself and his family. Ghassan is clearly quite a character, as stubborn in love as he would later be in matters of architectural preference.

'My mother, Souhila, was married before to my father's uncle. My grandmother, as was the tradition of the time, sought for her brother Nazim an arranged marriage. She spoke to her cousin who said she had a beautiful lady working with her, who was of a good family. And so everything was set up for Nazim, who was happy with the choice, and this was celebrated with a family gathering. My father walked into that room, took one look at the woman who was now engaged to his uncle and went mad. "This is *my* wife!" he cried. "*I* want this woman. Why didn't you tell me about her? This can't be! This woman is *mine*." My father gave the family so much trouble they had to arrange with his superiors to have him moved out of the city, again. Still nothing could shake him free of the belief that this was *his* wife, the mother of *his* children. She married the uncle, had a daughter by him, but within a year he got cancer and died. My father crept back into her life, came back at weekends and breaks, and would do things like take the daughter to the park. She was a widow with a child and here was a young man prepared to take her. They married.'

'What was it like growing up in Aleppo?'

'We belonged to a certain class. I wasn't allowed to go out on the street and play with the commoners, the neighbours' kids. We would sit on the balcony and watch them, listen to what they said,

their kind of speech. We stayed at home and read books and magazines. I remember at an early age treating myself every other week to another volume in the English Ladybird series, translated into Arabic, especially the histories – Alexander the Great, Napoleon, Julius Caesar, Hannibal. This took me to their world and their achievements.

'I grew up in the Jamilia area of Aleppo, which for the greater part was the new Jewish quarter. I remember in my grandmother's house climbing onto the kitchen table and from there I could look down into the courtyard of the Jewish synagogue. I have a photo of my grandmother at a wedding ceremony in the synagogue. Our upstairs neighbours were Jews. On the Jewish Sabbath I would go and switch the lights on and off and even cook for them. The Jews of Aleppo left en masse when in 1990 Hafez Assad allowed them to leave the country. Prior to that they were forbidden to go and so they would escape. They would leave the TV and lights on and vanish overnight, abandoning everything, even the furniture. This was their way. It was so organised that they would go to Turkey and cross over to Büyükada, the island near Istanbul, and there they'd get a passport and documents and then travel to America or Israel. All this was done very secretively. They would never say anything to anyone. There was pressure on them from all sides, of course. In the early 1990s I met my old neighbour, Janette. She and her husband, "Uncle Jameel", had many kids. They all left for America except for her and one daughter, Bella, who was my age. I said to Janette, "You are still here!" "What should I do?" she answered. "Where can I go? I'm over 90. I don't speak English. This is my home. This is where I *belong*." By 1992, the last of the Jews closed the school and the synagogue. Soon they were all gone. They were my mates. Funnily enough we were allowed to play with them but *not* with the others. It was a different society then.'

Often I ask people what their earliest memory is, finding in it some blueprint for the future, and Zahed was quick with his. It bore all the hallmarks of an omen. When later in life he related it to his father the latter could scarcely believe it because Zahed was less than a year old at the time. Zahed had gone with his father to the central park in Aleppo and remembers being carried on his shoulders. Suddenly the sky went dark and there began one of the worst rainstorms ever to have hit Aleppo. People fled in all directions and his father ran into a small guardhouse. There, still on his father's shoulders, he remembers peering through a flower-shaped window and seeing the people wading through water that by now had risen above their knees.

Another storm was about to take the whole of Syria by surprise, the sudden rise to power of the Ba'athists. I recently watched a work by the Syrian documentary film-maker Omar Amiralay who died on 5 February 2011, just forty days shy of the beginning of the revolution. It is one of his most highly regarded films, *Tufan Fi Balad el-Ba'ath* (*A Flood in Ba'ath Land*, 2003). The film was shot in a village beside Lake Assad, the huge expanse of water that had been created by diverting the Euphrates. The first interview is with a Bedouin sitting in a boat on the lake, a headscarf covering much of his face, saying his ancestral home is directly beneath him. And so it was for many people. A meticulously planned flood swallowed up their lives. The film then goes on to interview party figures who at the local school enforce the Ba'athist ideology – of which, incredibly enough, the creation of the artificial lake is presented almost as a parable. Something which struck me during my researches is that doorknobs were removed from all the doors in Syrian schools. *Where's the wisdom?* I had hoped the film would answer this. It didn't. I wonder if their removal does not, to some degree, signify a calculated withdrawal from young people's lives of anything that might be considered a private zone. The film is worth seeing for what it does not seek to articulate. The genius of Amiralay was to let people speak for themselves. The old adage, *give a man enough rope*. The result is a powerful indictment of an education system that is precisely Zahed's age.

'We were fed propaganda from day one. My age being what it is, I belonged to the beginning of things. I was born in 1965. Hafez Assad was then Minister of Defence. In 1970 he became president. I was five years old, already in school. We were so proud of him during the Sixth of October War in 1973, when the Syrians destroyed the defence line and gained some ground, causing havoc for the Israelis. Hafez was our leader, our rising star, and he was going to restore pride and honour to the Arabs, but later I realised it was all a show. Syria lost the Golan Heights. You could see gradual reform but we didn't know what was going on behind the scenes. Of course it took time for things to become clear. One day, when I was twelve, some visitors came to the school – I was in sixth year – and they selected from each class three or four kids who were special because they were artistic or clever or favoured by the teacher. I was one of them. I remember we were so proud to be selected. We went every Friday to another school and we became like the Hitler Youth of the time. "The blooms of the Ba'ath" we were called, or, more accurately, "the emerging Ba'athists". We had patriotic songs in which we were described as *blooms*. We thought it would be like the Scouts, which by then was a banned organisation. Any gathering outside the Ba'ath party was forbidden. The Scouts had more fun though. It was all a bit over the top. We had to salute the president every morning – we were taught he was the best sportsman, the best actor, the best musician, the one to aspire to… in other words his was the happy-face image of all dictators. We were given vouchers to go to the Ba'ath headquarters to receive our uniforms. I went there proudly, presented the vouchers and in turn was issued a plastic bag containing a uniform – a little hat, t-shirt, trousers, a scarf – it was all very socialist in style. The labels were in Russian. They were second-hand clothes imported from the Soviet Union. The white shirt I was given had two drops of blood on it. I'll never forget those two drops of dried blood. My mother washed them out, of course, and the following week I went in my uniform, feeling very special indeed.

'That lasted about four weeks and then they decided *everybody* in the school was a bloom of the Ba'ath party. Suddenly they wanted that propaganda system to be for *everyone*. It was so disappointing for me. They took away our beautiful uniforms and gave all the children a yellow t-shirt with the Ba'ath symbol, which is a map of the Arab world with a slogan printed on it, a blue scarf and blue hat. This was primary school. At high school you became a member of the Revolutionary Youth and the school uniform was now a military one, khaki trousers and tops, the girls in pale blue. We were lucky. The people before had no uniforms… but *we* had them. We took lessons on dismantling a Kalashnikov and putting it back together, what to do in a gas attack and so forth. We had a new subject, "Nationalist Education". Then the select ones joined the Ba'ath Party. They gave you a choice to join and of course many people did because there were benefits attached to doing so. I remember asking my father whether I could join and he said, "Forget it, the bastards… no, we are *not* getting involved." I was young and thought it was special. I was disappointed.

'The following year everybody had to sign a paper saying he was a Ba'ath party member. Even if you did not go to the meetings you were at the level of "supporter". The next step was to become a full member with special duties and then, after that, an "active" member. Active members became informers by default, writing reports on everyone else. They might have been nice people, friends even, but they were forced to judge us. Everybody knew where he stood – "negative radical", "supporter", "mute", "Communist" or "Islamicist". I was classified as a "positive radical", which meant I had no leftist or rightist or Islamic orientation. I was not positive towards them but neither was I active in any sense. I did not need to be put on their radar. An "active" member, regardless of what results he got, could enter any university. They were given so much extra. I was a mere supporter, one of the sheep. This was how they turned the country into a police state at every level – at work, at school, the workplace. Suddenly you could see trouble brewing. We had in a way enjoyed the peace. It was relatively easy-going but then, after 1982, things went bad. There was the war in Lebanon, the currency collapsed, and the British and Americans withdrew their embassies. I was young and in university and I discovered what kind of regime we had. I would argue with my father: "What has happened to people? It wasn't like this before. Why do you accept this? *Why* the silence?" And he'd reply, "Look at them. Can *you* do anything?" Some did try, of course. In 1982, we had the Muslim Brotherhood uprising, which was brutally crushed. The regime killed tens of thousands of people in Hama, and because we sympathised with the Muslim Brotherhood Aleppo was treated with great suspicion. Downstairs from where we lived there was a secret cell of those so-called terrorists. One night, at four in the morning, there was heavy knocking at our door. It was the secret police, armed to the teeth, who said to my father, "We are evacuating the houses. We are doing an operation." We started to leave when all of a sudden all hell broke loose. Outside there were troops everywhere, shooting like mad. My father realised from which direction the shooting came. We had a long balcony on the second floor. On the corner of that balcony were two reserve gas canisters. If a bullet hit one of them the whole building would explode. My father went out on his knees and dragged the two canisters indoors, away from the shooting. The troops, seeing this, fired at him. He was injured in the shoulder and burned by melting plastic which landed on his head. The corner was in flames but he saved the building.'

'And what happened to the people downstairs?'

'The bodies of two men, a woman and a little boy were removed from the house. This was 1982 and from then on we were punished just for being from Aleppo. At checkpoints if the police saw you were from there they would make you wait just to humiliate you. I had started university and they treated us like animals. My friends of 1982 participated in demonstrations. Some of them from my class were killed. I can give you their names. After the Friday prayers they demonstrated against the government. The secret police were filming everybody and then they went and got them one by one, just like that, many of them innocent people walking out of the mosque. Some of them were released in 1992, ten years later. One of them was my friend who lived across the road from us. I met him and he had completely lost it. Aged seventeen, ten years in Tadmor prison in Palmyra and released when he was twenty-seven, the best years of his life gone. And he was lucky because many people never came out. One day they arranged for the prisoners to escape and then they shot them in the desert like rabbits, hundreds of them, from helicopters.'

'Were you on this protest too?'

'I would have been but for the fact I was not going to the mosque at that time. I will tell you what really left a deep scar in me. It was the year of the University of Aleppo's silver jubilee. There were a lot of conferences and activities and so they shifted our classes to the evening because they were using the lecture halls for other activities. I studied chemistry. We had to do our lab work until late, finishing at nine or ten at night. One night I finished my practical… I remember I had my lab coat and books in my arms and was going back home. I was about to leave by the side gate when some soldiers shouted at me. "What are you doing? Stop right there!" "Wait a second," I shouted, "I'm a student here." I tried to get my student card out when one of them came and hit me with his Kalashnikov. Probably drunk, they starting kicking me… they hit me, swore at me. "You university students, you fuckers, you do-nothings, you play with the girls, you are terrorists!" They took it all out on me. I was really angry but couldn't do anything. Every time I tried to defend myself they hit me with the backs of their AK-47s and then I said, "Okay, what next?" I took all their punches. They dragged me to the headquarters of the *mukhabarat* in the university, the office of the secret police, which I didn't even know existed there at the time. They threw me in the room like some catch hunters made. "We found this suspicious character moving about in the middle of the night." The man in charge was a bit more civilised and said, "Leave him, I'll deal with him." They left, proud of what they had done. The officer said to me, "They are ignorant, excuse them, have a glass of water and go home." He didn't even ask me anything. I told my father what had happened. "These are the people we are saying *yes* to." My father still had some connections in the police. "Those bastards," they said to him. "We will punish them." Which they did, but it was not as though I had been given any justice. I had connections whereas others I knew who weren't so lucky were hit and simply had to carry on. That was the pattern, humiliation the name of the game, broken bones. I will never forgive them for that.

This, ultimately, was what made me leave Syria. There could be no life for me there while there were monsters like them about.'

When he left Syria forever in October 1989, Germany his destination, Zahed took his bicycle on the plane with him. At university in Aleppo he had been mocked by his classmates for still riding one. Bicycles were for children. *Abu Darrajah* they called him, 'Father of the Bicycle' or, for purposes of this prose, Abu Bicycle. At some point, years later, in London, his bicycle was transmogrified into a Honda SH125.

The first impression one gets from Zahed Tajeddin's sculpture is of there being very little between it and the ancient art he so admires, as if whole centuries have been blotted out of existence, but the longer one looks at it the more one begins to see a modern twist to the archaic, a smile that is perhaps not a smile at all but a grimace, a sense of play that might be actually the depiction of a struggle. Things are not what they seem at first glance. There is, too, a sense of an alchemical process such as that achieved in the making of Egyptian faience. Mostly sand in content but with a surface of the dazzling blue one

might associate with lapis lazuli or turquoise, the elixir used in the making of faience is a tiny amount of copper oxide. It is what gives the *shabti* or ancient Egyptian funerary figurines their otherworldly glaze. Zahed has produced a whole phalanx of *shabti* that he has called back to life and put to ironic use. Shoppers and protesters mingle. These figurines who are supposed to carry out the tasks required of the dead seem to have *other* ideas in their heads. There is in almost everything he makes an ongoing, ironic dialogue between modern and ancient. I asked him whether what he does is an escape from, or a confrontation with, the times.

'The simplest and most direct answer before I try to make it all fancy is that it is therapy. It makes me forget. It is like a drug.

Sometimes I am not even thinking. I read somewhere that the best or most precious time is when you do not *feel* time. When I am working on a sculpture I do not feel hunger or thirst. I can work till I drop whereas if I were doing something else I would get restless, I'd need a break or want to do something else. I began to realise to what degree this line of work is a part of me. At times it is mechanical almost. There is still a sense of beauty in the world. Maybe the making of these things creates or, rather, regenerates it and in doing so removes some of my pain and gives me hope. I don't really know to what degree that works. Sometimes it does, sometimes it doesn't. Where it definitely does help me is that it is *killing time*.'

(I note Zahed says *it is killing time* rather than *it kills time*. There is a world of difference between the two, the first metaphysical, the second superficial in nature.)

'There is an ancient Indian book, *The Panchatantra*,' he continued, 'which was translated into Arabic in the eighth century by the Persian scholar Abdullah ibn al-Muqaffa. *Kalīlah wa Dimnah* is considered the first masterpiece of Arabic prose. It is a collection of animal fables in which is depicted the relationship between the sultan and his ministers. It is all done through the speech of animals. The rabbit does this, the lion does that. It is, in a sense, what I do. I have always described the Syrians as sheep. A friend who influenced me said, "If you eat too much lamb, like the Syrians do, then you become a lamb, obedient and lazy… a *follower*. If you eat too much beef, like the Americans, you'll be tough and aggressive. If you eat too much goat, which is what Moroccans do, you're sly and cunning." In Syria we have all three – the sheep, the bull and the goat. I saw most of my peers as sheep – they were just following the system. They never raised their heads. The dogs barked and gathered them together. Some of them, though, were ready to challenge. I always saw myself as a goat. I couldn't accept what was around me. I wanted to climb trees. I wanted to chew bark and shoes and *not* eat what everyone else eats. I always question the things people do. I question my friends, my family, my religion… *everything*. I was never able to accept what I had been told. When I started working in archaeology I discovered that on cylinder seals you find these goats and sheep, bulls and lions, motifs that remain a part of our culture. Then I began to apply my own political views to them.

'There is a series I call *Acrobats*. You can see the influence of the Etruscan and Greek, especially Minoan culture, where you have the tradition of bull-leaping, women making acrobatic jumps and catching the horns of the bull, the most powerful part of him. I love the contradiction between the female, so delicate, and the aggressive bull. I love bulls too. Their power is beautiful which is why they are hungry for more and more of it. Those bulls I am making are a three-dimensional representation from cave art or what you see on Sumerian seals or in Anatolian art. Their shape is attractive to me. They are about beauty and pride but in a way they are dead too, more decorative than active. Some Syrians see these sculptures as

merely funny. They don't realise that when I put a goat standing proudly on top of a bull and the bull is bending down that the latter is our dying regime. We know the goat will never kill the bull or finish him off but he has his moment. That little goat has in his own way managed to get on top of that mighty and aggressive bull and have a little dance. This is my message. Stand up, *say* something and then maybe, if everyone does it, the bull will weaken and retire.

'Some people *see* it, of course. So yes, I play with these ideas. What has happened in Syria now is that finally people have been able to say *no* although the price is so heavy.'

'There is something else in your work that strikes me, and it is that the figures often tend to be on a mount or, as in this instance, raised to a height.'

'You need to go higher to see the truth. I love the poems of Nietzsche. You need to climb a mountain. The people on the ground never get anywhere. They do not see beyond the height of their own bodies.'

'And then, as if the old argument between gravity and grace has forced you in the opposite direction, there is your overweight Pegasus, which can't fly because it is too heavy.'

'It is another reflection on the time when I lived in Syria, but it is not only Syria but present-day Arabic culture in general. You know sheep and camels have two stomachs. They eat, store the food, and, when hungry again, re-chew it and swallow it back. This is what Arabs do. They regurgitate. We talk non-stop about our heritage, our glorious days, and of how we conquered the world and went all the way to China. *Enough!* Move on! It's finished! It's *history*! *Learn* something! You think of the Arabs now, so wealthy, and of how they could be so beautiful with their fortune. They are empty. They have fancy decorations but they can't fly, they are not going to go anywhere, which is why I portray them as this horse, this very powerful Arab symbol, which has become overweight. He tries to lift himself but with those little legs and wings he can't. Nothing will ever lift a beast like that.'

I suggested to Zahed that becoming an artist is always to some degree a decision, that there comes a point when something clicks inside you, and that it seemed to me the conflict in Syria and being so far away from it, living here in London, had determined his direction.

'I don't know if it is so directly related but it could be. I didn't identify myself as an artist, especially in practice, until my mid-thirties. Art for me was always something that ought not to be a profession or made commercial. It should be free in expression, and so for many years I never took it out of that area. I am one of those people who from an early age was good with my hands. I didn't see it as anything special and indeed for a long time, maybe because I have some Phoenician blood in me, and also because to an Aleppine trade is an irresistible thing, I did not even think of making money out of art. Money comes from *elsewhere* and so art could stay on the side. I didn't take it seriously as a profession until I finished with the gallery and went back to archaeology and was able to focus on what I like most, sculpture. I was around eighteen or nineteen when my addiction to archaeology began. At that time you could still go to the Friday market in Aleppo where you saw the farmers and peasants come, sell and exchange things, and some of them had little bags of beads, seals, broken terracotta and oil lamps. They found these things on their land and they would sell them. It was as casual as that. Also it was allowed at the time. People even took their finds to the museum and sold them there. "Portable antiquities" were anything from the ground that you could carry in your hand. You couldn't sell a column or large statue. Through this appreciation for little objects – cylinder seals, stamp seals, intaglios – you become curious about whatever the land reveals, what these people find and offer you.

'My particular joy was cylinder seals. They are carved on the surface and you could roll them on clay to produce a continuous image. That for me was magic. Then my attention turned to beads. These were peasant art, really basic, sometimes just little stones with holes in them that people would wear and appreciate. I think, too, the element of talismanic power in those objects had certain attractions for me. It is this personal relationship between man and objects. You create your own object, you carve it, you shape it, you adore it, it becomes precious and meaningful and of course beads have this magical role as well. In our culture the blue beads protect you from the evil eye. I always carry them with me, my little beads, what a friend calls my pillow full of treasures. They go with me everywhere. It was only when I went back to college that I was able to recreate this connection with sculpture. And then I discovered people wanted to buy it and so it had value not only for me, it had another, commercial, level, and if I was comfortable with it, well, *why not*. It is not working at something you don't like. So it was a combination of things. Also it gives one peace. Hopefully it will be recognised although I am not that interested. I am much keener in the process than in the product. I used to destroy everything I made. I never put my things out to sell. I would recycle the clay. When I began to sell things I had to start again. But now I was doing the things I most enjoy, that represent my ideas, my sense of duty and my reflection on the times in which we live. Above all, it is my drug.'

'I get the sense of there being in you almost a direct reconnection with the ancient as if there were nothing else in between.'

'I always ask people this question: if all of a sudden we had a time machine which way would you go, to the past or the future? For me it would definitely be the past. It is difficult to say *where* or *when* exactly, but definitely it would be the past. If I feel attached to it, it is not because I'm not enjoying the present but because I think we have lost a lot of the wisdom that earlier cultures and people had. We have become so very superficial. Look at what has happened to us in the last thirty or forty years. Once I could open up a radio or television and would know its structure and how things worked. Now I don't. Everything has become so strange and there is no longer the relation, the understanding, the organic growth and development of ideas to which one can still contribute. Everything has become alien to us. We don't really *know* those little devices we handle. Some thinkers and scientists and manipulators in the marketplace pull the strings and we are completely blind and dependent on them. I understood the mechanics of the bicycle. Now everything is covered, inside a box, and if something goes wrong with what's inside not even the mechanics understand any more, they simply replace the whole, so that connection with the development of ideas and of our growing as human beings has been lost somehow.'

'Which is why you go for the most primordial archetypes? With your archaeological research is this something you are trying to duplicate in your own work?'

'It is inspiration rather than duplication. In the early stages the best way to teach yourself or to learn about art is to copy the masters. This is what we all do, and the greatest master of all is God who creates all things or, as the famous hadith has it, *inna allāha jamīlun yuḫibbu al-jamāl*, "Allah is beautiful and loves beauty." You take the human body... animals... they are wonders, the way their lines flow. This is the work of a supreme being.'

'But then, in Islam, is the artist not damned because he is stealing from above?'

'I would say no, it is our blueprint. We believe that God created human beings. What I say here relates to sculpture. We were created from primeval mud. You get the same story in all cultures, whether Egyptian or South American. It is always the story of creation from mud. An Egyptian god sat at the potter's wheel and threw the first human, Horus, and then he blew his spirit into it to make it come alive. This is what modern science has been trying to identify, this first spark that turns material into a living thing. This is what artists try to do. We seek to be complete or perfect or to become through our achievements joined with our creator. That element is so important if we are to elevate ourselves and go above being just another human. It is copying, inspiration and development.'

'This goes full circle to when we first met in your shop, when you showed me those wonderful Phoenician beads, especially those with the tiny faces, the point being that the features were so fine you couldn't see them except with a magnifying glass and I remember you saying it was done as a striving towards God… to achieve the impossible.'

'I believe so. Craftsmen always push at the boundaries to make what has never been done before, to challenge our abilities, and show we can go beyond what is possible.'

'I was going to ask you about *Words*, one of your more politically inspired works.'

'It is a combination of several things in fact. The idea behind it came from lines of a poem by a Syrian friend of mine, Hares Yousef. As usual with an Arab poem it is full of good metaphors and images. One of the metaphors is of a man lying on grass, careless, in almost sleeping mode, and ignoring everything surrounding him to the extent that he is unaware that the tips of the grass blades beneath him have become like sharpened pencils blowing with the wind. That image stuck in my head. When I actually made the piece it was because I'd been invited to create a work in response to an English performance artist, Philip Lee. What he does is strip naked,

blindfold himself, cover himself in clay, and move amid the crowd. The performance I went to was in January, a bitterly cold day, and he lay naked and shivering on the floor in a foetal position. It was during the Syrian war and all that terrible pain. I thought to myself, *why are you doing this?* I think all those images came together at once. When Philip saw the sculpture he was very impressed but said, "That is not me, it's *you*." Anyway all the troubles in Syria had started and you heard the news, the commentaries, people talking and analysing … you heard voices coming from *everywhere*. Some of them made sense, others didn't, and it was very confusing and tiring because meanwhile the killing never stopped, the pain went on, and we had to deal with all these *words*. If you look at my figure, you see he is lying in a foetal position – it is related to Pompeii, those figures suddenly buried in ash, and his position is like theirs. Almost childlike, he curls in on himself in order to seek protection, a natural enough bodily gesture, but what the hands and eyes signify is something else. He is dying slowly… but he is not yet dead… his eyes are open and he is not blocking his ears. He wants to but he can't and of course he is on top of all these pencils representing all the *words* being said and written about him. The conflict had already been going on for a year when I did this sculpture. What I am saying is that it is a pain that you *have* to have… you cannot block your ears. I'm trying to, a lot of us are trying to, but you have to listen and you have to watch and you have to suffer. Also I like the archaeological look with all the horizontal scoring on the body, which I've done on earlier figures, and which in a way is suggestive of mummification. The face almost disappears inside the texture. These different effects I use are the accumulation of years of dealing with artefacts and their history. Sometimes it comes into my work intentionally, sometimes not.'

'Maybe this is a good point to discuss your coming to London.'

'It happened gradually. I didn't go directly from Syria to England. When I entered university I was frustrated by everything that was going on at the time. My fresh air came always from my trips abroad during the summer. I worked, saved money, and went to Turkey, the year after to Greece, Yugoslavia, Hungary, Bulgaria, and later on to Italy, France and Germany. Syrian money didn't go far so I slept in stations and tents, hitchhiked, and in 1987 I travelled by bicycle. In Greece, when I got into financial trouble, I drew postcards and sold them. This was my enlightenment, going and seeing other cultures, how young people lived, what opportunities they had when compared to mine. Gradually I needed to break free. I couldn't face Syria any more. I applied to do archaeology in Germany, got the applications, their acceptance, and I collected my stuff, my bicycle too, and left. I stayed in Germany for a few years. I met Anna there when she came as an exchange student. Then I travelled with her, came to England a couple of times, and three years later we got married. Then I had an invitation from a friend of mine, an Islamic manuscript dealer in London, to work with him. That was it. We never went back.'

'In terms of your mentality, well, your *soul*, did you feel it was a terribly alien environment?'

'I don't think so. Again I did not have that culture shock. Slowly, through my travels as a student, I began understand the Western mentality, the morals and behaviour, and I knew how to behave and respect them. Generally I am highly observant. I prefer to watch. I am more of a listener than a talker. This is how I gain my knowledge. When I came to London it felt normal to me.'

'Yet I remember us having conversations when you were feeling terribly out of place here. You wanted to go back to Syria or at least to divide your time between there and here.'

'This is a never-ending story. We are human. It is strange that we always define ourselves with our roots. The greater part of a tree is in air but I identify myself more with the roots than with the branches and leaves. My focus, on a spiritual level, is *back there*. I could never identify myself as a Westerner. I am always turned between two dimensions, the spiritual and the material, and so there is this longing. When I changed direction and went back to archaeology as a degree course, I started working on excavations there. This opened up a world I liked, the Syria I had always dreamt of… the land, its history and culture rather than the people. Archaeology gave me this dimension and it was then I started thinking of dividing my time between here and there, which is why I bought the house.'

'At the time I remember warning you not to burn your bridges because you never know what history will throw at you.'

'Yes, it is all shattered now. It is completely gone. All of a sudden this dimension of myself is not there any more. I can't even visualise the place. At times I have wanted to go back and I was even prepared to smuggle myself through the borders, but people said to me it is not going to help because it is no longer the place I knew. It would break my heart.'

'So does this turn England into a refuge or a prison?'

'Neither. I never came here as a refugee. I chose this route. I was not an exile to start with. I *chose* to leave Syria.'

'It would appear that rather than you having been taken from Aleppo, Aleppo has been taken away from you.'

'Yes, I feel that, although when I left Syria I was already in exile there. The city had become massive. The original Aleppines barely exist any more. They were lost in the flood of immigration, people moving en masse from the countryside. The old families were pushed aside and disappeared inside themselves. So this, too, was part of my struggle. The Aleppo I left was no longer the place I knew through my parents' eyes. A lovely story highlights what it had been once. Aleppo was one of the Arabic world centres for music. The great Egyptian singer and composer Mohammed Abdel Wahab, who was Om Kalthoum's predecessor, relates how his teacher told him that if he wanted to be accepted as a musician he first had to go to Aleppo and perform there. So he went to Aleppo to sing for a couple of nights. Wahab got to the concert hall and found only three old men in the audience. They sat, heads bowed to the floor, and listened. They said nothing. The next night the hall was completely full. The old men were testing him, you see. Already, in my time, that great classical tradition had died. There was no longer an Aleppine elite, those people who shared the same values, the same culture, the same music. I was born a ghost in my own city. The people, the politics, the mentality, became such that I felt my place was not there any more. It was bad enough that they accepted that regime and played by its rules but they lived with the corruption and became a part of it. I couldn't. Those people do not represent *my* Syria. I would rather be on the outside, and live a dream of a Syria the way I want it to be, than have to live inside that mess. My loyalty is not to the people but to the stone, the heritage, the history, the soil… the *dust*.'

'You never felt like an outsider here?'

'Of course! I will never feel fully at home here and this is London, which is so very cosmopolitan and with probably as many Arabs here as in Syria. It is the culture. You do not identify yourself with the same things even though I have now spent more of my life here than there. I don't know to what degree the first eight years or so of childhood contribute to your personality but when I listen to a song by Fairuz it makes me shiver, it elevates me with pride. I still miss the smell of jasmine in the morning, the breeze, the smell of the rain, the dust… yes, it is strange, but these things become special… these particular little details you will never find here. I remember in Germany my Syrian friends and I got together every Friday night and we baked Syrian bread and divided it between ourselves. I learned to bake my own bread, another form of alchemy. Also I think language is a very important factor. I speak better German than English because I studied it at university whereas English I picked up from the street and from communication. I never properly studied it. My English is more practical and is therefore full of embedded mistakes. Language is a powerful tool, so important and so delicate. Arabic is such a beautiful language. I understand it in depth, and I can enjoy it on an intellectual level, whereas here it is a struggle. I cannot express myself as I would in Arabic. I am like a craftsman without the right tools and this always created a barrier to experiencing the culture in depth.'

We were about to conclude but there was one more object Zahed wanted to show me. A familiar mischief was in his eyes.

'Here we have this very exotic goat or Capricorn and on the back of him a little bird. So here comes the story of my robin. Again it is one of the mysteries of my life. He is such a wonderful creature. I have my window looking out into the front garden and next to it is my desk with my microscope, my tools, speakers and CD player and usually when I do my restoration work I put on music, Fairuz or something classical. All of a sudden I noticed this bird throwing itself against the window over and over. The glass of my window is actually scratched from his beak. I thought at first he was flying against his own reflection and then he calmed down and stood on the windowsill with his head facing me. I thought, *what is going on here?* I have a little opening at the top of the window. So I opened it. He flew inside. I chased him about the room and he became frightened and started pooping everywhere. I caught him in my hands – he is the size of a table-tennis ball – and put him outside. It became a pattern. Every time I entered the room he appeared. Then I'd go out to my motorbike and he'd hop around me, follow me to the end of the drive, and watch me go. He will not do that with anyone else. A while later, when I went to do excavation work in Syria, he disappeared. I phoned home. "Have you seen him?" "No." "Are you putting food out for him?" "Yes, but he doesn't come." I came back from Syria. I brought my bags in and there he was, at the window. I have become a bit obsessed by him. People say he must be the reincarnation of my grandfather or someone from the past haunting me. And now my father always asks me about him. "How is *abul al'henna*?" This is the Arabic for robin, from henna which one uses for dyeing one's hair red. "Is he still coming?" I find it strange that he's so interested because in the old days he shot so many of those birds. When we were kids he would announce, "Let's have birds for dinner," and he would open the window. We lived on the third floor and behind us there was a garden with all these berry trees. I would go downstairs and he would sit in the window with his air gun and shoot the birds while I raced the cats to collect them. Then we would pluck the birds and fry them. They were wonderful… crunchy… you ate the bones and everything. All those birds he killed and he is asking after this one creature. I tell him my robin is a recall from his past.'

'What a horrible man! You too!'

'My father always took me hunting. He wanted me to be a man. He'd shoot birds or whatever and of course sometimes they were not dead, and so, pulling his knife, he'd say to me, "*You* kill it." I would do it too gently. "That is not the way," he said. "Do it in one stroke." Yes, I was his hunting dog. Anyway I did some research and learned that robins become quite attached to people. Now this is the strange bit. I found a BBC birdwatching site on the internet and not only do they tell you all about these birds but you can also listen to their sounds. What I did was to attach this to my speakers. I opened the window and I played for him the robin sound. He went completely mad. He got very nervous and then he disappeared for three or four months. I was really upset. What had I done? Then he came back. He always comes back – winter or summer, snow or rain – I'll go into my room and there he'll be, waiting for me. So the Capricorn represents me, with him on my back. Apparently robins go to Belgium to mate. You should see him when he comes back, absolutely wrecked, a broken soul, scruffy and miserable. The last I saw him was at the beginning of July but knowing him as I do he'll be back any day now. I'll know he's here because the first thing he does is shit on my bike.'

'I have always believed in the correspondence,' I said, 'between birds and people, especially when there is a death.'

'At the time, when he first appeared, there was no death.'

Syria, might it not have been Syria's imminent death? I gulped the question down. *Take care where you walk.* Syria will live, *inshallah.* The bird or, rather, talk of it had brightened Zahed's skies. Why throw a blanket over the cage? Sing it must, and may my friend continue to be its enchanted audience until, at the very least, the camels come home.

'I see him as a messenger,' Zahed continued, 'especially when related to certain things in my life. Then he gives me a sign as to some decision I have to make.'

'Such as?'

Old Phoenician, ever one to keep his cards close, Zahed smiled. *Where's the wisdom?* I might have guessed oracles are not to be tricked into the public domain.

'Classified,' he replied.

Jig Street

Where the Fire and the Rose are One

I was born into a condition of exile. I say this having no recollection of the word ever being used at home. It was measurable, this *whatever*, in the inaudible muttering of lips attuned to a language that no longer got a daily airing, a craving for the soups such as one's mother made, or, when the things in life did not fit the trajectory one was born into, a confused flickering of the eyes. It was, in other words, a state whose dimensions were reckoned mostly by absences. Maybe this was why it was never accorded a name, although, in truth, any of the several words that might have been used were not a little tinged with shame, as if their mere utterance would be to admit to some rape of the spirit. Soul is, after all, subject to damage. What one didn't want to do was release it from its cage for fear it would consume the world outside.

Often, though, it did slip out on parole, sometimes, most embarrassingly for me, when visitors came to the house. Softly, softly my father would pedal his sad historical theme, what his country had to endure, all of which was true, and then, just as the eyes of my mother began to roll a little, the metal teeth of the trap that had been set years before would snap shut and he would retreat into clenched silence. Anger would attach itself to the slightest cause. Touchiness was pervasive, unreason its precipitate. Any mention of the architects of peace would be sufficient cause to do battle. Yalta, where his country was betrayed by the Allies, and where his own fate was sealed, became for him a kind of satanic mantra or, rather, a mantra in reverse, an unlocking of negative forces. *Yalta, Yalta.* As he grew older he began to remake the world into what it might have been were it not for circumstances for which others, always others, were to blame. And yet what was Yalta to most of the people he spoke to? *Where* was Yalta? I wonder if he knew its name was derived from the Greek *yalos* which means 'safe shore'. (It is impossible to be a Pole and not be engulfed by history's ironies.) In later years especially, when his story had become reduced to a kind of verbal shorthand, usually prefaced by a feigned chuckle, he became like someone who had mislaid his wallet and kept looking for it in the same places. The historical scenarios he would devise got pottier by the minute.

When finally he lost his memory, or rather, when, most cruelly, what remained of it transported him back to scenes of imprisonment in the Gulag, as if he were fated to have to endure all those horrors twice, I would inform him that Poland was now free. This was breaking news each time, and once, summoning the words from somewhere unfathomable, where confusion mingled with pleasure, he replied in a shaky voice, 'I suppose I have to believe you.' As so he did, for another minute. The minutes, too, began to dissolve. Thus deprived, and forced into other gulags of silence, he became a much gentler man. Clarity, on occasion, would burst through the door that was slammed shut between him and the reasoning world. Once, hearing a Chopin prelude on the radio, he said, 'I want to lie down and meet him.' Anger, when it came, took the form of aphonia, a flinty stare. I mean not to criticise my own flesh and blood because the good in him by far outweighed the bad, even if for a child it seemed, at times, quite the opposite, but I would have the reader know the tragic consequences of being forced from, or, as in his case, not being able to return to, one's home.

Years later, after I left Canada for England, a willing émigré, I stood with my father on the shore of a lake near Bytów in northern Poland on what would be his last journey back. There was a white palisade of birch trees opposite. It was a conventionally pretty enough scene. 'Where in the world can one find such beauty as this?' he asked, mulled astonishment in his voice, and it was all I could do not to say *where you live now*. There were birch trees on the farm where I grew up, although admittedly no lake there in which they might preen themselves. The country, however, is not wanting in dark lakes shimmering with shafts of white. Apparently Polish birch was like birch nowhere else. And while it is true that the birch that grows in the east of the country is legendary, the birch near Bytów was like birch anywhere. The past had become for my father a lost paradise, such that at times his willingness to see was matched only by his willingness *not* to see. A great writer might describe this condition, as did Joseph Conrad in his short story 'Amy Foster', but even there, in the castle of language, Yanko's mouth opens to say something and no words emerge.

There is just one other anecdote I'll relate. This, too, involves trees. I think I was about thirteen at the time, already, in the thistly heart of rural Protestant Ontario, painfully aware of my 'difference'. Although born there, I was still from elsewhere. There were really only two ways to go, either to be more Canadian than the Canadians themselves or to be idea'd with stranger particles. What I am I am because of what I would not be. Anyway it was coming on autumn, the frost about to bite, the leaves of the maple ready to go up in a technicolour blaze. My father was chopping wood at the neighbour's, expounding on, and at times maybe even stretching a little, the historical parallels, as he saw them, between past and present in the Melian Dialogue from Thucydides. Its argument goes roughly like this: an embassy from the island of Melos goes to the Athenians suing for peace and the latter, politely but firmly, explain to them that peace, desirable though it might be, is not to their own advantage. *The strong do what they can and the weak suffer what they must.* Yalta, again. My father marvelled at those ancient, so very modern, voices, and, punctuating the blows of the axe, as if mimicking the sound of wood being split, our neighbour, no reader he, no slouch either, could only produce in response a 'Yep, yep, yep.' It was as perfect a picture of solitude as one might find in literature.

I wrote elsewhere, soon after my father's death:

> The path that took him to the Lubyanka Prison in Moscow, then to one of the Gulag concentration camps north of the Arctic Circle and from there, by a circuitous route, to England bore no signs that it would take him, *enfin*, to Canada. Strangely, perhaps, this last was for him the hardest to endure. Suffering has its own peculiar logic, which manifests itself not always in degrees but, rather, in its accumulated absences, and because nothing in the soul is measurable and because one rejects any form of cure, as if to cure would be to remove the thing one loves, the only answer is to go forth in bitter silence, and it is this, more than the vicissitudes of culture, politics or economics, that is the miserable lot of the exile.

This is not the place to describe those early Canadian travails, the poverty my parents had to endure, but suffice to say that for want of work clothes my father, a thousand miles from sea, wore out his naval officer's uniform doing the farm chores. *There's* something Conrad might have woven into a tale.

§

A couple of friends propose that I revisit my Canadian roots and in all solemnity suggest that were I to shake the earth from them I might find there some possibility of creative growth for the future. One of them in particular is fascinated by the small town of Kemptville, which he believes is my birthplace. A few years ago, on what would be his only visit there, he spotted at a local petrol station a female attendant with gold bangles, whose hair grows blonder, her legs longer with every retelling, such that by now she must straddle much of the northern hemisphere. There is, I believe, such a figure but she is visible only to wayfarers *in extremis*, usually before they sink beneath the waves. My friend, having spotted his siren, smells the possibility of epic and because his appetite is immense, and his talent too, I have offered up the town to him to do with as he likes. I have no further use for it. A while ago, it slipped into an impolite verse of his. Actually, and I am sorry to disappoint him, I was raised twelve miles away from Kemptville, in the heart of the country, which, given the social and mental divide between farm boy and town boy, is a considerable distance.

My other friend sees subject matter everywhere. I wonder sometimes whether he discriminates sufficiently, but just when doubt begins to gelatinise he'll produce a poem that proves his case. What works for him, however, does not work for me. What takes centre stage in my thoughts slips into the wings when I write. What settle onto the page are things which in the mind are of a secondary, or even tertiary, nature. Come scenes, faces I did not even know I'd forgotten.

The other night I had a dream about my horse, Bucephalus, a bay which my father rescued from the knacker's yard. I hadn't thought about him for decades. As to the matter of his name, much of the ancient world found its way into our lives, in the naming of pets and even cattle. This last was a terrible mistake. One should never overly familiarise oneself with what one day will be served up on a plate. My mother was largely to blame for this ill-judged nomenclature, her poetic sensitivity with regard to such matters being of a species that rather than heal only deepens wounds. Art, for her, is what is wept into being. My parents were never meant for the farm. Anyway Bucephalus spoke to me, in the dream, with an ease that made the idea of a talking horse not at all strange. There was none of the unnaturalness or amateur theatrics one finds in cartoon creatures when they speak, no flashing of gums, and nothing in the alignment of mandible, tooth and tongue that impeded ordinary human discourse. The fact that he was still alive after all these years did not surprise me either. I asked him how he'd been and whatever the answer was, which melted with much else in the dream, it was a droll one. After all, he was a droll horse. What I remember clearly, though, was that he told me he had been employed, very much against his wishes, in a massacre. Clearly this had a traumatic effect on him. I tried to coax more information out of him and all I managed to learn was that the said massacre was of chickens. I pictured trampled bodies, white feathers and blood. The dream concluded with him, in a heavy downpour, winning a race. Bucephalus was not, could never be, racing material. Would I have had this dream were it not for the fact I'd been working on this prose?

Already I flail about, spewing jumbled hierarchies. Things will not go in the order in which they originally came. What my friends recommend as a cure, metaphorical or otherwise, is, I believe, too strong a dose for any distemper I might have. I will go so far as to say their encouragement has positively stumped me. A metaphysic needs to be caught by other means, with nothing as silvery as memories. It will not be commandeered, not even by a talking horse. Also I am quite unable to arrange my memories in any manner that feels truthful to me. I spurn narrative. I believe one's *real* life is made up of clusters of varying degrees of brightness, which in the mind join up to make a constellation that is quite outside the dictates of chronological time. The body says otherwise. The body has a wristwatch attached to it – it sags in odd places and its shoelaces come undone. Also there's the small matter of whether I should seek to lay claim to what was never truly mine. It's not that I have become such a stranger to this area of my life as that I was a stranger to it at the time. Although I'm from rural Protestant Ontario and probably carry within me certain of its chromosomes, the sense I have of myself is of having come from other pastures.

§

I grew up on Jig Street. The merriment one might associate with such a name was nowhere in evidence. That it was called any kind of street at all must have been some kind of a joke because really it was a gravel road of approximately three miles, often impassable in spring when it became mud and in winter when it was the last to receive the attentions of the council snowplough. One waited for Lorne to come, the snow breaking before him in a frozen wave. In summer, when it was overly dry, choking dust would rise from beneath the wheels of the occasional heavy vehicle. One of those vehicles would claim the life of a favourite dog, Neptune. The setting down of these words brings his death alive. I see, yet again, the white film of dust over his shiny black coat, a goodbye to all things in his fading eyes. And then … *nothing*. When I rode my bicycle to school in the nearby village sometimes a pebble would get caught in the spokes, suspended there, and for a moment or two, if I were going at the right speed – not too fast, not too slow – it made a ghostly whistling noise such as whales make.

Midway on my journey, often I'd stop to converse with Deb Hare, always in his Sunday best, flat cap, smelly pipe in mouth, who would have been a young buck in the 1890s, so powerfully built local legend had it he could split wood with his bare hands. I was never struck until recently by the peculiarity of his name, which, I now learn, was a contraction of Delbert. I also discover that he was the local castrator, pigs his forte, one consequence of which is that I haven't been able to think of him in quite the same way any more. Goodbye, Deb. Further along lived Mel Weir, whom I can still see framed in the open hatch of the barn wall, an Old Master pitching manure. 'How are you, Mel?' 'Oh, still throwing shit.' There was no hint in his voice of an expletive. What he called it was what it was and if the polite world chose to call it manure, then so be it. Shit's shit. And then, as one entered the village, there was Margaret Porter, always so kind to me. She was a woman of mysteries. She seemed to converse with things or people unseen.

Adams General Store was the mercantile heart of the village.

The oldest Adams boy, Ray, was, and remains, my friend and one day he tells me he'll put into words what made that heart beat so loudly there. I shall leave the village to him to do with as he likes. I turn my bicycle around at this point.

There were only several farmhouses along Jig Street's entire length, smallholdings of rarely more than a hundred acres. They were, although nobody realised it at the time, doomed to extinction. Actually one might say the opposite – that Nature, victorious, would be allowed to reclaim them. The fields that so many generations fought to keep clear or later doused with insecticide reverted to scrubland; the birds and fauna one had thought gone forever made their return. Some deaths are not wholly unwelcome.

Sometimes, thinking back on my childhood there, its geographical coordinates are reduced to a metaphysic that eschews language. Jig Street becomes, rather, a state of mind or even, when I'm caught unawares, a state of mindlessness such as mystics crave. At night, lying in bed, I'd watch the play of light from an approaching car, which appeared first as a white rectangle moving slowly, slowly across the ceiling of my bedroom and where the ceiling became a downward slope it would speed up a little, split into white rhomboids and trapezoids, and, then, as the car turned the corner down at the Fitzgerald place, it became quadrilateral polygons and other shapes all too geometrically complex for me to be able to name. As the car got closer, and one could hear for the first time the sizzle of gravel beneath its tyres, the light took on ever more complex shapes that moved too quickly for me to be able to follow them with any exactitude, and for just those few seconds the room was like the inside, or so I imagined it to be, of a revolving prism. As soon as the car passed, the room was plunged back into darkness. The only variation in the pattern was when the car was my father's, returning home from the late shift at the factory where he also worked, when, with its cargo of unhappiness, it would turn into the drive. I'd hear the slamming of the car door, maybe just a bit louder than it needed to be, and then tired footsteps crunching towards the house.

This memory is coupled, for some reason, with the taste of wild strawberries. I do not harbour any comprehensive feeling for the country in which I was raised, although in certain particulars I probably do: I wouldn't be surprised if as an old man, once again, in imagination, I get down on my hands and knees, seeking those same berries. They were of a kind I've never seen elsewhere, conical in shape, and whose flavour had a charge unrivalled by other varieties. Some years ago, I did go looking for them again and was set upon by horseflies. I fled through the cedar trees, my arms beating the air about me, a hundred or more horseflies pursuing me, biting me, and it was as if all of nature were crying in a single voice, 'Get out of here, get out of here!' There are pastures one can never revisit, not physically, although other routes may take one there. There is an account of the Hungarian composer Béla Bartók, exiled in America, searching at night for the insects of his childhood. This would result in one of his most inspired compositions, the 'night music' (*adagio religioso*) of the second movement of his Third Piano Concerto, as God-driven a piece as any atheist could write. I think, though, only Rossini could do justice to horseflies.

What does any of this have to do with my chosen theme? Quite simply, *everything*. The movement of light across my bedroom ceiling coupled with the taste of wild strawberries belongs to another dimension, which ultimately, maybe even *because* of its incorporeity, is more powerful in its emotional impact than a whole flotilla of Yaltas. It finds its most powerful expression not so much in the whirligig of human affairs as in, say, a stand of birch trees. It is, sometimes, what breaks a strong man down. The business of going to live in another country is a complex one. We carry away from the first facts big and small and the question is which, in the second, exert the greater influence. And as we have only language by which to describe this state, what happens when we open our mouths to speak and, as with Conrad's Yanko, nothing emerges?

§

My earliest memory, unless there are others, others still waiting to be excavated, dusted off and labelled, is of finding an old pink pill in the grass behind my parents' house. Actually, and all credit here goes to my foraging eyes, it lay deeper than that, beneath summer's first green, down through the previous year's dead grass and then, deeper still, where contact with the earth had already eroded the pill of most of its vitreous glaze. I recall with exactitude not just its appearance but also its acrid taste and how, after a couple of chews, I spat out the pieces, as might a recalcitrant cat its medicine. I might even get fanciful here and say that I experienced early on life's bitter taste.

There was an old well by the house, its wide mouth covered by heavy planks of wood one of which I would lift and, seeing below the reflection of white sky and, as though punching a hole through it, my own silhouette, I'd drop various items, a whole set of chess pieces once. Queen, bishop, rook broke the mirrored image. *Plop, plop, plop.* The chess set was one of my parents' few treasures.

I wrote elsewhere:

> My father, in his memoirs, describes a chess set that he and his fellow inmates concocted in prison, which was made of the clayish bread that was their chief means of sustenance. Almost immediately it was confiscated, as if the moulded figures represented a serious challenge to the regime. Years later, in Canada, when he was still too poor to buy a chess set [after I had drowned his], he carved figures from black rubber stoppers that he brought home from his place of work. One side was left black while the other he painted industrial silver. The figures were purely representational and by this I mean the carving of them was crude. The significance they had, however, is beyond artifice. There are so many ways by which one may make a stand against hard times. Also he badly missed his game.

There was subtle pleasure in the interval between a thing dropped and the splash it made. The well was a grand acoustical instrument where a kind of spiritual music was made. There is in me still this need to disturb surfaces, to produce, as it were, my own concentric lines.

§

My mother was not so much an émigré as someone who'd been made to quit one planet for another, who, against the uncouthness of a raw, oxygenless existence, struggled to keep alive a poetic that in years previous had been her only escape. The Sussex Downs of her childhood were swapped for a landscape so flat an uprooted turnip constituted a Himalayan experience. She brought with her her pink ballet shoes. Where was the stage, though, and where the orchestra? If those shoes were a memento of childhood, what childhood was this, which was immured in pain and solitude? There is a species of English cruelty unmatched anywhere, which can take the form of gay laughter, a frivolous wave of the hand or a finely nuanced sentence. She had been made to believe she was plain. The photos demonstrate otherwise.

She brought with her a few books of sentimental value, among them a French prayer book in carved ivory covers, which a friend of

her mother's found in the Great War trenches. A pagan to the bone, I ran my child's fingers over the bas-relief of the Cross. There was not a single book whose pages I did not explore. The volumes my mother left behind in England she thought would be easily replaceable. Where were the village bookshops, though, that would replenish empty shelves? A reading of Stephen Leacock's *Sunshine Sketches of a Little Town* could hardly have prepared her for a country where she'd be unable to locate even a copy of that title. Such books as could be found were the ones that made their way onto a trestle table at the annual jumble sale where, aged eleven, I'd rush only to find there was no need for my haste. I was their only taker. I'd come away with books chosen not so much for their content as for their tactile qualities, which was just as well given some of them were missionary accounts of putting dresses on female savages. What mattered to me was the book as *book*, a sound vessel promising voyage. My mother, although she went more for content than appearance, may be held to blame for instilling the bibliomania that would keep me in penury for much of my life, and, even worse, she failed to inoculate me against an unhealthy inclination to write.

She also brought with her the quarto notebook in which she wrote out the poems she loved best, many of which she had, in any case, committed to memory and which still she can recite. Who, though, was her audience? The boy I was. She would recite to me, so melodramatically it's a wonder she did not lose her poetic licence, Lord Byron's 'The Isles of Greece' and, her voice all atremble, Walter de la Mare's 'The Listeners'. She conjured England and Greece. She had seen those purple Homeric skies beneath which *burning Sappho loved and sung*. What meant that 'burning' though? And who was that Traveller, 'a voice from the world of men'? I fancied him *me*, my proxy moving through dark English dales. Ghosts, so I hear, thrive best in a damp climate.

What, though, of my mother's *Englishness*? She'll dispute it even now, saying it was never any such thing, or, rather, that the world she was born into, and whose code she was expected to observe, was already dead and gone. That Englishness was, in certain respects, of a particular vintage, discernible only in people of a specific age, of a certain class, who ripened in the warm air of the 1930s and acquired their distinct bouquet in the chill of the 1940s. What, though, could have prepared her for a further baptism of snow and ice? Whatever it was she rejected for herself, she pushed onto me. A commoner by empathy, and she really did commune with the unfortunate, with regard to life's Ps and Qs the snob in her ruled supreme. She made me say *calf, can't, aunt* with long *a*'s as opposed to those which to her ear sounded like an out-of-tune banjo. What could have got into her head that she should have sent me to the village school on my first day, aged six, wearing shorts and sandals, carrying a satchel, some little English schoolboy wanting only for a Molesworth beanie?

There's perhaps nothing discombobulates a mind more than Englishness projected onto an Englishness it chooses not to recognise. The distance between the two is greater than between Patagonian and Chinese and what this amounted to in so remote a place was another species of exile, which a common language made, if anything, yet even more insufferable. The pain this induces is, because of its invisibility, one that is suffered in solitude. There were times when, like one of de la Mare's listeners, she would not answer a stranger's knock at the door, when, terrified, she ducked beneath the dinner table. I cowered there with her. She might have been avoiding Reverend James. Sometimes he came for tea and after taking a few sips would drop to his knees on the kitchen floor, in prayer. I remember his hands smelled of tar. Once he asked me whether I believed in God, to which my truthful response was yes, of course, I believed *in all of them*.

My mother, a Catholic by birth, although she can't pray she always lights the candles. She is, like so many Catholics who fall by the wayside, quick to defend what in practice she fails to promulgate. Religion and politics, the two things about which folk thereabouts knew the least, were what separated us from them. Catholics, although by name only, my parents were in league with dark satanic forces; Liberals, and this for my father was surely the greatest irony, they were suspected of pinko sympathies. It would be a mistake to assume Canada was not contaminated by the spirit of McCarthyism so prevalent south of the border. And to be in a remote place was to be among people who were not sure who their enemies were. A visitor came to the house once and all the while kept staring at my parents' copy of Mikhail Sholokhov's *And Quiet Flows the Don*, which on the spine of its dustwrapper bore a red hammer and sickle. After shifting uneasily in his chair for maybe an hour or more, he finally asked, 'Would you or your wife be, by any chance, members of the Communist Party?'

Such political and geographical uncertainties spread even to the school playground, where I overheard a discussion between two boys, one saying to the other, 'My mother says she'd sooner sleep with a Nazi than with a Frenchman.' Maybe, though, this was not uncertainty at all. The French, of whom there were none in our area, and who were therefore an unknown quantity, were roundly despised. They were, although nobody had ever met one, the *other*. What, then, could have possessed my parents to settle there, Jig Street of all the world's places? What devil of unlikelihood fed a god's mirth? And yet I feel, do I not, some affection for it. I could bicycle it blindfold still, maybe even pause here and there, banter with ghosts, confabulate a little.

I hear it still, in London, the pebble whistling like a whale.

§

I shall glide over my formal education, its early stages, pausing only to consider the woman who did her best to teach me. Although I did well in my studies, that is, before I fell to the demon of indolence, there was one area of great shame and that was my inability to learn the alphabet in its proper sequence. After the letter 'J' I was in enemy territory, but rather than sit down and actually learn the alphabet I spent the next few years trying to hide my handicap, expending more energy on concealment than I would have done in bringing abecedarian correctness to the fore. And even now my heart skips a beat when I stray into middle range, where the letter 'K' is like branches in the dark about to scratch me riding on my bicycle and 'Q' and 'R' (Queen's Rook) are even more dangerous obstacles. Why I should have had this trouble, when my name contains so generous a serving of the alphabet, was perhaps indicative of the awkward handle my name would become. My unpronounceable surname is the difference by which I live, the Doberman pinscher that shall be kept forever chained to me. And so, with regard to language's smallest particles, I managed for six years to avoid Mrs Morrison's alphabetically tuned eye.

What shall I say of this woman other than that she was some kind of heroine? She was the sole teacher of a one-room village schoolhouse. She taught six subjects to eight grades, which, if one multiplies eight times six, and then, allowing time for recesses, divides the product by the number of periods in any working day, was a feat close to mathematically impossible. She had to make time as well for the slowpokes who'd spend maybe two or three years in the same grade. Add to this the fact she would break off her classes to read us poetry and fables. She taught us Alfred Noyes' 'The Highwayman' which, so my unreason tells me, is not only the greatest but also the most erotic poem in world literature. I still remember the delicious shudder it gave me, the woman in darkness, pressing against her breast a red rose, which later would become the stain of blood that I can still see clearly through the deep night of that terrible passage.

Mrs Morrison had no children of her own and of her early life nothing by way of anecdote survives. She was married to a farmer by the name of Wilfred who hardly ever spoke. She led us in prayer each morning and I mouthed the words, unable to give them volume. She asked me once whether I believed in God and I replied, 'I believe in science.' It is not a position I've adhered to, but neither do I believe in the laboured divisions between religion and science. Any problems are invariably those of ethics. My answer brought tears to her eyes.

She wept thrice. She was a figure of huge strength, a pioneer in spirit, and this may explain why I remember so vividly those three breaks in her composure.

She wept to hear of my apostasy.

She wept on Remembrance Day, when she told us of how her brother had fallen on the very last day of the war.

She wept when the police came to the school once.

A Dutch boy and I had tried to protect ourselves from the bullying attentions of a certain Belgian boy who would attack for no apparent reason other than brute pleasure. One day the Dutchman armed himself with a small kitchen knife and I borrowed one of his painted wooden shoes. Was he the last of his tribe to wear wooden shoes? I was to hit the Belgian over the head, render him unconscious, and the Dutchman was to find some appropriate part of the body in which to lodge the knife. We had no specific plan as to what to do with the corpse. With a bit more forethought, and out of deference to the wooden shoe, we could have waited for him in the woods through which he normally took a shortcut home. It was a pleasant enough, rarely visited, spot, the emerald green of it whitened here and there with trilliums and the bark of birch trees, in short, a perfect scene for bringing about another person's demise. There was the rusty skeleton of an old car amid the foliage, in which, with a bit of care, we might have seated our Belgian corpse. A skeleton at the wheel of a skeleton, he would not have been missed. The day came. We waited for him by the side of the road, stupidly visible, at the edge of the village, in front of the Dutchman's parents' house. We hesitated, probably out of compassion for the murderee, which, when one is bent on murder, is a mistake. The Belgian fled. The Belgian's father, who aimed a shotgun at me once, phoned the police. The police came, and a tearful Mrs Morrison dutifully entered the information onto the school record that was to follow me through a good part of my life.

She had a limited intelligence, Mrs Morrison, but despite the many holes in her knowledge it was a net whose threads were strong enough to withstand anything hurled against it. A couple of years ago, I was speaking of her to my late friend Arcangelo Riffis. We were in his room, in London, which, because of the misfortune that claimed him, he had not left in almost a decade. The cigarette smoke was so dense a yellowish-brown covered the ceiling that was, when he first moved there, solid white. I had received news of Mrs Morrison's death a few days before. She died as she lived, mentally alert, and, luckily for her, fearless of the future. God was always near. I was telling my friend this and I was telling him, too, of how when she wished to test the fibre of an obviously guilty boy's feeble excuse she would ask to see his tongue. 'It's green!' she'd cry, 'you're lying to me.' An odd thing happened, which my friend and I both noticed immediately after. The clock stopped when I began talking of her, and, five or six minutes later, when I had finished, it started again. Also, a blackbird outside had stopped and then resumed its song, which of all birdsongs is my favourite. This, too, happened. Only recently have I heard more on the subject of birds and death, of how, when someone dies, they make a comforting presence. Could it be there are letters of other alphabets still waiting to be put in the right sequence? That bird, I'm sure it knew of whom I spoke. My old teacher seemed to be there, outside of time, in a room in a city in a country she had never been to. She had never been anywhere, it is true, but she did have a strange affection for Finland, such that on occasion she would have us sing, in an English version, which I have not been able to trace, Sibelius's *Finlandia*. What could have been her attraction to things Finnish, she who had never been anywhere? There is perhaps a mystery here, an answer to which I might have gently coaxed out of her had there been time enough. The response, though, may have been disappointment whereas the pleasure now is in being able to speculate as to what her secret was. I wonder if I'm the only one who remembers this. What would they have made of her in Äkäslompolo? Among my schoolmates, did any of them even know where Finland was?

§

Kemptville, where I went to high school, was more truly a scene of desolation than Jig Street ever was. I struggle against my own reluctance to write about this, and, in truth, the large boulder inside me will not be moved. All it does is teeter a little. The barbarities of rural life are usually visible or at least traceable. Small towns, on the other hand, conceal them with clipped garden hedges, the Rotary

Club and bridge parties. Savagery was part of the town's make-up, savagery among the elite. Only the poor ever paid for their crimes. I will leave it there. Small towns are said to be the same the world over, each with its attendant cruelties, but this is a meaningless platitude. All places differ, as do people. Some places are considerably worse than others. A blight hangs over certain parts of the world, which, although this has yet to be proven by aetiologists, political analysts and seismologists, may be discerned by those of even moderately sensitive natures.

The Jews were what made Kemptville distinctive. They were, to a child's eye, a world apart from the waspishness one associated with the place. Tough in business, which of course they had to be if they were to survive, many of them were refugees. I never had an inkling of any of their personal histories, which, in any case, I am sure they were reluctant to share. What, after all, is more terrible than to relate a tragedy that others find incomprehensible, or worse still, of no great interest? This, I believe, was my father's mistake, the fact that he thought a story told should have an audience. What the Jews of Kemptville did was to get on with life, secure their children's futures, which they did, of course, but with the consequence that the price of their success would be solitude. The children left home and the Jewish population dwindled to the point that there were not enough people left to form a synagogue. The old Russian Jew, Max Miller, had a small clapboard synagogue attached to his store. The general store was one from which he was never known to have willingly made a sale. Actually he did once make a multiple sale. I initiated a craze for the coloured sunglasses, yellow, blue and red, dating from the 1920s, the entire stock of which, to his puzzlement, he sold to me and my classmates. It was Max Miller who, according to David Brandes' brief memoir of the place, announced at the funeral of the Galician chicken farmer, Meier Landau (the same Meier Landau who related his marital problems to my mother), what others there assembled wished not to countenance: 'Gentlemen, we haven't had a *minyan* for several years. Let's face facts; no one is coming into Kemptville. The community is *oisgespeilt*, finished.' And *oisgespeilt* it would be. Today, as one walks down Prescott Street, through what used to be the business heart of Kemptville, before it dispersed to the town's edges, one passes boarded-up shop fronts or else bizarre

New Age ventures, such as belly dancing, which, given the average Kemptville figure, is not something one's imagination should too readily invite. When I was last there the general store in front of which Sammy Schneiderman spoke Polish with my father, which was from where my red, blue and white rubber ball came, was a hole in the ground, a digger turning on its slew ring, shovelling rubble, oblivious to those old struggles. One Jew alone remains in Kemptville, a poet who, although he rarely emerges from his house, seems to find the place affable. A poem of his, somewhat bizarrely to me, sings its praises.

At high school, in 1963, I was awarded a prize for a poem I wrote, 'The Wrecker's Ballad', which was based on a reading of Daphne du Maurier's *Jamaica Inn.*

> Beware of the flickering lanterns ashore,
> Of the cruel rocks which spell your doom,
> Of the towering white-capped waves that roar,
> And the rain-soaked sails and the falling boom.

I was not a little proud to step onto the stage to collect my ten-dollar prize, only to discover later that there'd be a cost for my pride. As I emerged from the school to go home, still flushed with victory, I was set upon and pummelled by some boys who accused me of being a sexual deviant because, after all, was that not what poets were? I am, in retrospect, just a bit grateful for those bruises. They would keep me necessarily remote.

An air of futility hangs over the place. A while ago, a teenager, recently split from his girlfriend, drove at full speed down Prescott Street and, where it and Clothier form a T, straight into the wall of the Bright Spot Restaurant. As a youth I used to frequent that place when it was Pete the Greek's *polis.* (I wonder if he'd read his Thucydides.) It was there, over French fries drowned in gravy, that I pontificated to a girl wearing jellybean pink lipstick on Roy Orbison being poetry in the way Gene Pitney could never be. She twitched a little. I heard later that the greatest profit made in such venues, which aim only so high and no higher, was in the plates after plates of French fries consumed by pimply teenagers between the hours of twelve and two. We were not, as we fondly believed, nuisances. We added to the gross national product. The Bright Spot went from Greek to Chinese. I had already quit town by then. I'd been gone so long nobody ever knew I was there. A month after the aforementioned incident, another young man committed suicide in identical fashion. The still visible signs of the first repair to the wall of the restaurant now bore the scars of a second repair, a darker shade of plaster smudged over the lighter, which had just about dried. It would appear the restaurant owner was going to wait a little before gambling on bringing the job to completion. Who'd be the third to go down Prescott Street? It's a sorrowful business when the young take their own lives, but what a deeply pitiful thing it is when one apes the other, as if choosing one's own path to self-destruction is just too much to have to construe. A fact terrible but true, something which newspapers have yet to twig to when speaking of such things happening in waves, is that this is how a bland world goes down, in dying echoes.

§

A joke has been doing the rounds. Someone is asked, if he could choose the time and place of his dying, when and where it would be. Ottawa on a Sunday afternoon, he replies, because the transition from life to death would be imperceptible. One Sunday afternoon, in the summer of 1971, I sat in a small park beside the Rideau Canal, very close to Confederation Square, deeply absorbed in a book, I can't remember which one. It would be terrible if it were Richard Brautigan, whom I was reading at the time. The day, as I would have good reason to recall, was a perfect one. Summer can sit heavily there. The day was fresh. The next morning I picked up a newspaper and read about what had taken place the day before, in that very spot, at that precise time. A man had been stabbed and he crawled, bleeding to death, from one small bush to another, where he expired. I worked out that he could not have been more than a few yards away from me, where I sat cross-legged with my back to him, oblivious to his fate. I find in this an analogy and yet for *what* exactly still eludes me. It may touch on the relationship between literature and life, in that an excessive love of the former can lead to blindness for the latter. On the other hand, it may have to do with the scene. Ottawa was, despite being the scene of my early adulthood and its vicissitudes, static. One could be close to, and miss completely, the great dramas of life and death. That was Ottawa all over, prophylactically sealed, immune.

Strangely, or maybe not so strangely, the years I spent there seem not to want to go into prose. All I will say of that period in my life is that I was foolish and wise in equal measure, subscribing, or so I thought, to some idea of Canadian literature, which, had I allowed it to, might have claimed me. The pressures, at that time, were to find oneself a distinctly Canadian voice. This really was a matter of the cat chasing its own tail. What I would have written had I remained there would not have been even remotely close to what I now write. This much is obvious. I had already become a gadfly of sorts but one whose buzzing was contained inside a small bottle. It was a trap every bit as deadly as the one I sought to avoid. There were good people too, the poet George Johnston for one, the street musician Sneezy Waters for another. Actually I had already begun to move in another direction. I picked up a little book in the Penguin Modern European Poets series and, reading for the first time Zbigniew Herbert's 'Elegy for Fortinbras', I knew my brief flirtation with 'CanLit' was all a pose.

Another figure in my life, a great encourager of my early poetical attempts, when suppression might have been kindlier, was the firebrand professor, Robin Mathews, whose lectures on Canadian literature were extravagant in their claims. One day, after I'd left university, I bumped into him in Byward Market and we went for a coffee. I could not invite him back to the squalor of my place, which, thick with flies, was situated above a fish warehouse. I dared to suggest that perhaps the Canadian poet F.R. Scott was not the equal of T.S. Eliot, at which point he pounded his fist on the table and, in what began as a whisper and slowly crescendoed to a whispered scream, he cried, 'Ma*rrrrrrrr*ius, don't tell me what's what! I know everything from *Beowulf* to Virginia Woolf.' It was too late, though. I had already settled on a divorce.

Ottawa is probably best rendered in one of my earliest solo ventures. A hitchhiker from the sticks, Jig Street all over me, I walked into a small bookshop off Elgin Avenue, Shirley Leishman, which in the 1960s was the closest to anything that could be described as 'alternative'. Actually the word had not yet been accorded its hip usage. As soon as I stepped inside the first thing I saw was a rack of New Directions paperbacks – translations of Rimbaud, Baudelaire and Lorca and a sprinkling of the Beat poets, Gregory Corso and Lawrence Ferlinghetti. What was it about those black-and-white photographic covers that they alone, together, signified a forbidden zone? It was somewhere I wished to go, and, in a sense, it is somewhere I wish to return to, where, in Stefan George's words, *Ich fühle Luft von anderen Planeten* ('I feel an air from other planets blowing'). All I understood at the time was that the line of my life would somehow run through that zone and that whatever form it took, whether secular or no, it was to be a pilgrimage. And returning to Jig Street with my dark trophies, I would read them with both puzzlement and vague recognition. At the same time, on a small crackly radio, I'd tune into 'Juicy Brucie', WBZ in Boston, who played music such as one heard nowhere else, and, one night late, hearing for the first time a tormented voice singing, 'Yonder stands your orphan with his gun, / Crying like a fire in the sun', I wondered if in the history of the world there was ever anything as new as this.

My decision, some years later, to leave Ottawa was anything but decisive. It was, rather, a journey, only vaguely planned, from which, as it so happened, I would not return. A year's travels through Europe and a detour of several months in Tunisia, which turned me into a fledgling Arabophile, would finally see me in England. I had, in a sense, completed a circle.

§

My first memory of London is of being on the tube, opposite me a man with mascara about his eyes, his hair dyed blonde, and with LOVE and HATE tattooed on his knuckles. I have always put great store by first impressions because for every misconception they might contain there are several truths and of those there may be one that unlocks the universe. It was 1974, and one could still see the occasional figure in a bowler hat, the last of a species, already laughable; the police tiptoed like blushing brides onto the scene of a crime; Old Chicago, middleweight boxing champion in the 1930s, was being stood another drink at the French House in Soho where Gaston Berlemont ruled supreme; the second-hand booksellers were mostly elderly misanthropes; the bosomy woman at the bakery on Earls Court Road, who sold just about the only edible bread available at the time, called me 'love'; Miss Ensing was chief reference librarian at Kensington; and spivs were still in evidence. Something, though, was beginning to gnaw away at the edges of this Norman Wisdom existence. It was as if I had arrived at the conjunction of two realities, the one of soggy tea and milky biscuits, and this mascara'd other with its creeping sinister edge. The 1960s decals declaiming love and peace had already begun to fade.

A few years later, the country was on the cusp of yet another of its silly revolutions, silliness being this country's bane, with a prime minister who, for all her imagined crimes, was hardly ever cited for the one for which she really was responsible, the unEnglishing of the English people. She who was from the corner shop betrayed the corner-shop mentality with which a mere island governed vast land masses. There's nothing like a good shrinking to amplify a hollow voice. Suddenly people spoke about how much they made or what they spent on their second or third mortgages. Young men sat with their legs spread wide, their word for 'thousands' *thou's*. Sleekness was all. Martin Amis caught it perfectly in *Money*. Greed was the new god and its priests were these boys newly graduated from the disco floor to the City. Mrs Thatcher loved them and they loved her. It marked the beginning of the end of English reticence. It marked the ascendancy of the philistine. Incredibly, even English humour ceased to be gentle. It was the spectacle of one group of besuited savages, shouting at the tops of their voices, at a wine bar on Hollywood Road, that I would later transpose to Leopardi's Naples:

> The mountain broods beneath its canopy of smoke
> While these revellers with their booming voice and pointed
> shoes,
> These plumed creatures whom progress loves,
> Make corridors in air.
> The pursuit of happiness brings them none.
> They drape the skeleton of all things with their festering
> pride,
> And fearing the tumble through endless space wage war
> upon silence.
> Should they win, where then my verses?

It was, in other respects, a thrilling time. Coming to London had engineered a crisis in me that forced me to rethink everything I had ever done. I had to learn how to walk anew, as it were, inside a gravitational field where things dropped did not necessarily go downwards. A compliment could be taken as an offence, an insult as a joke. The familiar, although things there might look the same, was a 'no go' zone.

All the poetry I wrote in Canada was now destined for the proverbial flames. I have a recurring dream of stepping into a book shop in Ottawa and pulling from a high shelf a slim volume, which, curiously, is issued in plain black cloth with no lettering on the spine. It contains not just the poems I really did write but also poems I never wrote. Could this be some writer's archetypal dream of exile? Maybe what it really says is that there is no escaping the bad one does. This is not to suggest that I immediately began to write better: on the contrary, for the first couple of years in London I wrote very badly indeed. I am not a little proud to have added to the store of poetry's worst ever lines: 'Equipped with dentistry of words, we strive / To disentangle truths from the grave.' Still the very fact of my being here served to rob me of the smug certainties with which I could indulge a parochial scene – Jig Street could no longer do it for me – but where was the voice that would accommodate this new, cosmopolitan one? Such was my struggle, and in many ways it continues. Also, despite my having an English mother, I could not claim birthright to a species of Englishness that'll forever elude me. I have always felt like some kind of foreigner marooned in the English language. The pity of it is that it's the only one I speak.

And yet, and yet …

As of late, unbidden, come wisps of the language my father so desperately tried to teach me. The words fall like feathers in the brain. I am mentally agile enough, just, to be able to catch them. A poor teacher, as was his father before him, and, perhaps, as I am to my own children, he tried to force me to learn Polish and the greater the effort he made the stronger my resistance. *What child will not speak his father's tongue?* I turned lowly intransigence into a high principle. Our sessions would often end in tears, the tears mine, fury his. I spat out that language. All things Polish were what kept me segregated from any fields I might have wished mine, such that its very sound was barbed wire to my ears. A pretty girl with braids, Polish, wearing a black patch over one eye, mollified me. She was called Jolanda, the *j* pronounced like a *y*. She was, in the space of only three hours, the first to make me fluent in love. Aged six, I wept to see her leave. *Do widzenia*, Jolanda. Although normally I spurn psychological explanations for one's shortcomings, I wonder if that philological struggle did not disable in me a capacity for languages. Only Latin agreed with me, but it wouldn't take up permanent residence in my brain. French, I mutilated. And what could be more gruelling than Polish with its myriad irregularities, its combinations of letters that were virtually unsayable? And yet, as of late, or, rather, after my father died, those words, as if themselves the floating ashes of language or else fireflies in the dark of absence, words I thought I had forgotten or which I had never absorbed in the first place, began to insinuate themselves onto my tongue.

Suddenly T.S. Eliot's lines acquire new force:

> And what the dead had no speech for, when living,
> They can tell you, being dead: the communication
> Of the dead is tongued with fire beyond the language of the
> living.

Was this not, then, my father *tongued with fire*? It was as if he belonged now to a dimension of pure sound, where meaning, which, after all, belongs to the exigencies of life, was no longer of use. The words were now without strings attached to them, free to go as they please. It seemed as though from time to time (*od czasu do czasu*) the world was being remade in accordance with those peculiar syllables. *Poziomka*, wild strawberry. *Jabłko*, apple, whose sound so perfectly conveys its shape. *Mój pies*, my dog. There were always dogs in the house. *Czy pan rozumie po polsku?* Sadly no, I understand very little. Often, though, I get the gist of what's being said. When my father and my uncle spoke, especially on the telephone, their most common expletive was *cholera*, with a silent *c*, which in Polish is a strong curse, a match for the strongest English ones, and when coupled with *jasna* ('bright'; again the *j* like a *y*), it is stronger still. If one accepts the argument, which I do only partly, that profanities are derived from what people most fear, *cholera jasna* bespeaks some old and widely shared misfortune. *Cholera jasna!* And now even those words I had never been able to pronounce, beginning with *prze*, for example – *przepraszam*, excuse me – or, more terrifyingly, with *szcz*, I'm now somehow able to manage. Quite by chance, I stumble on a word in my little English–Polish/Polish–English dictionary: *szczapa*, a piece of split wood, or wood cleaved with an axe.

And there, on my father's shelves, in Polish, *yep*, his Thucydides.

Polish had seemed to me the language of pointless sacrifice.

On the wall of my bedroom was a photograph, which my father put there, of a handsome boy who died, aged sixteen, fighting the

Russians in 1920, and with his haunting eyes, his cadet's cap at a slight tilt, he was all I could never be. That boy, long dead, surveyed my very existence. Once, in anger, I shouted at my father that maybe I, too, should die for Poland and fulfil his patriotic wishes, at which point he flew into a rage such as I'd never seen before or since. That boy was my father's family's offering to a country's martyrology.

Was Poland itself not Christ upon the Cross? Poland, which I was not to visit until I was nineteen, was a black cloud hanging over me. The irony is that when I finally got there it was a place of light. Its poetry I felt mine. The cafés were full of people deep in conversation, the women like women I'd never seen before, and in the mornings, as if the above, sexiness and intellect, were miraculously hybridised for the palate, a breakfast (*śniadanie*) of *naleśniki*, crepes with savoury cheese on the inside, topped with sour cream and then sprinkled with sugar, Polishness *par excellence*.

The truth of the matter is that although I wanted desperately not to be Polish I did not want to be Canadian either, but rather to be what any sane person might choose, Italian. This is not such an unusual affliction except that in my case the culture grew in isolation, the conditions there not at all favourable to its spores. There were no Italians about for me to emulate. My mother had an exaggerated love of all things Italian but she also sang the Isles of Greece. She was, before she ever pondered Canada's existence, decidedly happy in the south of France. There were three factors which doubtless clinched the matter for me.

The first was that my English grandmother sent me a photographic storybook called *Mario of the Po*, whose authorship is lost to me. I could with great ease superimpose myself upon this boy, who I fancied even looked like me. My grandmother was to me what she could never be to her own children, a sure diviner of my wishes. The books she sent me were magical texts.

The second was that in 1955 the great opera singer Beniamino Gigli, on the final leg of his farewell world tour, came, amazingly, to the Capitol Theatre in Ottawa. The capital of Canada was still, culturally, a village. It has since become a town. This was not something my parents could afford but go we did – a remarkable instance this, of gravity succumbing to grace – and I remember vividly the old man, already close to death, taking his bows against a red plush velvet curtain and me, as my mother had coached me to, shouting, *Bravo, bravo*.

The third, and perhaps most decisive, factor was going with my parents to an Italian deli, again in Ottawa, and, with this being my first direct engagement with Italian existence, being so overcome by the smell of hanging sausages, wooden buckets of olives, garlic, and Parmesan cheese that I wet my trousers. Soaked mentally as well as physically I would henceforth be *Mario*, and when, on my first day at school, about to be sacrificed to wild galoshed natives, Mrs Morrison called out my name, I corrected her, saying it was not Marius but Mario. 'Mario' I remained until my eighteenth year. What I had done, in effect, was to swap one species of émigré experience for another, one that had all the tunes.

Where was I before I made this mental swerve, this squeally on my bike?

'What is the language using us for?' writes the poet W.S. Graham.

An Iraqi poet tells me how for him the English language contains a sense of justice, which in turn has directed, morally, his writing of Arabic. There's something to ponder: justice, not *accuracy*, because

Arabic has so many more words with which to describe things than we do, but … *justice*. What happens, though, when the language becomes all tottery with euphemism? When it becomes debased with all manner of friendly fire? What I believe he refers to is good literature. Shakespeare's is a language of infinite justice. Although the circumstances of which the Iraqi speaks are vastly different from mine, fistfuls of terror as opposed to puffballs of peace, it was here, in London, that I came to appreciate for the first time the moral ascendancy of the long sentence as opposed to the staccato bursts that comprise the language of everyday North American experience. This is not to say the other is without value. American English has got its jive. Also it can be as sinewy, as beautifully wrought as the best English written here. What I'm saying is the language as ordinarily used, when reduced to the monosyllabic or else to a spluttering of arrested similes – *like, like* – only serves to abbreviate experience.

§

A few years ago, I went to an exhibition of El Greco at the National Gallery and seeing there his painting of Toledo, which is more spirit world than townscape, I felt something leap within me. I knew those turbulent skies from somewhere deeper than knowledge. There was a small print of it in my parents' house. What those skies represented was perhaps spiritual in nature, certainly troublesome, and sometimes I think I've moved beneath them ever since. There was also, at home, a reproduction of the Mona Lisa from whose steady gaze I tried to hide. I would barricade myself behind the sofa but no matter how often I tried to catch her out before she caught me her eyes were always ready to meet mine. Years later, when I helped my parents move from Jig Street to Kemptville, I checked one last time to see if everything from the house had gone. I climbed a cupboard and there, lo and behold, on the top shelf, lying face-down, serving as a lining, was the Mona Lisa. I found a hammer and a single nail, a three-incher, which may seem an overstatement but it was the only one available, and, hardly able to see for tears, I hammered the image to the wall, precisely in the spot where it had played hide-and-seek with me more than forty years before. What did the incomers make of it, the only object in an otherwise empty house?

Another image was of a photograph from a wartime issue of *Lilliput* magazine. It was the first female nude I had ever seen. She was walking nonchalantly onstage, not a stitch on her, absolutely carefree, one hand skimming the edge of a diaphanous curtain. There was sheer joy in the image. She was no victim of anything other than what time would make of her. Could she be still alive? Power was hers absolutely. She was not one of Bill Brandt's nudes, true, and in fact what made the image so startling was its total absence of artifice. Its sole object was to please. And yet there was nothing puerile, nothing in it to make men or women ashamed of themselves. When, a few years ago, I found that same picture in a rack of old magazines she was precisely as I had remembered her. She was on the cusp of laughter and the world would laugh with her. She, too, pricked my eyes.

A couple of images, revisited in London, bring me full circle.

The Mona Lisa, when I caught up with her in the Louvre, was being gawked at by a swarm of tourists, bastards all of them, who had no business ogling what was mine. Gioconda, bless her, looked only at me. *Goodbye, goodbye.* Our familial history is all echoes. A history of movement could be constructed, which would cover much of the globe. Whatever condition it is that I inhabit it is not one to which my own children, born here, have ever heard me give a name. I am neither exile nor émigré. I just happen to be in this place, and any interpretation I might put on it now is a combination of dubious hindsight, befuddlement, and not being able to afford to leave. I'm from Jig Street. God knows how I got here. The journeys all people make are, in a sense, inexplicable. They are hardly ever the consequence of one big idea but rather of a thousand small flukes. There's no accounting, though, for what goes on in the blood. *What I am I am because of what I would not be.* I am, only because I choose to believe what I was told once, the horseless scion of some old nomadic existence.

Acknowledgements

'The Poet, the Anarchist, the Master of Ceremonies', 'Swimming in the Tigris, Greenford', 'Once Upon a Time in County Cork', 'Ana Maria Pacheco's Journey to the Underworld', 'A Ghostly Hum of Parallel Lines' and 'The Goat that Stood upon the Bull's Spine' first appeared in *PN Review.* 'Swimming in the Tigris, Greenford' subsequently appeared as the Afterword to Fawzi Karim's *Plague Lands and Other Poems* (Carcanet, 2011). 'A Metaphysical Shaggy Dog Tale', 'Tehran in Stoke Newington', 'Three Chinese Characters' and 'Old Turk, Young Turk' first appeared in *The Bow Wow Shop.* A shortened version of 'A Tree Grows in Brixton' first appeared in *Wasafiri*. I am grateful to the editors of the above magazines.

Photographs, if not taken by me, come from various sources. A good many are, of course, in the possession of those about whom I wrote. The portrait of Martina Evans is by her daughter Liadáin, the portrait of Rajan Khosa by Bobbie Kociejowski. Thanks to Mirrorpix for permission to reproduce the photograph on p. 31.

Among those I wish to thank for their critical, editorial and practical help are Jarosław Anders, Michael Garrick, Michael Glover, Susan and Emily Johns, Bobbie Kociejowski, Gabriel Levin, Christopher Middleton, Eric Ormsby, Susan Pratt, Philippa Scott, Norm Sibum, Adam Thorpe and, of course, all the subjects of these pieces.

Also I thank Helen Tookey, for her diligence, Michael Schmidt, for his forbearance, and Grant Shipcott, for his imaginative eye.